Warren Oates

SCREEN CLASSICS

Screen Classics is a series of critical biographies, film histories, and analytical studies focusing on neglected filmmakers and important screen artists and subjects, from the era of silent cinema to the golden age of Hollywood to the international generation of today. Books in the Screen Classics series are intended for scholars and general readers alike. The contributing authors are established figures in their respective fields. This series also serves the purpose of advancing scholarship on film personalities and themes with ties to Kentucky.

Series Editor
Patrick McGilligan

Warren Oates

A Wild Life

Susan A. Compo

THE UNIVERSITY PRESS OF KENTUCKY

Scholarly publisher for the Commonwealth,
serving Bellarmine University, Berea College, Centre College of Kentucky, Eastern
Kentucky University, The Filson Historical Society, Georgetown College, Kentucky
Historical Society, Kentucky State University, Morehead State University, Murray
State University, Northern Kentucky University, Transylvania University, University
of Kentucky, University of Louisville, and Western Kentucky University.

Editorial and Sales Offices: The University Press of Kentucky
663 South Limestone Street, Lexington, Kentucky 40508-4008
www.kentuckypress.com

The Library of Congress has catalogued the hard cover edition as follows:

Compo, Susan.
  Warren Oates : a biography / Susan A. Compo.
     p.   cm. — (Screen classics)
  Includes bibliographical references and index.
  ISBN 978-0-8131-2536-7 (hardcover : alk. paper)
    1. Oates, Warren, 1928–1982. 2. Motion picture actors and actresses—
  United States—Biography. 3. Television actors and actresses—United
  States—Biography. I. Title.
  PN2287.O175C66 2009
  791.4302'8092—dc22
  [B]   2008048337
  ISBN 978-0-8131-9346-5 (paperback : alk. paper)

Manufactured in the United States of America.

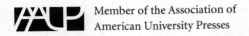 Member of the Association of
American University Presses

For Tony Wain, without whose friendship
I would be entirely stateless.

Warren Oates looked like he'd had the shit kicked out of him & didn't care. In his persona & characters there existed a brutality, tenderness, complexity & directness that no other actor of his genre could claim.

These qualities lived onscreen as compliments, not conflicts. Oates gave his characters a range like that of Charles Bukowski, a poet who could land a straight right in a downtown bar, honky-tonk or Juarez cantina. His stare, which often turned into a glare, came from his gut. It was the look of a shell-shocked soldier, broken lover or desert rat; his eyes focused out on the horizon. He mesmerized the audience in the way that he could pull qualities of the character he was acting up from his depths & then let them sink in or play across his face.

You got the feeling that not much scared Warren Oates. He was the guy you knew had your back as the shit started to break loose; he could throw a car into a four-wheel slide & then pull it up within inches of the camera or the cliff. With subtlety in his back pocket, he wasn't afraid to "go big," climbing out of a grave in Bring Me the Head of Alfredo Garcia or, in a mostly mute performance, losing his mind in Cockfighter.

He was the kind of actor who made Jack Nicholson or Harry Dean Stanton come to the set ready to ratchet the heat up a few notches or turn everything upside down. He was a true anti-hero who helped to change & at the same time personified cinema in the '60's & '70's w/ his unflinching brutal honesty.

—John Doe, musician/actor
Bakersfield, Calif.

Contents

Illustrations follow page 246

1

Population Boom

When the last firework had given up its ghost and the cookout embers had ceased smoldering, the population of a small town in the soft coalfields of Muhlenberg County in western Kentucky welcomed a late reveler. "I was due on the Fourth of July but I arrived a few hours late," said Warren Oates, who was born the morning after in 1928, in what he would refer to as "the little dirt town of Depoy," a coal-mining and farming community past its prime. Although Depoy had been through hardship before, this time it seemed a little deeper. The Great Depression was looming.

Depoy is situated some six miles from the Oates Valley, named for Major Jesse Oates, a Revolutionary War soldier of English, Scottish, and Welsh descent. Oates, something of a tearaway, fled North Carolina in 1796 after a duel, and he used his contested fortune to add to a large land grant and other property he had been busily accumulating in the new Commonwealth of Kentucky.

The colorful Jesse Oates was a third-generation New Worlder, born in North Carolina about 1756. By 1775, he had joined the fighting forces, and for a time he served under Colonel Francis Marion, the Swamp Fox of the Revolutionary War. When the battle moved southward, Marion shored up his troops with militiamen like Oates, who rendered such distinctive service that he was awarded the rank of first major.

Once the war was over, men were obliged to attend monthly military musters, and Oates did, despite his having great antipathy for another soldier in his unit. David Coghill, whom some regional histories identify as Jesse's brother-in-law, consistently attacked Oates, the smaller of the men. Oates grew tired of Coghill's bullying. "I'll kill him," he said to himself. At the next muster, when Coghill gave Oates his customary whipping, Oates threatened to shoot as Coghill begged for his life. Oates allowed Coghill to retrieve the gun he preferred, and then, when Coghill ordered him to fire, he did so, killing Coghill instantly.

Oates headed home, gathered some money and a pocket compass, and rode west. In a Natchez tavern, he saw a newspaper advertisement offering a reward for his capture. He quickly moved on to Kentucky and the Pond River country, where he sent for his family. He never returned to North Carolina; if he had, he would probably have been killed by one of Coghill's friends.

Oates married twice: first to Larahuma Stevens, the daughter of a well-to-do neighbor, on March 3, 1782, and then to Zilpha Mason on April 13, 1789. He fathered five children by Larahuma, including William, and twelve by Zilpha. The family lived on a plantation with thirty slaves at Harpe's Hill near Pond River. Harpe's Hill is high and picturesque, and the valley below is often referred to as Egypt because of its fertile soil and good drainage.

On August 10, 1831, at the grand old age of seventy-five, Jesse Oates died. His body is in an unmarked grave on Harpe's Hill, in a burying ground he set aside for that purpose.

Warren's father, Bayless E. Oates, was born one of six children, on July 16, 1886, in the pioneer house situated on the six-hundred-acre farm built by Warren's great-great-grandfather William Oates. Circumstances called for Bayless to be industrious, and he was that, as well as quiet and studious. In the early 1910s, he bought and began operating a general store located across the street from the farm. He and his brothers also had a gristmill, powered by a gasoline engine, in which they made cornmeal and a coarse animal feed known as chop, and they sharpened plow points for neighbors. His sister Kate helped with cooking and household chores, while another sister, Lillian, handled outside work: feeding horses, milking cows, and tending to sick animals.

In 1920, Bayless Oates married Sarah Alice Mercer, whom he had repeatedly traveled on foot or horseback to visit at the church she attended, two or three miles away. The couple set up house in Depoy on Bards Hill Road. In time she bore a daughter, who died after three days. Two years later, in the middle of a coalfield-wide union strike, towheaded son Gordon was born on March 14, 1924.

Four years later, at the tail end of the Jazz Age, which like a comet passed high over Depoy, a native son appeared who would put the place on the map. If you look up Depoy today, you will find Warren Oates's picture, although this tiny, slapdash town goes on about its existence pretty much oblivious of the connection. Fly into nearby Owensboro–Daviess County Regional Airport, and you will see a photo of Oates in the passenger waiting area. "That's my favorite character actor," said the airport's general manager, Tim Bradshaw. "And I didn't know he was from this area." Elsewhere in the region and across Green River, residents lay claim to country star Merle Travis, the Everly Brothers, and bluegrass visionary Bill Monroe. Slightly farther afield and further in the future, Paducah would offer up enigmatic actor Johnny Depp, but not before Depoy's Warren Oates imbued the screen with a talent as deep as Green River, which local legend holds has no perceptible bottom in some parts.

Although Oates left Depoy when he was thirteen, he would return in thought and in deed—once even to marry. And although he would live in the arty atmosphere of New York's Greenwich Village, the cowboy flats of Southern California's San Fernando Valley, the faux wilderness of the Hollywood Hills, the faded glamour of Los Angeles's Los Feliz district, and the dramatic Montana landscape, Warren Oates never really found a home. "I feel always in motion," he would insist. "You start moving a man around and he doesn't have time to adjust. It's 'The Grapes of Wrath' all over again."

Oates described Depoy as simultaneously pastoral—"rolling hills, trees dark in wintertime, filigreed"—and spartan, "strikes and guns in lunchboxes and always some war somewhere coming over our Philco radio, the second radio in town." He reported its population as anywhere from a meager ninety-nine to a handful of hundreds, depending on the effect he sought. At the time of his birth, Depoy held about three hundred families.

The village of Depoy had a circuitous development. In the early 1800s, a log cabin surrounded by a huge grove of oak trees became the area's first dwelling. Known as the Davis House, it was abandoned in the first decade of the next century, to the delight of a generation who used its setting for ice cream suppers and less fulsome outings until 1940, when the structure was torn down and the sheltering oaks were cut.

The town made its first bow as a place called Gordon (after a family who had a small store there) when a post office was established on August 31, 1874. Since the advent of the railroad, the area had had a depot ferrying both passengers and freight, but a post office made existence official.

During this time, the Oates family ran the farm, and Susan Slaton, Warren's Aunt Sis, operated a boardinghouse in a little town nearby. On the night of March 20, 1868, a group of men who stayed over left a ten-dollar gold coin beneath a breakfast plate as a tip. Earlier that day, they had visited the Southern Deposit Bank in Russellville and asked the clerk, Nimrod Long, to cash a bond. When he started to comply, the outlaws jumped over the bank counter. Long ran off, leaving another bank employee to fend for himself and load the sacks with money. Jesse and Frank and the rest of the James-Younger Gang made off with between twelve and fourteen thousand dollars.

In 1917, the town now known as Depoy was about to boom, albeit for a short burst. The Midwest Coal Company, headed by a West Virginian named Lepinsky, had purchased local coal deposits along with a country bank mine and was proceeding to commence operations in Depoy. Midwest Coal was about to rearrange the scenery, and soon, Muhlenberg County would lead the nation in coal production.

Spur track was laid to serve two mines in the number nine vein of coal. The existing mine employed 30 people; a new, larger undertaking would have some 110 employees. The foreman of the smaller opening was Bill Coleman, whose son Bobby would be a favorite childhood playmate of Warren Oates. Both mines were active until the coalfield-wide union strike of 1924.

The town struggled to recover from the strike and returned to a primarily farming community. Foreman Bill Coleman once again raised cattle and crops on land across the highway from the Davis cabin and near the house and general store owned by Bayless Oates. Times were hard: some parcels of land were offered for only two dollars an acre. Tobacco, corn, and hay could be grown, along with produce destined for the market in Greenville, a larger town four miles east of Depoy. One of Greenville's assets was the Palace Theater, which opened in 1901 and featured vaudeville acts before inevitably transitioning first to silent and then to talking pictures.

Bayless Oates continued to run the concrete block general store (one of five in Depoy), behind which John Spurlin cooked and served hamburgers. Depoy had two doctors, two blacksmiths, and two barbers. All enterprise prospered or stumbled in the shadow of a huge general store run by Adkins Camp and Tucker, a cradle-to-grave establishment so complete it had funeral supplies, including coffins. Their horse-drawn hearse was a regular feature of the community.

In the early morning hours of July 5, 1928, it was the services of Dr. D. G. Argabrite that were required at the Oateses' white weatherboard house on Bards Hill Road, just across the shallow creek from Oak Grove Baptist Church, which the family attended. The emergent baby boy had a set of determinedly kicking feet; a full head of dark, slightly wavy hair; bright, changeable, soon-to-be-hazel eyes; and a scowl that could convey a multitude of expressions even at this most tender age. Wary he was not. Warren Mercer Oates was ready for action, even if only within the confines of a modest home in a tiny western Kentucky town.

Older brother Gordon was transfixed by the new addition to the household, but even adulation has its limits. A few weeks later, Gordon walked with his father to spend the day in the general store, no doubt to relieve Sarah and "Aunt" Evie Bard, who functioned as a nanny, from the pace of life with a newborn and a four-year-old in the home. Father and son turned left from their house, went down the gravel road, and walked on to the store. The shop sold nearly everything, from groceries to dry goods, from block salt to wagons, but it was into the glass candy counter that Gordon would crawl. That morning, Gordon was at his usual post when his father stepped out for a moment. The little boy emerged when John Brizendene, a local wholesale grocery salesman, walked in. He was a tall man with white hair who often called on Bayless. He asked Gordon how he liked his new baby brother. "OK," Gordon replied.

Brizendene ran his hands through his white hair. "Well, see, I was thinking, I might be willing to trade you something for that new baby. I thought you might be in line for a billy goat and wagon. A white billy goat pulling a red and green wagon, a leather harness with brass rings, brass hubs on the wheels. You sitting up there, high in a decorated seat, the reins in your hands, the billy goat ready to go? You'd be driving this billy goat and red and green wagon all around Depoy."

Gordon raced out of the store and headed home to get Warren. As he hurried in the front door, Sarah asked Gordon what the matter was. He breathlessly explained he was making a trade for his brother. Sarah laughed and even cried a little, but she did not plan on parting with her new baby. Gordon reluctantly went back to the store, on foot, to explain. At day's end he came home on foot, too.

When Warren was old enough to walk, he would also go to the store. His father was usually immersed in a book and would not even bother to look up as customers entered. "My dad was an avid reader," Oates recalled. "He'd always go into Greenville and bring back seven or eight books. He'd read every one of them in the allotted two-week period. I'd go with him sometimes and he really got me interested in reading."

Depoy was for the young man "a splendid place," with "mainly a real community spirit. Sometimes the whole town would get together on a project, like all making mattresses one year, because they were too expensive to buy." Warren would make the rounds of the stores and go on to the post office. "The post office was in J. L. Taggart's store and that's where all the activity was because the trains would come through. They'd drop the mail off twice a day and the big deal was to go up and watch the train go through and watch the mail bags fly off the end of it."

In the early 1930s, the local mines were winding down, and work was thin both above and below ground. Labor unrest was prevalent, and in Depoy, several miners were killed, which, along with the prospect of work in another location, prompted a good portion of the population to move away. Loss in custom coupled with the fact that he had extended credit to people who could not pay soon meant Bayless had to shut down the store and pick up work when and where he could. Sarah, now suffering complications brought on by diabetes, took in boarders. It is unlikely that any of the boarders were as notorious as Aunt Sis's, but being surrounded by characters could not have failed to make an impression on Warren, who perfected his trademark squint by watching an uncle speak with an ever-present cigarette angling from his mouth.

"Our upbringing was strict and we had to walk the line," said Bobby Coleman. He was a Methodist whereas Oates was a Baptist, one of the few details that separated them. "We grew up rough, and we made do with what we had," Coleman asserted. The rough edges included both boys' taking up smoking well before the age of twelve. "Still, I would have to say no one could have had a better life," Gordon Oates said. "We had values and pride. Sure, there were ragtag kids and troublemakers, but we were told not to associate with them. Of course, when you needed a softball team, you played with them."

A man called Buren Gray had an old, dilapidated garage where he worked on rusted automobiles, most of which were out in the yard on the threadbare grass. As a sideline he sold bootleg whiskey, which he made up in five-gallon jugs. Bootlegging was tiring work—even if you sampled the wares—so for help he turned to the local kids, who would carefully pour the moonshine into pints and half pints. This gave Buren a little more time to sit in the shade and play marbles—he had a wide selection of taws—and hopefully keep his mean streak hidden.

"One day Buren had a little too much of what he sold, and he

decided to get on Speed Bard, a black boy we would play with,"
Gordon remembered. Speed's mother, Aunt Evie Bard, was the
Oateses' nanny. "All of us kids got together and ran Buren off!"

Soon, young Warren was exploring other ways to earn money,
working in the fields picking strawberries for two cents a quart,
suckering tobacco for twenty-five cents a day, or riding the mule
that turned the machine that made the sorghum or ground the
wheat. When he was a little older, he assisted highway crews by
loading sand onto trucks, a job he claimed created the deep, permanent furrows in his brow. "When I was about eight, in the
great road-building era around 19 and -35, -36, -37, a bunch of
us kids would pick up 10 cents or 15 cents a day shoveling sand
into the big hauler trucks for the guys who drove them at maybe
75 cents a day," Oates said. The kids would work for the truck-
ers the entire day. The trucks would then haul the sand down to
where the road was being built.

The kids would also hop the train to Graham, about four miles
away, and play on the tracks in all seasons. "In the wintertime
when the rails got cold, we were told never to put our skin on the
railroad track because you'd freeze there," Oates said. "Well a
friend of mine stuck his tongue on it one day going to school, just
before the train came. His dad ran in and got a kettle of hot water
and poured it on the railroad track to unfreeze his tongue."

As spirited as his friends were, Warren could hold his own
against any of them. "Warren learned to paddle his own canoe,"
Gordon said, "to the point where if he was confronted, he didn't
let anyone get in his way. If the big kids bullied him too much,
he'd hit them with a rock. He was not one to be backed down
quickly." And if there was no one to fight with, he knew he could
always turn to his best friend, who lived six hundred feet away.

"I would dread walking home," Bobby Coleman said, "because
I knew I'd have to fight with Warren. And I didn't want to get in
a fight with Warren! One day I found a knife and I ran after him,
chased him into his house. His mother screamed, 'Don't you cut
Warren!' and I shouted back, 'I would, if I could catch him.'"

The boys would play, running back and forth between T. D.
Clark's barbershop, Taggart's wooden store, Cie Shannon's brick

store, and the Oateses' concrete block structure. One day, when Warren was bringing molasses home, he could not resist galloping with the heavy glass jar brimming with the sweet, sticky substance. He tripped and fell, and the molasses spilled like tar onto the cement steps. He hightailed it away as he yelled to his friends, "'Lasses, boys, 'lasses."

Education took place in a two-room schoolhouse, and his teacher in the primary grades was a relation, Jeanette Earle. Having a family member for a teacher, Oates conceded, "made things much easier for me." A photograph of his class in 1934 shows Warren squinting slightly, hands poised on his thighs near the cuff of his off-white shorts. An errant tuft of hair divides his forehead. Next to him, looking like a perennial tough guy, is little Bobby Coleman. "Warren and I were average students," Coleman said, leaning heavily on the word "average." "We were ordinary kids, healthy. But Warren was the comedian type at an early age."

One afternoon in Earle's classroom, five-year-old Warren sat at his desk, waiting his turn while each of his thirty-odd classmates went through their oral recitals. When his moment came, he walked to the front of the class, turned to face the curious or distracted young faces, and began to recite a poem. "I wish I was a cat I do," he said, and he was hooked on performing.

The Oates Valley's Unity Baptist Cemetery, set on a series of low hills in Graham, holds many Oates and Earle remains as well as a large monument that marks the grave of Everett Green, a miner whose murder in 1936 set off a series of events that had a profound effect on young Warren. On the cold Monday morning of January 14, 1936, a procession of cars crawled through the tiny town of Depoy.

"The most impressive and dramatic thing I've seen in my entire life was the funeral for the first man killed in a strike near Depoy," Oates said. "It was like something out of Steinbeck. The miners drove his coffin on the back of a pickup truck through two counties. With all the traffic it took them three hours to go through my little town. They were going about five, ten miles an hour and that served to heat the miners up enough to declare open war on the strikebreakers. When they buried that man, that was the end of the strike, and the strikebreakers." The spectacle of the cortege, and its underlying message, did much to form the sensibility of a man whose life of comparative pageantry was tempered by a deep-rooted respect for the working man.

The Oates family, with dog Bingo and cat Sambo, was a social one, and friends came from across age and color lines. In a region where music was abundant, the family radio never did summon the Grand Ole Opry, with its tales of awful snakes and grieving flowers. Bill Monroe, the Blue Sky Boys, and the Carter Family were not an early (or late) influence on Oates. The first radio he encountered was at the hairdresser's. Then Bayless got one for the store, and young Warren would hover over it, listening to stories about holdups of Jack Armstrong, the Lone Ranger, wars in China, civil war in Spain. He savored any news of bank robber John Dillinger and paid "passionate attention" to the exploits of public enemy number one. "Dillinger was a fascinating person," Oates explained. When the Oateses finally got a radio in their home, it was always on, playing in the background. Oates remembered "everybody listening to FDR the day he got his second term . . . and I was only eight."

If the Oates family—wittingly or not—cultivated an educated air, it was equally true that when uncles Jim Oates and George Mercer, both veterans of World War I, came over, "you couldn't keep enough liquor in the house," Gordon recalled.

Mealtimes were serious affairs, with Bayless offering up loquacious prayers that were the opposite of fictional film patriarch Pa Kettle's "Much obliged." Once, a very hungry Warren stared longingly at a big plate of beans on the table while his father gave profuse thanks. The grace went on and on until Warren could not take it anymore. He got up from his chair and started chanting, "I'm going to chase those beans around the table, I'm going to chase those beans around the table," running busy circles around the chairs. When he passed his father's chair for the third time, Bayless clubbed him in the head, knocking him nearly unconscious. On another occasion, Warren ate so many tomatoes that he broke out in boils.

Six months after Everett Green's funeral procession, at the

conclusion of a day of play and work, the neighborhood gathered around a radio at a house on Harpe's Hill to listen to the Joe Louis and Max Schmeling fight. Louis's victory was all anyone could talk about at church that Sunday.

Warren always arrived at church early to light the fire in the winter, open windows in the summer, and ring the church bell, tasks for which he was paid seventy-five cents. "I don't know how to describe those Sunday mornings in the church except to say that it was just a perfectly happy time being there alone early in the morning," he said. "It was a little spooky but it was perfect. I'd get there early and play on the piano. The church was right across the creek from my house and the cemetery was up on the hill and I could see both of them. Joy and fear . . . It was a time of some of the purest moments in my life."

Oak Grove Baptist Church, along with the Methodist church and the lone evangelical church, composed the trinity of religion in Depoy. "When the doors of Oak Grove opened, we were there," said Gordon. "There was Sunday school at 10 a.m., Wednesday nights were prayer meetings. We were there. There was simply nothing else to do." The church also put on a series of religious plays, in which young Warren eagerly played parts. "I had an overactive imagination," he said, "and they let me run where it took me."

His imagination also took him four miles into Greenville. He and his fellow ruffians would hitch a ride on a wagon or, if they were lucky, on one of the town's pickup trucks. And although what he did mirrored many a prairie pilgrimage or citified retreat, Warren did not go to the Palace Theater just because he loved the movies. He also went for the girls. "Mr. Pittman was the manager of the theater," said Bobby Coleman, "and Warren and the Pittman girl were sweet on each other. So sometimes Warren got to go to the movies for free. Saturday—westerns—was the big day," Coleman continued. He and Warren would arrive at two o'clock, when, for eleven cents, they could watch a movie, a serial, and a cartoon. Oates's first film was a western starring Tom Mix.

When the matinee was over and dusk began to blanket the town, Warren and Bobby would go home, sometimes getting a ride with Bayless. Each time when they got back, Warren would do exactly the same thing. He would put a can on top of a broomstick to serve as a microphone, and act out all the parts. He got so good that the neighborhood kids who could not afford to go to the movies would pool their money to send him. "I think it rubbed off," Oates said. "I think maybe that's when I really got interested in acting."

Sarah Oates had instilled in both of her children the imperative that they leave the small town and gain a larger education. "Early on I knew I wanted to go to further schooling and not stay in Muhlenberg County and work in the coal mines," Gordon said. By the time Gordon graduated early from Graham High School in 1940, when he was sixteen (and Warren, eleven), Gordon had made the decision to leave his family and Depoy to attend business college in Louisville.

With his older son out of the home, Bayless realized that the little town was nearly spent. Since shutting up shop, he had worked where and when he could, and Sarah continued to take in boarders, but they were few and far between. "Daddy, when are you going to get me out of this mudhole?" Sarah would ask Bayless, and in 1942, he moved his family to Louisville.

Warren was thirteen. Like any other teenager, he did not want to leave his friends. All he had known, apart from westerns on Saturday afternoons, was Depoy. "My father moved to Louisville, and that's how I left my little town. I didn't want to go to Louisville, but I was forced to. I was ready to run off back to the country," he said. In some accounts, he colored the move with a hint of rebellion: "I knew everything about everyone; and they knew everything about me. I decided to keep moving." But as he traveled on U.S. 62, a road he had helped to pave, what remained of his childhood sunned on his shoulder.

Charles Dickens visited Louisville in 1842 and wrote, "There was nothing very interesting in the scenery of this day's journey which brought us at midnight to Louisville. We slept at the Galt House, a splendid hotel and were as handsomely lodged as though we had been in Paris. The city presenting no objects of sufficient interest to detain us on our way, we resolved to proceed the next day by another steamboat." Such a depiction of their city was said to have so perturbed some Louisvillians that they boycotted the writer's works.

A century later, Louisville was a city of 319,000, many of whom had been recently uprooted to higher ground. A devastating flood in 1937 prompted the move, which was followed by a period of rebuilding. It was into this teeming environment that in October 1940 the sixteen-year-old Gordon Oates arrived. After leaving his family in Depoy, he enrolled in Bryant and Stratton College in downtown Louisville, took lodgings in a large old brick home at 817 South Fourth Street, and worked nearby in the John R. Thompson Cafeteria Restaurant for meals or a full day's pay of $1.65. Within a year, he was working for the *Louisville Courier-Journal's* country circulation manager.

One early December afternoon, he took advantage of a lunch invitation from his cousin Nick Oates, who, along with his wife Sue, operated the R. N. Oates Uniform Company at 212 West Chestnut Street. Over their meal, they listened to the radio address given by President Franklin D. Roosevelt informing the country that Pearl Harbor had been bombed. Back in Depoy, his younger brother Warren was out playing in a field. "It was about 4 pm when we got the news," he said. "I was brought up on war reports, so I wasn't shocked."

Louisville was already a city in transition, led by a progressive New Deal mayor, Wilson Wyatt Sr. After the bombing of Pearl Harbor, Wyatt ordered extra guards to be stationed at the Louisville bridges that traversed the Ohio River and at the city's numerous war plants—Louisville would be ranked eighteenth in the nation as a war arsenal. Scrap metal and aluminum drives were initiated, and rationing of tires, cars, gasoline, and food was imposed. Powder plants appeared in Rubbertown and nearby Charlestown, Indiana, and chemical plants operated within the city limits. Louisville became the synthetic rubber capital of America as plants on Bells Lane used copious amounts of alcohol from the city's distilleries in the production of synthetic rubber.

Factories abounded: Mengel Company, where Bayless Oates would work, made wood products used in the war, and Reynolds Aluminum Company manufactured arms and other materials. At specially dedicated windows, Liberty National Bank sold war bonds. Ford Motor Company's Louisville assembly plant employed half a million people and turned out 93,000 military jeeps.

The city was overcrowded in every sense of the word: hospitals, public buildings, housing, and schools were inadequate to cope with the surge of people. By 1942, there were an additional 15,500 war workers.

It was a far cry from Depoy. Yet it was into this metropolis of exponential growth that Bayless, Sarah, and Warren would drive in early 1942. Stopping in the outskirts to fill up the truck's gas tank, they waited in awe as a woman attendant worked the fuel pump. When they pulled up in front of 1511 Morton Avenue, Gordon was already there, waiting to help his family unpack.

The reunited family carried crates and furniture, crockery and heirlooms into the home. The next morning, Warren Oates woke up in a new room in a strange house in an unfamiliar city. And he hated it. However strong his initial dislike, things were about to get worse. When he ventured outside, a hillbilly kid dressed in bib overalls, he quickly drew the attention of his citified peers. "The other kids wouldn't lay off me," Oates said.

It was in these overalls, and with a set of teeth that had the color and texture of chicken scratch, that he headed off to his first day at Eastern Junior High in September 1942. It was not pretty. He fought; he was truant. Soon his grades were appalling: Ds and Cs in math, social studies, and mechanical drawing. He somehow survived until summer, and then he headed straight back to Depoy. When it was time to return to Louisville, Oates resisted, to no avail.

In the fall of 1943, he started high school. Louisville Male High School on First Street between Walnut and Chestnut was a two-story brick structure segregated by sex and by race. "They didn't trust anybody," Oates said later. He was soon cutting classes, making a beeline for the Parkmoor Bowling Alley, the pool hall, and the roller rink. Spending time in these dank, dark, and anonymous haunts seemed a far better option than fighting other kids for his lunch money. Plus, he could steal a smoke. The truant and tough crowd were some solace, but they were not enough. "I hated the big city until I started going to the movies," Oates said. "I went every chance I got. The movies were the only thing that made [Louisville] bearable."

Movie houses with names like the Ohio and the Rialto lined the stretch of the 600 block of South Fourth Street known as theater row. Loew's Theater, designed in 1928 by John Eberson, was a picture palace in every sense: the Moorish marvel featured a ceiling replete with a star-studded sky over which wandering clouds floated. The fifteen-year-old Oates took note, but what was on screen mattered more. An engrossing *Batman* serial, *The Ox-Bow Incident*, and *For Whom the Bell Tolls* and *Casablanca* with his favorite actor, Humphrey Bogart, ran at Loew's, and Oates saw them multiple times.

He also found another refuge, one that does not meld with the image of a budding juvenile delinquent. "When I went to Louisville and was kind of lonely and inside myself," Oates said, "I discovered the local library. I read from A to C in most of the things that interested me, other than maybe heavy science, in this one corner of the library." Then he would move to the next segment of the alphabet. In the As, though, he found an author who held him in thrall. "Joseph A. Altsheler . . . had written a series of maybe 35 books: historical fiction, much in the manner that Zane Grey did about the West. Only he wrote about the earliest origins of the United States, from the French and Indian Wars on through, and he had heroes that went through a series of books. Maybe three or four books were about the same two or three guys." Oates remembered, "It was like a television series, only in novel form. I read every one of them, and then I got interested in the Indians, because he covered the Revolutionary War. He also covered the time in between, and he covered the War of 1812 and the Civil War. Then his two characters from the Civil War went out West."

Altsheler was a rustic counterpart to the ubiquitous up-by-your-own-bootstraps stories of Horatio Alger, and it was his popular book *The Young Trailers* that had the biggest impact on

Oates. The stories followed the exploits of young frontiersman Henry Ware and featured a character called Shif'less Sol who was a curious precursor to the kinds of roles Oates would play. Tales of high adventure, fires, fishing, and beaver streams with titles like *The Eyes of the Woods* and *The Riflemen of the Ohio* gradually forged Oates's ethos. Other installments on the French and Indian wars, the Civil War, and the West were equally captivating to the awkward, backwoods young man sitting in one corner of the library. When Altsheler wrote, "He would always remain a son of the wilderness, spending but part of his time in the houses of men," for Oates it would be more apt than any caption for his high school yearbook photo. True, he was rarely at school when class photos were taken, or on many other days.

His absence affected his already woeful grades, although he showed aptitude for sales and band and did reasonably well in world history and botany. He had the benefit of a "mean English teacher who forced us to read Shakespeare," kindling his respect for the classics. But a scholar he was not, playing hooky to go to the movies or anywhere else as far from a scholastic setting as he could get. Altsheler's schoolmaster Silas Pennypacker often taught his young charges outside the classroom, taking them out into the forests, where they would look for salt. Such an approach might have served Warren Oates better than did Algebra I.

One day he came home late after having cut school for two weeks straight. He found his father waiting for him. Bayless sat on his son's bed and said, "I don't know what I'm gonna do with you. I don't know what you are going to do with yourself."

Somehow that reached the teenager. "I knew I had to do something with my life," Oates said.

His brother was in England, about to participate in the D day invasion at Omaha Beach. Warren enlisted in the Reserve Officers' Training Corps and started thinking about joining the Marine Corps. By spring 1945, World War II was winding down, and an epidemic of remodeling hit Louisville stores. Gordon Oates returned from Germany to jubilant parents and a wayward brother. Warren had been in a car accident on February 29, and if it did not scare him straight, the rigors of the ROTC provided some direction.

But Warren was not keeping out of trouble. Just before the end of the war, ruffians beat up a friend of his named Billy. Warren ran home to get a Belgian pistol Gordon had brought back and then hunted down the culprits in front of a drugstore. "I stuck it [the pistol] in this one guy's stomach and said we were going to the hospital with Billy. He drove us over there and we sat in front of General Hospital with this pistol in his stomach until Billy got fixed up and came out. Then I told this guy to drive us back home. He did. Nobody said a word all the way back. We got out. I think it changed their lives because they thought I might shoot. They never did know the gun wasn't loaded," Oates said.

By spring 1946, it was obvious that Warren would not be graduating from Male High School. In fact, the only place he seemed to be headed was the state penitentiary. Although he had a few friends in jail, he did not care to join them. To avoid that potential reunion, he took a drastic step. Making good on his promise to keep out of trouble, he followed the logical course that had begun with his ROTC training. Patriotism in wartime and postwar America was all encompassing, and failure to serve your country in some capacity bordered on being morally suspect. So, on July 22, 1946, at the downtown Louisville recruiting station, eighteen-year-old Oates joined the U.S. Marine Corps. He might have chosen that branch of service for its emboldening motto, Semper Fidelis, but the grunt would again greet the arts in a tucked-away corner of the library.

His curly hair cropped short, Private Oates had his military photo taken on August 3 before being sent to Parris Island, South Carolina. His ROTC training spared him some grief: "Probably my being able to march and know a little something about a rifle and military drill saved me from getting a lot of knocks on my head," he said of his sojourn at the corps' clearinghouse.

In boot camp at Cherry Point, North Carolina, Oates had a memorable drill sergeant named Goodwin. "He used to carry a pet raccoon around with him and put it on the shoulder of the man who screwed up the most that day," Oates said. "He wanted to aggravate us and see if we had any guts."

Oates did have guts, but the Marine Photographic Squadron did not afford much scope for glory. Neither did the Second Marine Aircraft Wing Group, where he performed routine maintenance on helicopters. But his love of reading led him to the military library at Cherry Point, where he discovered an anthologized version of Eugene O'Neill's trilogy of plays *Mourning Becomes Electra*. What the machinations of the tragic Mannons meant to the boy from a stable, humble Kentucky family—one he would occasionally refer to as "puritan"—is difficult to capture, but he found their raw emotions to be heaven-sent. His feelings were strengthened when a theater group from Newberry, South Carolina, staged a performance of the play at the military barracks in 1946.

By 1947, Oates was stationed on board the USS *Palau*, an aircraft carrier then immobilized off the coast of Norfolk. After completing his two-year stint, he returned to Louisville as a reservist and worked as a passable but less than zealous recruiter. Later in life, he would occasionally embellish his military service, but he more often failed to mention it. "I wasn't a great marine, but at least I survived," he said.

2

A Good Horse

In April 1948, Corporal Warren Oates was a Marine Corps reservist in Louisville. He carried with him a Good Conduct Medal—which had been hard to earn, as it meant he had not caused any trouble whatsoever—plus a World War II victory medal, some souvenirs, and other perfunctory items. His service record was not remarkable, yet what it afforded him was life altering: the GI bill enabled him to go to college at no cost. Even for a Louisville Male High School dropout, it must have seemed like a viable plan. All he needed to do was pass the high school equivalency exam.

His arrival in Louisville on a spring day was no dramatic return. His mother and father still lived at 1511 Morton Avenue. He was bunking in his old room. To revisit haunts like Jack Fry's, the twenty-four-hour Saratoga Restaurant, the Hawaiian Gardens Dance Hall at Fourth Street and Broadway, and Club Madrid at 543 South Third Street was more standard operating procedure than fresh start. The low lights of the clubs and the marquees of the Ohio, Strand, and Rialto movie theaters spelled out "home." In his absence, though, a new venue had opened: the Scoop Theatre billed itself as Louisville's art theater and offered "French, German, Italian, Spanish, Polish, Russian, English, and Hollywood" attractions. And the Kentucky Theatre, formerly a house for the performing arts, had added a balcony and begun showing movies to accommodate changing tastes.

Oates took his high school equivalency exam and requested

that his decidedly lackluster high school transcript be sent to the University of Louisville. The university had an enrollment of 2,655 in the fall of 1948. At least one of the newly admitted underclassmen who went down Howdy Walk on the Belknap Campus that fall morning was far from worldly: Warren Oates may have been to Haiti, Cuba, and Camp Lejeune as a marine, but the insular, buddy-system corps had done little to turn him into a sophisticate. He still dressed in a "country" style and had a twang that stung like a hickory switch. "I was a total hick with a mountain accent," he said. "I didn't even talk like the city boys from the same state."

Oates took business math (business management was the first of many majors that would drift past him), typing, the rise of American civilization, and introduction to world literature, and received an F in every one. In fact, almost all his grades were Ds and Fs, with nary a C in sight. The mandatory English composition course seemed destined to be another washout, and if it had not been for the instructor, it probably would have been. That Oates got a B in the class is inconsequential. Because of its instructor, Warren Oates became an actor.

Weldon Stone was born into a Baptist family in Holland, Texas, on April 16, 1902. He grew up on a farm with his parents and a grandfather who had served in the Confederate army. Of medium height with brown hair and hazel eyes (he claimed Cherokee heritage), Stone began writing stories such as "A Ringtail Tooter" and "The Colt and the Pearl" while attending Baylor University in Waco. He eventually received a master of arts degree from Southern Methodist University. He also wrote plays, and in 1949, the Theater Guild Playhouse in Lighthouse, Connecticut, would stage a performance of his *Devil Take a Whittler* starring an unknown Kentucky-born actress named Patricia Neal. Neal played Kat Skaggs in the production, which was billed as an "authentic American folk fantasy" but nonetheless opened on July 29 and abruptly closed on August 3.

In the summer of 1947, Stone was a writer looking for a job, and one of the places he applied was the University of Louisville. An interdepartmental communication from Ernest C. Hassold to university president John W. Taylor makes for an entertaining read: "1. Mr. Stone has left his family on a mountain in Vermont and was eager to get home again. He seemed good to both Dean Oppenheimer and myself and I am recommending him for an assistant professorship at $4,000. 2. T. S. Eliot writes that he is not coming to Louisville till 1948 and will be glad to lecture but does not want to make a definite commitment too far in advance."

Unlike the world-famous author of *The Waste Land*, Stone was able to commit. A proviso of his hiring was that he teach a course in English composition. During his first semester of lecturing, Stone encouraged his instantly devoted class of budding actors and playwrights to break away from the university's current troupe, which typically excluded newer students. The upstart University Playshop rehearsed and performed in the student union building, while the established University of Louisville Players made a home in the Playhouse. Originally the chapel of a nineteenth-century orphanage, the Playhouse was a rustic Carpenter Gothic board and batten structure featuring stained glass windows and, unique for a theater, a core cruciform shape.

If the Playhouse had a patron saint, for some it would be Edgar Boyd Martin, although others still bristle at the suggestion. "Pop" Martin was a native son who entered a lifelong relationship with the theater in 1907. Within a few years, he was full director and had renamed the club the University of Louisville Players. He also became an instructor in the English department, where he formulated a groundbreaking class in play production.

In forty-five years, Martin oversaw four hundred plays and wrote for the *Louisville Courier-Journal*. But the pipe-smoking, impeccably dressed, energetic man did not cotton to younger postwar entrants such as Oates and his colleague, Mitzi Bornwasser. Martin believed that the renegade group "would rather work with Stone in experimental plays rather than in the Playhouse where the discipline was a little more rigorous," but Bornwasser, an ingenue and rising star in Louisville theater, took issue. "We didn't break off with Boyd Martin; he broke off with us," Bornwasser (now Friedlander) asserted. "He had his group of students, fine actors . . . but they were students in the 1920s! We were broken off *from*."

The relationship between Martin, the theater's director, and Stone, the often errant English instructor who also taught play-writing, was fraught. But Stone's students knew where their loyalties rested. "Weldon Stone was part of our group," Friedlander recalled. "He seemed very down home to me. I was not nearly so close as Warren was. Stone was kind of . . . oh, not a ne'er-do-well, but . . . he drank a bit."

As a reluctant student in English 101, oral and written composition, Oates was doing his best not to speak. "I felt strange even being in college," he said of his fledgling academic years. But on the first day of class, Stone went around the room, asking students what they wanted to get out of college. In Oates's case, it was less the answer he gave than the accent in which he gave it.

"Have you ever done any acting?" Stone asked him.

"No, sir," the student shrugged.

"We need someone like you down at the Playshop," Stone urged. "Why don't you go along and try out?"

Oates sheepishly did and was immediately cast in a student play called *Book Collecting*. "I didn't get the lead but I got the bug," Oates said.

He would later claim to have made his amateur stage debut in a play that opened two months later, but *Book Collecting* was the first time he acted at the university. As a March showcase commemorating the first anniversary of the University Playshop, three plays were performed at eight thirty on Thursday and Friday nights. In addition, Thursday, March 24, was "Playshop Day," during which the entire student body and faculty were invited to come by the student union for live music, free food (including Lady Betty cucumber wafers and Coca-Cola in cups), and a skit reenacting the brief history of the University Playshop. Oates performed in two of the evening's student-written presentations. He was a sentry in *The King's Bedchamber* by Les Gaddle and the rural reprobate Snippling in *Book Collecting*, written by a left-leaning student who had ginger-colored hair, which had earned him the nickname "Red" Vance.

To close the season, Weldon Stone was preparing to stage a play he had written, *Fine Pretty Things*, at the Playhouse. Boyd Martin, who later described the work as "a pretty bad play, a sort of hillbilly drama," reluctantly acceded and also agreed to the casting of Warren Oates as the protagonist Guy Hill. "That performance cinched Warren's determination to make the stage his profession," Martin later wrote.

On the successive evenings of May 16–19, Oates, the younger boy of a backwoods family, was first onstage in the big room of the Bland Hill log cabin in the Ozark Mountains in north central Arkansas on a chilly October morning early in the New Deal era. His debut was a delight; he brought "an easy sparkle to his performance and earn[ed] many laughs from the audience," Martin noted. After act 2 came the trademark coffee interlude during which the beverage was served in the theater's foyer along with Chesterfield cigarettes provided by the campus representative.

During intermission, the audience could leaf through the playbill and read about *Fine Pretty Things* as well as other recent plays, including *Chicken Every Sunday*. There was a prominent article titled "Portrait of Boyd Martin Wins High Praise." Oates's bio indicated that the actor playing "Guy Hill, Bland's Son" was "a freshman in the Arts and Sciences school who hopes to become a fine portrait and landscape artist but for the present is taking his acting seriously."

"The audience laughed at some pretty funny lines so I became the company's comedian," Oates said. But acting in the play offered more than a chance to become a cutup. The young man who, by his own admission, "even at the manly age of 20 still looked boyish" found in that part—and in the audience and critical reaction—the nudging toward an otherwise preposterous ambition: maybe he would try acting. "From there I got interested in the community theatres in Louisville," Oates said. "My reviews in the school paper were so good that I was hooked and simply had to become an actor. I slowly got into it, to the point where I lost interest in everything else in school." For all its hokum, *Fine Pretty Things* defined Oates's view of himself as an actor. "My identity was there with the people in the theatres and the playshop on the campus. That really was my total education. I was only interested in the theatre and what my friends were interested in. Some of them were interested in writing, and so we had a very unique sort of group, and they encouraged me in a sense."

And they were a unique bunch. After rehearsals and classes, the group that included Don Preston, who went on to edit Susan Sontag; Stuart Flexner, who became a highly regarded lexicographer; Bill Bauman, a bookstore proprietor who had been an expatriate journalist in 1920s Paris; and Weldon Stone all joined Oates, Bornwasser, Red Vance, and another student actor who got stuck with the moniker "Cheese" Kraft although his name was Joe. They gathered at the Hollywood Steakhouse or the Grand- ville Inn to talk about art, drink beer, and gossip—one topic of conversation was Earl Bircham, public enemy number one, who had recently been captured in Louisville after killing one police officer and wounding another.

Now when Oates walked across campus, it was with a pur- poseful stride, if not total gentility. One day a classmate, Ann Hart (now Marshall), joined him on a stroll, taking in the bright foliage and Oates's colorful verbiage. "His vocabulary," she recalled—"I just didn't hear that kind of language at home!"

During the summer of 1949, Stone taught an introductory drama course that covered William Saroyan's play *The Time of Your Life*. The story of a collection of oddballs and highballs in a San Francisco bar quickly became Oates's favorite, usurping the place held by the Mannons in the vastly more affected *Mourning Becomes Electra*. Stone's was one class Oates found it easy to attend, despite summer's distractions. On a particularly hot day, Stone made the comment, "The world is a stage and the stage is about morality," and Oates, previously slouched in his seat, sat up and took notice. He later said of Stone, "I had a great teacher in college who taught playwriting and drama, and I became inter- ested in acting. He's the one who got me into all this. He was a drunk and a romantic and I guess like me in many ways."

Weldon Stone did more than get Oates interested in acting. He provided a path to the joys and tragedies behind the words and enabled a poorly focused, sensitive young man from a hardscrabble background to both access and act on those emotions. Oates's mother might have wanted him to go to art school, but acting now had his full attention.

Before the end of the year, Oates appeared in *Nightmare*, a play by Bob White. This time he did not play a hillbilly—he was a horse who gave betting tips to his human friends. Bornwasser, who was also in *Nightmare*, insisted, "He was a good horse." Oates also played Private Dean, one of six soldier corpses in Irwin Shaw's *Bury the Dead*, a production that garnered special praise when it ran on November 17 and 18. Private Levy was portrayed by a friend named Marvin Goldman, whose uncle Milton was an actors' agent in New York City.

Oates and his mother and father were now living around the corner from their previous place on Morton Avenue, at 953 Edward Avenue in the Highlands neighborhood, just off Bardstown Road. Weldon Stone had a home nearby at 1745 Shady Lane, and Warren visited often.

Oates joined as many theater groups as he could, based on the practical belief that the experience he gained would only strengthen his abilities. His search for places to perform led him and several of his friends to the Carriage House Players, begun in the late 1940s by an actor named C. Douglas Ramey. Ramey, who would go on to pioneer Louisville's Shakespeare in the Park, would also be highly influential in Oates's life. Ramey "was an odd duck, very eccentric, a real theater person," said Bekky Schneider, who worked with him in later years. "He lived in the theater, and his closet was the costume room." His style was different from Stone's, but Ramey's rapport with his young charges was equally strong. An eastern Kentuckian who had studied at the Goodman Theatre in Chicago, Ramey knew acting. Ramey's weekly television show, *Songs of Faith*, made him a local celebrity, and his Shakespeare in the Park program inspired the Shakespeare movement in other cities and states.

Though his gifts to the community were rich, his circumstances were not. Yet his desperate straits may have indirectly fed his performers. "He would call you on Friday morning and say, 'Hey, I've lost my Juliet for tonight, could you do that?'" Schneider recalled. If the actor balked at her lack of preparation, he would be quick to assure her she could do it. "You went, 'If you think I can do it . . . ' and he'd say, 'Oh, sure you can do it,' and then you'd go do Shakespeare that night. He was pretty incredible." Oates said, "Doug gave a lot of us—meaning people who became professionals—some of our first experience." In Louisville's Central Park, the actor appeared in a summer production of *Macbeth*. Which part he played is not known, but given Ramey's legendary flexibility borne of necessity, Oates may well have appeared in a variety of cloaks within the Scottish play.

In February 1950, the University of Louisville dismissed Oates because of his poor scholarship. His four Fs and one C probably had something to do with it. But Stone ensured that Oates kept working, directing William Saroyan's *Hello Out There* and playing Walter Godkin in Carl Allensworth's *Village Green*. The playbill optimistically indicated that the student who had enrolled in fall 1948 would be a sophomore in the coming academic year.

In September 1950, Oates did manage to get readmitted to college, albeit on probation. His happiness was cut short, however. Coming home in the late evening of September 13, he was met with unexpected tragedy. His father had been doing repairs on the home, climbing up and down a wobbly ladder. He had fallen before dusk, hitting his head on a pile of bricks and fracturing his skull. He was taken to Louisville General Hospital, where he died at 10:10 that night. The funeral for the sixty-four-year-old Bayless, who worked as a watchman at Mengel Company, was held on September 16, and he was buried in Louisville's Cave Hill Cemetery, a large and extravagant memorial ground that includes a cave within its boundaries.

The bereaved family, Gordon, Warren, and their mother Sarah, soldiered on. Warren buckled down, improving his grades—slightly —and got a job. The Associates Discount Corporation located at 333 Guthrie Street was an automobile financing group that organized loans for new cars. "I knew then that wasn't what I wanted," Oates said, but he stuck with the job longer than might have been expected, and with a good deal more success and dedication.

Oates had his picture taken for *The Thoroughbred*, the University of Louisville's yearbook. On page 196 of the 1950 edition, his photo is in the second-to-last row of photos. He is smiling slightly between the wider grins (and better dental work) of sophomore classmates John R. Oakley and Helen F. O'Brien.

That fall, Oates did not take part in many school productions other than directing Weldon Stone's *Devil Take a Whittler*, which earned good notices. "Special recognition should go to director Warren Oates, whose efforts were well displayed by the great success of his cast," the school newspaper pointed out. "Sets for each of the three plays were well executed and the lighting effects achieved were excellent despite the distracting noises produced each time a switch was thrown."

Distraction during a performance was unlikely to faze Oates. It was collegiate life away from the stage that was proving tricky. And by mid-1951, his grades could not have been any worse. After a semester of all Fs in American government, the psychology of social issues, and life drawing, the university permanently dismissed him because of his poor scholarship.

Luckily for him, he was about to fall in love. On a hot summer evening in 1951, the twenty-three-year-old Oates barged out the back door of a diner across the street from Jack Fry's, the de facto second home for Oates, located at the intersection of Baxter and Highland Avenues. In the parking lot, a carful of teenagers loafed, affecting agitation at having to wait for the overworked carhop to come take their order. One of them, a pretty sixteen-year-old named Alberta "Bertie" Waddell (now Rutter), warily watched the dark-haired young man exit the back door, and she grew more surprised as he headed straight toward her.

"Your wish is my command," Oates said to Bertie, adding a little bow. "What would you like?"

"What a creep," she thought. "Your wish is my command?" Still, his appearance—sport jacket, shirt, and tie—captured her attention. It was a far cry from the sloppy jeans and wrinkled, untucked shirts her crowd wore. "I would like a big, tall glass of tomato juice with lots of ice," she said, deliberately choosing something she thought the diner was unlikely to have.

When Oates ran back to get it, she and her friends rolled with laughter.

Oates returned carrying a tall glass of thick red juice jostling with tiny rafts of ice. "I'm John," he said.

"What's he talking about?" she thought, before replying, "I'm Mary," catching the thread of the popular film *John Loves Mary*.

He reached for her hand and asked, "Would you like to step out of the car and talk with me?"

Bertie got out of the back seat. A ribbon held her curly, long blonde hair back, and she wore scruffy jeans with scuffed moccasins. "Can we see each other?" Oates ventured.

She told him her group gathered every night around eight o'clock at a swimming pool near the edge of town. After the pool was closed for the day, the space was converted into a dance hall, and dancing continued until midnight. When Oates turned up the next night, a relationship began, even if it was one based on a fib. Her date truthfully told her he had been in the service and also attended the University of Louisville, and Bertie was impressed. If she thought he had done a lot in his short years, though, it was because her suitor had cagily trimmed several years off his age. Seven years older than his high school date, Oates was also already behaving like an actor. From the theatrical flourish with which he had introduced himself to the shrewd way he had diminished their age difference, Oates was beginning a foray onto the romantic stage. The confidence that acting had given him could not be underestimated; it is impossible to picture the awkward Male High School hillbilly carrying on this way.

Oates would take her to Lighthouse Lake, where teenagers went to dance. "He didn't jitterbug or rat-race, so he would sit in a chair by the dance floor and watch me dance," Bertie said. "He would smile at me with that gapped-tooth smile and that mop of curly hair falling over one eye." Oates pursued the petite Bertie into what she felt was "a young, innocent romance, kind of like a first crush." She attempted to resist, but there was little point. "If he liked you, you had to like him in return; you didn't have much choice."

The high school sophomore and the college dropout dated casually over the next couple of years, with Bertie acutely aware of what separated them. Oates was strong willed, with complete confidence in his ability as an actor. "He always knew what he was going after and what he'd get," she said. "I always had no confidence."

Oates would meet her in his little red Willys Jeep, driving through the dust that drifted over from Rubbertown, and together they would go to Jack Fry's or Curtis's Doghouse on Shelby Street. Oates talked a lot about himself, about the University of Louisville, and about Weldon Stone. He would hang his head when he spoke about his job at Associates Discount. "I don't know what I want to be," he lied, before adding truthfully, "but I do know I don't want to be in an office. I cannot stand to be closed in."

After going to Jack Fry's or the diner, sometimes they would talk to the people who hung around outside Walgreen's Drugstore at the junction of Baxter and Highland Avenues and Bardstown Road. Oates would go in and steal bottles of wine for boys with names like Parky Philps. "Stealing wine made him look not like a stuffed shirt; he was one of the guys," Bertie explained. "He wanted to be one of the bad boys, black leather. He wanted to be the Fonzie. But he was the Richie. Sweet, well-mannered, quiet, gentle."

In 1952, Oates's almost alma mater, Louisville Male High School, finally consolidated after a prolonged and bitter controversy. The resultant Louisville Male and Girls' High School was born. "They said everybody was supposedly cutting school too much to go over and see the girls," Oates remarked. "I don't think that was so at all—they just found it more economical."

Although he was not officially enrolled in the university, under Stone's tutelage and the University Playshop's auspices, Oates was able to perform in a handful more plays there. In March 1952 he was Tokio in Clifford Odets's *Golden Boy*. And although he had lost a series of part-time jobs because he drifted away to rehearse or act, he had managed to hang on to his position at Associates Discount. When he wanted to, he had the gift of gab, and apprehensive car buyers were put at ease by his banter as he guided

them toward payment plans. Management began thinking about promotion for their salesman.

It was starting to look as if it was time to make or break his future. After rehearsal one night, Oates called for Bertie in the red Jeep he was thinking about selling and took her to Curtis's Doghouse. Standing above her, he said, "Bertie, I'm thinking about going away to New York to be an actor."

"Either you're either crazy or the biggest liar in the world, and I haven't figured out which one you are. If you think you can go to New York, you got something wrong with your head. I don't want to hurt your feelings, but you are no handsome leading man."

"I don't have to be handsome to be an actor," he answered quietly. But the damage was done. The couple did not speak again for several months.

On New Year's Eve 1952, Bertie called Oates in the house he shared with his mother.

"Thank goodness you're home!" she said.

"Where else would I be on New Year's Eve?" Oates replied glumly.

"Are you still serious about leaving for New York?"

"Dead serious. I don't know why you're so upset about my decision."

"But you have no money," Bertie insisted.

"I sold my car and my mother gave me a loan. My brother is not keen about me going. Nevertheless, he has decided to help."

"I'm sorry about what I called you. Will you forgive me?"

"Sure. It's not every day I'm called a liar and a nut. What are you doing tonight?" Oates asked her.

"I have a date," she said bluntly. "What are you going to do?"

"I'm just going to stay home."

"Well," she said, suddenly angry, "you can go chase your impossible dream while I stay in this jerk town. If you're hell-bent on going, I want to wish you all the luck in the world." She hung up.

In just over a year's time, Bertie would marry her date, one of the bad boys, and Oates would finally be on his way to New York City.

There had been very little rain heading into 1953, and the dust was still heavy in the west end of Louisville. The Rubbertown factories had agreed to finance their own investigation into the problem. Meanwhile, part of the city was abuzz with preparations for its 175th birthday party. A founding festival was in the works, and Douglas Ramey was preparing to stage *The Tall Kentuckian* at the amphitheater in Central Park. The musical, which would commemorate Abraham Lincoln's visit to Louisville, featured a large cast headed by Royal Dano. Every Louisville actor was in the production, including Warren Oates, who would refer to the large endeavor as his professional stage debut.

Before that, at the Playhouse in March 1953, Oates played a sixty-year-old man in Louis Verneuil's *Affairs of State*. "Mr. Warren Oates (Lawrence) is aging rapidly; he is adding at least 40 years to his chronological age with the aid of a little makeup and a great deal of talent to play Lawrence tonight," the playbill noted.

But Warren Oates had to make up his mind. His boss wanted to send him to an executive training course in South Bend, Indiana, a path his brother encouraged him to pursue over acting. "I just couldn't do it," Oates said. "I felt it was going to lock me in." Crucially, he had the support of his friends. "I had great encouragement from sympathetic, understanding people, and just good friends who were maybe more mature than I and could see my own kind of disillusionment and lost-ness," he said.

His brother, however, had done the research on acting as a profession. "I'd read there was a 700:1 odds that you'd ever make it or earn a living," he said, and he told his brother as much.

"I just must do this," Warren replied. "I promise you this: I will give it five years, and at the end of five years, if I haven't made it, I'll come back, and I'll lead a normal life."

Oates then rushed off for his drum lessons. The last play he would do at the Playhouse was also his first leading role. Waldo Walton was a young New York City apartment manager and aspiring musician in Howard Lindsay's *Remains to Be Seen* (which was made into a film), and Oates gave the part his all, taking drumming lessons and staying on long after rehearsals to play. "Since Waldo had to give several demonstrations of his dexterity with drums, cymbals and such, Warren practiced conscientiously before and after rehearsals and often far into the early morning after I had locked up The Playhouse for the night," Boyd Martin, who produced the play, wrote.

Oates took the play's theme to heart: Waldo has to decide between his safe, secure life and taking an artistic and romantic risk. When the arrival of Jody, an attractive, worldly band singer, tilts the scales, Waldo takes the leap, leaving his battle-ax boss Mrs. Bright in the lurch.

On May 8, 1953, the Playhouse's red curtain came down after the cast of *Remains to Be Seen* took its collective bow. Oates would do a few more plays in Louisville, but this was his last at the University of Louisville. Bertie Waddell was in the audience, feeling uncomfortable. "I thought, 'What does he want with me?'" she said.

On June 18, *The Tall Kentuckian* arrived in Louisville. Royal Dano, in his often repeated role of President Lincoln, would spend a portion of his time onstage looking down the dress of the actress playing Mary Todd Lincoln, portrayed on this occasion with unprecedented cleavage. In subsequent performances, the actress got a little perturbed. "HELLO" she wrote across her bust in eyeliner pencil. Dano had to work hard to recover his composure.

Dano had seen Oates perform and encouraged him to consider going to New York. It took Oates just under a year to make the leap. Before he left, he performed in *Dark of the Moon* in a production staged at the Brown-Forman Distillery at Eighteenth and Broadway. The facility had a space that served as a black box theater. Oates was extraordinarily convincing as both the mysterious Conjur Man and the earthbound bully, Marvin Hudgens, who made life difficult for the object of his affections, Barbara Ellen (sexily played by Mitzi Bornwasser), and her besotted witch boy, John. Set in the Smoky Mountains and written by Howard Richardson and William Berney, the play, which ran on Broadway and in London, is more of a curiosity today, but Hudgens's lines, such as "You black-bellied mule mouth, I'll manage you proper," seem written for Oates.

One night Mitch Ryan, who would become one of Douglas Ramey's Carriage House Players, was in the audience with his sister. As he watched Oates, Ryan's aspirations were confirmed: he wanted to be an actor. That night, Oates was already talking about leaving, but it was following the show's second incarnation that he had to go or lose face.

In September 1953, Oates escorted Bornwasser to the opening of the Kentucky Opera Association at Columbia Auditorium, where she was starring as Madame Fiora in *The Medium*. Oates was by her side afterward as she stood backstage while the audience cheered and pounded the wooden floors with their feet.

"Did you hear the people stomping?" he asked her at the cast party. Bornwasser said she did, but she was struck by the degree to which her date, handsome in a suit and tie, reveled in her triumph. It was not just that he shared in his friend's success; he embraced it entirely, and his empathy touched her.

During *Dark of the Moon*'s second run, in February 1954, Bornwasser, now Friedlander, reprised her role as Barbara Ellen in a hall beneath the Episcopal Church of the Advent. She was concerned about being thrown around onstage—Barbara Ellen belongs to everyone but herself, and Friedlander was pregnant.

After his last performance as Conjur Man and Marvin Hudgens, Oates left the stage and headed for the door, making his way toward the last of several farewell parties given in his honor, where he would make a brief appearance and grab a swift drink or two. "We had four or five going-away parties for him because he couldn't seem to get going," Ryan said. "He stayed around for parties." Oates's friend Bob Rowe called him a couple days beforehand. "If we have another party for you to leave town, man, we're going to drown you."

The partygoers—cast and crew members, friends, teachers, and rabble rousers—crowded into a tiny apartment not far from the theater. Toasts were made, dancing commenced, and people shouted to be heard above the celebratory din. But Oates could not get into full party swing that night. With a bus to catch at midnight, he bade farewell to the group and left with Mitzi and

Bill Friedlander. They got in Bill's spiffy black convertible, and Oates sat in the back as Bill drove on a last-quarter-moon night and Mitzi, in the passenger seat, tried to raise something suitable from the radio.

Next to Oates was his suitcase, and in his pockets were a letter of introduction to fellow Kentuckian Tom Ewell that Royal Dano had given him, plus the phone number and address of a New York agent, Milton Goldman, from his classmate Marvin Goldman. The Louisville streets were late-night still, but the rush of air hit Oates's face and toyed with his hair, raising strands from the fledgling bald spot at the crown of his head.

Bill turned onto Broadway, where there was a stir from the direction of the bus depot. He parked the car on the street and Oates jumped out, hurtling out of the car as if it were a starting gate. There was a short line at the ticket window, and the boarding docks were clustered with loners, lovers, and even a few families.

The Greyhound station at the corner of Broadway and Fifth was an art deco structure designed by Louisville native W. S. Arrasmith. Built in 1935, the two-story building was encased in blue enamel tiles, and its streamlined, modern curves suggested movement. Gordon joined his brother behind the terminal and handed him two hundred dollars.

"Put it in the back side of your billfold, for if you really get down and out," the older man advised. Warren thanked him, shook his hand, shook hands with Bill, kissed Mitzi a little too long, gave his suitcase to the porter, and climbed the steps to board the silver bus that had "New York City" emblazoned on its brow. He took a window seat, turned on its overhead light, waved goodbye with a flourish, and was gone.

"So they forced me to go," Oates would sigh, despite that he had been talking about leaving for the better part of two years. "I knew that's what I wanted to do but it was hard for me to leave my roots. I didn't want to leave them when I was in Depoy, [and] I didn't want to leave them when I was in Louisville."

Before leaving, Oates had met Weldon Stone for a farewell drink in Jack Fry's. They stood at the bar as the bartender, Effie, lined them up and owners Flossie and Jack held court beneath the stamped tin ceiling. Reflecting on the student who failed English 202, creative writing, the increasingly frail Stone, who would be dead within months, told his charge without a hint of charity, "You'll never be a playwright but you'll be a helluvan actor."

3

Hi, I'm Warren

Near Pittsburgh, it was hard to keep morning at bay through the gap in the bus's playhouse-sized window curtains. Not all passengers had drawn them. Some preferred to soak in the night ride's sateen sheen and, like Oates, take a little nip of something fortified between naps and to round off another cigarette. The trip to New York was long—almost twenty-four hours—but highways would be a familiar seam in Oates's life.

On the evening of February 20, 1954, the bus lurched to a stop outside New York City's Pennsylvania Station, 803 miles from Louisville. Oates had the address of a cheap hotel, plus a good sense of places where hopeful actors gathered, ranging from coffee shops to cocktail bars. New York would do fine for him: like the few other places he had been, it did not feel like home, but it promised things he loved, not least breathtaking troupes of beautiful women.

On Monday he went to Milton Goldman's offices at the Ashley Famous Agency after spending the morning setting up his account with a telephone answering service at Broadway and Forty-Sixth Street, the lobby of which was filled with Sunday-best-dressed actors looking for work. The answering service provided him with the number PL7-6300, one that would come to have a familiar ring for struggling performers. "Plaza" 7-6300 was the line for the Hayes Registry, an answering service–cum–casting agency set up by Sonny Hayes, a former singer turned impresario. Hayes had four hundred clients on his roster, each of whom paid $2.75

per month for the service. Oates added his name to a list that included Joanne Woodward, Peter Falk, Tuesday Weld, Martin Balsam, and James Dean.

Soon, Goldman had good news for Oates. He had secured for him an audition for a walk-on part on a show that would air in five days, going out live on Saturday night. Never mind five years: Oates had found work within days of leaving Louisville.

But he still needed a place to live and a means to pay the rent. In short, he needed a day—or night—job, one that he could quit at the drop of a hat. He got one at a coffeehouse in Greenwich Village. Pandora's Box was a prototypical bohemian espresso bar frequented by early beatniks, actors, and good-looking women, the last of which were so memorable that author Jim Harrison sang their praises years later in his work.

The Village was getting hot as a draw for artists. Oates's arrival there was one of a handful of times he would find himself on a cultural cutting edge, and he immediately loved Village life. The Village upheld the tenets of his personal faith: opportunity for vibrant friendships, passels of women to romance, scads of alcohol to consume, and cigarettes to smoke, all with the backdrop of art and possibility as similar intoxicants. "The chicks were wilder and the pace was faster. I dug that," said Village resident and Oates friend Steve McQueen, who was frequently seen riding around on his motorbike.

On March 6, 1954, Oates was assured of a walk-on part, but the appearance was not on just any television program. With or without its star, *The Jackie Gleason Show*, which ran on CBS in one incarnation or another between 1952 and 1971, was a Saturday-night powerhouse. Its host, a dipsomaniac despot in a sports shirt, was television's reigning behemoth, and a new sketch with Art Carney was developing a life of its own. *The Honeymooners* would soon dominate.

On the show that aired January 30, Gleason had been playing a naughty child who went around opening radiators at a party. While carrying an electric fan and a bag of flour in preparation for the next skit, Gleason had slipped and fallen in the puddle of carbon dioxide foam, breaking a bone in his ankle and his shin during the live broadcast. Carney's turn on March 6 as one of a series of guest hosts was a failure. It featured a sketch, which also fell flat, about a harried teacher in a classroom of hoodlums, one of which was a superannuated Warren Oates. For his efforts, Oates received his first acting pay of eighty dollars.

He began making the rounds and, as he put it, "learning the talk of the streets," but the living was tough. He went back to Louisville as often as he could, "because I was starving to death. I'd come back home and get fattened up." He was fortunate that the GI bill paid for the acting classes he was taking from Harvey Bogart.

Oates switched jobs, going to work washing dishes at the Stork Club, Sherman Billingsley's star-studded hangout, then the best-known club in New York. He made the most of his brief time there, meeting a stunningly beautiful young actress from a moneyed family. He wooed her for all he was worth and wound up in her living room hideaway bed. Like most actresses, she lived with a roommate, who also came back with a date that night. "She told me to be quiet, so I wouldn't wake her roommate," said Armand Alzamora, an exotically handsome actor who came to the city from Sleepy Hollow (then known as North Tarrytown), New York.

The next morning, while Alzamora and his date talked over coffee, one of the shapes in the living room bed began to stir, revealing her face. "She was a beautiful girl with long black hair and light blue eyes," Alzamora said. "I mean beautiful. Like Elizabeth Taylor. She said hello to me from this big bed in the middle of the room. And then she said, 'I'd like you to meet my friend.' She pulls back the covers just enough to reveal this gap-toothed guy who doesn't sit up, just reaches up his hand for me to shake and says, 'Hi, I'm Warren.'" Alzamora concluded, "I knew that to meet someone that way, I had to stay friends with him the rest of my life."

Oates soon asked the woman to marry him, but, under pressure from her parents, she refused. Warren's spirits sank, and he did what he often did in such situations: he drank. He left the Stork Club, never known to be the most understanding of employers. He worked off and on. Parts were scarce; meals were sparse. "The first two years were tough. I loved the literature of the Thirties and I went to the Village to see if that life could exist for me," he picturesquely told *TV Guide* a decade later. The reporter astutely observed, "He found the life was much like that of the Depression Thirties—at least for himself."

Waiting, hungover, in the lobby of his answering service, Oates started talking with an actor from Philadelphia. Oates told him that he was dejected because a beautiful debutante had jilted him. The hour was early, but the circumstances were grave enough to merit the other man's suggesting they get a drink at Patsy and Carl's Theatre Bar, an actors' hangout on Forty-fifth Street.

"Warren was broken up," the actor, Howard Dayton (né Harold Gelbstein), recalled. "He'd been drunk for a month. The girl was gorgeous and from old money; we're talking millions of dollars. I think the family was from Boston. The family begged her not to marry him, saying they were going to disown her if she did, so she broke it off."

The two men became fast friends. "He drank, I drank. Every day. We went to the same bars. . . . After a while I needed a place to stay or he needed a place to stay, and we found one, $4.25 a week or $15 a month. We moved in together." The place, a coldwater flat at Tenth and Bleecker Streets in Greenwich Village, was a fifth-floor walkup and the definition of arty austerity. Oates's space was a converted bathroom, and he slept on a board placed over the kitchen table. "He'd always come home drunk, so it didn't bother him," Dayton explained. They soon brought in another roommate, but not before they had one they had not invited. "We had a mouse that neither one of us could stand to kill. We'd throw shoes at it and deliberately miss. Eventually the mouse figured this out and was fearless," Dayton said.

Dayton was working as a hatcheck clerk in the 21 Club, and he got Oates a job there too. The club was high-toned, but it was welcoming, especially to at-liberty marines looking for a quiet drink, and others, blue- or red-blooded, seeking similar solace. Oates started out checking hats, "and after we checked hats, where do you think we went to drink?" asked Dayton. "21."

They also checked coats. They had an elaborate scheme for lining their own pockets: when a patron gave them a dollar for their service, instead of placing it in the required slot on the counter, the two young actors would leave the coats draped over their arms as they slipped the money into their own small stash. "People used to get caught all the time for stealing—they expect it—but when we got caught, they didn't fire us. I don't know why," Dayton said. Hat- and coat-check staff were always men—women were prohibited, as it was thought they could not resist making plays for the well-heeled clientele.

The 21 Club was the top. One night William Boyd, famous for portraying Hopalong Cassidy, came in after attending the opera. His appearance made an impression on Oates. "I was struggling along in New York City and William Boyd, who was a great opera fan, and his wife walked into the 21 Club one night around 11.30. She had on an ermine coat that was absolutely devastating and William Boyd had on a tuxedo." Oates continued, "The anteroom in the restaurant was full of distinguished and wealthy and intelligent people, and when William Boyd walked through that front door, everything stopped in total reverence. No one said a word. William Boyd came up and laid his hat and coat on the counter. That's a star."

When Oates recovered from his broken heart, life resumed a familiar consistency. "All we wanted to do was drink," Dayton said, "and, excuse the language, get laid. We would drink beer in the afternoons, go after work, after making the rounds. If we finished at 3 p.m. we'd go to the bar, get drunk, take our ten-cent subway down to the Village at five o'clock. Go home, clean up a little bit, go out to dinner," and onward out into the night. They often went to Louie's, an actors' hangout where Oates was well cared for. "For some reason those Italian people took me to their bosoms," he said. "They fed me when I didn't have any money." Another hangout was Sardi's, where they would go for afternoon drinks and snacks. "Preston Foster would be at the bar," said Dayton. "Paul Stewart, the butler in *Citizen Kane*. The original *Death of a Salesman* gang. Arthur Kennedy, Cameron Mitchell."

One day, in the Laundromat, Oates and Dayton decided to

forgo an extra load or two in favor of one-dollar martinis at Sardi's. "Warren smiled if he was miserable or happy," Dayton said. "But he wasn't able to hold his drink. And one drink was enough. There are happy drunks and mean drunks, and he wasn't a mean drunk, but he wouldn't remember anything. And Warren drank every day of his life."

Once, Gordon Oates came to visit and took the solids-starved pair out for thick steaks. He was struck by the camaraderie he found there. "They were almost like cults together, groups of friends hanging around," the older Oates remembered.

Excessive drinking was mixed—one could not say tempered—with ambition, with varying outcomes. "We lived two blocks away from Maurice Evans," Dayton said. In early 1955, actor, producer, and director Evans was casting the play *No Time for Sergeants*, directed by Morton Da Costa. "Warren and I went to get in line for the casting call, and it was so long we couldn't do it. If we'd been drunk we could have. So we decided to go drinking instead. We closed down the bars and then got to talking about how we knew where Evans lived. Why didn't we just go over and introduce ourselves, tell him how much we wanted the parts?"

The night was young—to them. "This was about two, two thirty in the morning, and we were really drunk. We go to his door, knock, and here answers this very proper Englishman in his robe and pajamas. He takes one look at us, totally drunk, and says, 'What can I do for you? Would you like to come in for coffee?'" They stumbled in, accepted the coffee, which Oates always drank black, and incoherently explained that they had read the play and were certain it held roles tailor-made for them. Eventually, they left. In the morning, when they hesitantly, sheepishly called their phone service, the two actors were amazed to learn they had appointments to read for the parts. They did—but neither one was cast.

Oates had been studying with Harvey Bogart, but he was at odds with the Max Reinhardt teachings his instructor embraced. "They allowed very little place for feeling, and feeling to me seemed the principal resort of an actor," Oates said. He switched to classes with Wynn Handman on Monday and Thursday evenings, studying basic and advanced action at his studio at 158 West Fifty-sixth Street. Handman's studio was a version of method acting minus the sense memory. Classes also involved improvisations "to find the truth in reality," Handman said, "and I sought to ground the actor in that reality. [Oates] gave a strong feeling like he came from the ground . . . a strong American spirit. He impressed me as an exceptional talent and he was a lot of fun to work with in class. He gave off deep feelings of the heart of America."

Through a friendship with a casting director at CBS, Oates tried out for a part that he did not get, but it still landed him a job: for $5.60 an hour, he got work as a so-called test pilot, taking part in stunts for the popular television game show *Beat the Clock*. The producers hired actors to work in front of the cameras during rehearsals, standing in for contestants, and if getting a custard pie in the face was funny, it flew. The trial runs also gave the show's producers a way of estimating how long it would take contestants to complete the uproarious tasks, such as lowering frankfurters suspended on fishing lines into bowls, retrieving marshmallows from Jell-O using only their mouths, and setting off a series of giant mousetraps.

In 1951 another actor had been let go from the job because he performed too well—he was able to catch just about anything thrown his way. The actor was James Dean, and Oates made much of following in Dean's footsteps, going as far as to say he took the job over from him. In fact he was equally resilient. Bud Collyer, the show's master of ceremonies, told Oates, "You're just like Jimmy Dean—you never give up." Dayton and Oates had a passing acquaintance with Dean, but he ran in a different crowd, in another part of the city.

There were parties almost every night and auditions several times a week. Armand Alzamora's girlfriend, Nashville native Betty Williams, was living with another actress, Diana Hale, on East Ninety-sixth Street. They often gave parties in their all-white apartment, which perilously featured spaghetti dinners. Williams, a pale brunette beauty suggestive of Bettie Page, was a consummate hostess. Her looks and charm were not lost on Oates. After several swigs of wine, he swept Williams up, tossed her over his shoulder, and proceeded to make off with her toward the nether tundra of the railroad apartment. Oates's distressed date ordered him to put her down, and he eventually obliged. Another evening the moveable feast took them to another apartment, where there was no food. Oates, in his cups, suggested that a beloved pet parakeet be taken from its cage and fried up on the spot. When his ludicrous request became an order, he was bundled out the door into the cold night and pointed in the direction of the nearest Automat.

"I met Warren in New York," said Millie Perkins. "He was dating my roommate, Patty, but he had a crush on me, as people kept reminding me. In fact I'm told he was dating my roommate to date me. But I was a model, and I never gave him a second thought. He was a struggling actor living in Greenwich Village," said the Jersey girl turned uptown girl who would soon hit major stardom by playing Anne Frank.

Oates was getting bits of work here and there, including occasional appearances on the inspirational program *Lamp unto My Feet*. The series aired on CBS from 1948 until 1979, when it was canceled because of declining viewing figures and the decision by many stations to air paid religious broadcasts instead. For a time, *Lamp* was a proving ground for actors, including George C. Scott, Steve McQueen, and Warren Beatty. Oates also had a couple very minor roles in the live drama series *Studio One*, which was a powerhouse but was already passing its ratings prime. In February 1955 he appeared off-Broadway in a revival of *The Wisteria Trees*, a Joshua Logan adaptation of Anton Chekhov's *The Cherry Orchard*. The City Center Theater production opened on Wednesday, February 2, and starred a lofty cast that included Helen Hayes, Walter Matthau, Cliff Robertson, and Ossie Davis. In his *New York Times* review on February 3, Brooks Atkinson found Logan's relocation of the setting from Chekhov's Russia to postbellum Louisiana something of a stretch. A box listing the cast featured Warren Oates second to last among "Guests at party."

In May 1955, Oates and Dayton flew to Louisville for the

Kentucky Derby. They drank mint juleps, and Dayton, a race-track fan, paid full attention to the races while Warren watched the women. "All the girls were running around him even then," Dayton said. "But then he always had girls running after him, always. He wasn't handsome: Tyrone Power or Montgomery Clift before his accident. It was the personality, and he was so charming."

Oates's appeal was a mixture of personality and appearance. He had the odd ability to look swarthy and malnourished at the same time. His light eyes—periwinkle, he insisted—and smile, then hampered by worrisome dental work, were charming, and his exuberance made his stature ("Six foot one in cowboy boots," he would say) seem taller than it was.

In New York Oates was seeing a dark-haired, petite woman named Roberta "Bobbie" Eis, whom he had met in a bar. She hailed from Paterson, New Jersey, from where she had felt New York City's gravitational pull. Feisty, fetching, and argumentative, Bobbie hitched herself to Oates with something like love, and certainly like fervor. For her, they were forever, and he was drawn in by her often troubled emotional state. "I think Warren thought he could save her," Dayton said. Bobbie was in therapy several times a week, and when she was not there, she and Oates were drinking. It was not the best template for a healthy relationship. Soon Oates was living part of the time at her place, at 60 West Seventy-sixth Street, just as Dayton stayed some of the time with his new girlfriend, Teddy, who was a schoolteacher. The men still kept their place on Bleecker Street, "for when we fought with our girlfriends or they kicked us out," Dayton said. Oates was "the kind of guy who'd go out with a girl two, three times, and if the girl said, 'I love you, will you marry me?' he'd say, 'All right,'" Dayton explained. "I know it sounds crazy. It was hard for him to say no about anything."

By 1956, Oates was working, if not regularly at least respectably, turning up on *Kraft Television Theatre* and *The Philco Television Playhouse*. Live television drama, although past its heyday, had not yet succumbed to the medium's migration west, where a purpose-built complex, CBS Television City, had opened in 1952.

For *Kraft Television Theatre*, he was one of several young marines stationed at Parris Island in *Murder of a Sand Flea* by James Lee Barrett. The play, which featured Rip Torn, was broadcast on October 10, 1956. Its content and dialogue caught the attention of Jim Kepner, who wrote in the pioneering gay activist magazine *One*, "Kraft-TV's 'Murder of a Sand Flea' had a tough Marine Sergeant say, 'Sure you're a hillbilly just like Owens over here is queer and I HATE queers.'"

On July 7, 1956, the *Louisville Courier-Journal* took note of Oates's progress. In "Bill Ladd's Almanac," the reporter noted, "Warren Oates, the Depoy and Louisville boy who appeared on 'Theater [*sic*] Guild' Wednesday night on Channel 11, had a busy week." A photograph accompanied the piece, showing Sarah Oates looking proud in a printed dress and costume jewelry, Gordon taciturn in a tie, and his cavorting young son, Gordon Jr., ensconced in their living room, purportedly watching the drama on TV. An antenna bisects the picture, and Gordon Jr., "who strongly resembles his uncle," points his finger like a six-gun at the camera.

The United States Steel Hour went out live. The episode in which Oates appeared aired on July 4, 1956, and also featured Paul Mazursky, Howard Dayton, and Robert Culp. The actors worked two days and received eighty dollars a day. The episode, "Operation Three Rs," was written and directed by Norman Felton, who would go on to create *The Man from U.N.C.L.E.* "I played a stuck-up Back Bay guy who'd just been inducted into the army and I got stuck with a special ed[ucation] class," Culp said. "Warren was in the special ed class. He was a hillbilly from I don't know where, and he went AWOL to be with his wife in childbirth back home. He came back, and I had to cover for him. It was a big mess—and that was essentially the story."

"We watched a tape of the show shortly afterward," Dayton said, "and Warren asked me what I thought of his performance. I told him I noticed he was looking down a lot. 'And that's not the character, that's you,' I said. 'You're trying to hide.'" Oates was grateful for the advice.

Culp and Oates became friends during two weeks of rehearsals, comparing notes and elaborating on a shared southern heritage. "We realized that we had to be cousins. There was no way not," Culp said. Culp began to bump into Oates at the regular haunts, including the Limelight, Downey's, and another joint, a long bar with a seedy reputation where Culp had a memorable encounter with a woman named Nancy whom he had seen dance in a play. He walked to the bar's back garden, overseen by a lone, pitiful tree, and saw the woman seated at a table with Oates, among others. "When she saw me, she tried to get out of her chair," Culp related, "and fell over backwards. I took her home, and we were never apart." The woman was Nancy Asch, and she soon became Nancy Culp.

A day after the July 4 *Theatre Guild* presentation, Oates celebrated his twenty-eighth birthday. Then, on July 7, he headed for Virginia Beach to start rehearsals for stock companies' theatrical productions. This time, at least, he turned up. Not so for summer stock in Hartford, Connecticut. "One day I got a call from someone in Hartford," Dayton said, "and they were trying to find Warren, who was supposed to appear in *Tobacco Road*." Oates was to play Dude, the son who is intrigued by Preacher Bessie (and her car) in the potboiler play. "I knew Oates was out on a drunk, but I said I didn't know where he was. They begged me to take the part—it opened in two days—so I did. When I eventually ran into Warren, he just shrugged it off."

Back in the city, the summer of 1956 was good to Oates. He appeared in a *Studio One* episode, "A Day before Battle." The live program aired September 3, 1956, as part of the series' "summer theater" and capped what Oates referred to as his triumphant week. "I had a part on 'Studio One,' I was working for 'Beat the Clock' and I was checkin' hats at 21."

In "A Day before Battle," Oates is the first on-screen, as would often be the case in his television appearances. Credited as "the prisoner," he plays a Confederate soldier who has just been captured and is accused of being a paper carrier or spy. He is placed in an outdoor cage to await execution, and his performance is as understated as it is riveting. He is very real flesh and blood, and though the "skin and bones" he was mocked for were the result of life circumstances rather than method acting, Oates managed to quietly steal the attention from the vaguely histrionic Union soldiers who control his fate. Oates had a lengthy scene with Jack Lord, who played one of the Union soldiers. Lord eventually shoots the prisoner in the back and then carries his limp body. It is difficult not to notice the dead man's checkered shirt rising and falling in rhythm with the crickets' chirping and frogs' croaking, yet Oates played the part with a great deal of skill.

Westinghouse's *Studio One* ran between 1948 and 1958 and was lofty viewing in terms of its writing and the careers it launched. The list of actors who made their debut on the show or appeared in it early in their careers reads "like a producer's wish list." according to a documentary made about the program in 1997. The show went out live, "top to bottom, all the way through. And that's a scary ride," said *Studio One* alumnus Charlton Heston. The series began as weekly ninety-minute teleplays, but by the time Oates started appearing, it had been trimmed to just an hour, reflecting viewer movement away from drama series toward other kinds of broadcasts, including films, which the studios had begun to sell to the networks, happy to snap up inexpensive programming that could be repeated many times.

On September 9, 1957, CBS broadcast a *Studio One* episode called "The Night America Trembled." Although Oates's role in it was less pronounced than that in "A Day before Battle," the program itself garnered more notice. It re-created Orson Welles's October 30, 1938, *Mercury Theatre* radio production of H. G. Wells's *The War of the Worlds*. In a career that eventually comprised more than one hundred television appearances and sixty films, this was the only time Warren Oates appeared as a card-playing, sweater-wearing fraternity boy. "Turn it off; I'm studying," says one of his classmates, in reference to the radio. But no one heeds his request. Then one of the card players begins to listen. "Trenton, that's where my family lives!" he exclaims. He is ruggedly good looking to Oates's almost doughy face, animated as he says, "Charlie, did you hear that? They're calling out the army!" Oates has a brief scene with the worried card player at a pay phone. It is nothing remarkable, except that it was the only time Warren Oates played opposite another Warren, Warren Beatty.

Buoyed by successes, Oates agreed to marry Bobbie Eis, who had become increasingly fragile. She had attempted to end her life more than once, and mired in this unhappy relationship that they thought commitment might cure, the two flew to Louisville. His mother gave her younger son her wedding ring for his dark-haired bride, and the family drove twenty miles to Floydsburg and the pretty, early English gothic Duncan Memorial Chapel. In the native stone church on July 27, 1957, a Methodist minister named Kenneth Dillon married a native son to a Jewish girl from New Jersey.

"Didn't you used to date Warren Oates?" Flossie Fry asked Bertie as she cleared tables at Jack Fry's. There were rumors that Bobbie was a dancer or of some other exotic pedigree.

While in town, Warren called in at the university and left a brief note for Boyd Martin, updating him about his life and career. He ended the note with a resigned, "I'm married now." The marriage was neither feted nor fated. "It was doomed," Alzamora said. There was no money for a honeymoon, and Oates was soon back washing dishes at Louie's. Howard Dayton, involved in his own romantic travails, did not even know his friend had gotten married. "He probably agreed one night in a bar, and that was it," he speculated later. Mitch Ryan was in New York that year and met Bobbie. "I have very little impression of her," he said, "but Warren didn't seem to like her."

In late 1957, two actors who were also husband and wife, Nick Georgiade and Anita Khanzadian, were putting together a showcase, a relatively new idea at the time. "I had every actor chip in, although I got everything for free except the rental at Steinway Hall," Georgiade said. "I got the coffee free, the pastries, the invitations . . ." The actors began rehearsing. Warren did a Tennessee Williams scene with Bobbie. The critics had been invited and everything was in place for the first night, but that morning, a subway strike began, and by nightfall, a blizzard had hit the city. The show went on, but to a tiny audience.

Friends were starting to leave New York City. Steve McQueen

went west; Robert Culp borrowed two dollars from Oates to make the trip ("Come to think of it, he still owes it to me," Oates said later); and Alzamora migrated as well. On January 10, 1958, Alzamora's girlfriend Betty Williams went west, boarding the Silver Chief in Nashville. At Memphis, she was joined in her compartment by a polite young man who asked if he could pass the three-day journey across the southern and southwestern states with her. He serenaded her with his guitar, and he asked her to marry him. At major city stops, the same thing always happened: a cluster of photographers boarded the train and pushed aside the other passengers, whose faces would often press against the glass compartment and gawk. Some newspapers' photo captions identified Williams as Natalie Wood. Her suitor they got right: Elvis Presley, on his way to Hollywood to film *King Creole*.

Reunited with Alzamora, Williams set about looking for a place to live. She found one in Hollywood, a Spanish-style marvel of a multiunit apartment building, near the corner of Fountain and Harper. Its name was Casa Real.

In New York, Dayton and Oates walked home one wet night. At Fifty-third and Lexington, they saw Montgomery Clift in a café, "sitting, drinking, reading, in such pain as a human being," as Dayton put it. As nightcaps go, it cast its pall, and Dayton went home while Oates returned to his wife. Their apartment on Bleecker sat empty. Then Dayton got a call to go west to do the *Loretta Young Show*. "They put me up in the Beverly Hills Hotel, I had a convertible, the sun was shining, it was a few days before Christmas, and I thought, 'Why am I going back to New York?'" He didn't.

January 1958 found New York City not so much an ice cream freezer, as socialite Elsa Maxwell had deemed it, as a morgue. Acting jobs were fleeing to the West Coast. The city's spirit had shifted less perceptively, but in television, the change was pronounced. Going, going, gone were the variety shows and thought-prodding dramas. In their place were a slew of game shows like *The $64,000 Question* and *Jackpot Bowling*, which was hosted by onetime Mr. Television, Milton Berle. West Coast westerns abounded: *Gunsmoke*, *Wyatt Earp*, *Have Gun—Will*

Travel, and *Bat Masterson* might have been in their infancy, but they had a strong grip. "Before I can turn on my TV set," quipped Bob Hope of their omnipresence, "I have to sweep the hay off it."

As early as the fall of 1956, once-popular shows like *Mr. Peepers* had been replaced by westerns such as *Frontier.* "The appetite of the television viewing audience would prove insatiable and westerns would ride live television off of the range. Television's center of gravity was shifting from New York to Los Angeles," writer Jon Krampner observed.

In Los Angeles, Robert Culp was making his own western series called *Trackdown,* which would air right before *The Jackie Gleason Show.* Culp felt his friend Oates was a shoo-in for cowboy boots and called to tell him as much. "These people don't have any money to bring you out, but if you were here, you'd have this part," he said.

"Do you really think I ought to come out there?" Oates asked.

"Warren, look. Walter Brennan can only last so long. Get your ass out here as quickly as possible and take advantage of this fact."

Nick Georgiade caught on quickly. "I kept hearing from all these actors that all the work was in California, so I said to my wife, 'If all the work is in California, why are we here knocking on doors in New York City?'"

"The theater is in New York City," Anita replied.

Her husband eventually convinced her to leave for the West Coast. But there were two problems: money and transportation. Georgiade arranged to deliver a car through an auto drive agency, and the couple prepared to pack up, managing to scrape together eight hundred dollars' traveling money. Loading the car, a 1951 Buick sedan, proved tricky, as the owners had crammed their belongings in the trunk, leaving only the backseat for "everything we owned, dishes and pots and pans. . . . We allowed ourselves each one suitcase and a box, and we filled it up," Anita recalled.

Oates had been forced to pick up menial work again. "I was between jobs and working in a coffee house," he said. "I overheard this young, unknown trio—Peter, Paul and Mary—talking about going to California. I said to myself: I'm going too. Live television is dying. The future is film, and I want to be part of it."

His ultimate decision might not have been prompted by anything quite that lyrical, but, according to one source, it was no less dramatic. Oates came home one afternoon to find his wife, Bobbie, sick in bed. Through the pain and delirium, she admitted that she had had an abortion. Viewing this as consummate betrayal, Oates unceremoniously left her.

From a payphone near his Bleecker Street apartment, he called Nick Georgiade. "Nick, you and Anita are driving to California. I'm going to ask you two questions, but please don't answer me tonight," he said. "The first one I will ask you is I would like to go to California with you and Anita. Please don't answer me today. Think it over. The second thing I want to ask you is I need to borrow a hundred dollars from you to go to California with. Don't answer me tonight."

Georgiade turned to his wife. "Gosh, it's a little crowded," she replied. "All our stuff is in the car." After thinking for a moment longer, she shrugged her shoulders and said, "Why not?"

On the early morning of February 4, 1958, in a car packed to the hilt, the three not so disparate souls headed west for California, "like the Okies," Oates would tell *Newsweek* thirteen years later. Oates had "a hang-up sack with an overcoat and two suits and very little else," but he was overlooking the intangible. His acting teacher, Wynn Handman, had encouraged him to go west, "to fly with my own wings," Oates recalled.

4

Have Gumption— Will Travel

To ride or drive across the continental United States in the winter of 1958 was to encounter a transforming world: fenced-in towns were letting out their hems to reveal ragged edges, and city limits seemed almost arbitrary. New buildings were often starkly linear or leaning toward whimsy, and a hitherto unnoticed breed—the teenager—could be found usually in clumps lurking sullenly or spiritedly beneath the neon signs of drive-in restaurants. The world of Tom Joad was in evidence too. In bas-relief, now shabby auto courts abutted the two-lane highway, sometimes with campsites right beside them. Route 66, the Mother Road of John Steinbeck's *The Grapes of Wrath*, had developed a split personality of good witch and wicked stepmother, weaving back and forth without control.

Much of this passed by Nick Georgiade and Anita Khanzadian and their passenger as they headed purposefully, side by side by side in the bench-style front seat of a 1951 Buick sedan. Once they had left New York, Oates had leaned against the passenger window and promptly fallen asleep, not coming up for air for at least nine hundred miles.

On the morning of February 5, they arrived in Louisville, where Gordon was living with his mother Sarah at 953 Edward Avenue. When Anita let it slip that it was her twenty-fifth birthday, a party was hastily organized. They celebrated, then left the next day laden with sandwiches and roast chicken that Sarah had prepared.

From Louisville, Georgiade drove on, stopping only to fill the car with gas and oil and to load up on sodas, snacks, and cigarettes. The car "sucked up oil like a vacuum," he said. "Every two hundred miles I had to give it oil. It was a wreck."

They pressed on to Albuquerque, where all three stayed in the same motel room. From New Mexico and on into Arizona, the roadside featured, like dangling charms on an unclasped bracelet, oblong billboards that promised attractions in just a matter of miles or exits. None could match the gravitas of the sign that simply read "California State Line." However prosaic, it symbolized what Oates would refer to as "the smartest move I ever made."

Along the way he had described to his companions his rationale for leaving. "If you're going to succeed, you've got to have a sense of knowing when the ball is about to stop," he would say, as the couple listened in agreement, "so you can get off and onto another ball. Or," he would laugh, "make your own ball." And then he would light up another cigarette.

The travelers had driven across several stretches of desert, with the car's burlap radiator bag hanging over the front grill. Barstow, California, offered yet more desert. They descended into the Los Angeles Basin, which appeared in the afternoon sun like a dry, rust-stained sink. Its dots of greenery were giant sparkler-like palm trees and scruffy cherimoya, chaparral, sumac, and toyon. Familiar Los Angeles landmarks came into view: Union Station, city hall, and the Hollywood sign, straddling Mount Lee like a row of crooked teeth. The new city felt wide open. Nick turned right off Santa Monica Boulevard, near the end of Route 66, and drove around the block several times before finding Harper, which did not have a street sign. They pulled up in front of a Spanish-style apartment building on a grid-straight street. A straggly stretch of grass skirted the Casa Real's eight apartments, one of which was occupied by Howard Dayton and Armand Alzamora. For Oates it was the welcome wagon, having his friends there to greet him. Together, the trio would live in similar places on neighboring streets with names like Hayworth and Havenhurst and Laurel in the coming months, and it would be fine, as long as they were within walking distance of Sunset Boulevard and, more to the point, a small but significant stretch of it known as the Sunset Strip.

Anita Khanzadian was thrilled with her new digs: "It was a wonderful building. It had a Murphy bed in the living room and a walk-in kitchen. I thought I [had] died and had gone to heaven. A dressing room!" Oates's days of sleeping on tabletops were over.

Oates quickly sized up the expanse of Los Angeles, and it confirmed what he had heard: it would be difficult to navigate without a car. Alzamora came to his rescue, finding a 1946 Mercury for him, and it was in this somber sedan that he drove to begin work in a significant role on *Have Gun—Will Travel*. To find work in New York had taken him two weeks, and in Tinseltown, three weeks. "He got hot right away," Dayton said. Alzamora also took note: "Warren got work very quickly. He was a star in no time."

Oates was set to make his debut on the televised western landscape as a wily and tenacious no-account. Although he would make the garb and gab of the Old West his own in art and life, for now it was still artifice for a child of the Kentucky coalfields.

Have Gun—Will Travel was number three in the ratings, and it was noted for its superior writing and stylish craftsmanship. The series starred Richard Boone, a seventh-generation nephew of Daniel Boone. He played the elegant sophisticate Paladin, a former West Point man who advanced through the ranks unhampered by a first name, in place of which he had a calling card with the words "Wire Paladin San Francisco," accompanied by the requisite etched chess piece. (For a time, the popular cards were available to fans of the show who sent in a self-addressed, stamped envelope.)

The series aired on the CBS network from 1957 to 1963, and Oates first showed up in the broadcast of May 10, 1958. "They sent a mutilated cat to a young girl as a wedding present!" went the teaser. Oates played the soberly named John Bosworth, a bad seed who is one of the groom's vicious half-brothers. "It ain't easy sending a gift to a girl who's got everything," John declares sensationally from his berth in a cabin on the North Fork Road. Paladin has given up his hotel suite to the young newlyweds but is drawn into their plight after the disturbing gift unsettles the winsome bride. He travels out to the brothers' ranch and meets the father, an eccentric and interestingly drawn codger who keeps an owl named Jasper for a pet. Paladin takes on his case and nails the half-brothers for attempted arson. Following his conviction, John follows Paladin into the alley and attempts to kill him. Instead, his brother Ed is killed, and Paladin shoots John in the leg. Oates's performance is compellingly gritty, mean, and even a touch humorous. He is pathetic, painful, and disturbing. And he is already a visual shorthand for viewers.

In *Television Westerns*, Richard West notes that from 1946 to 1978 there were 119 network series in the western genre, or 150 counting syndication. At the western's pinnacle, 114 of the three networks' 160 shows were so-called oaters and horse operas. Over two hundred heroes shot, punched, and roped their ways out of scrapes and tight fits. Oates rarely played the hero. Instead he was a rascal or worse among stronger and more traditionally handsome, better-spoken men. He seemed to have been born into this world of horses, cacti, mules, donkeys, chickens, and loyal dogs and was equally at ease among stuntmen and stand-ins, sweet damsels and tough gals, and a whole lot of crazy fellows, on-screen and off. There were boots, guns, and saddles with canteens and pots and pans hanging from them. It was rumored that the least popular actors were assigned the crockery-heavy saddles. There were American Indians, Mexicans, Brits and Berbers, cooks and barbers, and when they needed menacing or merriment, Oates was the man to provide it. His squeezed-up eyes, already ornamented with lines like cracked clay, and his toothy grin defined his character, as did his walk and his general deportment, which made him seem taller and lankier than his actual height of five feet, ten inches. Oates had a definite attraction to Harry Carey Sr.'s stance, particularly in *The Three Godfathers*. The posture was putting his left hand on his right elbow and leaning to one side.

Robert Culp was trying to get Oates more work; he wanted

him for his series *Trackdown*. "I kept pushing and pushing and pushing to get him on the show because he was just such a natural, for God's sake," Culp said. "After those initial roles he began to work for a lot of people, and he began to refine that Warren Oates quality that was his until it was more and more specific. He was a stylist, and he was a natural. And if you had an individual personality or a style that was unique, you would be guaranteed work."

And work Oates would. Never mind that he did not really know how to ride and would, for a time, head his horse toward a tree to come to a stop. "Warren learned to ride on the set," said stuntman Loren Janes. "Wranglers and stuntmen taught him how to ride and how to do things. He loved stuntmen. When you go on a set, a lot of the stars, they don't talk to anybody, and they're mean to everybody all the time and they complain all the time. Warren wasn't like that, and the stuntmen loved him."

For his next role, Oates headed not toward the nearest live oak but south, to the threatened waters off the coast of San Diego.

In Jerry Steiner, Oates had a tireless and dedicated agent who loved both him and his work. "I had just gotten to California when my New York agent merged with a very good agency in Los Angeles," Oates told *Films Illustrated* in 1971. "They had people like Yul Brynner, Keenan Wynn and so on. They had ten actors and 40 really fantastic writers and I was the only guy in the whole company who wasn't working. I guess they had to get me going or kick me out," he said with typical self-effacement.

Steiner had received a call from a casting director at Warner Brothers, who said he had seen one of his client's *Studio One* performances. The call sent Oates to Warner Brothers, then casting a World War II submarine movie. Oates got in line with fifty other guys in the wardrobe department as the director, Gordon Douglas, "walked up and down the line, like a misplaced Colonel," he said. "He stopped in front of me and there was some mumbling going on with the casting director." Oates stood still in anticipation.

"You look like John Huston out of work," Douglas said. "What's your name?" Oates answered, and Douglas shrugged, "Well, you'll do."

Up Periscope, which starred James Garner, was scheduled to be shot using a process called Technirama and filmed in Hawaii but was eventually modified to Technicolor and stage three on the Warner Brothers lot in Burbank, with the naval base and beaches of San Diego fleshing out the requisite scenes. *Up Periscope* was one of a small school of submarine movies that included *The Enemy Below*, *Run Silent Run Deep*, and *Torpedo Run*.

Preproduction on *Up Periscope* began on July 15, 1958, with the cast and crew decamping on July 19 to San Diego, where they stayed at El Cortez Hotel. Oates and other underlings arrived by train before being taken onboard the USS *Tilefish*. The *Tilefish*, commissioned in 1943, had a deck three hundred feet long and only seventeen feet wide, and virtually all of that surface was soon covered with film and sound equipment, cameras, reflectors, and parallels. Add to that above- and below-deck navy personnel totaling sixty-two, six officers, and a movie crew of fifty assorted actors and the director, and the sardines analogy became truly apt. As the *Tilefish* made its way through groundswells at a surface speed of nine knots, many onboard nibbled saltine crackers and tried to avoid seasickness. "You know something?" Garner said. "I'd like to be back on my horse."

Oates's role was Seaman Kovacs, a goofy, hungry hick whose always-eating shtick proved humorous enough, but the uncredited part offered him little opportunity to sink his teeth into anything other than a white bread sandwich. He eagerly plays with a knife and fork, champing at the bit before getting off the first of his eight lines. "Argue, argue. That's all you guys do is argue," he says between mouthfuls. It is little wonder that the film's running sheets indicate that Warren "Oats" rarely needed more than one take.

At El Cortez Hotel, Oates roomed with an actor who was less than happy to be bunkmates. "I was a city slicker, and he was definitely a country boy," said Edd Byrnes, who played the submarine pharmacist, Ash, his last role before breaking into the national consciousness as Gerald Lloyd Kookson III, the jive-talking, comb-packing Kookie on the television series *77 Sunset Strip*. Byrnes, an actor from Brooklyn, had just starred in the series' precursor, a movie called *Girl on the Run*, and was miffed by his minuscule role in *Up Periscope*. But that was not all that got his goat. "The worst part is, I have to share a room with a guy called Warren Oates. Where the hell did that guy come from?" Byrnes asked. "I thought it was a big inconvenience to share a hotel [room] with another actor," he continued. "I wanted my privacy, and Warner Brothers was just being cheap by having everyone double up. They were always trying to save money."

Byrnes had been given a sip of stardom, and he took to it as if it were fine champagne, the color of his Brylcreemed locks. He had driven to the location in a flashy sports car while other non-marquee actors schlepped in on the train. Byrnes had a definite taste for the high life, and Oates, still green, did not fit his concept of it.

Douglas was an understanding director with plenty of experience getting the best out of novice actors and tender egos; he had received his start directing *Our Gang* comedy shorts. He was also fond of practical jokes, as Oates would find out. By July 22, cast and crew had returned to the Burbank lot, where Oates had a two-minute scene alone scrubbing dishes in the submarine's galley. "Gordon told him, 'Keep moving around, putting all the pots and pans away, doing all the work until I call 'Cut,'" Byrnes remembered. Douglas also suggested that Oates improvise, and he did, talking to himself while cleaning up the dishes. "Warren was doing all this stuff, busy, busy, busy," Byrnes continued. As he launched into his monologue, Douglas cued everybody else to quietly exit the soundstage. "He never yelled 'Cut,' and we walked all the way out of the soundstage. The cast and crew were all out on the street, and Warren was in there waiting for 'Cut.' After about ten minutes, he comes out and asks, 'What's going on?'"

That the scene did not make the final version might have proved galling, and Oates would sometimes dismiss his role in *Up Periscope*, claiming he did not know he was in it or saying, "I was the guy eating sandwiches." But in 1971 he gave *Films Illustrated* a less reconstructed version of his film debut. "I took the script home and read through it, looking for my part," Oates said. "I had one line [*sic*] to say, but it was the thrill of my life.

Douglas gave me little things to do along the way. I was a skinny guy, skinnier than I am now, anyway, so we worked out this thing where I was eating all the time."

Variety noted, "Warren Oates, tyro thesp who graduated from the University of Louisville only last year, made his film bow in a featured role in Warner Brothers' Up Periscope." A featured role is not bad, even for an uncredited actor. And for playing a small role, Oates was more prominent than Byrnes, factoring into the film's boiling point scene in which he wrestles—shirtless—with hotheaded Seaman Peck (Richard Bakalyan).

The week it opened, in March 1959, *Up Periscope* did well, taking in $29,000, making it the week's leader. "Lent is blamed for denting first run box office," noted the *Hollywood Reporter*, adding that the film brought in $89,000 in fourteen "nabes and ozoners" (neighborhood theaters and drive-ins).

Going into the dog days of his first summer in Hollywood, Oates had now appeared in a fistful of top-rated television shows and a Warner Brothers movie. His roommates Dayton and Alzamora were not finding as much work, but Nick Georgiade had been courted by Lucille Ball's Desilu Studios and was studying acting with the famous redhead. Their lives life centered around similar themes as they had in New York, namely, women, work, and drink. To satisfy these ends, a unique watering hole had opened on the Sunset Strip, and Oates wasted no time in making it home. Chez Paulette had a beatnik vibe that reminded him of his Village days at Pandora's Box, but he was no longer starving, nor struggling with the espresso machine. Instead he lounged, finding a chess partner in Mort Sahl, a drinking companion in Pernell Roberts, and conversation with old friends like Steve McQueen.

Chez Paulette was located at 8537 Sunset Boulevard, across the street from Dean Martin's restaurant, Dino's. It offered a different environment in a city where coffee shops still dwelled largely in the land of Edward Hopper: counter seats and tired waitresses in starched aprons. Chez Paulette was chic yet comfortable, proffering coffee, food, and wine. Sometimes the last two were twinned. "The New York Steaks are dipped in wine and broiled in butter. They are the most," an ad for the restaurant boasted. It could not have been more Oates. Chez Paulette was elite yet easy, serving drinks, habituated by colleagues and pretty women and even prettier waitresses (among them Sally Kellerman), and laden with impossibly rich food. He ate there with friends consistently.

Occasionally there was food at home. One night Alzamora and Oates arrived at their shared apartment at the same time and were overcome by a horrific smell accompanied by smoke. "We came in, and there was Howie Dayton in some army shorts, frying pig knuckles," Alzamora remembered. "I wanted to surprise you!" Dayton said, but the two were more gut-wrenched than delighted. Besides, explained Alzamora, "I was the cook of the group, and I know you *never* fry pig knuckles."

In the afternoons, when the apartment was usually empty, another person made saucier use of it. Steve McQueen found it handy for romantic trysts, and the notoriously spendthrift actor would leave a five-dollar bill on the nightstand, much to the annoyance of Dayton, who found it tantamount to brothel keeping. The roommates themselves had devised a system of leaving an item of clothing in the front room if they were "entertaining." That Oates was still married was of little importance.

Oates had been working. He had played Deke in an episode of *The Adventures of Rin Tin Tin*, a series based on the exploits of "Rinty," an irrepressible canine, and Rusty, his human cohort, played by Lee Aaker. In "The Epidemic," which aired at seven thirty in the evening on November 21, 1958, on ABC, Deke fires a shot during a bank holdup, accidentally destroying the town's only bottle of anthrax vaccine. Deke's younger brother Hal is unable to flee because he is suffering from exposure.

It was not Shakespeare. However, a show Oates had recently completed came closer to having the Bard walk into a bar. His agent, Jerry Steiner, had been at Dick Powell's Four Star Productions and persuaded a secretary to give him a script for *The Rifleman*, a new western television series about a man, Lucas McCain (played by former baseball star Chuck Connors), and his motherless son on the frontier. Oates read the script and went along to meet Sam Peckinpah, the young director, unaware he was about to shake hands with a man he would be asked about more than any other person, thing, or event throughout the rest of his life. Peckinpah would alter the course of Oates's career and personal condition and accompany him roughshod through landscape lush and spare, spread out over wild nights and woeful dawns. He would coax copacetic performances out of the actor, and their friendship would in many ways be the pure stuff of fatalism.

Oates would seat himself at "a long table of people who make comments about Sam," but as a close friend, Oates was particularly insightful and even poetic about one of the most controversial directors in the history of film. Peckinpah was "wild as a bat," as Oates would say, but he was quick to qualify that he was "gentle with me as an actor. I don't think he's a horrible maniac, he just injures your innocence. And you get pissed off about that."

In "The Marshal," Oates played Andrew, one of the Sheltin Boys, a vicious gang of brothers who, as Peckinpah biographer David Weddle points out, are "the first of many such rabid jackals . . . who would trot through Peckinpah's landscape in search of fresh meat." After being found "sleeping with the owls" (a euphemism for being drunk), Andrew turns over a few saloon tables and gets into a knife fight. "We ain't spellin' men," he explains before placing an X as his mark on the hotel register. It is observed that the boys are "so country they never been inside anything but a corral." Weddle writes, "Peckinpah was fascinated by the perverse vitality of such characters, and lavished on them much more attention and humanity than he ever did to the steel-girder figure of Lucas McCain. He had begun to break down the stereotypes of TV westerns by introducing villains who were more complex, interesting, even sympathetic than the clench-jawed heroes who gunned them down."

Sheriff Tomlinson, played by R. G. Armstrong, is killed, and then Andrew Sheltin shoots up the bar two more times before turning his gun on the show's lead, Lucas McCain. Andrew brags about having shot the rifleman, an excess of ego that eventually provides for his comeuppance. Subtle it is not, but playing such an uncouth character of mayhem would become Oates's bread and butter. In "The Marshal" he fared far better than usual in the hands of Peckinpah, who cowrote the episode in addition to making his directorial debut in the medium. The frisson among the men—including Armstrong, who, like Oates, would become a Peckinpah player—proved electric and the charge far ranging.

Hollywood was turning out to be far more hospitable than Manhattan, and the ease of life suited Oates's nature. Off-camera, he was part of the furniture at Chez Paulette, sitting at a front table, drinking, talking, smoking, and watching women. He also had his eye on a young brunette he had seen working the cash register at Schwab's, smiling sweetly and offering sultry, husky, precocious replies to customers' remarks.

The girl in question was Teddy Farmer, an eighteen-year-old Phoenix native. Farmer was as attractive as she was determined, the type of girl who became a popular high school cheerleader after overcoming the onus of being an awkward and shy transfer student. After she graduated from high school, she came to California initially to find her father, and stayed after her aunt convinced her to try modeling. She went back to Phoenix, where she told her high school sweetheart and fiancé Jim Chase, "I've got to try this for six months," before making the move to Hollywood. She used what money she had to secure an apartment a block away from Schwab's, the drugstore and lunch counter at the medicated heart of celluloid Hollywood. Within a few days, she got a job there alongside another young new hire, an eighteen-year-old Seattle transplant named Marlene. "They let a couple of the older women go," Teddy recalled. "I guess they decided they wanted younger ones in there, and of course the older ladies hated us!"

Television audiences did not hate Warren Oates, even though he played roles that were often ornery. By now he was working regularly, particularly in another Four Star production, *Wanted: Dead or Alive*, which starred Steve McQueen as a bounty hunter. *Wanted* was a spin-off of Robert Culp's *Trackdown*, and when it debuted on September 6, 1958, McQueen was making $750 a week. In "Die by the Gun," Oates played Jesse Cox, and then he was retained as a recurring character. McQueen would change dialogue if it did not meet his approval. He seemed to care for his role as Josh, saying he made the revisions because "I look out for him when no one else does." His attention to his part was crucial to the series' success, and McQueen would be earning $100,000 a year by the show's last season.

Oates's photograph in the *Academy Players Directory* shows the visage of a young man looking reflective and hopeful, and by the end of 1958 such optimism was merited. He rounded off the year with an appearance in *Playhouse 90*. In the featured drama "Seven against the Wall," he left his western duds behind in favor of gangster garb—the show was based on the St. Valentine's Day Massacre. But he was back on the range as Jed Hakes for *Gunsmoke* in "Snakebite." The legendary show had a reputation for its cast's camaraderie, and by the time it was broadcast on December 20, Oates had much to feel festive about.

Nick Georgiade and Anita Khanzadian had rented a big house on Gardner and decided to host a New Year's Eve party. On December 31, 1958, as a wildfire burned in one of the canyons above Sunset, Oates and his friends had a relatively subdued celebration: the air outside was thick with smoke, and inside the house it was not much better. Cigarette fumes clouded conversations and clung to clothes, bottles, and glasses like heavy weather.

Teddy Farmer's New Year's Eve was far more fraught. She had moved into a little guest cottage behind one of the large homes where the fire now burned in Benedict Canyon, and the flames were getting closer and closer. She was forced to evacuate, and given half an hour in which to do it. Luckily, at her young age, she had not accumulated anything beyond what could fit in one hasty carload.

As 1959 began, Oates was earning enough to move out on his own. He rented an apartment north of Sunset on the steep and winding Gould Avenue, where he would live at number 8186. It offered a great view of the stretching city as well as proximity to Chez Paulette, which was virtually at his feet.

Now homeless, Teddy moved in with her coworker Marlene, sharing an apartment "in a big musty old building" on Carlton Way, close to the intersection of Hollywood and Vine, and near an overpass of the Hollywood Freeway. One night Teddy decided to walk down to Hollywood Boulevard to get a newspaper. At the newsstand, she accidentally knocked a movie magazine off the shelf, and she decided to buy it too. At their apartment, Teddy and Marlene pored over the magazine, which had an article about a place where all the movie stars, particularly Marlon Brando and Ricky Nelson, went, called Chez Paulette.

"Let's go find this place!" they agreed. They drove up and down Sunset Boulevard five or six times until finally they decided to pull into a gas station that allowed parking. It was right across the street from Dino's, and from that vantage point the two could see Chez Paulette, set back from the sidewalk in an arcade. "Marlene and I went in," Teddy said. "This was the day of the beatnik, so there were all these women with black hair and dark lipstick—or no makeup. There was a front table with about eight very rowdy guys there, so we sat in the back drinking coffee for three hours or so. And as we left—there were venetian blinds in the front window—I turned around to see that someone from the front table was peeking out the blinds."

"One of those weirdos at the table is looking at us, Marlene," Teddy told her friend as they headed toward the car.

Three nights later, the women decided to go back, this time decked out in black stockings. "We still wore makeup and did our hair because we weren't too pleased with our appearance," Teddy said. They were invited to sit with a guy they mistook for the actor James Darren and his friend. In actuality he was named Jimmy Cimino. After they said good night, Marlene and Teddy were walking back to their car, parked at the gas station, when Teddy heard footsteps running behind her.

"Are you hung up on Jimmy Cimino?" the guy from the coffeehouse asked her.

"I hardly know the guy."

"That's all I wanted to know."

"I didn't know who he was," Teddy admitted. "But he'd been sitting at that front table again."

The next time Oates was strutting around in a pair of black-and-white pinstriped pants. "He wasn't a fashion guy," Teddy insisted. "They were like mattress ticking, just really tacky." Oates was looking at her and pointing, making a phone gesture as if to say, "Give me your phone number." She asked Jimmy Cimino who he was.

"That's Warren Oates. You don't want to know him."

But Oates wanted to know Teddy, and he pursued her, telling her he was an actor—and that he was twenty-eight instead of thirty-one. She fell for the age line but found it hard to believe that he was an actor. "Yeah, right," she thought. "These good-looking guys over here, the slick guys are actors. This guy, never in a million years."

But he continued to make a play for her, and soon they began dating. "He just zeroed in," she said. "This man of the world, wild man. This was the first time in my life where somebody had said 'I want you,' and it scared me to death. I really didn't think I wanted anything to do with him."

On their first date, they went to a snazzy Italian restaurant, and Oates surprised her by pulling out a letter written in a large script. He asked Teddy to read it to him, and she obliged, relating a message from Oates's eight-year-old nephew, Gordie, back in Louisville. If it was a ploy, it worked. Then she asked Oates if he had ever been married.

"Yeah, yeah, I used to be married," he replied. "But I'm not now. She's in New York, and I'm here."

"Well, now, are you divorced?"

"Well, yeah, she's in New York and I'm here."

Teddy could tell he was not divorced, and she made it clear she had no interest in going out with a married man. "When you're divorced, come talk to me."

Entanglements aside, they went out for a week, during which they necked like crazy, with Oates angling for more. He asked her to come up to his house. "I'm sorry," Teddy said. "I'm just not ready. Not till I'm married."

"Well, Teddy, I'm a man," Oates replied. "I just can't do this."

He raised his glass in a toast to his date. "To us," he said, "as long as we are." At first blush, Teddy thought his words wonderfully romantic.

A pursuit of another kind was about to come to fruition as Oates worked again with Robert Culp on *Trackdown*. Culp was now living in Encino, in the San Fernando Valley, with his wife

Nancy and their infant son Joshua. The actor rode to work on his motorcycle, "a windbreaker over a black knitted turtleneck sweater. He had on Levi's, cycle boots, dark glasses," wrote the intriguingly named Boots Le Baron in the *Los Angeles Times*. Evidently, Culp, and most likely Le Baron, was a fashion guy.

Culp was also a dedicated writer. One storyline he had scripted for *Trackdown* was structured around a role for Nancy, who was finding her way back to acting after becoming a mother. Labeling her "a female Brando," Culp presented her with a part that was challenging and creative. It was also country miles from the usual roles for women, western or not, centering on an outlaw's widow who seeks revenge against the man who killed her husband, yet she essentially wants to die herself, and does. To complete the storyline, Culp wrote a part for Oates, whom he credited as bringing him and his wife together in New York City. Oates's character would shoot the leading lady and then ask, "Did I do right, Mr. Gillum?"

"He nailed it," Culp remembered. "It was a straightforward, simple question from a simple man who had just done a simple thing, but it was devastating. It was like the end of the world."

Trackdown, which dwelled in a comparatively cerebral corral, caught the notice of columnist Cecil Smith, who wrote in the *Los Angeles Times*, "Television's western craze has brought a new and rather unique brand of cowboy to the theatrical scene. He's as far removed from the 'yup' and 'howdy' brand of the old movie western hero as you can get—a serious, articulate worker in the theatrical vineyards, trained in Actor's Studio or Neighborhood Playhouse, as familiar to Shakespearian tights as the form-fitting jeans of the TV cowpoke. Typical of the breed are such performers as Steve McQueen, Richard Boone, and Robert Culp."

For a few Wednesday nights at seven thirty on CBS, viewers could see Oates in subsequent episodes of *Trackdown*, playing different characters. As they watched him effortlessly ease into the skin of a hillbilly cowboy or a wild-eyed hick, the folks at home may not have realized the actor was likewise theatrically trained.

5

Bullfights and Boots

Warren Oates had a given name that lent itself to westerns, themselves often less than respectfully referred to as "oaters." Over his considerable career, he played characters named Deke, Jed, Lute, Sonny, Drago, Bowers, Mobeetie, Tate, Kemp, Dink, Korbie, Buxton, Hode, Ves, and Jace. He was Speeler, Orville, Rabbit, Stark, Hanes, Jep, Shep, Clem, and Cat Crail. He was Private Hurd Maple, Troy Armbruster, and Silas Carpenter. He was Weed, and he must have enjoyed that. He played Muff, which could not have been lost on him. He was both Willet and Coyne Gashade and Perce and Frank Clampett. He was Lyle Gorch and entirely Arch Harris. "I can't tell you how many times I've played a guy named Billy Joe," Oates said. "When I finally did a 'Gunsmoke' Dennis Weaver was directing his first show, and the character I played in it was Sweet Billy." He was forgetting the previous *Gunsmoke*s he had done in which he had played Jep Scooper and Seth Pickett.

"At first, I played the neurotic hillbilly son or the third man on the horse, then worked my way up with tremendous success to being the second heavy on a horse," he said. Of another role, he explained, "I was the fourth heavy, the nutty son who was quiet and would suddenly explode. If you exploded well enough maybe next time you got to play the third heavy." He also offered the descriptions "I was usually the guy on the fifth horse from the horse closest to the camera" and "I was the second hood to

step out of the black '49 Chevy." Oates brought forth piano players and gangsters, rogues and rubes, arsonists and androids. He
even played an insurance investigator. But the one type he seldom
played was a married man.

The year 1959 treated Robert Culp and Warren Oates dis-
parately. "I couldn't get a job in '59 at all," Culp recalled, "so
I went to fairs and rodeos and did trick riding." Unlike Culp,
Oates did not have leading-man status, and there was plenty of
room for the kinds of roles he played.

Nick Georgiade too had found work, being cast as Enrico
Rossi in the series *The Untouchables*. The relative success allowed
him and Anita to stay in their big house, which was a boon to
many of their friends. "In my huge kitchen was a breakfast nook
that could actually seat ten people," Georgiade said. "Every
morning when I would get up to go to work, the kitchen would
be filled with actors: Howie Dayton, Steve McQueen, Wayne
Rogers, Armand, Vic Tayback came for a while. They'd be in
the kitchen playing cards. The poker was a penny and the most
you could raise was five cents." Anita would be in the kitchen,
wearing an apron and serving coffee to the troops. "They had
nothing to do and nowhere else to go," Georgiade sighed. "I felt
a great empathy because none of these guys were working except
for Warren."

Warren was taking roles such as that of Charlie in an episode
of *Buckskin*. Tom Nolan, a child actor in the series who has since
become a writer, explained,

The premise of the series was a hotel in Montana in 1880.
I played the son of the man who ran the hotel, and the stories centered around the various guests. James Coburn was a
guest, as was Warren Oates. Warren played the son of Edgar
Stehli, a great character actor. The plot was, the old man was
dying and he came to seek reconciliation with his son, who'd
become a criminal but didn't want his father to know this.
In the scene where he meets the old man, he pretends he's a
success. The emotions he brought to the scene, he was grief
stricken. He was wonderful in it.

"Charlie, My Boy" aired in some areas on Monday, April 6, 1959. In other regions it was preempted by a political convention; the episode eventually ran in the Los Angeles market five years later, when NBC revived *Buckskin* in an afternoon slot.

The morning before *Buckskin* gave way to blowhards, Oates was flown by charter aircraft to northern Arizona for work in another Gordon Douglas film. *Yellowstone Kelly* was purportedly about Luther Sage Kelly, a mountain man and native of New York's Finger Lakes region who roamed the country in the 1870s, trapping, surveying, and working as an Indian scout. Kelly had a memorable calling card: a grizzly bear's paw. Decades later, this detail popped into the mind of a copywriter working on a pitch for U.S. savings bonds. "His calling card had claws on it," ran the subsequent full-page advertisement for savings bonds that appeared in the bible of hunting and fishing known as *Variety* early in 1956. The advertisement caught the eye of someone at Warner Brothers, who promptly registered the title *Yellowstone Kelly* with the Motion Picture Association of America (MPAA) on February 1, 1956.

The movie's star was Clint Walker, one of infamous agent Henry Willson's discoveries. The flamboyant Willson, who guided the career of Rock Hudson, among others, had spotted Walker working as a bouncer (or, in some accounts, as a deputy sheriff) in Las Vegas. Hollywood tagged him "the gentle giant," and the well-developed, if one-dimensional, actor got the lead in television's *Cheyenne*. That Walker starred in *Yellowstone Kelly* was a reflection of the studio's old system of operating.

Oates was never under contract to Warner Brothers. "Strange thing," he said, "I could work in the [Warner Brothers] film department, but I couldn't get a job on TV. All those good-looking guys had the jobs, you see?" A shift toward more realistic dramas, he said, eventually gave him the chance he needed.

Realism was not at the fore of *Yellowstone Kelly*, however; an early memo indicated that any film about the man would be "highly fictionalized." Warner Brothers handily found roles for three prominent players from its television series: Walker, Edd Byrnes, and John Russell, from *Lawman*, who was picked to play

Gall, the Indian chief. Burt Kennedy, who would direct Oates a total of four complete times, wrote the script.

The film was shot near Flagstaff, Arizona. Whereas the Yellowstone Valley was inclement, heavily blanketed in snow, Arizona had a comparatively hospitable climate that, along with its proximity, would help keep costs down—and budget was never out of sight on a Warner Brothers production. That, as the studio suggested, 114 Navajo actors lent realism to the efforts is laughable. In their central casting wigs, they were convincing Sioux only compared to cast members Andra Martin and Ray Danton, who also played Native Americans.

On location, Oates got the flu, as did most of the cast except health-food addict Walker. Oates had another misfortune when he was thrown from his horse during a cavalry charge. He suffered lacerations to his face and nose, and he learned enough to grab onto an overhanging branch the next time his horse veered off into a clump of trees. By now, his former method of stopping was unintentional.

Oates did not have many lines, but the first few set the tone. "Well, well, well," he says. "What yuh figure he is, Sarge . . . Sioux or Cheyenne?" and "Why don't you ask 'im?" were fairly standard Oates fare. The MPAA monitored the proceedings, and the line "April, hell!" was an early casualty that nevertheless made it into the film's final version.

Motion Picture Daily's assessment that the movie's "names may well bring out to theaters that part of the so-called 'lost' audience which has been lost because of TV westerns and action dramas" proved correct. *Yellowstone Kelly* opened strongly and was generally well received by reviewers (none of whom mentioned Oates's performance) and the public. To watch *Yellowstone Kelly* today, however, is to see a stiff, dated, and even silly film. Clint Walker resembles a fiberglass Muffler Man as he wanders through the scenery; Edd Byrnes plays it to the hilt; Ray Danton is wasted in face paint. Oates, however, makes the most of his time on camera. The fun he is having is palpable. But perhaps the *Los Angeles Mirror-News* said it best when it later recognized the film as "a throwback to those Technicolored cavalry versus

Indian days before the movie western went somberly psychological, tense and black-and-white."

Oates checked out of the Flamingo Motel (which later would lose its *o* and remain as "Flaming") on April 16 and, after a few drinks at the Hotel Monte Vista, boarded the ten o'clock Southern Pacific bound for Los Angeles. His seatmate was Gary Vinson, who had played a lieutenant, and the two actors slept and talked, drank and smoked as they rolled through Williams, Needles, Barstow, Victorville, and on into Union Station just after breakfast. Jerry Steiner had borrowed Oates's car and was waiting to pick him up on the gray, drizzly morning.

Steiner dropped Oates off at his house above the Strip, and he slept until early evening, when he was ready for action. It had been raining on and off for much of the day, and low clouds now hung over the hilltops of the Santa Monica Mountains, which crested the streets surrounding Gould Avenue. Oates dressed, a bit flashily, before walking down the labyrinthine road to Chez Paulette. He had a steak and a few drinks, asked after friends, and slapped a few more on the back. Taking stock again, he saw Teddy sitting with Jimmy Cimino. When he caught her eye, she waved him over and gave him a warm embrace. She knew he had just returned from filming a movie, and she asked him about it.

Oates wasted no time. "Are you going to come to my house tonight?" he asked. Cimino pretended to be out of earshot, but he had heard it all before.

"Yeah," she replied. "I think I will. I'll think about it."

He did a double-take, then exaggeratedly looked at his watch. "How long do you need?"

"Give me half an hour."

Oates walked back to the bar, careful to keep looking over his shoulder lest Teddy try to slip away. He walked over to the table every few minutes. "Have you decided yet?" he kept asking. Many of the patrons had left for the night, and it looked as if it might start to rain again. Oates sat down in Cimino's chair and looked at Teddy. She was perfect. Her wavy, wheat-colored hair seemed to have an understanding with the night's weather, and although she was petite, it was evident she could look out for herself.

Cimino came back, and Oates ran out of patience. "Okay, where's your car?" he asked Teddy.

"My roommate has it. Where's yours?"

"My agent has my car."

Cimino, silent until now, said, "I'll take you."

The three drove up the hill in Cimino's sports car. Oates held Teddy's hand, his arm draped over the passenger seat. Once they arrived, he nearly jerked her arm out of its socket trying to untangle her.

They ran up the steps, the shrubs rustling in the breeze. He opened the front door and then suddenly dropped her hand. "Get behind me. Somebody's in here," he said, in a low voice. Picking up a lamp, he announced, "Come on out, whoever this is."

A light turned on. "Surprise!" shouted Teddy's crowd from Chez Paulette.

"Welcome home!" rejoined Oates's.

"He wouldn't talk to me all night," Teddy recalled. "He thought he was going to get lucky." Guests began to filter out, Teddy kept drinking wine, and eventually she and Oates were left alone. They both got lucky.

Oates was at his usual place in Chez Paulette one night in early May when Armand Alzamora walked in and announced he had just gotten married in Tennessee. Wasting no time, Oates commandeered a bottle of champagne and shook it portentously. He popped the cork, which flew like a space capsule straight at Alzamora, hitting him in the face and knocking him out cold. After a visit to an emergency clinic on Santa Monica Boulevard, Alzamora went home, bandaged up, to his new bride Betty. Unfazed, Betty took one look at him and said, "You've been out with Warren."

Oates's next role was not looking to get lucky—he was being forced to. Veering far from Oates's usual terrain and well into the realm of the art film, his character Boots in *Private Property* (or, as it sometimes excitedly appeared, *Private Property!*) was one of a pair of "motorcycle-booted, switchblade-packing young drifters pursuing an evil mission," according to the press release. An opening scene took place alongside the Pacific Ocean, but this clearly was not his usual West.

transported his young companion across the border for immoral purposes.

They checked into San Diego's La Pierre Motel and later went dancing ("The man could not dance," his new wife said) at the Hotel del Coronado, which had recently stood in for a Florida resort (as Jack Lemmon and Tony Curtis stood in for women) in *Some Like It Hot*.

Back in their upstairs motel room, the newlyweds heard gunfire. Oates ran out to the balcony and saw police cars having a shootout with another car. He leaned over the railing as his new wife screamed for him to get back. "There were bullets flying right below him, maybe fifteen feet away," Teddy said. "I had to pull him away from that so I wasn't a widow before I was a wife."

The skirmish involved two teenagers, one of whom had taken his parents' car and headed toward Tijuana. They fled from the police because they were afraid that if they were caught, they would lose their privileges. What they lost was greater. Both teenagers were shot and killed.

As omens went, it was not good.

6

A Diamond, a Daughter, and a Drunk

Southern California insomniacs with a penchant for movies till dawn might have tuned into the Lindy—as in ink pens—Theater's "Four Uninterrupted Movies" starting at eleven o'clock on KABC, channel 7, on Sunday, September 27, 1959. Among the gems *Shadows of the Thief*, *A Very Big Man*, *Alibi*, and *Uncle Azry*, they would have seen a guest interview with Warren Oates. It was Oates's first—and practically last—such appearance. He would make a point of shying away from television talk shows and interviews and anything that presented him, a private and even shy man, as the focal point. On the late-night broadcast, it is very likely that he spoke about his most recent role, which again had taken him to the Warner Brothers lot.

In the fall of 1959, he was a twice-married man with a new bride and a baby well on the way. To many of their friends and colleagues, such as producer Stanley Colbert, Teddy was "sweet, uncomplicated, and highly supportive of Warren." Teddy and he now shared his Hollywood Hills house on Gould, along with Oatsie de Blanca, a white cockapoo with a penchant for car rides, a black dog named Perrita, and Tiger the calico cat. Friends Robert and Nancy Culp had given them two parakeets, and at times the expectant couple were so broke Teddy had to go down alleys gathering pop bottles to have enough money to buy birdseed.

Meanwhile, Oates was having an ongoing affair with the wife

of a business associate. "How long do I think Oates was faithful?" Howard Dayton asked. "I don't know. Twenty-four hours?"

Oates had been working on a film with the tentative title of "The Life and Death of Legs Diamond," directed by Budd Boetticher, whose own life was the stuff of myth. Boetticher had been trained as a bullfighter before working in the movies, where his first credit was as a technical advisor on the Tyrone Power epic *Blood and Sand*. By the late 1950s, he was turning out superior western films like *Buchanan Rides Alone* and *Seven Men from Now*. After Boetticher made *The Rise and Fall of Legs Diamond*, he would return to Mexico and remain for eight years, losing his wife, his sanity, and every penny in the process. Oates would refer to his director years later as "that dear old mean, hard man, Budd Boetticher."

Boetticher said that he loved his characters' loneliness and that villains were as important to him as heroes. His short and tight movies almost certainly caught Peckinpah's eye. His preferred cameraman's work did. "Lucien Ballard was my cameraman," Boetticher wrote in his 1989 autobiography *When in Disgrace*. "Of course the only way Lucien was not always going to be my cameraman was if some other director beat me to him." Although Boetticher got his cameraman for his next film, making it would sour his patience with Hollywood. "It was time to make 'Legs Diamond,'" he wrote, "and get the hell out of Hollywood for a while." Boetticher and Ballard joined leagues when they realized that their producer, Milton Sperling, was hobbling the film. "So to try to do *something* different, we decided to film Diamond in the 1920s fashion—shot for shot, nothing fancy." There were no dolly shots, very few pans, and no foreground setups.

The producer's reaction to the day's rushes was swift. "I thought you said Lucien Ballard was a good cameraman," Sperling demanded of Boetticher.

"Please quote me correctly. Lucien Ballard is a great cameraman."

"Well, that's your opinion. Yesterday's stuff looks like it was shot in 1920."

Legs Diamond was a Jazz Age gangster known as the Clay

Pigeon because he survived numerous gunshots in several attacks. In the film, Ray Danton, a dark-haired young actor who would go on to become a notable director, played Diamond. The show is all Danton's: his is a coldness that makes Pacino's Scarface ooze with humanity. Danton was not the most convivial man in Hollywood, and although he had played a series of delinquents and malcontents to great effect, Legs Diamond gave him a chance to stretch.

As Diamond's tubercular brother Eddie, Oates is not given much to do apart from coughing convincingly and then being shot while convalescing in a Denver sanatorium. Reviewers tended not to notice him, but the notes accompanying a 2007 screening by the American Cinematheque in Hollywood found that "Warren Oates is perfect as Diamond's sickly brother and initial partner in crime."

The Rise and Fall of Legs Diamond is complex, with a fine script by Joseph Landon. It looks striking, not surprising given the presence of Ballard, who would become a Peckinpah stalwart and also amass an impressive body of work. The film has a place among other gangster chronicles, although at the time of its release, the studios, reviewers, and audiences did not know how to handle it. Still, a *Los Angeles Times* reviewer suggested, some audiences "may cotton to Legs as a sort of hero. Cunning he is, but as cold-blooded as any back alley thug." A tougher world was not very far off.

But as the holiday season of 1959 approached, Warren Oates packed his Triumph, whistled for Oatsie the dog, waited for Teddy, and then drove east to spend Christmas in Phoenix with his in-laws. "Warren loved my mother, who he called Mamacita," Teddy said. Louise Farmer was, at five feet two inches, tiny. She was also attractive and effervescent, and she always appeared happy, making her a good match for Oates's own conviviality. Plus the drinks flowed as they did at most holiday occasions, making the new year seem like a very bright prospect.

January chill—not in the least a Southern California oxymoron—represented a comedown from the balm of the central Arizona desert. Teddy was no longer working at Schwab's; she had taken a job at Los Angeles Motor Car Dealers, handily located across Sunset from a coffee bar called Pupi's.

"I was on the switchboard," Teddy said, "and dealers would call in with license plate numbers and I would tell them the address of the owner of that car, so they could send them a letter seeing if they would like to trade their car in. The president eventually offered me a job as his secretary. I said I better not because I'm pregnant and I won't be working that long." In fact, Teddy had another reason for refusing the promotion. "Every day from where I was sitting I could see Warren at Pupi's playing chess with Mort Sahl and everybody. I thought if he's not going to work, I'm not going to work. So I quit."

"Pupi's was the most typical place I ran into Warren," said writer B. J. Merholz. "Madame Pupi, as we called her, specialized in Italian pastries, a big platter of tennis ball–sized puffballs they'd pile up two feet tall. I'd go there at ten thirty if I'd been working at the typewriter early, and I would do coffee. Then I'd come back around two, three o'clock and do coffee. My problem was I'd be there having coffee in early afternoon and Warren would come by and we would schmooze for thirty, forty minutes or so, and before he left, Jack [Nicholson] would come by for another thirty, forty minutes."

Pupi's, which opened in the mid- to late 1950s, sat on the south side of the Sunset Strip, in the historically upscale portion known as Sunset Plaza. It had a striped awning over sidewalk tables, but the little flagstone patio was the real attraction, along with some Perspex that blocked the wind coming up from the great sweep that separated its patrons from the wider Los Angeles Basin below. Oates spent a lot of daylight time there, but once the sun was over the yardarm, Chez Paulette sounded her siren call. There were other spots along this portion of the Strip, all within a three-block walk: Cyranos, Via Veneto, and the intriguingly named Sea Witch. But Chez Paulette and Pupi's took the lion's share of Oates's leisure time.

With Oates earning only when he was working, it was touch and go in early 1960. "Every now and then he'd get a paycheck, four hundred dollars for doing a western, or a residual would come in, just in the nick of time," Teddy said. From January 15 to June 15, there was a writers' strike, brought on by issues concerning residuals for movies shown on television and the creation of a pension plan. No script that required a single word change could be filmed; it was either shelved or made as it was.

For Sam Peckinpah, the break in the action was critical: he was putting together a new series to be called *The Westerner*, and he quickly joined a breakaway group of writers who sought to resolve the strike to keep working.

Oates had not worked for a while, and the rent was due. "Our rent at the time was $195," Teddy said. "Warren went to the bank to get a $200 loan just to pay the rent. I think he went to the bank at ten thirty in the morning. He came back at seven at night. He didn't have the $200 to pay the rent, but he did have two new jackets, both of them beige, both of them khaki kind of colored. They looked identical except that one had a little brown piping on the front."

Teddy said, "Warren . . ."

"Teddy, I . . . you know, I got the money and I went to Schwab's. And I was just walking to my car and I see this jacket in the window."

"But you got two of 'em!" she exclaimed.

"I know, but look at it. This one's got brown on it, Teddy."

"How do we pay the rent?"

Oates said he would borrow money from a friend.

"Do you know what we did with *that* $200?" Teddy asked. "We took all of our friends to Cyrano's to celebrate the fact that one of Warren's movies or shows was on the air that day. And that $200 went away."

Oates would soon be working on a new series created by Rod Serling, *The Twilight Zone*. In the episode titled "The Purple Testament," Oates had a small role driving a Jeep on maneuvers in the Philippine jungle. Serling had served there in 1944 under extreme conditions; the premise, that a soldier slated to die could be identified by a pall cast over his face, might have been formulated then. The effect was achieved by excessive lighting, combined with overexposure of the film. "The Purple Testament" did not run the night it was scheduled to appear, however, because its director, Richard L. Bare, and lead actor William Reynolds had been involved in a plane crash that killed one of the five people onboard.

Unhampered by the writers' strike, Oates did several other shows during the spring, including the popular *77 Sunset Strip*, even though his *Up Periscope* roommate Edd "Kookie" Byrnes had not warmed to him. But with one or two exceptions, the hostility or indifference of other actors did not bother Oates.

One weekend in February, Oates and a very pregnant Teddy, who would turn twenty on February 9, drove down to San Diego to walk across the border and then take a Tijuana taxi to the bullring. They sat in their usual seats, and some time after Warren finished his customary cigar, a little girl with blonde hair came and sat on his lap, put her arm around his neck, and proceeded to watch the bullfight. "I'm looking over at Warren and saying 'Who's this?'" remembered Teddy. "After about ten minutes, we hear this voice in the back saying, 'Jennifer, you get back up here,' and the child kissed him on the cheek and went away."

Back in Los Angeles, in late March, Teddy realized she was going into labor. Oates drove her to Queen of Angels Hospital near downtown and then spent a portion of the restless night with Teddy in the hospital room before announcing, "I've got to go home and get my script for *Johnny Ringo*."

"He goes home, and he doesn't come back and doesn't come back. So finally I called the answering service. I said, 'If Mr. Oates calls in, will you tell him his wife is in the hospital having a baby?'"

When he returned to the hospital room, Teddy was awake. "How's little Kelly?" he asked. They were going to name the baby Kelly whether it was a boy or a girl.

"Jennifer," Teddy replied.

The new parents were worried they would not be able to take their infant home, having heard that the hospital kept the baby until the birth was paid for. But that was not the case. Jennifer Oates was born March 27, 1960, and the hospital allowed her proud parents to take her home.

By that summer, with the writers' strike resolved, Peckinpah was at work on *The Westerner*. Set around a drifter named Dave Blassingame (Brian Keith) and his mongrel dog Brown, the show was as distant from stagy cowboy shows as it could be. Even Brown, far from a faithful hound, was described by his master as "just a bunch of skin wrapped around an appetite."

The episode titled "Jeff" was broadcast on September 30, 1960. In an intricate morality play in which realism effortlessly mixes with dreamlike imagery, the titular character is a prostitute in Mexico whose father asks Blassingame to retrieve her. In its opening scene, in a grungy bar on the periphery of life, a drunk sits alone at a table, muttering to himself. Eventually he falls over and is dragged away. Oates's "drunk" is uncredited, brief, and nearly silent, but his gritty impact and tangential integrity offer a thumbnail sketch of the performances he will give for Peckinpah over the next decade and a half.

"The first *Westerner* Sam ever did, Warren is a background character, a drunk in a bar," said writer Garner Simmons. "Sam really looked for people who were unique, in outlook and in look. Warren was not your average everyday movie star, which is what attracted Sam. Warren's ability to put forward an everyman quality was hugely important to the films Sam was making, and also to Warren himself."

7

Meanwhile, Back at the Raincheck

Warren Oates had longstanding groups of friends who, like whiskey and rocks, blended with hesitancy. Some were divided geographically (Montana, California, New Mexico), others by era, and still others by temperament. Oates's friend Bob Watkins remembered a volatile dinner party rounded off by two rowdy personalities. "Sam Peckinpah and Dennis Hopper were very much alike in that they both got totally out there and were always intense. They want drama every five minutes and they'll create it. Some people will hang around them because the energy is wild, but if you're a real easygoing person, you'll get nauseous from the rush."

Oates, who could veer from laid back to full throttle in a heartbeat, took the rush in his stride. He had an enormous number of pals, a handful of whom were close and a far greater number who were passing—or passing out—acquaintances. And the sectors sometimes collided in an unassuming bar in the heart of what would become Boystown in the not yet designated city of West Hollywood. The Raincheck Room, located at 8279 Santa Monica Boulevard, near the corner of Crescent Heights, opened in the early 1960s and was owned by Zell Davis and Phil Pearl, colorful characters in their own right. In its lifespan, which ran a few years past the legal drinking age, it served as a kind of rumpus room for actors and show people. Taking its name from the little tickets the bartender would give to those receiving but not then wanting a drink, the Raincheck endeared itself to many who would find the stubs more quickly than they found their car keys as they attempted to make their way to the door.

The Raincheck had a bulletin board where people in town from New York could sign in (or sign out). The drinks were cheap, the food was good, the service was fast, and the place was small enough that it was always bustling, an "in" place to go. Dennis Hopper played darts; Harry Dean Stanton sat back one night while Oates got into a fight.

"I think he thought a guy was hitting on his wife," Stanton said. "Warren slammed a beer bottle on the table and chased the guy out into the street. Somehow out there they must have made up because they came back, sat at the bar, and Warren bought him a drink. That's when the guy said, 'You know that beer bottle you had? It didn't break.'"

Teddy Oates also factored into another brawl. "My girlfriend Micki and I took Warren out on his birthday. We all went down to the Troubadour to see Richard Pryor. About ten minutes before Richard Pryor was finished, Warren says, 'I'm going on down and will meet you guys at the Raincheck.' So we wait ten minutes for the show to be over, and then Micki and I go down to the Raincheck. There's Warren sitting way down the bar. So she and I sit at this end of the bar, 'cause there's no room down there."

"Hey, Warren, we're down here," Teddy waved to no avail.

"Some poor guy who didn't know me, didn't know Warren, didn't know anybody, happened to lean over my shoulder to order a beer. Warren came from that end of the bar to this end of the bar, tackled the guy."

"Get away from my wife!" Oates growled before he and the man fell into a table of eight people having dinner. The Raincheck's sizable bartenders vaulted over the bar, took Oates off the guy, and sent him off into the summer night to commemorate his birthday in the air scented with night-blooming jasmine, orange blossoms, car exhaust, spilled beer, and charcoal-broiled hamburger.

As a bartender, Alex Rocco saw it all, serving drinks and New

York steak sandwiches that came with a baked potato for $1.75. "The Raincheck Room, that was our lives. I would see someone and think, 'Oh, there's a screwdriver. There's whiskey on the rocks.' I'd know their drinks. Warren was everything. I used to have to hide Warren behind the darts room when his wife came in." Rocco continued, "All the calls came from the wives and the girlfriends and Rocco was the go-to guy. We had everybody. Rock Hudson would come in and comb his hair the other way, wear sunglasses, trying to hide out. I would spot the celebrities, who was cruising, who was picking up, the whole nine yards. Warren would sit at the far end of the bar so he could clock the room for either Teddy coming in, or a chick."

The Oates family had left the Hollywood Hills and meandering Gould Avenue for the comparatively bucolic San Fernando Valley, but they would not stay there for long. Still, their temporary home on Milbank Street in Sherman Oaks was better suited to life with a child. Teddy's memories of Gould are not scrapbook material: The house was dark; it had steep steps leading up to it; and she was a young mother often alone with a baby. Her husband had developed the habit of saying he would be home at a certain time and then rolling up at any given hour. "If Warren wasn't home when it got dark, I'd put Jennifer in the car and drive around, either go to the drive-in or something until he came home."

On one particular night, she waited in the car until close to midnight with the baby because she was too scared to go up the steps and be in the secluded house alone. Oates pulled up, smelling of gin, and proceeded up the steps. "Don't say anything to me," he said.

"Where have you been?" she asked.

"Oh, you don't want to know."

Inside the house, she put the baby to bed and then questioned him further. Finally, he blurted out, "I've got cancer of the mouth. I'm going to die. There's nothing we can do about it."

"OK," she said calmly. "Did you see a doctor?"

He rattled off the name of one in Culver City near Twentieth Century–Fox. "I'm going to die," he repeated. "Don't tell anybody." Then he shut his eyes and went to sleep.

The next morning Teddy was making coffee when her husband woke up. "Now Warren," she ventured, "Where do you want to be buried? Do you want to be buried here or in Kentucky or what?"

"What are you talking about?" he asked, reaching for a cup of coffee.

"You know, cancer of the mouth."

"Did I say that? Oh, God."

Oates would not be home for much of 1961. He would be making two movies: One had a small budget and is now as good as forgotten. The other became a classic.

In the first case, Leslie Stevens was again employing his own inventive savvy that made him a thinking man's Roger Corman. His next project, he told the *Los Angeles Times*, was "way out in left field."

On Monday, January 9, 1961, Oates left a pregnant Teddy and joined James Mason, Rip Torn, Neville Brand, and Kate Manx en route not to the ballpark but to a resort some twenty miles off the coast of Southern California. Chicago Cubs owner William Wrigley had developed Catalina Island's principal city, Avalon, into a gambling haven in the 1920s. Part of the less developed majority of the island would stand in for Carolina in Stevens's next movie, "The Land We Love," which would be retitled *Hero's Island*. "We can no longer afford the luxury of a twisted neurosis," Stevens said, referring to the testy political climate of early 1961. "In effect the time has passed to look at the twisted side of life, of America."

Hero's Island, set in 1718, follows a collection of indentured servants as they experience their freedom for the first time on Bull Island in Carolina. Stevens was again looking to work quickly, eighteen days, but this time United Artists put up $250,000. "What we are calling it is the idea picture aimed at the intelligent market—whoever that market may be," he said. The top salary was $10,000, but the actors would get a share in the profits. "The idea is not to destroy an actor's position in relation to his feature price, but to make him feel he is doing something commensurate with his dignity and ability," Stevens explained. "Is it New Wave?" he asked. "American history is the last place you'd expect to find New Wave! Is it art house? Yes and no. Yes, in the sense that it will try to be art on a New Wave budget; no, if you equate it with Bridget Bardot and sex."

Private Property's dismal fate had demanded that Stevens distance himself from sex, which meant vivacious Manx, as Devon Mainwaring, would be doing no colonial skinny-dipping. Still, her presence as an American Bardot of the limited release added punch to an otherwise straitlaced affair. Devon and her husband Thomas (Brendan Dillon) and their two children, Cullen (played by Morgan Mason, James's son) and Jafar (Darby Hinton), have made a home on an island off the Carolina coast. They are menaced by local fishermen (Rip Torn, Neville Brand, and Harry Dean Stanton), one of whom kills Thomas, leaving Devon alone to raise her two children. Kindly family friend Wayte (Oates, in a unique bit of casting) becomes a stand-in father and husband. A mysterious stranger, Jacob Webber (James Mason), arrives, and the widow Devon warms to him, despite that he is, he confesses, a pirate. Webber intends to avenge Thomas's murder, and a battle ensues in which Devon rescues Webber. He does not stay with her, however, but rather returns to his life on the high seas.

Hero's Island appears lavish in comparison with its predecessor, *Private Property*, and it also makes far more concessions to commerciality. Manx is appealing and engaging. Oates appears earnest, speaking in a dialect that is part Somerset, part sundown Kentucky. In scenes with Harry Dean Stanton, he is careful to keep him in his sights. Oates and Rip Torn are occasionally on-screen together, and after the salty air has turned Torn's hair curly, they begin to resemble each other so strongly that it is fortunate that they wear light and dark clothing, respectively, just as sports teams wore opposite-hued jerseys in the days of black-and-white television.

The sound track by Dominic Frontiere is streaked with glissando, and while the landscape is pure California coastal, it is no more obtrusive than it is in other, bigger-budget films. James Mason's speech, revealing his true identity as a pirate, is played to the hilt—the corn is high—but the plot twist in which he leaves the island is surprising.

When *Hero's Island* premiered in Charlotte, North Carolina, in September 1962, the city's mayor and local scout troops came along, but that was about it. The *Hollywood Reporter* thought it was "a worthy effort," citing Oates's performance as "able." Oates told Boyd Martin it was his first sympathetic part, a fact Martin duly reported in his column for the *Louisville Courier-Journal*.

Oates made a lasting friend during the filming of *Hero's Island*. He was always well liked on set, and it was not unusual for him to come away laden with names and numbers of new drinking buddies and good-time pals. But Harry Dean Stanton, a fellow native Kentuckian who was as wild as he could be withdrawn, would be more than just a fair-weather acquaintance. Stanton and Oates were like twin cyclones.

While *Hero's Island* was being filmed, Teddy had gone into early labor. Before going into the hospital, she called Nancy Culp. "To this day, I don't know why," she said. "Nancy Culp and I had never been close in any way, shape, or form, but when I knew I was going to the hospital, I called her house. Her maid answered the phone, and I told her, 'Tell Nancy Culp that Teddy Oates is going to Beverly Hills Doctors Hospital.' And it was some kind of psychic thing because I must have known this woman will take care of what needs to be taken care of."

Together Nancy and Robert Culp chartered a plane to Catalina and retrieved Warren. He was there when the premature baby girl was born. He returned to location the next morning, during which time the baby died. Nancy Culp stayed with Teddy in an adjacent room for the next two days.

On March 27, 1961, Jennifer Oates turned one year old, and her father was there to celebrate her birthday. The party featured all the requisite trimmings: balloons, bunting, a pony, a clown. In the backyard shade of the Oateses' San Fernando Valley home, children squealed and ate cake and ice cream while their parents drank and ate barbecue. Teddy, expecting again, kept the party in its paces, ever the dutiful hostess.

For the rest of the spring, the family scraped by in the house under the scrub oaks, their lives reinforced by residual checks from television work and the promise of more. A cat they had yet to name had joined their ranks—Oatsie the dog had been stolen—and there was an array of Southern Californian wildlife: raccoons, possums, skunks, and the occasional wandering coyote.

Despite being pregnant again and looking after a one-year-old, Teddy cooked and kept house. Hired help would have been welcome, but their financial circumstances could not support it. Oates was gone much of the time—working or propping up the bar at the Raincheck Room—and his career was climbing like a bougainvillea vine up a trellis. His next film role would be his highest-profile part yet.

Sam Peckinpah was three years older than Oates and from a considerably different background, that of an affluent family rooted in California's Central Valley. Oates and Peckinpah each had done a hitch in the Marine Corps—the latter served in Korea—and although Oates was not one to champion his lackluster service record, the Semper Fi ethos informed both men. They both lived hard, enjoyed a drink, and, despite their macho exteriors, cared passionately about their art. They had worked together on *The Rifleman* and *The Westerner*, and Peckinpah, about to make his second feature film, promised Oates a small but substantial part over whiskeys one night in the Raincheck.

Peckinpah's father, David, whom he revered, had died the previous autumn, and Oates had lost Bayless much earlier. For men prone to wildness, the absence of a patriarch against whom they would not have rebelled left the internal landscape wide open and the night always young.

Ride the High Country had begun when Metro-Goldwyn-Mayer hired producer Richard Lyons to make a low-budget western to come in at $800,000. Lyons had been intrigued by a script about two aging gunfighters up for one last hurrah as they shepherd a shipment of gold down from a remote mining community safely into town. The film that became *Ride the High Country* was rumored to have been offered to Budd Boetticher, who had often directed the film's prospective lead, Randolph Scott, but Lyons denied this, insisting he had seen portions of *The Westerner* at the urging of his agent at William Morris, where the series' director, Sam Peckinpah, was also a client.

The movie's credited screenwriter was N. B. Stone Jr., a man who had a deserved reputation as a serious drinker. The first draft that Lyons drew out of Stone was dreadful, so Lyons went to the person who had recommended Stone, writer Bill Roberts, for an explanation. Roberts rewrote the script into something workable, and then the two stars, Randolph Scott and Joel McCrea, were secured, but only after they decided to change roles because of McCrea's reluctance to play a villain.

The script went to Peckinpah, who retooled it further, adding a pivotal coda. Shooting—cinematographer Lucien Ballard was in place—began in mid-October, and Oates was cast as Henry, one of the notorious Hammond brothers. "Inbred, lice-infested, slavering, they nevertheless possessed two qualities Peckinpah felt *almost* redeemed their many shortcomings: a surprising sense of family honor and a wild vitality," writes Peckinpah biographer David Weddle.

Oates said good-bye to his daughter and wife, whose brother came to stay with them as Teddy entered the latter stages of pregnancy, and took the bus with the rest of the cast north to Mammoth Lakes, in the Sierras near Bishop, California. The lush and intensely dramatic scenery would reflect the ascent and descent as the group journeyed from town to Coarsegold and back.

As a Hammond, Oates joined James Drury (in a role Robert Culp turned down), L. Q. Jones, John Davis Chandler, and John Anderson as a bad-blooded breed apart. Richard Lyons recalled that after Peckinpah wardrobed them, he instructed, "'Now you guys are a unit. I want you to stay away from the rest of the cast. You are the Hammond brothers. You eat by yourselves; you live in the motel by yourselves. You hate everybody here!' And he kept them all as a unit and it worked." The story is intriguing, if apocryphal. John Davis Chandler, who played the youngest Hammond brother, Jimmy, remembered no such seclusion. L. Q. Jones, who played Sylvus Hammond, added, "One of the things most people don't understand about Sam is when he does action, everybody is involved in it, not just the people fighting. So you are prepared to do anything that needs to be done. Ron Starr [who played Heck Longtree; his former job as a car salesman was his only acting experience], poor devil, was the new one and Sam couldn't stand him and practically ran him out of the business. All the others in *Ride* had been actors a long time and knew how to act."

In relation to the rest of the cast, Mariette Hartley, who played Elsa Knudsen, was less than a seasoned professional, but she had come through the ranks as a stage actress. Her short locks, used to such realistic effect in *Ride*, were the result of her recent performance in *Saint Joan* in Chicago. Whatever the method of the ensemble performance, one thing was certain. As Hartley said, "They were really Sam's repertory company, and they scared the shit out of me. They were big drinkers, and what the hell did I know; they were very loud."

If the Hammonds were sent away to solidify in the Sierras, it was not for very long. Just as the mining camp scene in Coarsegold was about to be filmed, snow was forecast, and MGM ordered Peckinpah and his cast and crew to return to Los Angeles. He pleaded with the studio, but it did no good. The director was so livid he opted to ride home on the bus with his cast rather than travel in the studio car. He gave his bus mates instructions for their six-hour ride back to Los Angeles. "I don't want to see anybody sober when we get off," Peckinpah told them. Chandler explained, "He had gone to the local store and bought out all the booze, and he loaded all the booze onto the buses."

"Man, what a ride home that was," Hartley said. "Five miles down the road toward Los Angeles it stopped snowing, and he hit the tequila like I have never seen. Sam was the kind of alcoholic who would become cold," she said. "He generally started to drink about eight or nine in the morning—most of them did—but not this hard and not tequila. He was sitting behind me like a demon, taunting. I don't remember the words, just the tone."

Chandler sat next to Peckinpah in a more reflective mood as they neared Los Angeles. He asked Peckinpah, "Do you always want to do this [make films]?"

"Yeah, pretty much. I'm thinking this may be my last one. It's not worth going through all this nonsense."

"What would you have done if you hadn't gotten into this?" Chandler asked.

"I seriously considered being a Buddhist monk at one time."

The actor was nonplussed. "Buddhist monk as in . . . ?"

"Buddhist monk as in going and living in China," Peckinpah said.

Chandler remembered, "That didn't make much sense to me at the time because China was killing monks."

When the bus finally pulled into the parking lot in Culver City, L. Q. Jones guided the director toward his Corvette and promptly drove him home. The actors also returned to their homes, rested a bit, and then headed for nearby locations that included the Santa Monica Mountains and Griffith Park's often mined—cinematically—Bronson Canyon. Filming resumed with a scene in which Oates's character is forced by his brothers to take a bath. The actor's reluctance was so palpable it fooled Mariette Hartley. "When he was given the bath, I'm not sure if he wasn't as surprised about that . . . the way it happened. Knowing Sam and how evil he was at times, and what a wonderful director because he loved to improvise—I'm not sure that they didn't just grab him and put him in the water. And when he gets up and looks like Hitler all wet and everything, and the camera just stays on him, I was there the day that happened, and it was so powerful to watch."

Though it was not improvised, the action did involve a shift, as Oates told Garner Simmons. "That scene came about in a strange way. It originally involved my reaching into a hole and pulling out a rattlesnake by the tail. So they had this pipe they were going to put down in the ground and put the rattlesnake down the pipe headfirst so that his tail would be sticking out for me to grab. . . . Because Sam insisted that its mouth be open, there was a chance I would be bitten. So I said, 'Oh, shit!'" Oates approached the assistant director and insisted that a medical attendant and ambulance be standing by. "Then after lunch, Sam came up to me and said they had talked it over and decided to do something else. He looked at me and I looked a little ripe, and he said: 'They're going to try to give you a bath and you don't let 'em. Take out your knife. Cut 'em. Kill 'em. But don't you let 'em give you a bath.'"

Peckinpah yelled at the actors and crew throughout the sequence and promptly fired a soundman who had accidentally let a microphone boom descend into a shot. It was a tactic he had learned in the Marine Corps, to destroy morale and then rebuild it, with the effect that the newfound loyalty was to him alone.

Action that was improvised involved chickens. The chickens and their wrangler had been dismissed by the production manager, who thought they were no longer needed on set. But "Sam told [writer] Frank Kowalski that he needed another chicken scene," Chandler said. Once they were recalled, the birds were placed in a way that led to a very tranquil scene, which then cuts to Armstrong's bloodied face and is followed by the movie's shoot-out. "Warren is in the barn, and he is so brainless that he gets mighty disturbed by these chickens that are running around squawking in the yard because of all the shooting going on," Chandler related. "Warren stood up in the balcony of the barn and was so incensed with the chickens he just started shooting them."

"Warren was one of those actors who didn't lose his concentration," Jones said. His intensity also registered with Hartley, who as Elsa is sexually menaced by the Hammonds. "I can tell you I was truly, bona fide terrified during the dancing, during the wedding, and then the door opens and it is Warren who comes first," Hartley said.

The story—centering on two lawmen, Steve Judd and Gil Westrum, marginalized by age and circumstance, and a young straggler, Heck Longtree, who bring a shipment of gold from a mining camp known as Coarsegold to the tiny town bank in Hornitos—is certainly lyric. Peckinpah described it as a film about "salvation and loneliness," and it is also an homage to his late father. *Ride*'s oft-quoted line, the biblically inspired "All I want is to enter my house justified," spoken by Judd to Westrum, was a phrase favored by the elder Peckinpah, and it resonated greatly with his son. It is a beautifully patriarchal sentiment and is possibly the key to why the director is regarded, often mistakenly, as macho. A woman has a guaranteed place at the hearth, whether or not she is working outside the home. For a man, given this maxim, that place is something that must be earned.

In their documentary *Sam Peckinpah's West: Legacy of a Hollywood Renegade*, Tom Thurman and Tom Marksbury describe *Ride the High Country* as "one of the last classic Westerns and one of the first truly modern ones." Its elegiac bow casts a shadow over the vanishing American West. "Today the ranch is gone," Peckinpah lamented to writer Richard Whitehall. "There are motels. It's all gone."

Water serves as a baptismal font—it is no accident that Oates's Henry resists immersion before his brother's wedding. His emphasis on the "h" in "What?" sails across the dust like the emptiness of his soul. Yet he is not without humanity: he speaks the word innocently, and during the wedding, his jacket is buttoned up to the top in a childlike attempt at civility. His character is described in the script as the "dirty one of the group, badly in need of a haircut, wears filthy clothes, chews tobacco, parts his thin beard with thumb and forefinger of the hand when spitting, called Hene-ry by the others." Elsewhere, the direction calls for him to shout "the rebel yell."

Razor magazine described Henry as "a diseased inbred gold prospector who first walks into the film in extreme close-up with a crow sitting on his shoulder and a sneer on his lips." Indeed, this is the closest close-up in the film. "With the appearance of the crow, the movie shifts from light adventure to dreary deceit, cheating, and eventually murder," said author John M. Marzluff, whose book *In the Company of Crows and Ravens*, cowritten with Tony Angell, examines the birds' symbolism and habits. "Nothing is mysterious with Henry's crow. But what is interesting to me is that Henry's familiar is really an innocent young crow, complete with pink mouth and begging wing movements. . . . Maybe there really is a bit more to Henry than the dark side we really see?"

The film's editor, Frank Santillo, employed flash cuts that bring the audience up close. When MGM production head Sol Siegel viewed a rough cut in January 1962, he was pleased. However, Siegel left MGM shortly thereafter, and Joseph Vogel took over production. Vogel hated the picture and said he probably would not release it. Peckinpah promptly countered that he would buy the picture himself so the studio would not have to release it. It was a suggestion that got him barred from the lot.

A public preview in Los Angeles won favor with the audience. The next day's reviews were outstanding, even if Oates's performance was largely overlooked. Eventually *Ride* was *Newsweek's* film of 1962 and appeared in *Time's* top ten during a year that had also seen *Lawrence of Arabia*, *To Kill a Mockingbird*, *The Miracle Worker*, and *Days of Wine and Roses*.

Oates had been away, advancing his career and supporting his young family. It enabled him to enter his home justified. "Instead of being the rebel who was going out and getting drunk every night and having a good time, he got really serious about making a living at acting," Teddy said. "Before that, it was more fun. He was definitely not into making money, because he would do a half-hour western every three months and earn four hundred dollars and that was it. And he didn't care if he had to live on ninety dollars a week unemployment; that was fine. He had no desire for money or anything like that until the first child came. Then all of a sudden, wham! Let's go for it."

Sherman Oaks was not home to the Oateses much longer: financial straits plus a booming housing market prompted them to sell and move to less costly digs. The family found themselves in an apartment on Laurel, close to Schwab's, Pupi's, and Chez Paulette, to say nothing of the Raincheck Room.

On November 7, 1961, while *Ride the High Country* was being made, a playlet Warren had done called *Somebody's Waiting* appeared as part of *The Dick Powell Show*. Directed by Arthur Hiller, it is primarily a showcase for lead actor Mickey Rooney, who portrays a sorry soul who finds redemption from friends he did not know he had, plus the love of a fallen woman (Susan Oliver). As a fellow sailor called Bruno, Oates appears without a trace of trail dust. For an actor seldom described as versatile, he demonstrates a reserved, even elegant sophistication in the seamy port-of-call surrounds.

8

It's Chicken One Day . . .

By the time Stoney Burke started trying to win his Golden Buckle, it was looking less likely that Warren Oates would be playing a leading role any time soon. He rationalized this: "I'm happy as a character man and I want to stay a character man. The world is full of Tony Perkins types," he told *TV Scout*. And the role of Jack Lord's sidekick and often side ache Vesper P. Painter was made to order. Ves was, in Oates's words, "a rural American petty con man." But then he added a stinger. "Bad guys are all the roles available to a freelance actor and that's what I have been."

He more lightheartedly informed the *Charlotte (NC) News* that his idea of Ves was a man "full of fun and petty larceny. Always stealing something for someone and running away. I guess you'd call me a rodeo camp follower, friend of Stoney's—if you could call him that—who works his little business on the side. I just get a rake off for any suckers I can hustle. I'm a ten percenter."

Ves Painter was the perfect skin for Oates in which to bide his time and develop a character he would refer to as "hip country." Hip, reservedly: With Ves, it was as if Edd "Kookie" Byrnes got tangled up gelled-head first in a washing machine ringer and then spat straight out into the rodeo dirt. Ves may have never seen a comb that was not attached to a chicken, but that did not keep him from having a wavy way with words, mashing them into a cornpone lingo all his own. In the wrong actor's hands, the character would have been insufferable. Oates's good-natured interpretation lassoed the proceedings and made off with them. Ves "doesn't ride, doesn't work, doesn't anything—he just gets his jollies watching others," Oates said.

John Erman was the show's casting director, and he also directed a couple of its episodes. "Leslie Stevens had done a movie with Warren, and Leslie sort of got to know Warren and used a lot of Warren's personality and his vernacular in the scripts," Erman said. "Ves Painter was a prototype for a lot of very great characters to follow," said screenwriter Gordon Dawson. Ves "was Warren all over the place. The little cur at the foot of the head of the show, who absolutely stole the show."

Jack Lord, with whom Oates had appeared in *Studio One*'s "A Day before Battle" in New York, was a Brooklyn native and former Cadillac salesman who had studied in Sanford Meisner's Neighborhood Playhouse. By the time Stevens offered Lord the lead in *Stoney Burke*, Lord had been in two movies with Gary Cooper and was determined to emulate his idol's success. He told Stevens that he would be the only star of his new series about a rodeo cowboy, and he prepared to read the script. For his role as Stoney, Lord would receive $3,500 a week, to Oates's $750, the amount also paid to Robert Dowdell (who played Cody Bristol) and Bruce Dern (as E. J. Stocker).

The pilot, filmed in December 1961, saw Stoney suffer a setback after drawing the meanest bronc in the rodeo. The debut featured Stevens's wife Kate Manx, Ruby Lee, and Philip Abbott along with Oates, Lord, and Dowdell. Dern and Lord immediately crossed swords. "I knew his name was Jack Ryan, and the first thing I ever said was, 'Why'd you ever change your name from Jack Ryan to Lord?'" Lord didn't answer, but he continued to rile Dern with his constant references to Gary Cooper. "It was Coop this and Coop that," groaned the man Oates would nickname the Rattler.

A March 1962 screening report on *Stoney Burke* from the William Morris Agency read, "Revue's WIDE COUNTRY is very similar to this; stars Earl Holliman & this show's Jack Lord are both excellent in virtually the same roles & most likely wd hv the same appeal. Lord has had less TV exposure than Holliman, who had his own TV series; Thus Lord may be fresher to TV audiences.

The two boys who word [*sic*] with Lord make a good team. In concept & projection, both shows are essentially 'Route 66' or 'Wagon Train' with a rodeo background—ie, character stories & in this sense cd enjoy longevity."

The series went into production in June 1962, and the steady salary enabled the Oates family to leave their cramped apartment in Hollywood for a big house on a huge plot of land, again in the San Fernando Valley. Their new home was on Zelzah Avenue, at the end of the line and near the last vestiges of civilization in Encino. Oates told a reporter that he lived "in a house on a big lot with a lot of oak trees, so I've got a lot of work to do," although it is unlikely he spent much time raking leaves or performing any other domestic duties. Managing the house was Teddy's remit.

When Jennifer Oates turned three, she acquired a pet rabbit named Mr. Buggins (which eventually fell prey to a raccoon). Chickens ran around in the backyard and had to be negotiated during a party for, as the banner proclaimed, the Stoney Burke Bunch.

Oates was friendly with Bruce Dern but closer to Robert Dowdell, not least because during the long breaks between filming, Dern, a fanatical runner, would go off on a sprint rather than stick around the smokers. "Warren smoked way too much," said Dern. "He wasn't an athlete like I was." The difference did not hinder Dern's fondness for Oates, though. "He was just the easiest-going, most natural guy I'd ever been around in my life," he attested. Oates had established a reputation for an on-set temperament that tolerated almost any adversity. To go with the flow was much more difficult for the Rattler, who Oates laughingly insisted was always trying to stir things up. "The nickname stuck with me for a long time," Dern conceded.

"Bruce Dern never stopped complaining about everything," guest actor Michael Anderson Jr. said. "He hated Jack." On the subject of Lord, Oates tried to stay silent. "Warren wouldn't ever dis[respect] a fellow actor," Anderson said. "He would just stay out of the way and do his own thing."

With guest actors like Anderson, Oates exercised his discretion, but he wasted no time in sharing his thoughts with Bruce Dern. Dern recalled,

> Warren and I both had something in common: neither of us cared for Jack Lord. He looked at Warren and I, who in the show were young actors, but he thought we were trying to steal every fucking scene! And we weren't. I mean, my line every week was 'Stay with 'em, Stoney,' and Warren's was to invent some little limerick that he'd say, and that was it. Warren had a little bit more to do than I did, and poor Dowdell, he didn't have a goddamn thing to do.
>
> He [Lord] did not like the little people. And to him the little people weren't just the people behind the camera. They were people who weren't stars.

One-time guest star Mariette Hartley echoed that sentiment. In "Bandwagon," she played the daughter of a wronged man, and her performance drew Lord's ire. "I had just gotten into town and just started doing television," Hartley said. "He [Lord] was quite nasty with me. I had just gotten the script the night before, and there were a lot of words about graft and finances. I was kind of tripping over my lines and was very nervous. He didn't cut me a break at all."

"What do you do when you're on stage?" the show's star asked her.

"Well, when I'm on stage, Jack, I get these lines a good month before I perform." She pointed out that because she worked a lot, she must know what she was doing.

"He kind of got it," she allowed. "But Jack and Warren just weren't the same kind of person. Anybody who walks out of a hotel room in Hawaii fully made up is not a Warren Oates style," she said of a future Lord incarnation.

More than a decade later, when Lord ruled the airwaves as the king of *Hawaii Five-O*, Oates admitted that although he did not remember Lord with any particular fondness, he had learned something from him. He attributed "professionalism and discipline" to the maligned but perfectly coifed actor.

Dern had no time for charity. After seventeen episodes, Stoney would have to stay with 'em without E. J. Stocker. By the time Stoney was asked to throw a rodeo match, Stocker was not around to provide moral support.

Dern's well-heeled background in Chicago's exclusive North Shore community of Glencoe, peopled with relatives who included a poet laureate and various political bigwigs, piqued Oates's curiosity. "He was very fascinated by it because I was trying to be Warren, and Warren wasn't trying to be me, but he'd never seen anybody like me. We were so opposite. I ran from it all, and that's one of the reasons Warren and I got along," Dern said.

Ben Johnson appeared as a judge in the show's episode "Point of Honor" and also served as the series' rodeo announcer and stuntman for Lord. The tall Oklahoma cowboy cut an impressive figure, especially to Oates, whose adulation ran along the lines of what he felt for *Hopalong Cassidy*'s William Boyd. Oates admired Johnson's personal code of honor ("honesty, realism, and respect") much as he did Boyd's white hat, stardust, and business acumen. In Oates's looming mythological phase, he would connect Johnson (and Boyd) with the White Knight, placing both among a group of men who "hang in with the Knights of the Holy Grail who are after good, and those are the kind of men I admire. . . . Ben Johnson to me is the living epitome of the western cowboy who knows what the hell he's doing on a horse, a world champion rodeo rider, steer wrestler and all around cowboy, a great gentleman, and my friend . . . the living American working cowboy who is a star."

As an assessment, it was both slightly dizzy and absolutely founded. But Oates's relationship with the nearly teetotal, essentially upright, and conservative Johnson rested uneasily on one caveat. "Ben Johnson was the only guy that Warren didn't want to know he got high," Bob Watkins said. "Anybody but Ben Johnson. He was such a father figure to Warren. 'Don't let Ben Johnson find out—he wouldn't approve of it.'"

During *Stoney Burke*, Oates's highs were more or less restricted to the alcoholic variety. High jinks, however, could come in any form, and although the Raincheck was a long trek away at the end of a day's shooting, it always seemed to be on the way home. There he would drink, flirt with women, and hide from his wife, or drink, hide from women, and flirt with his wife.

In September, Teddy and Warren headed for Las Vegas, where his agent, Jerry Steiner, married singer-actress Joanie Sommers ("Johnny Get Angry" was her signature, if salacious, hit in which she sang about wanting a caveman to rough her up). The Oateses were among the sixty guests, including Juliet Prowse, Tony Bennett, and Efrem Zimbalist Jr., who packed the Little Church of the West in Sin City.

Before *Stoney Burke* went on the air, its actors did their pre-publicity. For Lord, it was easy finding something to talk about. "Coop, you know, was painfully shy to the day he died," he told *TV Guide* in an article that appeared in November 1962. "He'd drive his eyes to the ground and once in a while look up to see if he was making eye contact. He was big, *big*. And I'm going to make Stoney *big*."

Oates was not emulating any great actors or proclaiming high ambitions for Ves. Instead, he emphasized his childhood in and around Bayless's "real old cracker barrel general store" as providing fodder for Ves. Leslie Stevens was doing his bit as well, taking a decidedly Dickensian turn with Hal Humphrey in the *Los Angeles Times*. "The worst of TV is better, and the best is worse," the indefatigable writer-director-producer said of the state of airplay. Humphrey concurred. "TV's economics and a fetish for having the same characters come into your living rooms every week have combined to turn the medium into a cyclical gristmill populated with doctors, fathers and mothers, cowboys, happy emcees and now rodeo riders," he wrote.

ABC focused its campaign for viewers on Lord, touting the show's lead as "a classic hero in a modern setting," not knowing then that it was a nice mesh of cowboys, classic cars, and midcentury modern architecture. The ad in the *Los Angeles Times* was emphatic. "Jack Lord stars as Stoney Burke, whose hour-long dramas buck and bronc out of men who ride the rodeo circuit. Stoney is paid to flirt with death. Tonight he also flirts with an unbridled heiress on his own time."

When Stoney Burke flirted into town on Monday, October 1, 1962, he had competition. Earl Holliman's *Wide Country* also appeared that season, but *Burke* had more of a buzz. Debuting at nine o'clock, an episode titled "The Contender" attempted to capitalize on its lead-in, the fifth season of *The Rifleman*, which kicked off at eight thirty with a two-part drama called "Waste," written by Robert Culp. The season premiere of *The Danny Thomas Show* at nine o'clock would find that "Danny is back doing business at the same old stand," but it was uncertain whether Stoney's Lord could prevail over Marjorie Lord and the kids. "Talented people, these," the *Los Angeles Times'* preview had promised of the *Stoney Burke* team.

By the time Andy Griffith started on CBS at nine thirty, the rodeo cowboy had drawn the meanest bronc in the competition and realized that the path to winning the Golden Buckle would be a bumpy ride. A shadowy agent attempts to sign him, dismissing Stoney's sidekick with the words, "Ves, you're the smallest time there is." A custom convertible owned by legendary western tailor Nudie makes an appearance, replete with cowhide seats, tooled leather paneling, six-gun handles for gear knobs, saddle console, and prairie-sized dashboard pockmarked by myriad silver dollars. Twin Texas longhorns serve as cow-catchers; as Ves observes, "I guess the horns are to stick policemen."

Stoney did not win in his first televised outing; neither did he clean up in the ratings. But *Variety* was positive, invoking a comparison with a popular doctor series of the day: "'Ben Casey' on the hoof," the reviewer called it. "Particularly strong in support was Warren Oates as sidekick Ves Painter, who will be developed as a sometimes buddy whose loyalty is supposed to be shaky in a human way."

For Oates and the show's producers, Stoney's "bow-legged friend" who was originally to appear only in the first episode had more than earned his place; Ves Painter would be wandering around the padlock or propping up the bar drinking several small beers for the duration. Ves often appeared elevated, atop a water tower or straddling a wooden fence, like some kind of one-man lookout chorus. Men like Ves did exist, according to the champion cowboy Casey Tibbs, who was a double and also produced the show's rodeo segments. "There really are characters like him. Some ride, some just hang around, but nobody ever wants to run 'em off." Ben Johnson concurred. "It's like carnival people; they just go from one spot to another, a lot of them," he said.

The part was Leslie Stevens's gift to Oates. "I owe Warren Oates infinitely more than he owes me," Stevens said. "I modeled the character on him, and all I do is emphasize parts of his own personality." There was a lot of invention and borrowing, as well as some added touches. Although Ves's lingo may have seemed improvised, that was not the case. "Because Leslie was a writer, he monitored that show fairly well," Erman explained. Addressing the other men as "Sporty" was something Oates picked up from a rodeo rat. What soaks through his rodeo duds is the character's humanity; Oates allowed his own personality to imbue Ves with humor and kindness.

It was that same kindness that impressed Michael Anderson Jr., the son of the noted British director. Both Andersons made appearances on *Stoney Burke*. Anderson Jr. found his way into an episode titled "Gold-Plated Maverick." "It was the first time I ever played an American, and I kept myself pretty much to myself," he said. "I met Warren, and I liked him immediately. I could tell he was authentic, and that's what gravitated me toward him. I realized that he wasn't polished like a lot of the other actors."

Anderson's theatrical background eventually led to a little confusion. "In England if you like working with a fellow actor, you buy them something," Anderson said. So he had a leather-bound script cover made with Oates's name on it. Then he phoned the production office and inquired where *Stoney Burke* was shooting that day, went there, and knocked on Oates's trailer door.

"Well, hey kid, how are you?" Oates said.

"Fine, fine. I have a present for you."

"You do? Why, why would you do that?"

Anderson explained that it was traditional in England. Oates opened the package.

"I don't think anybody has ever done anything like this," Oates told him. And then he gave him a quizzical look.

"No, Warren!" Anderson said. It never occurred to him the decidedly American actor might misunderstand his intentions. But Oates was tickled, and the two men became friends.

"Gold-Plated Maverick" is an endearing episode about a pampered yet neglected youngster (Anderson) who is set among the Stoney Burke bunch to rope and ride his way to maturity. While it is true that Anderson's accent slips in and out, what is more noticeable is that, in the many scenes he shares with Oates, the older man reacts with kindness and a lot of theatrical elbow room.

Stoney Burke was a surprisingly textured and superior series of its time. Fans of dark motels with blinking neon, dirt streets populated by big cars with little fins (Mercury was a sponsor, touting its new Comet), bus depots, cocktail bars with starlight-glitter ceilings, and tailored western wear by way of Beverly Hills found a spiritual home in *Stoney*.

That the show is enjoyable today is the result of its clever dialogue, strong cast, neat stable of extras, and deft hand in its selection of guest stars. In the fourth broadcast, "Point of Honor," which aired on October 22, Harry Dean Stanton and Oates shared a scene by a honky tonk's billiards table. The sheer delight of these two actors bouncing lines off each other is as cozy as baize. Leslie Stevens's chum James Mason was an early—and uncredited—guest star, playing a downtrodden soul named Enoch Gates in "The Scavenger." Mason stayed in character throughout the shooting, a big change for the elegant and sophisticated British actor. The very touching episode "Joby" follows cowboy hero Joby Pierce (beautifully played by Robert Duvall), whose fear of the spotlight masks a difficult past. His mentally frail character talks to horses. "A lot of people talk to horses," Stoney tells Ves. "Yes, but he hears 'em talk back," the less than sympathetic scoundrel replies.

A spitfire Elizabeth Ashley appeared in "Tigress by the Tail," and the salty, sultry actress "cursed like a sailor," as Edward Asner, who was also in the episode, recalled. (Fortunately, by the time she wrote a tell-all memoir, Ashley would also sing like a bird.) In "Tigress" she played Donna Weston, a worldly, wealthy journalist who, after a bout of reckless driving, has been "sentenced to six months of martinis without olives. I'm a woman," she tells Ves. "Do you know what that is? We cry at weddings and laugh at funerals."

Ves is nonplussed and can only shake his head and surmise, "You can feed cat food to a tiger, but that don't make her a tabby."

Donald Freeman captured Ves's character for a story in the *San Diego Union*. Freeman wrote, "That's Ves all right, a cowpoke Falstaff to Jack Lord's Prince Hal (or just possibly a troublemaking Tonto who can resist anything except temptation). Ves, a great role for an actor to sink his teeth into, is played by Warren Oates and to watch him week after week, he certainly understands the subtleties of his character." Freeman went on to relay some particular Ves-isms:

"I got a guilty look about me. I got a way of squintin' my eyes that—well, just let somebody break a window or steal a hubcap and they run me in . . ."

"Ves," says Stoney, "I know the truth isn't in you, but if you want help you gotta level with me. . . . Why'd you bust outa jail?" Ves shrugs. "You know a better place to bust out of?"

"Did you leave the bar at any time during the night?" Ves is asked on the witness stand. "Well," he grins, "I did step outside once to flush the carbon tetrachloride outa my lungs."

In another episode, when the rodeo is threatened with cancellation, Ves seeks to right things by heading straight for the local women's club. "There's only one thing tougher to beat than a state senator, and that's li'l old ladies marching around in them club-toed shoes wearin' campaign buttons that say, 'Watch yourself, daddy, we got the vote!'"

"Ves Painter," Freeman concluded, "is the world's unlikeliest hero's best friend."

By midseason, the show had received enough attention and good press, if not stellar ratings, for the cast to be invited to ride in Los Angeles's Christmas Lane Parade. Entering its fifteenth year, the parade had become a handy forum for promotional staff wishing to position their stars before a seasonally giddy throng.

As the stars went gliding by in natty convertibles, they could wave to the crowds and get free publicity mixed in with good cheer.

The parade took place on December 1, 1962, under clear night skies in the Los Angeles suburb of Huntington Park, just southeast of downtown. Some 350,000 people crowded the sidewalks of Pacific, Slauson, and Florence Boulevards to see fourteen high school bands, four youth bands, seven drum and bugle corps, fifty marching groups, and two hundred television and movie celebrities. Chances are the crowd was more transfixed by the grand marshal, platinum-haired actress Jayne Mansfield, but Oates was in the parade too, waving for all he was worth.

The new year, however, would bring sadness. Oates's mother, Sarah, was in declining health, and he flew home to visit her just after Christmas. He stayed by her side in the hospital until she passed away on January 12, 1963, at Kentucky Baptist Hospital in Louisville, at the age of seventy-three. The *Louisville Courier-Journal* noted she was "the widow of a Western Kentucky merchant," but the headline spoke a little louder. "Mother of TV Star," it read, "a star on the Stoney-Burke television show" who "has appeared in many television and movie roles."

Sarah was buried beside Bayless in Cave Hill Cemetery. Earlier, at the Arch L. Heady Funeral Home, Alberta Rutter came by to pay her respects, opting to visit early in the morning so Oates would not see her. "I didn't want him to compare me to those famous actresses he'd appeared with," she said. She left a simple card, which she signed "Mary."

During the second half of *Stoney Burke*'s season, the viewership continued to prove largely indifferent to Ves's witticisms, although some critics were wise enough to catch on to these simulated pearls of wisdom. But by the time *TV Guide* ran a feature on Oates in its May 11, 1963, issue, the branding iron marks on the fencepost read like hieroglyphics saying, "Adios and sayonara, Stoney," as Ves might have put it. The writer noted, "As played to the hilt by the hitherto obscure actor Warren Oates, Ves Painter is also bringing something new to a television season that has managed to avoid the fresh, the daring or the original. [Ves] is breaking a tradition almost as old as the movie Western, and at the same time carrying on another tradition which goes back to the very beginnings of English drama."

For a jive-talking ne'er-do-well, it was heady stuff. Dudley Saunders in the *Louisville Times* reported that Oates's "rube image . . . got him a regular part in the Stoney Burke TV series. He sought to shake that image by becoming a voracious reader and scholarly conversationalist." Such conscious effort was in evidence when Oates told the *Charlotte (NC) News* that he had spent a good deal of time at the Thomas Wolfe house in Asheville, North Carolina. The house, he claimed, "was my meat," and the curators might have been interested to learn that he "used to hang around there and steal little bits of paper from that place."

Stoney Burke never won his Golden Buckle, and the series ended after one season. It did, however, make history as the first series from which spin-offs were suggested. "Kincaid," "Border Town," "Mr. Kingston," and "Tack Reynolds" were all posited as prospective new series. Where other programs would bow out in glory, Stoney's last roundup, "The Journey," was in keeping with Stevens's style. Stoney, sick with blood poisoning and desperate for money to send home to his family, is railroaded into accepting a job driving a truck for the order buyer. Megaton, the uncontrollable horse that threw Stoney, has a one-way ticket to the slaughterhouse. Ves turns up after storming the barricades by leading the gatekeeper astray. Originally in favor of the plant—the man who deals in animal trade of any kind will prosper, he believes—Ves witnesses the buzzards circling overhead and Burke's tightening anguish. Together they decide to open the holding pens and set the condemned horses free. The animals scatter, except for Megaton, whom they have loaded onto their truck. The fiery stallion will serve not as pet food but as a means of rekindling a man's pride. In the last, long shot, Megaton rears up as Stoney Burke regains his ambition.

The indefatigable Stevens moved on to his next project, which would have a place for Oates. In the meantime, Oates was not unemployed for long. He also appeared in a different format: a comic book tie-in for the show depicted a brightly blue-eyed Ves, replete with five o'clock shadow and half-moon teeth, acting as a liaison between Stoney and a Hollywood celebrity. It might not have been vintage Ves, but it was a nickel and dime immortality.

"If it'd gone two years, I may never have gotten out of it," Oates said of *Stoney Burke*. But he had affection for the show as well. "I played a wild, four-eyed character and that's one of my favorites because I had 32 episodes to deal with the character, and you don't get that opportunity in a movie." And whereas Ves might have been fond of saying, "It's chicken one day and feathers the next," Oates had something a little wetter on his mind. "I'm goin' fishing for two weeks, starting the opening day of trout season," he told *TV Guide*.

And that was precisely what he did.

9

. . . And Feathers the Next

After Oates went fishing, he went hunting. Fern Lea Peckinpah (now Peter) recalled, "My brother Sam, my husband Walter, and Warren all went on a hunting trip where they were meeting my older brother. Somehow there was a flat tire, and they were off the road, and they were stuck." Oates volunteered to go off in search of assistance and then, from out in the middle of nowhere, returned with hot tea and help. The eventual help was a given; it was the tea that was the Oates touch.

He sometimes joined the group on deer hunting expeditions in the mountains of California and Nevada, not far from the ancestral Peckinpah patch. "In my family with my grandfather, you either ate or you didn't by what you killed," Fern Lea Peter continued. "Also, shells were expensive, so you better be a good shot. They would string up the animals and gut them, and the liver and heart were always cooked there."

Oates was an indifferent and even conflicted hunter who would one day abandon the practice. His daughter Jennifer was along when her father went deer hunting in the Sierras. "He shot and wounded the deer, but the deer kept running, and Dad kept chasing it. He'd run back and forth, back and forth, and I guess a hunter saw him running and running, and the other hunter put the deer down. That was Ralph, and up until last year Ralph was still around, but he got a little mangy," Jennifer said in 2006. "He was very pretty, with eight points."

Back home on Zelzah Avenue on the night of June 4, Oates

and Teddy, who were expecting a child in late summer, got dressed to go to Bruce Dern's twenty-seventh birthday party. Dern was married to Diane Ladd, who had decided to throw a costume party. Oates slicked back his hair, coaxing a cowlick, climbed into britches and suspenders, and christened himself Butch the Bad Boy. Teddy, heavily pregnant, was Shirley Temple. "It was," Teddy said, "the best party I have been to in my entire life."

Oates spent most of his brief respite from work at the Raincheck, Pupi's, and Chez Paulette, where he would drink, play chess, and gab. Although he would sometimes call his wife and tell her to rustle up beans and cornbread because he was bringing friends home for supper, he was out much of the time. At Chez Paulette he found a fellow live wire in young, blond actor Will Hutchins, who had been in *Sugarfoot*, a popular western series that ended its run in 1961.

Like Oates, Hutchins frequented Pupi's, as did Jack Nicholson, by now an Oates acquaintance. Pupi's had the special advantage of being a great place to eavesdrop, even if the proprietress did not entirely welcome her clientele. "Madame Pupi was a very strange lady, and she didn't like all of us actors hanging out there, I guess. We weren't spending too much money," Hutchins said. One day she took a particular dislike to writer B. J. Merholz and turned the hose on his car, which happened to be a convertible. The volatile Madame Pupi (Marge Drury) was not around for long, though. "She ended up taking poison and crawling under her house and dying," Hutchins said. "One of the legends of the Sunset Strip. Pupi's closed after she died, and we all had to hang out at the Plush Pup."

Oates continued to have brief affairs—usually one-night stands—but they did not prey on his conscience. Women, like booze, were a dizzy and irresistible lure. But he had developed another passion that turned into a habit, which led to an obsession and lifelong addiction. Warren Oates was in love with the stock market. Friends at Schwab's or Pupi's would find him perusing the newspaper's stock report in the intent manner some people devoted to the trade papers. Walter Peter was a stockbroker and would run into Oates, often over coffee at Pupi's. "Warren was a good student," his wife Fern Lea said. She thought he did not look the part, "very skinny and wearing outrageous outfits like plaid pants," but when it came to Wall Street, he might as well have been dressed in a suit and carrying a briefcase.

The barnyard menagerie at the Oates household had dwindled to only one duck and one chicken. Teddy suggested to Warren that he take this mismatched pair to the pet shop. "Make sure you say not to put them in the same cage," she told her husband, "because the rooster jumps the duck." She didn't think much more about it until she was writing a check for cat food in the pet shop. The owner looked at her warily. "Did you bring in a chicken and a duck recently?" he asked.

"Maybe," she cagily replied.

"That rooster wouldn't leave that duck alone!"

There were summer parties, all of which were potluck, and a luau to which Marty Kaplan came dressed as a witch doctor and promptly fell over the very pregnant hostess. "No wonder Timmy came out early," Teddy said.

The house had two dens, one of which the Oateses turned into a bar with a slate floor. "Warren was heavy-duty on slate, natural things, not carpet," Teddy said. "And we'd taken the door off the closet; I think the stereo was going to go in there. He would go into this little closet with the door open and put the earphones on and listen to music. I'd go up on the roof and put the aerial up, or I'd go into the side yard and move the cord of wood so I could make a play yard for the kids." Oates had a brief handyman phase during which where he decided to do some woodworking in the garage. "It took him four or five months to make a three-piece spice rack. It was never quite the right size for the spice bottles, but he made it, and I used it on the back of the stove."

There were outings at Zuma and Trancas beaches, and one photo shows a pregnant Teddy wearing a homemade bathing suit with a carefully placed watermelon appliqué over her belly. "He was always into the ocean, being alone," Teddy said. "My idea of going to the beach was to go to State Beach, where everybody went, and you hear the music and all of that. Warren's idea of going to the beach was to go down to where there was nobody . . . no other people and you're by yourself."

In August Oates was off again, this time to California's Sierras for a movie called *Mail Order Bride*. Teddy's due date was imminent, so again she called for her brother, who would help when she brought the baby boy home. Timothy Brien Mercer Oates was born at Cedars of Lebanon on August 4, 1963.

Mail Order Bride, made for $700,000, shared personnel with Peckinpah's elegant, lyric *Ride the High Country* in the forms of producer Richard Lyons and film editor Frank Santillo, but that was about all they shared. *Bride*'s screenplay, based on a short story that had appeared in the *Saturday Evening Post*, was by Burt Kennedy, with whom Oates would not always work with gusto. "The things I did with Burt Kennedy," Oates told a National Film Theatre audience in 1971, "everybody wanted me to play that [Ves] character and I refused to play Vesper P. Painter again."

But in August 1963, the body of Ves Painter was still warm, and his gamey soul inhabited Oates's performance as Jace, "one of five rough-looking cowboys" who was "young and wild," according to the script's notations. The appearance of Oates's teeth provides a good gauge of a production's sensibilities: When his choppers are flawless and straight, as they are here, the production is mainstream and unimaginative. When gaps, an overbite, and other dentine irregularities are apparent, the movie or television show likewise has a touch more bite. Oates had recently had his teeth capped and, as a result, stopped putting his hand over his mouth in private conversation, a habit Nick Georgiade had noticed early on. "He'd put his right hand to his mouth, covering those teeth."

But it is a perfect smile that Jace possesses in *Mail Order Bride*, where he appears as best man in Lee Carey's (Keir Dullea) arranged marriage to a willful young widow named Annie (Lois Nettleton). Lee, the unruly orphan son of a man named Will Lane (Buddy Ebsen), has come to straighten himself out so that he might earn his father's inheritance. As part of that goal, he reluctantly agrees to marry the comely Annie, although he would rather spend time with cattle rustler Jace.

The *Los Angeles Times* opined that "Warren Oates plays a chief heavy with double-dyed villainy," and the *Hollywood Reporter* concurred. "Oates is good as Dullea's conniving drinking buddy." *Films and Filming* was closer to the mark, finding him a "not very villainous one-note heavy." *Product Digest* deemed the film "a generally enjoyable though unpretentious picture that is helped by the scenic beauty of its high Sierras locale, filmed in Panavision and Metrocolor. . . . The story moves along credibly until it is approaching the climax; then the heavy [Oates] seems to be voicing the script writer's uncertainty as he says, 'I'll think of something.'" But *Variety* nailed it. With Jace, the script turned "a merely colorfully ornery critter into a first class and totally absurd heavy and the picture never recovers from this mortal blow."

In the fall, Teddy went with Oates to Hawaii, where an episode of the series *Combat!* was being filmed. They spent a month there, time enough for Teddy to witness philandering actors and a whole lot of misbehaving. "Don't tell me you're the only straight one here around this," she told her husband, who did not reply.

"Forever I had wanted to get married again in the United States, and Warren said, 'What difference does it make? We're married.' And then he wanted to do it, and I said, 'What difference . . .'" Teddy explained. That their relationship was less than perfect was apparent.

It was not a big part, but it was a big picture, and Oates and Michael Anderson Jr. were doing some daytime celebrating in the Raincheck. Warren had been there much longer than Anderson, who was not much of a drinker but still wanted to mark the occasion of landing a great role in what should be an epic film, directed by Sam Peckinpah. Peckinpah had been in the Raincheck earlier, as had John Davis Chandler. Even L. Q. Jones had come by for a bit, although, like Anderson, he did not drink. He explained, "Somebody had to carry the bodies home." Anderson was sipping a Coke when Oates suddenly decided to go home to eat, invited Anderson to come along a little later, and gave him directions to the house on Zelzah Avenue.

The handsome young actor pulled up in front of the big house with the awning of oak trees at six o'clock. He was immediately impressed by the size of the home, having thought of Oates as a little guy lucky to get a day's work. The night was young, even if it had kicked off early in the forced darkness of a regular haunt. As Anderson was getting out of his car, a woman appeared at the front door, waving him off. "Dinner's off," Teddy told him. "It's been canceled."

"What's the matter?" he asked.

"Warren . . . he went berserk and he's got a gun. Dinner is off!"

Anderson was torn between getting in his car and offering to help the obviously distressed hostess. "Holy shit," he thought, "this lovely guy I've been working with, completely bonkers. I had no clue he was even capable of something like that." While he stood there, frozen in indecision, Teddy came outside, carrying a small child and leading a young girl by the hand. She bundled her children into her station wagon and drove away. Dinner was definitely off, Anderson realized, and he headed home.

In February 1964, a whole lot of movie people decamped to Durango, Mexico. Among them were Warren Oates and L. Q. Jones, both of whom were equally at home in television and in film. "The money was in pictures, but if you got a good TV series you could make more money than the people doing movies," said Jones, adding that not that many actors transitioned between media. "If you worked in television, you were an enigma, and god help you if you made a commercial! Warren jumped back and forth because he was extraordinarily talented. Nobody was ever any better at doing what he did. He was a hellacious actor—and he looked at things differently than most people." Besides, Jones continued, "Warren loved people, and he loved to work."

That *Major Dundee* is scattered, sprawling, and disorganized is a given. The movie was in trouble before shooting even began. Although it was originally envisioned by Columbia Pictures as an opus in the tradition of *Lawrence of Arabia*, a change in management at the studio resulted in its budget being reduced from $4.5 million to $3 million, effectively putting Peckinpah on notice before his creative juices were in full flow. And to rein him in was to ask for rebellion.

Further, the movie's producer, Jerry Bresler, was a fellow in his fifties who had produced *The Vikings* and a couple of Gidget movies—hardly a match for Peckinpah. In 1963, Bresler had been given a lucrative deal with Columbia, and he was in the market for a film in which he could cast Charlton Heston, contractually obliged to the studio for one more film. Bresler had developed a rapport with the leading man when they worked together on *Diamond Head*. After reading the treatment for *Dundee*, Heston was reluctant to commit unless a very strong director was attached. Bresler's first choice, John Ford, was making *Cheyenne Autumn*, but after Bresler watched *Ride the High Country*, he believed Peckinpah was the right choice for the story of a deluded Civil War officer hell-bent on revenge, accompanied by a ragtag band of scoundrels and cutthroats crossing often hostile terrain. Peckinpah agreed and also recognized the opportunity to traverse central Mexico, from Durango to Mexico City, across wide swaths of desert and temperamental streams. He headed south to secure Mexico City's Churubusco Studios and to scout locations.

Back in Hollywood, Bresler was not amused by the logistics of Peckinpah's vision but at this point was unwilling to rattle his director. The script, by Harry Julian Fink, would do that. For a start, it was far too long. Filming was pushed back from December 1, 1963, to February 6, 1964, to allow Peckinpah and writer Oscar Saul to put together a revised script and to clarify its concept. Bresler was omnipresent during the filming, definitely not optimal Peckinpah working conditions, and he surely took note as the director fired a whopping fifteen people, including wardrobe supervisors. Gordon Dawson, head of Columbia's wardrobe department, was called in to help, and his innovative style, informed by a strong sense of realism, led to a productive collaboration.

Dawson would also prove instrumental in Oates's career. The two men first met in the fitting room at Columbia Pictures, before Dawson had been summoned to Mexico. Dawson said,

Warren Oates was playing a rebel in his rebel outfit, and [in the film] he'd been living in it for three years when we first see him. So we had to burn the nap off and, depending on how aged it would get, rub paraffin in it so it would get that greasy, grimy look around the collar. Rubbing in umbers and painting each thing was really a work of art, and it was done on a dress dummy. The problem was, you'd do one and you'd spend all your time doing it and it was perfect, and then you'd have to do ten more of the sons of bitches for all the doubles.

Destroying clothes got me involved with Sam [Peckinpah] because he certainly never looked at me when I was in the fitting rooms doing all the wardrobe fittings. I was just the guy picking up all the crap after they threw it off, and putting it back on hangers.

Oates was conscientious enough to return his wardrobe to the racks, which was not lost on Dawson. "Ask the wardrobe men who the great actors were—the great actors were the ones who hang up their wardrobe at night."

On location in Mexico, Dawson tried to avoid Peckinpah's wrath. The director was on a roll, shouting and drinking throughout, although Senta Berger (who played Teresa Santiago) maintained he was a very shy man who loved classical music.

In Durango, the actors and crew were lodged at a couple of hotels. "Warren stayed at the Casablanca, and me and the big guys stayed at the Posada Durant, which was only eighteen rooms but a beautiful hotel," Michael Anderson Jr. (who played Tim Ryan) said. "I saw Chuck Heston and Jim Hutton and Jim Coburn every night, but the other guys were over at the other hotel. A lot of these guys would just hang out until they fell asleep at 3 a.m." Dawson confirmed that "there were two different levels of actors working on *Dundee* and two different levels of crew. There was the high crew and the crew that couldn't even eat at the tables. Finally Heston and some of them said, 'If we have tablecloths, they have tablecloths. If we get served, they get served.'" Getting served, however, was a liability. "It was the worst caterer in the world," Dawson insisted. "Everyone got sick." Oates, often ill while away on location, was no exception.

On the night of February 25, 1964, however, most of the cast gathered at the bar in the Casablanca to watch Sonny Liston fight Cassius Clay. "I won four hundred bucks on that fight," Anderson boasted, "and I had no clue who I was betting on." Anderson was happy to be working again with Oates, whom he called Kentucky Mountain Man, though he recognized a much deeper side of Oates. "He was also complicated. I didn't see a lot of that, but I knew about it. Warren's face was like a god-damn road map. All those guys were hard-drinking, woman-izing, hard-living character actors. They were fascinating to be around. The bottom line is you couldn't not love Warren. He lived a hell of a life." Oates reminded Anderson of another of his friends, turbulent actor Sal Mineo. "The reality is, he was dark like that."

By the time *Major Dundee* began filming, Oates had acquired the habit of taking a camera along with him. Eventually he would bring a movie camera or camcorder, but on *Dundee* he photo-graphed scenery and his fellow actors and crew. "He took the best picture of me that's ever been taken by anybody," said Anderson, who would photograph Dennis Hopper for the cover of *Rolling Stone*.

In *Dundee* Oates is not on-screen for long, even considering the scope of the film, but his part provides impact. He is O. W. Hadley, a Confederate prisoner who is as uneducated as he is prejudiced, but he is somehow adrift from the action. Writer Matt Wanat noted, "Hadley, played brilliantly by Peckinpah regular Warren Oates, seems withdrawn from the other Southerners as they swim in the river."

Oates would not have refused a role in any Peckinpah offer-ing, but Garner Simmons suggested one reason he was eager to play the renegade. "O. W. Hadley is a great role, and Warren took it because it was an opportunity to deal with death," Simmons said. "Here is a character that ultimately is going to die in a very dramatic fashion. He's a character you like, but he goes AWOL. You know he's lying, but you like him despite all his faults. And he winds up being killed by his own commander, a really powerful moment."

John Davis Chandler, who had played the younger brother of Oates's Henry Hammond in *Ride the High Country*, was the unappealing Jimmy Lee Benteen, who was also headed for an untimely end. Chandler, who had been perusing the script, bemoaned his character's presumed fate to Oates one afternoon in late March, about halfway through the twelve-week shooting. "That big river fight they're having tomorrow," Chandler said to Oates, "there's nothing about my character dying, but I don't see him indicated through the rest of the script. I think Sam's got me disappearing and that's it. I'm out of here as a result tomorrow." Chandler thought it would be terrific if Benteen lived.

"I'm going over to Sam's place tonight," Oates said. "I agree, it'd be great and an ironic sense of justice if your despicable character lives through the entire thing and rides out with him in the end. Let me get a little tequila in him tonight and we'll do some talking on it, and I'll talk to you tomorrow."

Chandler was hopeful—an ironic twist was never lost on Peckinpah, and tequila had its powers of persuasion, as did Oates, whose opinion the director respected. When Oates ran into Chandler the next day, he said, with a wink, "Your character lives."

"It didn't amount to anything," Chandler concluded. "I was still making minimum [six hundred dollars per week], but it was better than the breadline."

Halfway through production, the film faced more problems. Ironically, the man who saved Peckinpah's bacon had not been his first choice for the lead. "I was talking to Sam one day," Chandler said, "and I asked him, 'When you were putting this thing together, who was your first choice for the major?'"

"Brian Keith," Peckinpah responded.

The film was falling behind schedule despite shooting six days a week, using every single daylight hour, and continuing into the cold Durango nights. The company was starting to fray under the mental and physical strain of working with an increasingly erratic Peckinpah, who often directed his actors with an ambivalence akin to dismission. Columbia's vice president of creative affairs,

Arthur Kramer, arrived in the Mexican desert to tell the director he was to be replaced. What happened next was a behind-the-scenes maneuver tantamount to the parting of the Red Sea. Charlton Heston said that if the director went, he went. Richard Harris, L. Q. Jones, R. G. Armstrong, Warren Oates, Ben Johnson, and Slim Pickens followed suit. Then Heston put his money where his ultimatum was: he would give up his $200,000 salary if the director were retained. The studio turned on a dime, wasting no time in accepting Heston's offer.

Peckinpah remained, but he was losing the plot, as were most of those involved. Drastic weather conditions, inedible food (Jones found maggots in one of his craft meals), and polluted and unsafe rivers in which actors and stuntmen could not help but fall made for tense relationships among men not known for being genteel. Such abject circumstances can have a positive outcome in one sense, though, as Jones noted. "Everybody in our group kept forcing everybody else to do things better."

Peckinpah's predilection for impressionistic slow-motion sequences ("I can kill three men, take them to the graveyard, and bury them before he gets one on the ground," Howard Hawks said), used to groundbreaking effect in his next effort, originated during the filming of *Dundee*. During the film's river battle, which took five days to shoot, Peckinpah had actors, stuntmen, and their horses repeat action again and again. But it was not just his notorious perfectionism at play. "Sam was using the sequence as a drain to pour the studio's money down," writes biographer David Weddle.

On the last day of April 1964, *Major Dundee* wrapped, fifteen days past schedule and $1.5 million over budget. Peckinpah would ultimately be barred from the editing room; Bresler took over and slashed one-third of the film's running time. Storylines were left open ended, strange sound effects were added, and an unforgivable score, including jolly songs by Mitch Miller and the Gang, was added. All that was missing was the bouncing ball. Even the device of Tim Ryan as narrator was hobbled.

Audiences and critics in 1965 watched a movie whose extended version the *New York Times* would refer to four decades later as "the smoking ruin from which Peckinpah's masterpiece [*The Wild Bunch*] arose." But that was retroactive cold comfort. *Dundee* was hard to like. Yet, pitted against its contemporaries, its superiority seems evident. Critics expressed their unease: Richard L. Coe wrote in the *Washington Post*, "In the case of 'Major Dundee,' the choppiness of events, the listlessness of scenes and the non sequiturs of actions are sorely clear." But a review in the *New York Times* heralded the cast and the outdoor vistas, concluding, "Mr. Peckinpah does have an eye. He has a lot to learn, but his education should be worth paying for."

Oates was asked in 1971 about the blackballing of Peckinpah. "I remember the incident," he said. "What I know would be hearsay, and I'd rather not comment, except that I would defend Sam. He was a serious man, and he was trying to make a serious movie. The subject matter wasn't the greatest in the world; you know, the chase and all of that." Ten years later, Oates explained, "'Major Dundee' didn't work out because they had the rein on him and Sam can't tolerate a rein. It's like putting him into a martingale, one of those things that keeps a horse from tossing its head."

Dundee is difficult. But the expanded version, released in 2005, benefits as much from its appropriate new sound track as from the restored footage.

What Oates took away from *Dundee* was unexpected: it involved a sense of place and the rekindling of his social conscience.

> I think Mexico reaches a lot of people in many ways. We had a fine Mexican doctor on our film [who,] . . . when he wasn't busy with us, was always off on the fringe of the set, trying to administer to the people, these peasants, medically. And the children! You see a lot of lovely children down there. The Mexican government provides medical services for them, but in some instances the literacy rate isn't high enough for them to understand that if they take this vitamin pill it will help cure their rickets and their sores and things like that.
>
> I suppose that was the most disheartening thing I saw there. You could see the enormous need for some kind of

deep-reaching education. It's slow because . . . it can't be done overnight.

In his next film for Peckinpah, his character would say of Mexico, simply and sincerely, "I don't see nothing so *lindo* about it." But he most certainly saw its beauty.

Dundee was not an easy experience to come down from. It was hardest of all for Peckinpah, who would ask that his name be taken off the film before he regained his composure.

Oates was soon spending a lot of time a few doors down from the Raincheck, at 8325 Santa Monica Boulevard, where the Players' Ring Gallery theater group was mounting a production of Ken Kesey's landmark novel, *One Flew over the Cuckoo's Nest*. The book's film rights were owned by actor Kirk Douglas, who cowrote the original stage version with Dale Wasserman.

The play, starring Douglas, fared well regionally, but when it got to Broadway in November 1963, a couple of scathing reviews sealed its fate. Wasserman was quick to distance himself from it. His reworking of it, which is the defining live theater version today, appeared in Hollywood on January 12, 1965. John Erman, who had worked with Oates on *Stoney Burke*, directed the play. "It was an interesting turn of events because I was just sort of beginning to get my feet wet as a director when I got the assignment," Erman said. "Kirk Douglas had played [McMurphy] to begin with and he was so unpleasant in it that the show hadn't succeeded. I wanted somebody who I really believed in and I wanted somebody who was different and had his own kind of likable charm." That someone was Oates, and Erman sent him the script to read.

Oates called him and asked, "Well, what part do you want me to play?"

"I want you to play McMurphy," Erman replied.

"The lead? I've never played the lead. Are you sure?" Oates asked.

"Yeah, I'm completely sure."

The Players' Ring and Players' Ring Gallery were unique venues, pioneering first-class Broadway and off-Broadway plays in a small setting. Nonetheless, *Cuckoo's Nest* would be their swan song; thereafter, they were bulldozed to make way for a shopping mall. Erman met Oates and the other main actors, Priscilla Morrill, William Smith, Robert Doyle, Richard Brander, and Penny Kunard, at the Equity-waiver theater for rehearsals in late December.

"We began to work on it," Erman said, "and he [Oates] wasn't having the easiest time finding his authority, the 'leader of men' syndrome that the part needed to have." Erman told the rest of the company to take a few hours off. "I just worked with Warren alone on the stage. I got him to imagine that the other actors were there and play the scenes as if they were there. But what I was trying to do was bring him up into a kind of acting that he hadn't done before. It was hard and it took a while, but it worked."

The public responded, attending nightly eight o'clock shows as well as performances on Saturday nights at ten forty-five. The play was a hit except with the *Los Angeles Times'* Philip K. Scheuer, whose sensibilities were severely offended. "It is a vulgarization in language, theme and action. . . . What was hard to believe was that the man, a strutting, shouting cock of the walk from start to nearly finish, would have been permitted to rage unchecked as long as he did, or that the woman, on her part, would have been allowed to subject him to such 'therapeutic' tortures such as the shock treatment and, finally, a pre-frontal lobotomy without having been challenged by qualified medical authority more than she was." But it was not all bad for Scheuer: "I must admit that the players knocked themselves out—sometimes almost literally—to get the shocks across under the high-voltage direction of John Erman, and very often succeeded." He had good words for Oates. "If anybody could have, Warren Oates was able to bring out McMurphy's possibly likable qualities above McMurphy's ornery rantings and posturings. Oates, in the part originated by Kirk Douglas, reminded me of a young, very young John Huston."

"Everybody came," Erman said—"Sam Peckinpah, everybody in town who'd heard about the fact that Warren was doing this in an off-Broadway theater and that he was *good*. I think he was the reason that play got the kind of attention it did—I don't think that would have happened without Warren." Actor Jack Klugman was knocked out by Oates's performance. "He was sensational, he really was," Klugman told writer Tom Nolan in 2005. "He was better than Jack Nicholson [who would play McMurphy in the film version]. He was perfect, he knew that character. And there's a certain arrogance about Warren." Erman said, "I imagine Jack Nicholson saw it [the play]. Jack was very much part of that theater group. Oates was very different. He was such an original in it. I can't tell you how good he was—he was just wonderful. *Cuckoo's Nest* was a watershed for Warren, and for me."

Richard Brander, a peripheral actor who is now an acting teacher, played the faltering Billy Bibbitt. "John Erman asked me to be in the play," Brander said. "I didn't want to be an actor, but I agreed to do it because I admired Warren so much." The two men became friends, and Oates would visit Brander's ranch. Brander said of Oates's character, "The way Ken Kesey developed the role was really for a cowboy—boots and all—and that was perfect for Warren." Brander's only direct scene with Oates came halfway through act 2. "I used to love doing the one scene I had with him because each time he would give me something different. I'd be studying with Sandy Meisner during the day, and I couldn't wait to get to the theater. Before we'd go on, Warren would say to me, 'Where do you want to go tonight, Brander?' and you never knew what you were going to get. But it was brilliant. It was *his* play."

Cuckoo's Nest was the talk of the town, and Oates was the cock of the walk. "Everyone would come backstage and congratulate him," Brander said. The night Sam Peckinpah came, Brander and Oates joined him afterward in the Raincheck. "He was a little ahead of Warren and I in the drinking," Brander said. "I could only have one or two drinks—I was a lightweight—but I could be a designated driver." His comparative sobriety was of little use that night when Sam insisted on driving Warren's huge truck.

"No way," Oates growled. "I want to live."

"I'm going to drive, damn it," Peckinpah insisted, taking the driver's seat. Oates wrestled with the wheel, but Peckinpah kept fighting him off, saying, "I'll drive! I want to drive!"

"It was a wild ride back," Brander said. "It was like a scene from a movie. I was in the backseat, bouncing along."

Randle P. McMurphy's impishness affected Oates. The bio he provided for the playbill read, "Warren Oates (McMurphy) claims to have come to Hollywood in 1954 to write Academy Award and Emmy acceptance speeches for fun and profit. However, not being acquainted with enough of the nominees, he turned to acting for a living. Since then he has appeared on numerous TV shows, including Stoney Burke, The Fugitive, Outer Limits, The Corrupters, The Untouchables, among others. This year he has completed roles in the films Major Dundee, Fields of Honor (title to be changed), and Mail Order Bride."

Cuckoo's Nest ran for four months with Oates as McMurphy and Morrill as Nurse Ratched. When they left the show, they were replaced by Michael Witney and Mary Gregory. Cuckoo's Nest lasted another week before closing on April 11, 1965.

"Fields of Honor," starring James Stewart and many, many on-screen sons, would be renamed Shenandoah, and Oates's part (Billy Packer) would fail to make the transition. In his playbill bio, Oates did not mention The Rounders, in which he had ample screen time but was not credited. A goofy, cloying western based on a story by Max Evans, The Rounders paired Glenn Ford and Henry Fonda as aging cowpokes frightening the horses in Sedona. Harley, Oates's character, is an amiable rustler who in one scene rides a horse that knocks him out. He comes up swinging and wearing the cheesiest grin west of Wisconsin. All that is missing is the sound of cuckoo clocks.

"I think the only author who liked what I did with his work was Max Evans," director Burt Kennedy wrote in his memoir, Hollywood Trail Boss. The movie does have a kind of giddy bravado. The red rock and tall pine Sedona backdrop is breathtaking, and although the actors were intent on chewing the scenery, the viewer might be advised to focus on it rather than on the action.

During filming, Oates looked over his script and asked Kennedy, "Why don't I say this instead of the way it's written?"

"Warren, say anything you can remember," his director replied.

10

Cloudy and Cool

During a particularly rough patch, Warren Oates's wife Teddy plucked up her considerable courage and suggested that her husband moonlight as a taxi driver. Teddy was no shrinking violet—she had danced with Mick Jagger, Kareem Abdul-Jabbar, and Henry Fonda and had rustled up cornbread and beans on a moment's notice for Jack Nicholson—and she did not need to dig deep to summon up what she knew would be received as audacity. "I'm an actor," her man wasted no time in replying. "I'm not a cab driver."

Indeed, Oates held deep convictions about his craft. "I try to be as precise as possible if it's a fictional character. I read the script five or six times to the end. I think about it as long as possible. I draw on my own experience. I imagine the [character's] physique from head to toe. I try to find a small relevant detail, then I draw that detail from someone I know, someone I observe or a detail that comes to me. I also take into account the acting of the people I'm working with, and try to understand the essence of each scene," he explained. "I don't truthfully know how a part comes together for me, except that if I believe in it, I can probably do it. I'm not really a smart guy. If they asked me to play Hamlet, I'd just have to stick to the script." Oates did not actively build his career. Instead, his approach reflected the Zen that would come to captivate him. "I don't talk about my theory of acting, I haven't one. The only thing in the world you can do is hang out your shingle and say 'I am.'"

How he was captured on film varied a good deal, depending on his health, his weight, the consecutive number of late nights, and the demands of the role. "The camera distorts me. It just twists me all around," Oates said. But he lived comfortably in his looks, proclaiming he had "a face like two miles of country road. Every night I've stayed up, every woman I ever chased, every drink I've ever taken—shows. I don't work in spite of my face—I work because of it—and I know that for a fact. Anyway I wouldn't trade one of these lines or scars for the memory it carries."

He blew hot and cold on the character actor tag. Sometimes he wistfully embraced it: "I'm not angry because I'm not the leading man. Whatever they give me to do, I do. I don't want to be typed but I have learned a lesson in patience and resignation. If it's an anti-hero they want, I'm more than happy to oblige." On other occasions, he expressed real gratitude for filmmakers who were willing to cast him in something other than a part that sent him straight to wardrobe. "I feel maybe most uncomfortable in a Western role because my image of the Western man is John Wayne, and I'm just a little shit. When I think of the Western role I think that the man has to be bigger than life, bigger than the screen. And I feel less comfortable working in those because I feel the most inhibited."

Oates explained, "I didn't intentionally set out to be a villain. I do what is given me to do and from there I evolve my attitude and comment. Heavies are closer to life than leading men. The heavy is everyman—everyman when he faces a tough moment in life. It's the heavy that has to do with the meat of life." And he felt no burden from playing miscreants. "I believe what Camus says. When the curtain rings down, your job is done. The responsibility is pitched to someone else as to what the meaning is of what you've played. What you represent is always one aspect of a moral question."

For the man who told his son he took drama classes to chase girls, his favorite movie moment was a telling one. "If I had to pick one scene from all the films I saw that affected me the most, it would have to be Fred Astaire singing 'It's quarter past three and there's no one in the place but just you and me. So set 'em up

Joe.' It was music and dancing, but it was really theatre. It cap-suled all the mysteries of our business in just that moment."

Ready to instill a love of the outdoors in his infant son, Oates whisked Timothy away to the California mountains near Bishop. Equipped with camping gear, cowboy grub, and the requisite fire-arms, he staked the tent, set up camp, and thought about pre-paring a fire. His enthusiasm was not tempered with practicality: When his young child began to squall, demonstrating his unhap-piness with how lunch had conversed with his tiny system, Oates panicked. Attempting to change his diaper, he was confronted by a mess for which he was thoroughly unprepared. He did a make-shift botch of changing the child, packed him and their equipment into the station wagon, and hightailed it back to civilization and his wife.

The Oateses had moved again, this time to 15321 Kingswood Lane in Sherman Oaks. The new home, reached after climbing thirty-five steps, was sprawling, with a pool, a large yard, and the San Fernando Valley's then semirustic appeal.

Oates made a pilot for *Bob Hope Presents the Chrysler The-atre* called "The War and Eric Kurtz," in which he played Joe Grover. The plan for the sixty-minute program, which aired on March 5, 1965, was to follow captives at a German prisoner of war camp through the perspectives of officers, the camp com-mander, the chief medical officer, and the man who supervised the food provisions. The show also starred Martin Milner, who later said, "I'm not sure how serious an attempt it was as a pilot, but it was a pretty good show." Whatever its merits, it was not picked up.

Meanwhile, Teddy tried to be a loving wife and a storybook mother, sewing skirts for children's dressing tables and making doll clothes. But a pushover she was not. Nor, for all her feminin-ity, was she girly. When Oates asked her if she would like "some-thing fuzzy to wear" for her birthday, she invariably opted for a toolbox, a pool table, or a tape recorder. But she was also bright, and she needed something to do, especially with her husband often away on location. Her role as a mother, in her husband's eyes, was to pamper the children until they were eighteen, make their breakfasts every day, and then suddenly unloose them into the world to fend for themselves. Teddy begged to differ, believing Jennifer and Timothy should be taught early on to be as self-sufficient as possible. It was a difference of opinion that led to arguments and, of course, drinking. One evening, when Armand and Betty Alzamora were invited for dinner, Betty arrived early and found Teddy in the kitchen emptying out bottles of wine before Oates got home.

The womanizing, Teddy tried not to think about. When Oates was with her, she felt almost secure. "This was a guy who worked with the most buxom broads in the world, and he didn't give a care. That wasn't his idea of beauty. He made me feel like I was the most gorgeous thing that ever walked, and it was kind of hard for me to accept that he really meant that, but he did. He did not look at a woman in a bikini."

But she needed something in which to immerse herself other than being a wife, a mother, and a drinking companion (invited or not) at the Raincheck. She and her friend Micki got involved with the Sherman Oaks Junior Women's Club. The San Fernando Valley edition of the *Los Angeles Times* abounded with notices of their activities: a Shades of Summer party that featured a Christmas boutique as its highlight; a dance in an Encino garden decorated with Japanese lanterns, cherry blossoms, parasols, and flying fish; swim parties; tree planting, and a Roaring Twenties Junior Club Dance replete with "midnight buffet."

Oates occasionally went along, but the country club milieu was a world away from location in Durango, rehearsals at the Players' Ring, and late-night gab fests with Harry Dean Stanton at Barney's Beanery. Stanton had given Oates a guitar, and he took it to locations with him, asking actors he liked to sign it.

Whatever their gentility, the Sherman Oaks Junior Women's Club did not always sit around wearing white gloves while sipping tea. "I somehow got elected to something I wasn't even running for," Teddy said, and she went out to celebrate. Eventually Micki gave her a ride home, and she accepted Teddy's invitation for a nightcap. Oates appeared in the foyer, put his hand across

Micki's chest and told her, "Nope, you're not coming in." She tripped and fell over, her hairpiece landing after her like a loopy punctuation mark. She collected herself and then her hair, went to her car, and drove home.

"Where the hell have you been?" Oates asked his wife, who tried to convince him of the innocence of the evening. A few nights before, Teddy had expressed frustration with his always being gone. After she intimated she had considered leaving him, he responded, "How can you want to leave me? I go on location, and all these broads are everywhere. And now the only one I want doesn't want me."

In early 1965, Monte Hellman was browsing in Martindale's bookstore in Beverly Hills. The tall, thin, and quiet man with curly hair was born in Brooklyn to Missourian parents on July 12, 1932. He went west early—his mother had a lucrative business selling real estate in Palm Springs—and lived in San Francisco, where he acted briefly, but he quickly gravitated toward directing. In Los Angeles, he collaborated with Roger Corman on several quick movies and directed *Beast from Haunted Cave* in 1959. His work with Corman led him to work with Jack Nicholson in *The Wild Ride*.

Hellman and Nicholson had recently returned from the Philippines, where they had worked together on *Flight to Fury*. They had approached Corman for further financing, and Corman agreed, provided the movie was commercial. "A Western is commercial," the producer offered. "My first movie was a Western and I still believe in Westerns." The two men were willing to go along with the western theme when Corman said, "Well, if you're going to make one Western, you might as well make two."

The first of the two movies featured a curious script written by a friend of Hellman's named Carole Eastman, who used the pen name Adrien Joyce because of its perceived androgyny. Nicholson had wanted his friend B. J. Merholz to write the script, but Hellman favored Eastman, an actress and dancer who had appeared, uncredited, in *Funny Face*, and would eventually write, with Bob Rafelson, *Five Easy Pieces*. "Several friends submitted ideas,"

Hellman told writer Brad Stevens. "Carole submitted a script that wasn't producible but was very interesting, and I had faith in her talent, so we decided to go with her." Eastman and Nicholson were given office space in the Artists and Writers Building in Beverly Hills, but Eastman soon bolted, unable to concentrate alongside Nicholson, who favored a frenetic atmosphere in which to write.

Based on a Jack London story, Eastman's script was about two bounty hunters who escort a woman across the desert so that she can exact her revenge on men who may have killed her husband and child. Along the way, they are joined by a malevolent and dispassionate gunfighter, a role earmarked for the prebreakthrough Nicholson. The story was existential and dreamlike, then unusual qualities for a western. The female character was singular. Tough, nearly monosyllabic, and almost entirely unsympathetic, her closest parallel was Maureen O'Hara in Sam Peckinpah's first film, *The Deadly Companions.*

As Hellman perused the shelves of books at Martindale's, his mind was not so much on them as on the casting of this film. He had been considering Sterling Hayden and Dana Wynter, but something nagged him until another face cropped up in his thoughts. "I don't know why he was so much on my mind. Maybe I met him somewhere else; I know he was a friend of Jack's," Hellman said. "I'd seen Warren in a production of *One Flew over the Cuckoo's Nest* here in Los Angeles, and it just suddenly popped into my mind: Warren Oates, Millie Perkins, and Will Hutchins together as a unit. I was so excited by this I instantly went to a pay telephone booth and called Jack. He was excited too."

The entire movie was shot for $75,000, under the table and under union radar. A hefty portion of the amount went to the wranglers, who were unionized. The film's financing hinged on securing the services of Will Hutchins, whose name would enable them to cast the other three actors. Corman anted up $5,000 for the two projects reluctantly: he was unhappy with both scripts.

Oates quickly agreed to appear, despite the paltry pay he was offered. He liked Nicholson and Merholz (who would play a minuscule role), and the idea of an offbeat bunch of actors in the desert intrigued him. Plus, he had an instant rapport with Hellman. Their birthdays were very close to each other, Oates's on July 5 and Hellman's on July 12. The two men shared a passion for chess and equal zeal apportioned to women, drinking, art, and solitude. "It was one of those silent friendships," Hellman said. "I never really felt that I knew Warren, but it was as if I knew him so well that there was room for that much more mystery. I knew he was a poet."

That poet was in ascendance. Oates was moving beyond being a jobbing actor who was great company on the set, a ready drinking partner, and a sympathetic ear. Maybe it was the guitar from Stanton; it was as if his soul were suddenly strumming with the tenor of the times. The admittedly wild-streaked Kentucky boy who voted for Goldwater was becoming a hippie. "He was a shy man the way many actors are," explained Robert Culp. "He was nobody's fool; he was just a flower child. Inside of Warren there was a terrific humanist." The camaraderie Oates would find over the next few weeks would open up his life like a giant, unwieldy road map that he could never again fold into place and compartmentalize. The country and landscape were changing, but Oates did not so much change with it as mold it to suit his worldview.

Millie Perkins was born in New Jersey and had been a teen model before starring in *The Diary of Anne Frank*. She had been taking acting classes with Merholz and Nicholson—Hellman was also in the class—to ease the transition from perceived child star to more mature roles, and she had become aware of Hellman and Nicholson's project. She liked the role of the unnamed woman, with its vague motivation and background. She also remembered Oates and his crush on her from their time in New York City, but she did not give it much more thought. Before driving to location, she and Nicholson went to Western Costume Company on Santa Monica Boulevard near Western Avenue, a cavernous building that was almost funereal, apt considering its proximity to Hollywood Cemetery. The two actors selected their costumes, and Nicholson expressed disdain for the hat Perkins picked out.

Will Hutchins arrived in Kanab, Utah, to find his costume already selected. He had also experienced his teen idol turn, having starred in a popular television western. "I liked my duds a whole lot better than my *Sugarfoot* outfit, which reminded me of a Buster Brown hand-me-down," the famously good-natured Hutchins said. "Warren Oates looked properly heroic and Millie Perkins and Jack Nicholson were clad in his and hers matching outfits—very Freudian."

Hutchins brought along his new wife, the former Chris Burnett (now Chris Sanchez), who was pregnant. A western movie devotee, she fell in love with Kanab, which is located in a nest of mountains and red buttes. "It was a real one-road place, gorgeous, dry, and dusty, with the Grand Canyon nearby. We'd go to Rosie's Diner for dinner every night," Chris said. Hutchins remembered, "I'd slip a nickel into the jukebox and play Chet Atkins' 'Cloudy and Cool.' My sainted ex, Antonia Christina, would accompany Chet by performing pseudo-Arabic dance to the haunting melody . . . while seated." Sanchez clarified, "People were smoking dope, of course."

Kanab was Mormon country, so alcohol was outlawed, which meant the cast and crew had to be creative. "We invented a drink during *The Shooting*," Hellman said. "We couldn't get any vodka, so we would drive across the border [three miles into Arizona], and manage to get some rum. And so we invented the rum tonic." The nearest Arizona town also had a bar called the Buckskin, and it received heavy patronage.

The Shooting, though it would be the final title, was one of several names for the movie being made. It was also known as "Gashade" and "The Tragical Death of Leland Drum." It was shot in sequence over fifteen days, and the actors were often less than pampered. Kanab had sprouted up to serve the film industry, which began making westerns there in the 1920s. Its Parry Lodge was built in 1929 to house and water the actors. Hellman and Nicholson stayed at the lodge, with the rest of the cast and crew down Center Street at the Brandon Motel. The newly built Frostop Drive-In provided sodas and burgers, but it was Rosie's Diner that became their temporary dining room, with its heavily buttered bread and equally soothing jukebox.

Shooting began some thirty miles away at a little set off the

Old Paria turnoff, where a few false fronts had been hastily built and used in *Gunsmoke* episodes as well as the *Gunga Din* remake *Sergeants Three*. To the east of the Paria River lay the remains of the Pahreah town site, completely abandoned until 1911, when prospectors came looking for gold. An early scene in *The Shooting* takes place at a mine, where Leland Drum (Merholz) was shot. Soon after, as Hutchins, playing Coley Boyard, was asked to run up and down a hill carrying a split flour sack for several takes, rain started to fall. As flour turned to paste, so did dust turn to mud.

A few days' lull in production ensued, to wait for the mud to dry. Because the movie was being shot in sequence and using natural light, scenes and scenery had to match from day to day. During the hiatus, Oates, who had driven to Kanab in his pickup truck, found he was in his element. He wrote songs on his guitar, knocked back across-the-state-line liquor, and breathed in the outdoors and anything firelit—from campfires to joints. He also resumed his pursuit of Millie Perkins. "I was aware he had a big crush on Millie. He was making the moves there," Chris Sanchez said. "Warren was a cutie," she added, saying that he reminded her of her first love, Roy Rogers.

Though he was less conventionally good-looking, Oates and Perkins side by side made for a mightily attractive couple. As an on-screen pair, their beauty matches the film's scenery, although in the movie they are not romantically entwined. No matter how sullied they got (at one point Perkins stopped to spit out a large amount of dust she had swallowed), the two continue to almost shimmer on-screen.

Perkins was more drawn to Oates this time, but, like Oates, she was married. She was also far less of a drinker and not interested in taking drugs, including pot. So she shrugged off Oates's obvious advances—obvious to the entire company. What she could not fend off was his kindness, and the amount of fun they were sharing. "Warren understood the common folk and that's why we got along. I grew up by farms and everything, and I was more of a country person."

Nicholson was not entirely pleased. He also had a thing for

the porcelain-pretty Perkins. He was often awkward with Oates during filming, and their arguments would halt the action. "They would scream at each other, and I always felt Warren was right about the interpretation, but since Jack had the instincts of a star, he probably was right too," Perkins allowed.

Perkins took riding lessons with Oates in Kanab, where horses were provided by Calvin Johnson, a Mormon rancher. Johnson later told Perkins, "You and Warren are the only two people here who know how to treat a horse." She noted, "Everyone was trying to pretend they were cowboys. They'd go up and jump on the horse, they'd swing over, but the horses were trained to be treated in a certain way." At one point, Nicholson decided he wanted Perkins's horse. "Her horse listens to her. Why should she have that horse?" he questioned. Perkins surrendered her steed, but the swap did not change anything. Nicholson's former horse obeyed Perkins, and hers began to act up under its new master.

Each evening they would return to the Brandon Motel, unite at Rosie's Diner for dinner, and start again the next morning, with coffee brewed ever stronger. The strains of Chet Atkins began and ended their working day like reveille and taps.

When filming resumed, Oates and Nicholson were soon battling again. Fortunately, they did not have a huge blowup. While they argued, Perkins and Hutchins would sit on their horses and wait it out.

Meanwhile, Oates and Perkins, on-screen and off, were blending well. "Warren would have been great in silent films," Perkins said. "There's something in him that was longing." In the evenings after work, some of the actors would gather to throw the I Ching and talk about mysticism. Oates was interested but kept his distance. "He was too much of his own guy to get involved in anything like that," Hutchins said. "He wasn't a joiner." But if the group was playing a game, that was different. "He was a tough poker player and a tough chess player, and I don't think I ever won a game or a match he was in," B. J. Merholz said.

He might not have been a joiner, but good times suited Oates to a T. "While we were on location, we couldn't see any footage, so I would call Los Angeles and ask how the dailies were," Merholz explained. "I had to drive many miles to get to a phone, and when I got back, Monte asked how the dailies were." As Merholz started to reply, Oates grabbed his guitar, climbed on top of a pile of junk mixed with some rocks, and started to sing, "I never saw grapes that couldn't make wine / Never saw rushes that weren't just fine." The assembled group laughed and applauded his spur-of-the-moment serenade.

The next morning, a little later than usual, Oates joined the table in Rosie's. "Cloudy and Cool" drifted as usual, but there was a new waitress who had come in to help. She was pretty but not sophisticated, and one of the crew mocked her manners, while another guy made a pass at her. Oates made a special effort to talk to her. He asked where she grew up and what she liked to do, apparently with nothing more than human interest on his mind. Watching this, Perkins started to melt. "Warren was *talking* to her," she said.

That night, Perkins slipped into his motel room.

Hellman said he never really had to give Oates any direction, but *The Shooting* was also the only time the two men would disagree. Well into the trek, Perkins's character goes off to give the bearded man (played by Charles Eastman) a drink of water. The man is stranded in the desert, hampered by a broken leg, and entirely hopeless.

Oates felt this moment would be a good time for his character to have a soliloquy. Hellman did not agree. Their standoff, which took place in the morning, stopped the action as surely as the rains and mud had. Oates, in a way that would have made Douglas Ramey proud, decided his character, Willet Gashade, was Hamlet and that he needed a soliloquy to give voice to his internal dialogue. Hellman agreed with his character interpretation, saying, "That's right, that's exactly what's happening," but he did not feel a speech was necessary. "You are speaking for the other people," Hellman told him. "You are talking to yourself and for yourself, but you're also talking to them and for them."

Even after eighteen takes, Oates refused to budge, so Hellman elected they break for lunch and talk about it over some food. Director and actor reached a compromise, to shoot it both ways. After lunch, Hellman ordered the microphones brought in as close as possible to Oates's location in the desert sand. Technology and budget being what they were, "We just couldn't hear him," Hellman said, but he told his actor, "Okay, we have both, and we'll see how it works out in the cutting room." Hellman remembered, "It was like pulling teeth to get it out of him, but that's the only time we ever had a problem. We did more talking about the character in *The Shooting* than we ever did again. Warren and I really got it all out."

The interchange provided insight for Hellman. "I realized . . . how intellectual his approach really was. He pretended not to be an intellectual, he pretended to be just a very simple person. He was a very complex person and approached his role from thought and then as it became him, as he became a character, the emotions would take over. He would forget about all the thought."

Perkins now had some concerns about her character's motivation as well. "Just do it," Hellman replied. "I don't have anything to tell you. We don't know why she's here."

"But Monte, did somebody kill her child?" she would protest.

"No one ever told us, but I tried to pretend that was it," Perkins explained.

Hellman was acutely aware of the prevailing mood in the desert setting. "I don't remember *The Shooting* as being a relatively happy experience from the point of view of the actors. The crew was a little disgruntled because they didn't really know what kind of picture we were making, and you know, they were very much underpaid. They felt I was a little uncommunicative as far as trying to explain. I tell people what we're going to do, the day's work, but I don't necessarily get into a lot of stuff like 'We're going after this, trying to make this kind of movie.'"

Jack Nicholson's wife Sandra visited the set with their two-year-old daughter, Jennifer. Hutchins's expectant wife Chris doted on the child and said she intended to name her baby, if it was a girl, Jennifer. Oates overheard and later came up to her. "Warren said something very sweet to me," she recalled. "He said he thought I was the most graceful pregnant woman he'd ever seen."

Then Perkins's husband, Robert Thom, came to Kanab. Perkins and Oates were having an affair, but it was not much deeper than the passionate moment one of the crew had caught them in. "I loved my husband," Perkins said. "I wasn't as close to Warren at the time he was visiting for a few days but Warren and he would talk while I was out shooting. He didn't know about anything between Warren and me." One night, she and her husband went to dinner at the Parry Lodge. "You know what Warren said to me?" her husband asked her. "He said, 'Well I guess you put in your time.'" Perkins internally sighed. She took it to mean Oates empathized with how uncomfortable it was for a husband to be on the lot while his wife was shooting.

"It's hard for an actor not to fall in love with an actress he's working with and vice versa," Hellman said. "I think in his [Oates's] case there was more than just an attraction."

Before the film's delirious, climactic chase scene, Hutchins was given a different horse with which to charge gunslinger Nicholson. Having ridden a dud for several days, Hutchins received a jolt. "They gave me a real buster, more horse than I ever knew. I rode like the wind. It was an exhilarating feeling. Jack could never have caught me in a million years." Nicholson took note. When it was time to start the next feature, *Ride in the Whirlwind*, he would claim that horse for his own.

An hour-long traipse across the sand awaited the cast on their final day of work, and Nicholson, who was producing as well as acting, worried about the schedule. "We can't afford the time," he told Hellman as they walked. "By the time we finished arguing, we were there," Hellman recounted.

The Shooting ended in a haze. Hutchins and his wife got ready to leave, saying good-bye to the cast and crew. "We loaded our cars and pledged eternal allegiance," he said. "Tough returnin' to reality. That show," he added, "Jack and I were both Taurus, Warren's Cancer, Millie's a Taurus. There you are, case closed." The director, too, was a Cancer.

During the few days' break between the two films, Oates and Perkins left Kanab together. In his pickup truck, he drove sometimes slow, sometimes fast, over a dipping and climbing two-lane road where the breathtaking view complemented their feelings. He and Perkins were very much in love. "Warren was my romance," she said. "He was charming, kind, romantic, and not 'bad' naughty, just naughty enough to be fun and alive." Shadows of clouds looked like black ponds in the desert landscape, and the couple held hands, sitting close on the truck's bench seat, with the windows rolled down and a country station on the radio. "Make the World Go Away," lushly arranged, would have played as the two lovers plotted to keep it at bay. In Los Angeles there were commitments, in his case a marriage on the rocks and a love that did not quite fit. Like a loose-fitting wedding band, it was forever slipping, being lost and found, then lost again. "He never said anything bad about Teddy, but he never said anything about it being right," Perkins said. "Driving down and being totally without any responsibility and without any problems, it was everything you wanted life to be about, but you weren't going to have it all the time."

They stopped in little towns and danced in the only bar. They held each other beneath the stars and a same-patterned quilt. They ate in greasy spoon cafés unless Oates could find his favorite, a family-style restaurant. They pretended he was a rancher and she, his cowgirl. "We were at the peak of our youth," Perkins said, and Oates was perfecting his approach to living. "He went along with life as it came along just because he lived in the moment and in the now."

When they said good-bye in Los Angeles, Perkins would be returning to Kanab to make *Ride in the Whirlwind*. Oates had an episode of *Branded*. The lovers would be together again, but the circumstances would be far from the same. "It was like a dream world," she said. "And having Warren by my side, it was heaven."

Upon release, *The Shooting* would run anything but in sequence. In late July, Hellman began to edit the two films, a process that took six months—quick work for two movies. "We thought they would be a couple more Roger Corman movies that would play on the second half of a double-bill somewhere," Hellman told Brad Stevens. Nicholson was tireless in making sure they saw daylight, but the French distributor with which he secured a deal went bankrupt, holding the films' fate in limbo for the next three years.

The films were eventually sold to the Walter Reade Organization, which offered *The Shooting* to television, and on January 24, 1969, it was broadcast on WTTV in Indianapolis. But attempts to secure a theatrical release continued.

The Shooting was lyrical, confounding, beautiful, and too much for its targeted audience. After a run at the drive-ins to cash in on Nicholson's rising star, it premiered at the Royal Theatre in Los Angeles on January 12, 1972. Ron Pennington in the *Hollywood Reporter* recognized a minor classic and a minimalist masterpiece. "What makes the film work so well is the magnificent style Hellman achieves throughout," he wrote. "It is strictly a visual film and Hellman creates an urgency and tension through his images and his sharp and calculated editing. The performances are all excellent but not in the usual terms. With the exception of Hutchins, who gives a delightful portrayal of an innocent and simple-minded cowboy, the roles are extremely underplayed with a stoic delivery and manner." David Castell noted in *Films Illustrated*, "The film has only one major performance, that of Warren Oates as the bounty hunter, which is supported toweringly by Hellman's direction."

Oates later told an audience at the National Film Theatre in London how he felt about Hellman. "He's a very careful, precise, patient man who says very little. He's a marvelous man, intelligent. Without comparing him . . . I like to say he's the only Antonioni we have." Hellman would return the compliment. "In *The Shooting* he [Oates] was at his most heroic," he said. "The character is as close as I can get to the way I saw Warren." Hellman received a lasting accolade when his cast and crew watched the final product. "They saw the picture and everybody to a man came up to me and apologized for having been, you know, so ornery." Oates said that the film offered him his "shot at being Bogart." He added, "No one bugged us. We had a few wars but you can't make a film without a war or two. I think bumping heads actually helps. In television this is where you often lose out. It's all done too quickly."

Warren Oates was not an actor to stay still. "I can't stand not to work," he would often say, plus he had his family to provide for. Before the summer of 1965, when the Watts neighborhood of Los Angeles would burn in anger and frustration, he completed several more shows. One of them was the "Judge Not" episode of *Branded*, which, oddly enough, took him back to Kanab. *Branded*, with its opening ballad by Dominic Frontiere, starred Chuck Connors as Jason McCord, an honorable soldier who has taken a fall for his superior. With some of its sixty-four episodes shot in color, *Branded* was memorable and not a little campy, prompting it to be comically referenced years later in the Coen brothers' 1998 cult hit *The Big Lebowski*.

"Judge Not" opened the second season of *Branded*, and again Oates appeared first on-screen, his agate-like face a template for what audiences could expect. He is gallows-bound Perce Clampett, a prisoner who, despite being called "just a kid," looks a little long in the tooth. He is aboard a stagecoach on which McCord hitches a ride, unaware that one of the passengers—an officer—was present at McCord's court-martial. In an odd twist, Clampett has a twin brother, Frank, so Oates played back-to-back twins (although he was credited only as Perce), having just portrayed Coyne and Willet Gashade in *The Shooting*.

The year ended with Oates and Teddy together but starting to fray. If, as he frequently said, he did not have a home, he was finding a way to make the road his natural habitat.

On January 25, 1966, he went to Madrid. *Return of the Seven* was an attempt to capitalize on 1960's *The Magnificent Seven*, a huge hit starring Yul Brynner, Steve McQueen, and Robert Vaughn. By comparison, the sequel had, for example, Jordan Christopher, a singer who owned a disco and was making his acting debut. Robert Fuller provided some marquee glow, but the rest of the cast, apart from Brynner (the only holdover from the original), Oates, and the imperial Emilio Fernandez, were a fistful of dullards. The film's musical score by Elmer Bernstein incorporated the familiar rousing theme, large as all outdoors, which nearly dwarfed the marginalized seven.

The location, originally Mexico, was moved to Spain, where the law required that a portion of the cast be citizens. Thus Julian Mateos, Virgilio Texiera, and Elisa Montes appeared where Peter Falk and Telly Savalas might have been. Oates, who did not travel particularly well, was in for a bad time. As the plane took off, his career rose along with it: this was a high-profile film. But prior to landing in Alicante, Spain, the plane dropped five hundred feet, silencing the actors and their director, Burt Kennedy.

Oates played Colbee, a girl-crazy gunslinger ("Violent, virile, he kills many men—and leaves many women!" exclaimed the trailer) with a set of very white teeth. His character is introduced in the film when he falls out a window. Then he runs, and Oates was a lively runner. But by the end of filming, Oates was rail thin, and his pallor had gone from golden to ashen. Traveling between Alicante and Colmenar de Oreja, he managed to contract hepatitis B, and he became sicker than he had ever been in his thirty-seven years.

During a campfire scene, he delivers a lengthy speech peppered with braggadocio about his having romanced, in one night, "half the women in Sonora" and claiming that he "would have gone through more if I hadn't a pulled a leg muscle." His performance has a perspiring humor, all the more impressive because Oates was running a high temperature, 102 and rising. Because of his illness, he was warned off alcohol, and he did not have to be told twice. "That saved me, because I began to turn to other things," Oates said later.

Return is weak, with only Fernandez around to up the ante. Some of the sets are as false as the dialogue, and the action is as predictable as the church bell ringing seven times as the survivors ride off. But although it disappointed at the box office after it opened at El Rey Theatre in Los Angeles on November 2, 1966, *Return of the Seven* represented a step up for Oates. "Much hilarity comes from Warren Oates. Oates nearly steals the picture. He's that funny," wrote Glen Hawkins in the *Los Angeles Herald-Examiner*, and the *Hollywood Reporter* deemed it his "best outing since 'Mail Order Bride.'"

"Western style leisure clothing is always popular," advised the press book regarding how theater chains might promote this film. Oates would have to hang on a bit longer, but before too long, he would be able to change out of his duds.

On July 25, 1966, however, he would go to work on the Janss Conejo Ranch in nearby Thousand Oaks on a film that, in the right hands, could have been a classic. But instead it became an obscure novelty with a cold-steel core.

After *Ride the High Country*, Oates had come across a book by E. L. Doctorow called *Bad Man from Bodie*. Oates was impressed with it and mentioned it to Robert Culp, who wholeheartedly agreed. Both men believed the novel, published in 1960, would be a great project for Sam Peckinpah, so Oates took his paperback copy to MGM and placed it on Peckinpah's desk. "That was Warren's gift to Sam for no good reason particularly," Culp said. "There may or may not have been anything in it for him."

The book caught the eye of a producer who shared an office adjoining the director's. He took it into his office, read it, and immediately optioned it. The director he chose might have been the antithesis of Peckinpah, but he was also one who often had room for Oates. Burt Kennedy went to work on the project, changing its name to *Welcome to Hard Times*.

"If Sam had made that movie, it would have been a classic forever," Culp said. In Kennedy's hands, it drove Doctorow to declare it was the second-worst picture he had ever seen. "I was afraid to ask him what the first one was," Kennedy wrote. It is, however, superior to *Return of the Seven* and much darker than *Mail Order Bride*. Henry Fonda stars as Will Blue, a curiously somnambulistic lawyer in a tough town, Hard Times. Janice Rule is Molly, his working-girl love interest. Molly was an unsympathetic role originally intended for Rita Hayworth, who pulled out after breaking her hip in a fall at her swimming pool. Her blouse, however, made the final cut: Arlene Golonka, who starred as the baby-doll-voiced Mae, was given the garment to wear. "It was a beautiful old blouse," Golonka said, "but being out in the sun so much, as it got hotter and hotter, I started smelling Rita Hayworth."

Oates played Leo Jenks, riding into town perched atop a funeral carriage he has appropriated, unaware of its putrefying contents. (Jenks mistakes the coach, with its plumage and luster, for one that belonged to a circus.) He camps out on the periphery of Hard Times, polishes his gun, and provides light comedy with his jack-o'-lantern teeth and stock quizzical expressions. In a bare and blustery Christmas sequence, Janis Paige as Adah sings carols, and Jenks respectfully joins in, sitting on some boxes. He is also called on to signify the arrival of spring, and as he runs around the paddocks, whooping and hollering, he symbolizes the childlike wonder that the rest of the ensemble, including a child, Jimmy Fee (Michael Shea), cannot muster.

Welcome to Hard Times has problems of pacing and intent, and the specter of a town that should be pitied is one that director Kennedy cannot quite bring into focus. The premise is there, but by the time the body count, including Jenks's, who confronts the menacing bad man Aldo Ray, piles up, the film is at an obtuse crossroads, with one signpost reading "listless" and the other "haphazard."

After opening at New York's Festival Theater on Fifty-seventh Street in May 1967, *Welcome to Hard Times* closed quickly. It turned up on television some seven months later, a retreat to the small screen so hasty that the National Association of Theater Owners protested.

Golonka said the movie's location, in what is now the center of Thousand Oaks, felt remote, but for Oates it was an easy drive home. What he found there, though, was a mood as abject as that in Hard Times. Oates often responded by heading for the Raincheck.

Director Norman Jewison was wrapping up work on *The Russians Are Coming, the Russians Are Coming* when he began to formulate his next project. A native of Toronto, Jewison had wanted to make a film about an intelligent black man stuck in a tiny Mississippi town in the early 1960s. Martin Baum, Sidney Poitier's manager, had also read John Ball's novel *In the Heat of the Night* and recognized how right it would be for his client, who had recently won the Academy Award for best actor for *Lilies of the Field*—the first black man to achieve such an accolade. Producer Walter Mirisch had purchased the novel's film rights, and writer Stirling Silliphant, a friend of Poitier's, had written a chatty but powerful screenplay. Momentum was growing for the film to be made on the Goldwyn lot in Los Angeles.

Jewison quickly made Mirisch aware of his interest in directing the film and was summarily dismissed. "No, no, Norman, it's not for you," the producer said. "We're not going to spend much money on it. . . . The movie's too small for you at this stage of your career." The director might have left it at that had he not gone skiing—and if his son Michael had not broken his leg on the slopes. While Michael was being treated in Sun Valley, Idaho, Jewison struck up a conversation with a couple in the waiting room, Robert and Ethel Kennedy. At a New Year's Eve party in the Kennedys' private lodge, Jewison mentioned *In the Heat of the Night*. Kennedy was emphatic. "It's very important, Norman, that you make this movie. Timing is everything in politics, in art, and in life itself. Now is the time to make *In the Heat of the Night*," Kennedy pronounced.

Jewison told Mirisch he would agree to the tiny budget of about $1.5 million with the caveat that the movie be made on location. Following a couple of rewrites, one of which pushed the book's central character, Sam Wood, into the periphery, Jewison began to cast the movie. He knew he needed an established actor to play the redneck sheriff opposite Poitier's urbane policeman. When his first choice, George C. Scott, was unavailable, he secured Rod Steiger. For the remaining roles, he wanted relative unknowns. "I didn't want the actors' histories in past movies to get between the audience and the storyline," Jewison said. "I looked for people who had little or no screen time."

That would prove a boon to jobbing actor Warren Oates. With some seventy television shows and about a dozen films to his name, Oates's airplay miles might have qualified him as a frequent flier, but he was still traveling economy.

Edward Asner tested for the important part of police deputy Sam Wood. "I thought I made a helluva impression," Asner recalled. "I went home that night, and so did Norman, but he went home and turned on some program, maybe it was *Stoney Burke,* and he saw Warren in this TV show and decided that's who he wanted for that particular role. So I immediately wanted to find Warren wherever he might be, and kill him."

"I was aware of his [Oates's] work, or he wouldn't have been there," Jewison said. "But frankly I was auditioning in Los Angeles most of the actors I could find from the South. I had people from Texas, I had people from Kentucky, and people from Missouri, and people from Oklahoma. And we worked very, very hard to get the Mississippi sound in all the accents. But Warren was very good and he had this twinkle in his eye. There was something about him; he had so much energy on-screen."

In the Heat of the Night would begin filming on September 19, 1966. Earlier that summer, Jewison and two assistants had scoured the southern states for the right location. Paducah, Kentucky, was considered, as were Joplin, Missouri, and Memphis. "Then Sidney Poitier spoke up," Jewison said. "Sidney said there was no god damn way he'd go below the Mason-Dixon Line for the eight weeks we'd need to shoot the movie. Earlier in the year, Sidney and Harry Belafonte had flown to Mississippi to deliver money to a civil rights group led by the activist Stokely Carmichael. After they had been picked up in a small airfield in Greenville, a bunch of crackers followed their car. Sidney had no desire to expose himself again to white Southern hospitality."

For several weeks in the fall of 1966, Sparta, Illinois, originally intended to be Wells, Mississippi, became Sparta in that deepest of southern states. Located in Randolph County, the town, then with a population of five thousand, is forty-five miles east of St. Louis, near the borders of Missouri and Kentucky. It was rural and quiet—and long on community spirit. Sparta also had a sizable minority population who coexisted reasonably well with their white neighbors. For the time being, at least, residents were united in one thing: no one believed their town was about to appear in a major motion picture.

"A lot of people thought it was a bunch of baloney," said Jack Bivens, an Illinois state trooper assigned to movie security who also served as Rod Steiger's stand-in. "Oh yeah, they're going to make a movie at Sparta." Richard E. McDaniel, whose parents owned a funeral home, remembered, "People just came to the back door one day and said they were making a movie and wanted to rent the place. Dad thought sure, they're never going to." But an item in the weekly *Sparta News-Plaindealer* on September 15, 1966, made it official—almost. A film would be made in Sparta, and it would be called "In the Heat of the Sun."

There was little sun on offer when the cast and crew arrived at their lodgings in Augustine's Motor Lodge, forty-five miles from Sparta in Belleville. Bivens explained the move: "We had no motels around here, nothing that would house them." While the majority stayed at Augustine's, Jewison rented one of the town's toniest homes and drove around Sparta, causing a stir in his white Jaguar convertible. For the first few days, the top was firmly up, as buckets of rain fell.

Buses took the cast to and from Sparta, and the unseasonably cold autumn played havoc with the filmmaking. In a pivotal scene outside the diner, the actors' breath is clearly visible, and the foliage is decidedly turning as Harvey Oberst (Scott Wilson) is chased from a dog's-eye view through the woods. An autopsy scene in the funeral home was put on hold because of condensation.

Jack Bivens invited his mother in nearby Chester to come watch a movie being made. Myrtle Bivens, whose maiden name was Newton, had grown up east of Owensboro, Kentucky. "I introduced her to Warren Oates, and when they got together, those two were like long-lost cousins," Bivens recalled. "He was an old hillbilly boy who came up in a common atmosphere right there in the fields of Kentucky. My mother got a big kick out of it, and they knew names of a lot of families." Oates's stand-in was a local named George L. Kirkland. "Sidney Poitier and Warren Oates were just down-home country boys. We always got along good. One night Poitier, Oates, and my cousin and I were passing time so we all got into a dice game in that alley behind the theater," Kirkland told journalist Patrick Gauen, adding that the movie on the marquee was Poitier's *A Patch of Blue*. Kirkland's car, a Plymouth sedan with a Confederate license plate and extraordinarily large tail fins, was used as the vehicle in which a group of hayseed racists (one of whom was played by Kirkland) try to run Poitier's Virgil Tibbs out of town.

James DuBose authored *Searching for Sparta*, which looks at the relationship between the town and the film. DuBose recalled Oates carrying three-year-old Spartan James Neilson around on his shoulders at the Gulf, Mobile and Ohio railway station, and he described how residents like Rich McDaniel sat with Oates in the car to keep warm. As they waited out the weather, Oates grilled him about his college career.

Sam Wood provided Oates with the opportunity to examine his role in a new way. Wood is neither stock nor caricature, although in the wrong hands he could have been both. "I tried to see him as a man who had real problems. I wanted the audience to see him that way too," Oates said. There is humor in the scenes between Steiger (who played Bill Gillespie) and Oates, and in the scene in the diner where he never gets his pie, but Oates and Jewison were united in their desire to keep his performance subdued. "It's easy to unconsciously steal a laugh, but we hoped to preserve Sam's dignity and avoid anything that would reduce him to a cliché statement," Oates said. Wood "was written a little, we felt, on the clichéd side and I was anxious to make the film very real," Jewison said. Oates "was very concerned that it not be someone we've seen before. He was on a constant search for that kind of unique character. Of course he's also the source of a lot of humor in the film. The way Stirling Silliphant writes and the way I direct, regardless of how serious the picture is, or the situation is, I always try to inject a little bit of humor here and there because I believe that's what life is all about."

One night Oates and Jewison were waiting out the rain in a police car. "We shot quite a bit with Warren at night—he was driving around in the police car—and he was all the way through the film, there for the whole shoot, practically, so I got to know him quite well as an actor-director relationship," Jewison said.

A lull in the conversation came, and Jewison looked out the window in the dark, at the light-falling rain. "There are strange things done in the midnight sun . . . " he began.

"By the men who moil for gold," replied Oates.

"The Arctic trails of their secret tales / That would make your blood run cold," Jewison continued.

"The northern lights have seen queer sights / But the queerest they ever did see . . ."

The two men looked at each other. "Was that night on the marge of Lake Lebarge / I cremated Sam McGee," they shouted in unison and then broke into laughter before completing the entire fifteen stanzas of Robert Service's poem "The Cremation of Sam McGee."

The rain let up and shooting resumed, this time with a slightly more anticipatory pace. It was late, and the long day was about to end. But while others made their way to the buffet and bar at Augustine's Motor Lodge, Jewison and Oates had other preoccupations. "We couldn't wait to come back into the car so we could recite to each other," Jewison said. Some time near midnight, they got their wish. "A bunch of the boys were whooping it up / in the Malamute Saloon," they began, launching into another Service poem, "The Shooting of Dan McGrew." Oates, Jewison was thrilled to find, knew every stanza.

Sam Wood may have been denied his slice of pie, but Jewison made sure Rod Steiger got his. "I wanted Rod's gut hanging over his belt," Jewison said. "I wanted him to look like the stereotype of every beefy, bigoted police chief in the South." At dinner, Jewison made a point of saying to Steiger, "That pecan pie sure looks good tonight." Such method dining did the trick, but Steiger's method acting affected Oates. "I think Warren had his eye on Steiger as someone who had a tendency to go over the top," Jewison said, and Oates's quiet assessment prompted him to turn in a performance that was far more muted than his previous work on film. Oates's tendency toward the manic—rapidly blinking eyes, fault-lined forehead, yee-hawing laughter—is entirely absent from

In the Heat of the Night. "He was up against Steiger and Poitier, and I trusted him as an actor," Jewison said. The director also enabled him to leave his cowboy hat at home, and the horse in the studio lot stables. "Off a horse and into a patrol car," Jewison laughed. "He had a warmth which I liked very much, an honesty he projected. He wasn't abrasive in any way but he was tough. When he said something, you believed him, which is what film acting is all about. He was very subtle, very confident. He knew where he was going." Nonetheless, the director concluded, "Our special bond was actually through poetry."

When the cast and crew wrapped on November 9, they were all aware of the significance of the film they had just completed. They knew that shock waves would be felt when Poitier's Virgil Tibbs slapped the face of bigoted industrialist Eric Endicott, the first black man to hit a white man on film. Consistently regarded as one of the best movies of all time, *In the Heat of the Night* has an import and a quietude that were intentional in equal parts. Its debut score by Quincy Jones is subtle; Ray Charles sings the theme, with lyrics by Alan and Marilyn Bergman. Jewison used music sparingly and was said to have nixed Sam the Sham's hit "Little Red Riding Hood" in favor of "Fowl Owl on the Prowl" (sung by Glen Campbell) in the scene in which Ralph Henshaw (Anthony James) does some greasy-spoon dancing in the diner. Since budget constraints were never far from the surface during the filming, it could not have hurt to save the extra royalty payment.

Cinematographer Haskell Wexler, who had recently won the Oscar for his work on *Who's Afraid of Virginia Woolf?* adopted a documentary-style technique for *In the Heat of the Night* and simply used a handheld camera. He also employed a forced development film technique, shooting at a lower light level than the exposure of the film called for. Working with less light made setups much more expedient and gave the film its grainy feel. Cars' headlights were replaced with high-powered bulbs so they could be captured more effectively, but their glow is often eerie, as is the cross-shaped reflection from the approaching train engine in the movie's opening sequence. "Part of the lighting at night is because

I didn't know any better," Wexler said, but many scenes—the tight lens on a cadaver, the first-ever overt use of a 500 mm zoom as Oberst runs across the bridge—suggest not so much happy accident as brilliance at work.

Jewison noted that the film started several careers. The extraordinary Wilson went on to star in *In Cold Blood* opposite Robert Blake, who had also tested for the role of Oberst.

"I'm really one of those sub-plots running through the picture, an arm or leg of it," Oates said in 1967. Oates looks different in the film, appearing all of his thirty-eight years, pudgy faced and hazel eyed. He is no tanned ruffian, and his use of his hands at the steering wheel while driving past Delores Purdy's (Quentin Dean) house is slight but evocative. Dull-witted Sam Wood has hidden depths and a deep sensuality. When Purdy, the object of his lust, comes clean about their relationship, she tells police chief Gillespie that Sam has been riding by her house every night to peep. "He says, 'Hey little girl, you know what the coolest spot in town is?' And I say, 'No Sam, I guess I don't.' He says, 'A cemetery, that's where. Know why? 'Cause they got all them big, cool tombstones. Ever stretch out on a tombstone, 'Lores? Feel all that nice, cool marble on your body?'"

"In 'In the Heat of the Night' I don't feel I'm a heavy," Oates said, "just a man with a few problems. You see, I'm a police officer and also a peeping Tom. They closed the set in a nude scene," he continued. "Quentin Dean is the girl I peeked at and I was one of the few guys who got to stick around. She's a talented girl. She handled the situation with great dignity and modesty so we didn't lose any respect for her."

Back in Los Angeles, Oates went home to an empty house. While he was away, he had missed the Los Angeles premiere of *Return of the Seven*. But that was not all he had missed: Teddy had begun divorce proceedings against him.

On October 26, 1966, she initiated the process, citing "extreme cruelty," and on November 5, Warren Oates was sent divorce papers at their Kingswood Lane home. Teddy had moved with the children to Marlin Place in Van Nuys. "The [film] locations are killing us," Teddy said to Oates. "I'm starting to hate you.

Every time you get a job, I hate you for taking that job. I know you need to, and we need to have it, but I don't want to hate the father of my kids. I'm going to leave you because I don't want to hate you."

The divorce began on November 7, 1966, but the estranged couple were far from through with each other. "My first wife, Teddy, was not an actress and she did not understand," Oates said later. Bobbie, for press purposes at least, had been erased.

"We were used to seeing Warren by himself," L. Q. Jones said. "Teddy was with him on *Ride the High Country*, and she was gregarious; she loved people. She was just unhappy with the business that Warren wasn't around. That she did such a great job with her children, it couldn't have been easy. The biggest child was Warren. How do you get around Warren? Teddy put up with it for as long as she could and finally had enough."

"About two or three weeks after he taught me to play chess, I checkmated him in three moves. I'm not a good chess player," Teddy said in 1993. "He just wasn't paying attention."

Alone on the evening of November 21, Warren Oates did not have to think about his first Thanksgiving as a newly separated man. Instead, he could watch an episode of *The Big Valley* in which he limped and shouted through the role of an incompetent safe robber named Duke, ordering "Put her [Linda Evans as Audra] back in that sack!" In the shadow of Santa Clarita's Vasquez Rocks, he had played it for laughs, but more important, he had gone one-on-one with Barbara Stanwyck and, as the guest star, was every inch the screen legend's peer.

11

Beyond the Valley of the Summer of Love

At midlife in the middle of the 1960s, a newly separated Warren Oates did what many single men did, or dreamed of doing. He took his new Buick convertible and moved to the marina.

Securing a quintessential bachelor pad with a view of docked boats and yachts and their fluid blue path to the wide-open Pacific, he might have been content, but the failure of his marriage had devastated him. "It really hurt Warren; it really, really did," said L. Q. Jones. "I don't think very many people realized just how unhappy he was. He was unhappy because he loved Teddy, and the main thing was, he was still confused. He couldn't figure out why they couldn't get together and why they couldn't fit in the business. I think Teddy believed the business changed Warren, and she wasn't happy with that," Jones continued. "I don't even know if she'd admit that to herself. But it did change him. It changes everybody."

Oates took the split hard, and he took to hard liquor. The television executive and producer Norman Powell remembered going to visit Oates in the marina one midmorning and being met by a shambled man much worse for wear. Oates was not alone. He had Sam Peckinpah for company. "Warren was the only person I know of who got really close to Sam that Sam didn't screw," Jones explained. "He didn't like anyone close. But Warren was probably as crazy as he was. Warren was a piece of work." Powell begged to differ. "Oates was a nice human being, pleasant, and not nearly as difficult as Sam."

Oates bought a boat, a twenty-nine-foot sloop he christened the *Yonder*. His daughter Jennifer occasionally went onboard. "I went out on the boat, but I would only allow him to cruise around the marina. I wouldn't let him go past the breakwaters because I did not want to go in the real ocean. No."

Some adults, not as sensible, threw their caution to the wind. Oates's brother Gordon came to visit. He had been out to visit Oates and Teddy several times in the past, joining in their impromptu potluck parties and what Warren referred to as his "famous bean suppers like our old maid aunts made." He would cook the beans for two to three days and serve them with green onions and fried hot-water cornbread to friends who included hungry, out-of-work actors.

Gordon drove his rental car to the marina, which was just north of the expanding Los Angeles International Airport. When he arrived, he joined Oates and Peckinpah aboard the *Yonder*. "He and Sam were onboard talking in all these nautical terms, first mate this and that, Mister so and so . . ." This went on for the entire sail, so the older Oates needed a plan to keep himself from contemplating mutiny. "I just started looking for the beer," Gordon said. "But it was easy to see how he got along with Sam."

However, Peckinpah's sister, Fern Lea Peter, said, "Warren was a lot more sober than Sam, and I don't think the drinking was so much aboard as after." She and her husband Walter went sailing one day with Oates, Peckinpah, and the actress Mary Murphy. Back ashore, they went to Oates's apartment. She and Walter, who had two children, left in the early evening. Later that night, they were awoken by a phone call. "Sam is drunk. He's threatening to hit me!" a frantic Oates shouted. Apparently Peckinpah was certain Oates had made a play for Murphy. "I think Warren had enough sense not to do that, but Sam didn't see things that way, especially when he'd had more than enough," Fern Lea attested. Peckinpah eventually fell asleep, using a box of Kleenex for a pillow. Fern Lea regretted that Oates forgot to take a picture.

The *Yonder* met an unusual fate: It ended up going straight. Oates asked an acquaintance to look after the boat when he went on location, leaving Teddy to take the phone call from the Long Beach Police Department.

"Mrs. Oates, do you have a boat?"

"Yes," she replied.

"Well, I think you're going to have to come down here, because we had to confiscate the boat."

The friend who was looking after the *Yonder* had had a run-in with the Coast Guard and refused to let them board, giving chase until finally running the boat aground. "I guess he had stuff on there that wasn't supposed to be there," Teddy said. Oates eventually donated the *Yonder* to the SeaBees.

Oates kept in touch with his old friends: Alzamora, Dayton, Georgiade. Nick Georgiade was a regular on *The Untouchables* and was spending most of his free time in Vegas, where he had fallen in with a heavy crowd. "I got very friendly with everybody in the Sinatra clan except Frank Sinatra," Georgiade said. Sinatra, it transpired, was no fan of *The Untouchables*. "He hates that fucking show you're on," Dean Martin told a nonplussed Georgiade.

Armand Alzamora had pretty much given up the business to manage apartment buildings and, from time to time, serve as Oates's driver. Howard Dayton was driving too, a cab, when Alzamora called to suggest they meet Oates for breakfast at Pupi's. Dayton was reluctant at first. "It seemed like he had no time for me; he was busy, and any time I went to talk to him, he had a million people around him, wanting him to get them jobs," Dayton said. He felt awkward as he sat down to eat with his old friend. "I don't think he'd changed at all," Dayton allowed. "I changed. I was envious."

Coming off the high of *In the Heat of the Night*, Oates worked on films in late 1967 and early 1968 that were not his most memorable. But if Oates was in a holding pattern, it was one that cut a wide swath, veering from Walt Disney to John Fante. Television work included the staple *Gunsmoke*, an unsold ABC pilot called *Attack* in which he played a marine stationed in the South Pacific during World War II, and an episode of *Dundee and the Culhane* (where he would put his feet in cement for the Western Walk of Fame at Apacheland Studio). Other than that, he had time on his hands. Time on his hands was time to drink. And time to drink was time for the Raincheck.

Michael Anderson Jr., married with two children and living in a little house in Beverly Hills, got a strange call one day. "I get this phone call, one of those dirty phone calls, a breather. And I don't hang up on those phone calls; I'm fascinated," Anderson explained. "But I get this phone call, and it's disturbing."

"Hello, who is this? Hello? Do you know me? Who are you?" Anderson was met with silence.

A month later, he got another one. "'Hello, who is this? Hello?' Now the breathing is a little more pronounced, and I can't hear anybody laughing, but whoever it is is staying on the line. 'Goddamn it, who is this? Who are you?'" Anderson demanded.

One more month passed, and then another phone call came. "OK, I don't know who the fuck you are, but I'm calling the damn cops. Do I know you?"

"You," came the reply, "are . . . my . . . Mexico . . . lover."

"Who the hell is that, my Mexico lover?" The caller hung up.

"It haunted me for a year," Anderson continued. "He never called again. One day I go to a bar; I can't remember its name because I didn't go there often. All the guys went there. Anyway there's Warren sitting there and he goes, 'Michael, how are ya? Good to see you.'"

"You're doing well. I haven't seen you in ages," Anderson replied.

"No, you haven't *seen* me," Oates said.

"You son of a bitch!" Anderson said, giving his friend a neck hug and a few words of advice. "Don't be doing that."

"He never thought in a million years I'd pick up on it, but it was so typical of the kind of impish spirit he had."

"Impish" is a kind word. "Childish" might have been closer to the mark. Oates was living on his own, and it showed. "Warren was totally taken care of all his life and then let out into the world, where he didn't know how to do anything," Teddy said. He frequently came over to see her and the kids in their Van Nuys home. A few years earlier, Teddy had painted two portraits, one of herself and one of her husband, and she hung them near the fireplace. Warren kept staring at these two pictures. "You know," he finally said, "I've been wanting to tell you something for months. That's a painting of Bobbie." The two women, it transpired, looked very much alike.

"Is it?" Teddy took the painting and threw it in the fire.

That Valentine's Day, he sent flowers and a card to his estranged wife. Millie Perkins also received a present. "Warren sent me this beautiful collage without a name on it, but I knew it was from him. It was the most romantic Valentine collage I've ever got in my whole life," she said.

The Summer of Love was still a few months off, and although Oates and Teddy made several attempts at reconciliation, few were quite as telling as Saturday night, March 8, 1967.

Alzamora, who had been the designated chef when he, Oates, and Dayton lived together in the Casa Real, had arranged, a year and a half before, for a party of friends to dine at Henri Charpentier's in Redondo Beach. Charpentier was the famed chef and originator of crêpes suzettes who had come to the Southern California seafront after World War II and set up a tiny restaurant at the corner of Diamond Avenue and the Pacific Coast Highway. It was a long way from the French Riviera, but Hollywood stars had palates that aspired to approximate those of crowned heads of state, so they flocked.

By the late 1950s, Charpentier was leaving the cooking to an assistant and spending his time socializing with the fifteen to twenty diners who managed to get reservations. Waiting lists ran from two to five years. Charpentier died in 1961, but the waiting list remained, and so the restaurant carried on until it closed in the late 1960s.

"The twelve of us rented a bus," Alzamora said, "and drove down to have this last meal." It was a ten-course feast including lobster, soup, a beef pastry, and roast duck with all the trimmings, rounded off by crêpes suzettes. The diners included Warren and Teddy Oates, Armand and Betty Alzamora, Will and Chris

Hutchins, and Pernell Roberts and his wife. They ate and drank and engaged in revelry, conversation, and laughter. When it was over, they all went bowling.

About a year later, Alzamora was on the sidewalk outside Schwab's when a clerk came rushing outside. "Aren't you Armand Alzamora?" she asked. Flattered, he replied in the affirmative. "You need to come in and pick up your film," the young woman told him. Perusing the piles of photographs that evening, he and Betty came across one from the dinner at Charpentier's. Pointing at each couple, they soon realized that every single one, save for themselves, was separated or divorced. From then on, the meal was referred to as the Great Divorce Dinner.

Around the time Alzamora was prompted to pick up his photos, Hutchins had just missed Oates at a party. Biding his time, Hutchins found that "no one was very friendly apart from Norman Jewison and a sweet gal who came up to me and asked, 'Are you wearing patchouli?'"

"Yeah, I'm wearing it," Hutchins replied.

"I'm wearing it too," said the beaming blonde, whose name was Sharon Tate.

The Summer of Love would last longer than a season, yet it would be the very essence of ephemera. Within a couple of years, Tate and others would be killed by members of the Manson Family.

In May 1967, Norman Jewison went to San Francisco for an advance screening of *In the Heat of the Night* and was unnerved by the audience's laughter. "I've ruined the movie," Jewison thought, certain it was condemned to failure. "They laughed," Jewison mourned to the film's editor, Hal Ashby. "Not at the movie, man," Ashby replied. "*With* the movie." *In the Heat of the Night* opened in New York on August 2 and at Grauman's Chinese Theatre in Los Angeles on August 23. It was met with emphatically approving reviews. Joseph Morgenstern in *Newsweek* cited its advance reputation as "word of mouth verbose" and found the film an "intricate, moving . . . labor of love." Oates's "craven patrolman is fine," the reviewer added.

The movie was a hit, and if Oates's performance as Sam Wood

was not always singled out, he was proud of it and aware of its significance to his career. Don Alpert of the *Los Angeles Times* commented that Oates had a face that was more familiar than his name. He added, "Oates's plight, if indeed it is one, is that there can just be so many leading men and he doesn't happen to be one." Such cold consolation was followed by Oates's refrain that he was happy with where he was in his career, but the anticipated success of *In the Heat of the Night* enabled him to project. "I feel I can guide my life better now," he said. "I don't want to be type-cast as a—what?—some are gangsters or heavies. I don't want that kind of routine." Despite 1967's relative leanness, Oates told Alpert he was not interested in doing another television series. "Unless something special came along I wouldn't want it right now." But he was mindful of what his stint as Ves Painter on *Stoney Burke* had done for him. "That series did a world of good for me. Not only here but overseas."

The man with an apartment and a boat in the marina was starting to feel his rootlessness more acutely, and Alpert took note. "Home for Oates is a problem," he wrote. Oates admitted, "I never did adjust to the city. Not that I want to go on a farm. But I just can't adjust to a posh saloon either. I can't get involved in that world." He concluded, "I can't seem to find a home here," and Alpert asked where home might be. "Man," he answered, "I just don't know."

The article's publication prompted a fan letter, a relative rarity for a man who would acknowledge, "I don't get fan letters from little girls but I do get them from doctors, lawyers, writers, and professors." It is hard to know what occupation Marilyn J. Morris of Rosemead, California, held, but her sober yet sensitive letter to the *Los Angeles Times*, printed on August 13, read, "I was glad to see Don Alpert's article on Warren Oates. I have followed his career as closely as possible, from Stoney Burke to now. I regret to say, however, that this has been rather difficult as he is very seldom mentioned even in the trade papers, much less in a national publication. I really cannot understand this as surely he is one of the best character actors around and is immediately recognized by most everyone."

He was indeed often recognized, and he was not entirely comfortable with it. Teddy recalled,

> He loved acting, but he didn't want the adoration. We would try to go to Bishop or Mammoth or someplace, and we would stop in the most remote, dinky little café, and there might be two people who looked like they'd never seen a television set or gone to a movie. But they'd take one look at him and they'd go, "I know you. You're that guy," and that would be the end of us being able to just sit down and have a meal. I mean, he enjoyed it once he got into it, but I think it bothered him because he really couldn't have any privacy. And that started way before he was a well-known actor. He just had that kind of face you recognize.

His face was recognized not just by people who looked as if they did not own television sets. "Every now and then he'd come into Schwab's, but then he had to stop because everybody would bug him, come out of the woodwork," Dayton said, referring to would-be and struggling actors. "They were parasites."

Oates did a telephone interview in late summer during which he spoke frankly with the *Louisville Times*' David McGinty. Oates came across brimming with bravado, yet the thread of displacement sneaked in like a kid at a small-town movie theater. Still, he started off strong. "Some people panic in this business but I went through all that about four years ago," Oates told McGinty. "I'm tough as nails now. I'm a hard-hearted so-and-so." He said he felt his portrayal of Colbee in *Return of the Seven* led to his being cast in *In the Heat of the Night*, although that was not the performance that had caught Norman Jewison's eye. He explained that he did not have a publicity person. "My brother thinks I'm a damn fool not to have one," Oates told the paper from the city Gordon Oates called home. He expressed no conflict about playing the parts in which he was typically cast. "If they're heavies, fine," he chortled. "I don't give a whoop and a holler."

McGinty was aware Oates had been married and asked him about it, receiving a reply that referred to Bobbie. Oates labeled "a mistake" his first marriage, which he said had lasted about five months. He allowed that he would return to Louisville for visits, but he insisted, "Like they say, you can't go home again."

Also away from home were a couple of British subjects who meandered into *Cimarron Strip*, a ninety-minute series that gave Stuart Whitman the opportunity to head up a western, a genre about to fall prey to urbanization. Whitman played Marshal Jim Crown, whose jurisdiction is the Oklahoma Panhandle to which the series title refers, and he had a Scottish sidekick, an English barmaid, and a youthful photographer (played by Randy Boone) to keep him company. When the show was reissued in 1996 as ten separate films, Whitman selected "Battleground" as his favorite. The episode, which starred Oates alongside Telly Savalas, Randy Boone, R. G. Armstrong, and L. Q. Jones, has Oates's Mobeetie riding into town on a rail and atop a pig before menacing the Scotsman MacGregor (Percy Herbert) with a cowbell. That the series brought Oates back for another episode, "Nobody," is not unusual, but that his character was repeated is: it meant that, for once, his gap-toothed, villainous nutcase did not die.

Back in his marina abode, Oates got a call from Teddy one evening. She wondered if he could provide airfare for her mother to come to Los Angeles. When "Mamacita" was met by both Teddy and Oates at LAX, she exclaimed, "Oh, I'm so glad you're back together again."

"And so therefore we were," Teddy said. "And back he comes. That lasted maybe three or four months, and then he left again."

By all accounts, the writer John Fante should rank as a soul mate—or at least a kindred spirit—of Warren Oates, but by the time the groundbreaking, hard-drinking author put together a television script with his sometime writing partner Frank Fenton, both men of modern letters were nearer the ground than the height of their powers.

Something for a Lonely Man might have the tinkling-piano title of a dark cocktail bar muted by low clouds of cigarette smoke, but in fact it took its lead from Ralph Waldo Emerson. Its anti–western hero Big John Killibrew, played by Dan Blocker, spouts lines from "Self-Reliance" while pursuing his quest. Oates played Angus Duren opposite Susan Clark, and *Daily Variety* acknowledged that "Warren Oates as Miss Clark's lazy older brother was a standout." The movie eventually aired on NBC at nine o'clock in the evening on December 7, 1968, and garnered respectable ratings, finishing in the top twenty. But Oates was not happy about his role, which was essentially edited out of the ensemble piece's second half.

Tom Nolan, who had appeared with Oates eight years earlier in *Buckskin*, was also in *Something for a Lonely Man*. Nolan talked to Oates about his performance in *In the Heat of the Night*, and Oates told him that a friend had urged him to take out an advertisement about his role in *Something*, a suggestion he laughingly refused. That his failure to do so might have had repercussions troubled Oates not one jot. "He just couldn't follow that line of reasoning," Nolan said.

Between setups, Nolan also spoke with Oates about the Vietnam War. "Warren didn't express a position on the war itself, but he was most insistent, even irate, on the need to recognize and honor the loyal service of young people in the armed services, specifically kids from his old neck of the woods." Oates told him, "Whenever the politicians and the generals decide we have to go fight somewhere, it's those good old boys from where I come from who always sign up first to put themselves in harm's way, no questions asked, and go do what needs to be done, what nobody else is willing to do."

Nolan was returning to acting work after some time away, and Oates was generous in his encouragement to the young man. "After this, you won't have any trouble getting work," were his parting words.

"Horse" might have been the name of Oates's next role, but against preconceptions, this time he was a butcher. In late 1967, the Center Theatre Group began as an offshoot of Los Angeles's Mark Taper Forum, offering a new play every six weeks. Under the auspices of Gordon Davidson, the new group sought to invigorate and modernize theatergoers' experience, and Oliver Hailey's play *Who's Happy Now?* was part of that plan. Hailey, who grew up in Lubbock, Texas, had written a largely autobiographical, inventive work about a nasty man (Horse) who possessed inexplicably redeeming qualities. Given where he was at the time, it was the perfect vehicle for Oates.

During rehearsals, others in the cast—among them Peggy Pope and star Betty Garrett—became exasperated with Oates because he was drinking and missing both rehearsals and lines. But he straightened up for the show. "Warren was wonderful in the part. He was so mean, but at the same time you had to kind of love him," Garrett said. Pope recalled, "There was one very endearing thing Warren did. He'd been doing a lot of mean cowboy films, and he got to do this play, a mean man, but he had something inside him that women . . . There was something about him that was really lovable. It was not an easy part to do, and Warren knew that. He had this history of playing mean characters, so he told the actor Malcolm Atterbury, 'Whenever I get too mean, give me a look.' They arranged this between them. Warren said, 'If I went too far, I'd look over at Malcolm.'"

It worked. The *Los Angeles Times'* Cecil Smith found it a "howlingly funny, darkly desperate probing for the roots of human existence that is an unforgettable experience. It is a beautiful play and beautifully performed and quite the best thing the Center Theatre Group has mounted in its brief tenure in the Mark Taper Forum." Oates handled the part of the beer-loving, song-hating, misogynistic butcher in Sunray, Texas, with aplomb. Smith called it "a marvelously made performance." Oates's character, described in the play's notes as a large, boisterous man in his mid-thirties, was torn between his wife (Garrett) and his love for a waitress, Faye Precious (Pope). The role called for bouts of meanness tempered by crying jags. "I ain't gonna be the only person in this bar drinking! Two is gonna drink!" Horse commands.

Although the play signified a brave and cagey move in what was something of a barren year, the answer to "Who's happy now?" was "not Warren Oates." He was struggling under the failure of his marriage and the resultant separation from his children. "He would talk about [his split] very frankly," Garrett said. "I remember sitting in the bar in the Mark Taper, and he told me

Check Out Receipt

Chester Public Library (CHTP-ZCA)
618-826-3711
www.chester.lib.il.us

Thursday, November 8, 2018 3:02:23 PM
22138

Item: 31205004342349
Title: Practicing Catholic
Material: Book
Due: 11/24/2018

Item: 31205004631006
Title: Warren Oates : a wild life
Material: Book
Due: 11/24/2018

Total items: 2

You just saved $53.00 by using your library. You have saved $924.47 this past year and $1,903.86 since you began using the library!

Thank You!

about the whole thing. He was very upset." Pope, however, was unaware of Oates's personal difficulties. "Warren Oates seemed single to me!" she said. To Garrett, he rationalized his drinking by claiming to be part Arab. "What was his name? Avrum! I remember it because I wrote a risqué limerick about it," Garrett said.

While it might have been William Saroyan's irascible sage from *The Time of Your Life*, the other spirit haunting Oates was clear. "He was a pretty happy drunk on everything except gin," Teddy said, and it was gin that prodded him into a nasty exchange with Teddy. He had had Timothy and Jennifer over the weekend and was heading toward the downtown theater, where he would transfer his four-year-old son and seven-year-old daughter to their mother in the parking lot. Oates was drinking heavily and in a huff. Teddy and her friend Micki had taken a trip to Mexico, and this did not sit well with him. When his wife pulled into the parking lot in her Pontiac Firebird, he was clearly livid.

"Where have you been?" he growled. She explained that she had been to Mexico to deliver some powdered milk to an orphanage for the Sherman Oaks Junior Women's Club.

"I don't believe you," Oates said, certain Teddy and Micki had gone there to meet men.

Teddy insisted that his jealously was both unwarranted and patently ridiculous, but Oates would not let up, saying things the children could not quite hear yet were able to grasp. She drove away with Timothy in the backseat and Jennifer next to her, visibly shaking. "Why don't you find a different man?" her second-grade daughter pleaded.

"He was hurting," Teddy recognized.

Who's Happy Now? ended its scheduled six-week run in mid-December. Christmas was bittersweet for Oates, but he did not reveal that perception to his children. He came to the Van Nuys home late on Christmas Eve to help Teddy assemble the gifts, and he was there the next morning as they marveled at their presents under the tree.

The day after Christmas, the *Los Angeles Times* printed a brief item to the effect that Oates's Pecos Productions was merging with the Muhlenberg County Investment Company, which owned the film rights to Arthur James Halstead's "Blackfire" and another property by William Tinsley. Both his roots and branching out were on Oates's mind.

Also on his mind was attempting to salvage his marriage. Teddy suggested they resume dating, never expecting that the very next day a moving van would appear, filled with his bachelor furnishings. "This is dating?" Teddy wondered. But he stayed in the Marlin Place home for a little over eight months. "He started looking at houses to buy, big, huge houses. And I thought, 'I can't let him buy one of these houses unless I plan to stay.'" The big purchase was put on hold, and again it was Oates who did not stay.

The following year, he would make four movies in a row, including one in which, the *Louisville-Courier Journal* noted, he would have costar billing, "which means above the title, with William Holden, Robert Ryan and [Ernest] Borgnine." He would be so busy in 1968 that he would turn down a three-picture deal with Sergio Leone.

On January 10, Oates appeared in *Run for Your Life* with Ben Gazzara, enlivening the character of psychopathic Deputy Potter, a man who favors bourbon with a beer chaser and does not usually let women buy his drinks. Potter and a fellow policeman (Strother Martin) make life difficult for already hard-pressed Paul Bryan (Gazzara), but Potter is eventually double-crossed into justice. "I was bribed into coming to this state!" Potter cries upon his arrival in California.

In late January, Oates went to a party on a Sunday night at the Factory in Los Angeles after going to the Pro Bowl at Los Angeles Memorial Coliseum. He was not particularly a football fan—sports usually failed to captivate him—but he was playing a safecracker in a football heist caper to be called *The Split*, which had begun filming on January 15 for MGM. The film's star, former football player Jim Brown, sauntered through the nightclub in a white silk Nehru shirt and coral beads, while Oates made less of a fashion statement in bell-bottoms and a dark turtleneck. Gossip columnist Joyce Haber described the party's atmosphere as "wild" before noting it was attended by "at least three girls who strongly resembled Candace [*sic*] Bergen," as well as "Ernie Borgnine, Julie Harris, Diahann Carroll, and Warren Oates."

The Factory was truly a former factory, near the corner of Santa Monica and Robertson Boulevards in what is now West Hollywood. It had been renovated for the then-princely sum of $500,000 and was managed by a man named Ronald Buck. Outfitted with nineteenth-century pool tables, church pews, barber chairs, Italian chandeliers, Indian heads, wood paneling, overstuffed armchairs, old coin games, and stained glass windows, the Factory was the scene for its members and guests who bellied up to the burnished bar. Male bar staff wore blue work shirts and Levi's and were as handsome as they were groovy. Gossip columnists noted the club's prevailing scent of marijuana and the Rolls Royces that waited bumper to bumper to be valet parked.

On February 18, Oates and Teddy were back at the Factory, eating a late-night Sunday dinner. The food was about as heavy as the experience of the bearded hippie selling beads on the main floor. The couple were marking Teddy's twenty-eighth birthday, presenting a celebratory front while drinking pink champagne and eating beef brisket. They were happily interrupted when Stella Stevens, in a slinky gown, stopped by their table with word of the Academy Award nominations. *In the Heat of the Night* had received seven, including for best picture, the blonde actress related. Then Stevens carefully couched her next remark, telling Oates that he was not among the best supporting actor nods.

"Ah, Teddy," Oates said, crestfallen.

Norman Jewison was equally surprised by Oates's exclusion. "We thought he would get a nomination," the director insisted.

The Split was the first theatrical release to receive an R rating. When it premiered at Los Angeles's Vogue Theatre on October 16, 1968, *Soul Illustrated* recommended it as "exciting and intriguing." The *New Yorker* found that it suffered by comparison to Stanley Kubrick's now classic *The Killing*, and *Time* did not mince words when pronouncing it "dreadful." The *Hollywood Reporter*, however, noted that Oates continued to "impress, particularly in a snappy and amusing episode with a harlot."

The Split has a good deal of style, although the fight scenes provide an embarrassment of fake punches. It is a low-budget *Ocean's 11*, but Brown is captivating, and the rest of the cast, including Diahann Carroll, Gene Hackman, and Donald Sutherland, are strong.

The movie ends as McClain (Brown) ponders his escape to Mexico. For Warren Oates, such a decision did not require much thought. And although it was unusual to have an epic Peckinpah turn essentially book-ended by Disney properties, Oates was no stranger to such extremes. A couple of weeks before he left for Mexico, Oates played Cornish immigrant John Blythe in "The Mystery of Edward Sims," a two-part episode of a Walt Disney program centered on a frontier reporter named Gallegher. By the time the show aired on March 31, however, it was not Walt Disney's but rather Sam Peckinpah's wonderful world of color that Oates and others were in up to their necks, and in some cases over their heads.

12

All Sam's Films
Are War Films

As decisions go, it was not one that called for much mulling over. To Teddy, an estranged wife still very much in the picture, the choice was cut and dried. Her husband should stay home in Los Angeles and make another film with Burt Kennedy, "The Sheriff" (which would become *Support Your Local Sheriff*, starring James Garner), rather than run off to a remote location in Mexico with Sam Peckinpah and company.

"No, Warren, do this one," Teddy insisted, about the work that would keep him close to home. She knew how precarious their relationship was and that another separation would end it.

Oates did not equivocate, either. It was not so much that his loyalty to Peckinpah trumped his feelings for his family. There was a wild card: a wonderful script. "He knew that was the better film," Teddy acknowledged of his decision to go with *The Wild Bunch*.

With a sweeping script by Peckinpah and Walon Green, *The Wild Bunch* begins in a 1913 Texas-Mexico border town and follows a dissolute band of men, Pike Bishop, Dutch Engstrom, Lyle and Tector Gorch, and a Mexican national named Angel as they flee south to escape mercenaries led by Deke Thornton. Angel is eventually abducted by General Mapache's bandits, but after brief deliberation, Bishop, Engstrom, and the Gorches demand Angel's release.

Oates's character, Lyle Gorch, has a last name that suggests a rural gap between him and society, but the performance he would give is more understated than his Henry Hammond in *Ride the High Country*, minus the rapidly blinking eyes and brow furrowing that were Oates's equivalent of playing to the rafters. In a pivotal scene, his clouded eyes shift into shard-sharp focus before he says "Why not?" to Bishop's command, "Let's go."

"'Let's go. Why not,' are my two favorite lines in cinema," said British writer Charles Higson. "It might not look like much on paper but for me this is magisterial scriptwriting: the whole meaning of the film condensed into almost nothing." It is also open to a variety of interpretations. When the Bunch attempt to retrieve Angel, is it to honor a moral code or to face certain annihilation, or both? Robert Culp wrote in *Perfect Vision*, "The whole book of Peckinpah's Ecclesiastes burns in Lyle's eyes as he turns back to Bishop and croaks, 'Why not!?' No more words are necessary, just those. And it begins to open for us then, the tragic feeling, the knowledge and the hating it of what they are about to do. They are going to hopeless war against a whole army, just literally throwing their lives away, not to do something noble or selfless as in the case of 'The Seven Samurai' (though they *do* 'save the village' by decimating General Mapache's army, it is completely an irrelevant side issue), but to pay off a mistake, to obliterate their error as Oedipus obliterated his vision."

When he left to make *The Wild Bunch* in mid-March, Oates did not know that he was riding out on his marriage. But Teddy did. "It had a lot to do with my lack of trust, and because I had been on a couple of locations. It would be hard for me to believe that Warren was the only straight arrow there." In just over a month, though he would still fight for it, his marriage would be over.

Ben Johnson's assertion that Peckinpah and Oates were a lethal combination held sway. "Warren liked to party pretty good, and so did Peckinpah, and that was all you needed to start the parties, is have Peckinpah and Warren to get together," the actor who played Oates's brother Tector remembered. Johnson had a great fondness for Oates, who returned his feeling with a healthy shot of respect. They had worked together on several occasions, but it was while making *Major Dundee* that the two very different men became friends. "We got to be pretty good buddies on *Major Dundee* because we spent an awful lot of time in Mexico together, and a lot of pretty rough times down there," Johnson said.

Oates would be late in joining the others in Parras, in the state of Coahuila, Mexico. Located one hundred miles east of Torreon (the nearest thing to a big city), Parras had the requisite desert, ample trees, a river, and a disused vineyard at Hacienda Cienega del Carmen. An earthquake in 1916 had rendered the garden spot a comparative ghost town, which in movie terms made it almost irresistible. Parras had been scouted as a location by Chalo Gonzalez, Peckinpah's right-hand man, driver, and uncle of Peckinpah's wife, Begonia Palacios. Peckinpah gave Gonzalez the script and two thousand dollars. "Find me locations," he instructed. Gonzalez was the first man to be hired; he would also be the last to go. "I knew a teacher who worked for the government and was in charge of all the desert areas in Mexico," Gonzalez said. When Gonzalez returned to Los Angeles, Peckinpah was elated with the findings.

Bo Hopkins was a young actor who had made a few television appearances before being cast in the role of the murderous hothead Crazy Lee. He arrived in Mexico ahead of Oates. "For two days I read his part, and I started to fantasize about it. I'm thinking, 'Damn, if he don't show up, I'd love to play this part,'" Hopkins said. But Oates arrived, and the part of Lyle Gorch was spoken for. Hopkins shared a room with Dub Taylor, while Oates had digs in a huge house with Archie Butler, Ben Johnson, and L. Q. Jones, who was quick to notice that Oates was disappearing a lot. At first he chalked it up to all-nighters, but then the absences grew more frequent, and Jones became an accomplice. He knew Oates was having trouble in his marriage, but at first Oates would not talk about it. "I couldn't help him," Jones said. "We all were trying to help him, but most of us were as screwed up as he was." Soon, however, Oates began to talk. "He'd sit there by the hour jawing about what he was trying to do. Warren was a country boy, and he didn't quite know what to do. He and Teddy got started together. He loved working with Sam, but he also loved Teddy. All you can do is listen, send him out to get drunk, and off you go again."

Off he would go, and there came a point at which he was really gone, not an optimal condition for working on a Peckinpah project. Filming began early and ran late, fourteen to eighteen hours a day. On Saturdays they would wrap around three o'clock, in time for lunch before a party started, culminating in fights—and jail for some. Monday would bring work all over again.

Ben Johnson believed that Oates and Peckinpah were bonded by past sorrows. "Warren opened up to me once or twice in his life, talked about his growing up and a lot of things that had happened to him along the way, and he, like Peckinpah, had had a lot of things happen to him that shouldn't happen to a young guy, and he just never did forget it. Maybe he was trying to get even with somebody along the way, you know?" Johnson said.

What Peckinpah did not realize was how far, literally, Oates was going to save his marriage. "We would have had to bury Sam if he found out what he was doing," Jones said. What Oates was doing, according to Jones, was catching a small plane from Parras to Torreon at seven thirty in the evening, and flying from there to Los Angeles. "He'd see Teddy for literally an hour and then reverse the process and be back the next morning, or maybe at noon. He'd do this three times a week. It was tough, and one of the few times I knew Warren to get really testy." If a plane was delayed, there was a failsafe. "I'd know if Warren was back or not because the body wouldn't be there," Jones explained. "Then I'd go in and b.s. Sam. But Warren was always back. He was sometimes back with thirty minutes to spare, but it didn't make any difference. The only reason I knew was because we were living so close."

That Oates was flying to Los Angeles and back from a remote Mexican location is uncertain. Chalo Gonzalez said there was a two-seater Cessna that Warren would use to fly to Torreon to talk to Teddy by telephone because he could not communicate from Parras. Oates made this trek "for about a week. After that, he stopped doing it, so maybe they patched things up."

To leave at all was risky, but it confirmed Oates's insider status on a Peckinpah film. Traipsing to and fro hurt his performance during the scene in which the Bunch discover that the bounty they have looted from the train station amounts to nothing more than a hill of laundry washers. On that day, however, Oates was not alone in his lack of preparation. None of the actors were ready. After being dressed down by Peckinpah, they shaped up.

By then, Oates had gone native, wearing a serape and a floppy hat and smoking a cheroot. He had hired a local kid to carry his chair around, make sure his drink was full, and secure him a shady spot.

As work on the film outdistanced the irreparable rift at home, Oates fell deeper into his role of Lyle Gorch, a dim and volatile ember of a man who has moments of pathos and empathy. Lyle's childlike aspect is apparent in several scenes, one of which was the actor's favorite. Pike Bishop (Holden), Dutch Engstrom (Borgnine), Angel (Jaime Sanchez), Sykes (Edmond O'Brien), and Tector Gorch (Johnson) are passing around a bottle of whiskey that Lyle does not get until it has been drained of its contents. He is left dry and not high, and he hurls the bottle into the dirt. "That day, that moment even, I made a great step in my progress as a comedian," Oates said about the vignette. "Effectively you could play that scene in different ways. My character realizes that the others, instead of giving him a drink, do something else to him." His chosen reaction, he explained, was gauged so the others would not be goaded into violence, and indeed, Oates's understatement helps provide one of the film's few light-hearted moments.

Touched with a similar innocence but potentially very dangerous was a scene that comes after the Bunch wrests control of the portion of the train transporting the arms shipment. Oates said,

> By then I really knew my character. After I killed off the two soldiers who were sitting on the front of the flatcar, Sam wanted this one shot where I'm supposed to be really enjoying the ride. I pretended I was the engineer like a kid might do and the Mexican engineer always gives a little toot when he's going to move the train. . . . So that's what I did.

Bill Holden, who was riding with the engineer, reached over and floor-boarded the thing and off we went at about 30 miles an hour. I was riding in the cattle car between the engine and a flatcar. As we picked up speed I saw this old man and a little boy sitting in a field watching their sheep. I thought it was beautiful and wished my wife and kids were there.

Then I realized people were yelling and jumping off the train. I looked out the door and saw we were going to hit the flatcar across the bridge. The engineer hit the brakes and they were squealing and sparks were flying, but we were going too fast to stop. I couldn't jump because we were on the bridge over a dry riverbed and it was maybe 30 feet down. We smacked into the flatcar and the car behind us rode up on top of the car I was in. I watched it all happen just like it was in slow motion. Then I jumped off the train and ran down this embankment.

Gordon Dawson said, "I'll be a son of a bitch if Warren didn't pass me saying, 'I beat it again, I beat it again!' And man, he had to run over the arched flatcar, down the side of the embankment to the sandy wash, and then up the stream to pass me. That could have been a major disaster."

"I was alive right then and I knew what that meant," Oates said.

The Wild Bunch was scheduled to allow for seventy days of principal photography and allotted a budget of $3,451,420. Dawson insisted that extra ammunition be sent along to Mexico, and it was justified. Actors were equipped both front and back with squibs—powder capsules hooked up to copper wire sewn into garments and set off by a remote trigger mechanism. The dangers when they exploded were palpable, as Bo Hopkins found out. "They'd been putting wires on me all day, all up my legs and on my chest. They asked me if I wanted to wear a T-shirt, and I said, 'Oh no, I want to feel it so I can react.' Like a dummy, I didn't know they went off and caused blisters."

Oates later said,

In "The Wild Bunch" the first time I ever shot anyone, rehearsal after rehearsal a man kept coming and I kept raising the rifle higher. He said, "I won't do it next time," but sure enough he came in, ten feet away and a piece of that powder hit him in the eye. It takes careful planning when you're dealing with lots of men and horses and equipment and gunpowder, whether it has slugs in it or not. And you never know when these guys are going to charge in . . . or substitute something. It's the inevitable realism that's around Sam's set. It never hurt me. I've been scared a few times but it never hurt me.

Given the intensity and exhaustive nature of the shoot, time away from filming was not entirely fueled by excess. David Weddle writes, "Peckinpah would have occasional bouts with the bottle over the next four months, but only occasional." But as Ben Johnson foretold, Oates and Peckinpah managed to knock a few back. "Drinking was part of the culture," Garner Simmons said. "Today you've got guys having double lattes and thinking they're on the cutting edge, whereas with Sam and Warren, drinking was a way of digging deeper inside yourself and loosing those demons as well as those angels who bring you to a place you wouldn't otherwise be. It's like what Lincoln said about Grant: 'If more of my generals would drink this, I'd buy it by the case.'"

"When Warren was around Peckinpah, why, it was a disaster all the time," Johnson said. "You know, they'd get on the jug, and it was a continuous party. It was a bad scene when they both got together. . . . I kept both of them from getting killed a thousand times, I guess." Chalo Gonzalez had been observing the camaraderie between Oates and Johnson. "Warren and Ben Johnson were different. Warren thought crazy things, and Ben Johnson, he didn't drink much. Warren did, but they were very good friends. They agree about everything, mostly when they talk about acting. Both of them had the same answer: 'It beats working.'" And it probably did when it came to a scene involving the disused winery and, in particular, a wine vat. The Gorch brothers decamp there with three women from the village, and both Tector and Lyle shoot holes in wine barrels and soak in their showers. Oates said,

They had cast these three rather rotund ladies from the neighborhood, and Ben Johnson and I knew they were shy and backward and we had to do a scene with them. We were shooting in a bodega or distillery. The distillery had been closed down by the government, but they had left behind cases upon cases of brandy that had just been agin' and agin' and some rather sour wine which we *didn't* get into.

But we got into the brandy and we literally helped the ladies get into it and loosened them up quite a bit. By the time we went on to do that scene, we were all rather loose-lipped and the ladies didn't care and we certainly enjoyed ourselves. We weren't disrespectful to them: we just all had a good time.

The scene came off well. Then later on we had to get 'em into the wine vat, so we thought if the brandy worked once, it'd certainly work again. So when the three ladies showed up, we just started on 'em with the brandy about two hours ahead of the scene, and it certainly did work out well.

I remember one lady did a slow roll-over in that vat and she looked like an enormous whale surfacing. What appeared was a pair of big synthetic fiber aqua-blue tights on her massive buttocks. Of course they couldn't use that scene and we had to do it over again. Even the Mexican censor enjoyed it but he wouldn't allow us to keep it in.

A waterlogged moment in which Tector Gorch pulls out one of his female companions' breasts and measures her nipple against his thumb was also axed. Although Ben Johnson later laughed off the wine vat episode, allowing that his wife never let him return to Mexico, it shores up something Bo Hopkins said about Johnson. "Ben had a quiet mischievousness about him," Hopkins insisted of the man Oates would compare to the White Knight of the Holy Grail.

Johnson also had his hands full in other aspects. "When we were in Mexico, we kind of relayed Peckinpah," he said. "I took care of him awhile, and then Warren would take care of him, to keep somebody from killing him or something." Peckinpah needed most of all to be saved from himself. Oates said,

Sam . . . had a bad case of the piles. Bloody. And he was working in a lot of dust. He wouldn't quit, he wouldn't take the time to get it [treatment] done, because I think he felt that they would fire him. So he stuck there. And he'd climb up on the camera and you could see all the way down the side of his leg this red, brown, dusty, bloody, stinkin,' smellin' mess that would drain out of him. But he fuckin' wouldn't quit. They wanted him to go to the hospital and take it out, but he said uh-uh. Finally they persuaded him to see a specialist because he wouldn't let anybody there do it.

The specialist came on a Sunday afternoon, when friends gathered at the large home Peckinpah was renting. They walked in past a mariachi that had been hired to play softly outside his window, commencing wistfully at ten o'clock that morning.

Peckinpah told the doctor that he would agree to the procedure if it could be done in the kitchen by a kerosene lamp, with the promise that he would be back at work on Monday. The doctor insisted a hospital visit was necessary, and Peckinpah refused. "He went through the whole fuckin' movie like that," Oates marveled. "He'd get a shot in the ass for pain, or whatever, and that son of a bitch stuck up there every day. Finally it began to clear up toward the end of the picture . . . but the incredible fight that man has . . ."

After eighty days and, astoundingly, only twenty-five accident reports, actors, crew, horses, ants, scorpions, vultures, and a dark-eyed, defeated bird on a length of string were spent. The epic intensity had flailed right down to a whittled hush. With shooting over, Peckinpah was said to have wandered to a quiet spot on the set, inconsolable.

Working on *The Wild Bunch* was, Oates said upon his return to America, "the toughest thing I ever did." The crew and cast "probably had to work twice as hard as they were used to." But, he added, "I don't think I have ever been in a movie or any aspect of my life where I have had so much excitement, joy, or sadness than the four months we worked on that film." He told the *Hollywood Reporter*, "Sam's a perfectionist and when you're in the boonies for four months, tempers get short. Pressure was brought because of the way we shot. Every shot Sam made was with three cameras, one a wide lens for a master shot, another for a medium, and another for a closeup. The grips, wardrobe, everybody, had to jump double time because when we moved into a medium we were still shooting with three cameras. Even while Sam was breaking down the action, the cameras were still encompassing a wide area, a lot of overlapping action."

Back in Los Angeles in time for his fortieth birthday, Oates was exhausted but circumspect. "This is the lesson I learned in Mexico," he said: "When man leaves the society he's dependent on and faces the basic essentials, he changes faces and becomes more peaceful, a wiser man, a happier man."

Ten years later, Oates was asked if he had ever acted in any war films. He did not miss a beat. "All Sam's films are war films," he responded.

What *The Wild Bunch* meant to cinema is oversize. What it meant to popular culture is immeasurable; its impact reverberates. For Oates, the role of Lyle Gorch was not necessarily career making, but it was certainly life altering. He would spend the remainder of his life cultivating or recapturing the camaraderie he had felt over the seventy days he was on set. If his companions fell short, fell asleep, or were otherwise unavailable, Oates felt bereft. The loss Sam Peckinpah experienced alone on the soundstage was something Oates would always seek to fill.

The film was ruthlessly edited by the studios, and casualties included a flashback in which Pike Bishop is crippled, a scene in which Thornton and Pike are trapped in a bordello, and Mapache's army battling Pancho Villa's men. Oates said,

The flashback scenes, I don't know if they had a great deal of significance to the film. It may have said something about the relationship between Bill Holden and Robert Ryan, but I don't think it promoted the film, the structure, and the story. I think one enormous battle sequence with the Federales and Pancho Villa [was cut]. There was a great deal of care and concern put into that sequence because it was taken from old

photos of the Mexican Revolution. . . . I think the train station was cut out of the film in some states in order to insert
a cartoon! They chopped that out, and I couldn't understand
it, you know?

Oates was about to decompress by making a G-rated film for
Disney. In the time he had been away, his marriage had collapsed,
and *In the Heat of the Night* had won five Academy Awards,
including best picture and, for Rod Steiger, best actor. Martin
Luther King Jr. and Robert F. Kennedy had been assassinated,
and the Democratic National Convention would soon turn into a
deadly melee between protestors and the Chicago police force.

Oates spent less than a month at his apartment in the marina
before heading out again, barely enough time to grasp the pieces
of his failed marriage. The divorce settlement was being finalized,
and there were stocks to be divided: twenty-five shares of Standard Oil, one hundred of World Airways, and fifty in Foremost
Dairies. An outstanding $594 on a Baldwin piano would have to
be paid, as well as incidental doctor and dentist bills. Child support and alimony were being worked out.

Against expectations, Oates's next film attempted to deal
with weightier issues than the standard Disney fluff. It follows
a rancher, Smith (Glenn Ford), in whose outback shack a young
Indian suspected of murder has taken to hiding. Smith believes
the young man to be innocent and takes up his cause. The project had the participation of the Indian Actors Workshop of
Hollywood, which had been established by native actor Jay Silverheels (who would play McDonald Lasheway in the film) as a
casting office for American Indian actors who, as late as 1968,
were just beginning to be placed in roles previously occupied by
Anglos or, occasionally, Latinos. Acting classes were held in the
Echo Park Methodist Church, and several actors from the workshop would appear in the project, which downsized in title from
"Breaking Smith's Quarterhorse" to "Everybody Loves Smith"
to its eventual release as *Smith!* One role not filled by a native
actor was that of "conniving Indian" Walter Charlie, played by
Oates.

Oates overplayed Walter Charlie but calmed down when required, and his Salish was serviceable. (Overall, Oates's utterances in Native American languages outpaced his often exasperating attempts at Spanish.) *Smith!* is a likeable enough message movie, but Rex Reed in *Holiday* magazine saw it differently. "The movie insults Indians by portraying them as childlike, simpleminded creatures incapable of taking care of even their most basic needs. . . . Somebody should teach Indians how to sue."

Oates was working nonstop, partly because he had hired "a personal manager, a publicity man, and a business manager to control my life because I was very confused," he said. None of these employees would be advised to rest easily: Oates was notoriously lackadaisical about the business side of his career. When he returned from Mexico, he found a script pushed under his door. He read it with increasing unease—he did not think the part or the project was right for him. Yet he agreed to make the film. "I thought, 'What the hell, it's in England,' and just came over and did it," he told *Films Illustrated*.

Oates went to England in the fall of 1968, when the country was not so much swinging as reveling in psychedelia. The movie he would make, *Crooks and Coronets*, was not a reflection of mid-1960s London, however; it was almost as if that part of the decade had yet to happen. Instead *Crooks and Coronets* (also known as *Sophie's Place*) was an attempt to re-create an Ealing comedy, classic 1940s and 1950s British cinema exemplified by films like *The Lavender Hill Mob* and *The Ladykillers*. Unfortunately, its script, by director Jim O'Connolly, and its overall sensibility fell wide of the mark. Subtle it was not.

Oates played Marty Miller, a smalltime gangster who joins his partner in crime, Herbie Hassler (Telly Savalas), in a scheme to rob a stately home. *Crooks* was filmed over a period of two weeks at Shepperton Studios in Teddington and at Cliveden, a lavish home and grounds that were part of Lord Astor's estate near Maidenhead in Buckinghamshire. The film also featured Dame Edith Evans (as Lady Sophie Fitzmore), a doyenne of British acting known primarily for her role as Lady Bracknell in Oscar Wilde's *The Importance of Being Earnest*. "She's great," Oates raved. "She's so old but she's young. She thinks and talks and acts like a girl, but it isn't a put-on. It's just her. She's wonderful."

Nicky Henson played the young Lord Freddie Fitzmore, a nice but somewhat dim minor royal who invites Marty and Herbie to stay on at the home, Great Friars, and help devise a security system for it. Henson was starring in a West End rock musical version of *The Canterbury Tales* and was collected each morning, bleary eyed after performances that bled into wee-hours socializing. Henson was alert enough to notice the disparity between friends Oates and Savalas, who would become a huge star in the United States and the United Kingdom's first American television superstar as lollypop-loving detective Kojak. "Warren was in awe of everything the way Telly wasn't," Henson said. "You had this brash, confident, not very talented man and this very talented, shy, polite man, Warren Oates. Warren Oates was extremely polite and in awe of the English actors, particularly Edith Evans."

A pert and pretty young British actress named Vickery Turner played Annie. She had heard of Savalas but not Oates, but that would change. Savalas got to keep the picture's blue Rolls Royce, but Oates went home with the girl. "It was a huge shock that Warren Oates and Vickery got together," Henson said. Yet after watching the film, it becomes less outlandish that the lass from one of England's home counties took up with the Kentucky-to-Hollywood hillbilly. Oates's character, Marty Miller, flashes an eager grin when Turner's Annie offers him "Cake, sir?" A naughty postcard vignette in which Annie milks a cow while Miller gets a gander at her comely gams is equally unrestrained. By the movie's penultimate scene, Turner and Oates are wedged together side by side, dressed to the nines, with Oates's arm around his future bride's tiny waist as they stroll offscreen.

Christine Hazel Turner was born on April 3, 1940, in Sunbury, Surrey, a southern suburb of London. She was briefly a reporter for the provincial newspaper, the *Croydon Advertiser*, before deciding to become an actress. After earning her place in the Royal Academy of Dramatic Art, she made her 1963 London stage debut at the National Theatre in *The Crucible*, directed by Laurence Olivier. To wider English audiences, she became familiar after she played Eileen in Ken Loach's version of the seminal novel *Up the Junction* by Nell Dunn.

Vickery Turner, as she was now known, was blonde and adorable. She was also driven, sharp, and multitalented: in 1965 her play *Keep on Running*, about youthful romance and sexual inequality, was produced on BBC Television—no small feat for a woman working against the old boy network. It was unexpected that this English rose grafted with a whisper of London Lolita would see something in a decidedly American actor from the fertile hills of Kentucky, but when they parted, it was with the understanding that she would be joining him in Hollywood. A few days before, Oates had made a call to Armand Alzamora with a curious edict. "I need you to help me find a house. I've got a new English wife," Oates instructed.

On November 5, which Vickery would have noted was Guy Fawkes Day, Oates had his own fireworks and ashes to deal with. He was served with final settlement papers: Each of his children would receive $150 per month in child support from him. Teddy, for whom his feelings were more complicated, had been awarded $700 per month in alimony.

Before the end of 1968, Oates made a trip to Louisville with Timothy, now five, and Jennifer, eight, in tow. While there, he met Dudley Saunders from the *Louisville Times* for an interview at the Brown Hotel. The meeting did not get off to the best start. Saunders explained,

> Hands jammed deep in his pockets and looking a bit sleepy, Oates had plowed into the hotel lobby and apologized for being 15 minutes late for a luncheon interview. The interviewer, still puffing himself, admitted he had been 14 minutes late. Newsman and actor traded tales about the young day's woes between lobby and restaurant.
>
> A mug of draft beer arrived and Oates ordered a corned beef sandwich. . . . Oates bit into [the] sandwich and ordered another draft. He was beginning to relax.

Oates told Saunders, "If things keep going the way they are now,

I'd like to buy a little farm back here, have a couple of horses, and start living like a human being between pictures." This was the beginning of a professional relationship in which Oates often expressed feelings and opinions he kept more sequestered from the Los Angeles press corps. Perhaps it was Saunders's comfortable, insightful writing style. It is also very likely Oates let down his guard a little because he felt close to home. Saunders would touch base with Oates for the rest of the actor's career, observing that his acquaintance was always courteous but rarely totally at ease.

"I've done four pictures this year, one right after the other, and I'm worn out," Oates said. Saunders noted that his subject spoke with "only the slightest hint of the country accent he uses in most of his character roles. Some of his expressions are pure Kentucky, but only a speech authority could pin down his accent. He is slender, medium tall and not as big or burly as he appears on screen." Oates continued, "I used to feel I had to take any job that came along. But now I can pick and choose. I can say no today and know that somebody else will offer me a part tomorrow. Right now, I'm interested in branching out into different roles and getting away from being typecast." This confidence was forged from a year's steady, to say nothing of diverse and groundbreaking, work. But he was also rethinking the business side of his career. He explained, "I fired the business manager in London and took on a new one. I've got to go back to California to replace the agent. I think I've got a good press agent."

What he did not say was that Vickery Turner had a hand in these dealings. "When I met Vickery . . ." he began telling Kevin Thomas of the *Los Angeles Times*. "I took over," Vickery finished.

Oates concluded his luncheon with Saunders by saying he planned to go skiing and skin diving and sail his four-ton boat, the *Yonder*. Presumably he planned to do all these activities on the same day. He would be back in Los Angeles for only the briefest time before going to the Mojave Desert to make a movie called, at that point, "The Prison Story."

But Oates was in a reflective mood, and he decided to go to

Depoy for the first time in more than twenty years. He took Timothy and Jennifer, as well as his brother Gordon and Gordon's two sons, Robert and Gordon Jr. They drove first to the white weatherboard house where Warren and Gordon had been children. "My children got bored quickly," Oates said. "They went out picking hickory nuts and dropping them in the creek, and playing in the churchyard across the creek like we did."

Early in the new year, 1969, Oates typed a letter—writing a letter at all was rare for him—to his ex-wife, telling of a visit to a couple of their friends, after a fashion. He started it "From You Know Where, CAL, Sunny Wed, 1969," but amended, "Forget WED, it is Rainy Monday duh 20." He continued,

> Hello my little DARLING,
>
> I have been off on a toot. That's Irish for singing in the streets and then when the cops come and pick you us [sic]. I visited with WES BISHOP at FRASCATTIS Wed. at the usual hour and plyed [sic] myself generously with strong drink. The table got smaller as more folks arrived, the conversation louder, and hour later and everyone hungrier and all split to do their thing I to the Raincheck to dine sumptuously on steak. . . . Somebody came by on a crutch and mentioned skiing. Well that's all I needed—a reminder—at 3.30am I was on my way. Bob Ginter and Sally had more room than they could use so of course I stayed with them. My room was on the first floor and I had a marvelous view of great mounds of snow that might be considered cars. They were very surprised to see me at 9.30 Thursday morning. I was too tired to enjoy anything but bed and sleep Thursday after the long drive and too exhilarated to rest properly. They went on to the slops [sic] and left me with a steaming cup of coffee and staring at a roaring fire.

If he could have seen his future in that fire, it would have looked equally compelling.

13

Leaving No Turn Unstoned

Warren Oates had one showpiece song that he played on his guitar, which he had had various cohorts sign as if it were a stuffed toy autograph hound. There is no way to know what the melody was, but the lyrics, which he wrote "a little crocked one morning at 4am," went like this:

I'm a careless heart, a wandering lover
and there ain't no way I'll settle down
the diesels whine way over yonder
and the mystery of that other town.

Match that restlessness with a touch of reverie and no fixed abode, and you have a lonely, wandering soul searching for a whole lot of twin cities. What Oates needed was a mobile space for his journeys.

Detroit had an answer. It might have been anathema to Volkswagen van–driving hippies and camping purists, but for Oates the recreational vehicle was anthemic mobile heaven. Once the twenty-eight-foot Open Road entered his life, it never left. He decked it out with Indian rugs and blankets, a cow's skull next to incense burning atop the dashboard, and an eagle feather hanging from the rearview mirror. In the back was a bed covered by a pinto hide.

"Warren's numerology number was a five. That's the traveling number," Teddy said. "And it never fit anybody like it fit Warren

Oates. I mean, he was a traveler. He wanted to go, go, go, go, go. And not to get away from anything, but just to go toward things, you know? Just to see as much as he could, fast as he could."

Oates had at least two Open Roads, one with a brown stripe and a blue one, but they had the same name. Each was christened the Roach Coach. The roof he had outfitted with twin domes, like the poached-egg eyes of his *Outer Limits* character, so he and a passenger could perform the cowboy change—switching drivers without stopping—or stand up while in motion. More than once, Oates left the wheel while driving to go to the back and retrieve a beverage or two. In the Roach Coach there would be music playing, classical or country, as Oates loved Merle Haggard, Waylon Jennings, and Willie Nelson.

In late 1969 Oates already had both a 1960s hangover and a strong anticipation of the 1970s, a decade for which he was ready. The style and tempo of the 1970s would suit him to a T, just as one of its primary predilections would as good as kill him. "In the '70s it was not uncommon for people to say that having cocaine was like drinking a glass of very nice champagne," Garner Simmons said. How the drug found its way into Peckinpah's and Oates's lives is irrelevant. One Peckinpah biographer singles out Oates as bringing the drug to his friend's attention, but that is a little like bringing mountains to Montana. By the mid-1960s, cocaine was available in both Hollywood and the back of beyond.

As usual, Oates was a fixture at the Raincheck Room. The bar's proximity was a contributing factor to his selection of a temporary home in a towering white skyscraper on the Sunset Strip. In late 1968 he had moved to 1147 Horn Avenue, where, Teddy insisted, their son almost fell off the balcony.

Oates also went to the movies, including one in which he had lost the lead. "'Cable Hogue' was done as if you and I were in Denver, Colorado in 1863 and we went into the opera house to see an opera," Oates said. "And this happens to be an opera about the West. It's almost an intimate stage play. . . . That's an element of Sam that I think is genius. If you haven't seen 'Cable Hogue' you've missed maybe his pure soft being." Garner Simmons commented, "I find it interesting that Warren saw himself as that character, his ability to see himself as a leading man. It's something he saw in himself."

Oates was in frequent touch with Vickery Turner via transatlantic phone calls. His new lady was writing a script about women's liberation called "Trust in God." In it, a group of women embark on a series of bombings at such locales as strip bars and the Playboy Club. "Men don't understand what the women's liberation movement is all about," she said. "They're either frightened by it, or amused, or bored." Or they might adopt her future husband's cant: "All I know is that there are too many and I am too old," he replied, when asked for his opinion on the women's movement. Clearly, Oates and Vickery were not reading from the same feminist manifesto.

But Oates had the opportunity to apply his political conscience when Robert Culp invited him to a screening of a documentary he had had made with partial backing from his friend Bill Cosby. (Culp had been hoping to work with Oates and Peckinpah on a project about two men aboard a World War II surplus PT boat in the Caribbean, but Peckinpah's volatile relationship with Warner Brothers sank the ship.) The documentary, *Operation Breadbasket*, was shown at screenwriter-director Richard Brooks's house in Hollywood. "It was a bit of a polemic, about black economics in the United States, and I showed it to a bunch of attorneys," Culp explained. He also asked Oates, whom he had not seen in a while, to come over and see it. When a few viewers began to question the legitimacy of the film's position, Oates reacted quickly. "Why don't you just give the guy a chance, for Christ's sake? Look, it's his picture; he's made it. Be quiet and respectful of this whether you agree with it or not." Culp was touched by his friend's efforts. "I think he may very well have disagreed with a lot of stuff that was in the film, but he made this impassioned speech. I was astounded. I'd never heard him open his mouth like that before."

Oates's politics veered from self-professed conservative anarchism to occasional moral outrage. "I guess I'm a conservative radical. I used to be a conservative anarchist but I've reduced it now," he said. "I don't believe that anybody can run my life but myself, or ruin it either." But when it came to political issues, he usually did not take a stand. "Actors aren't citizens, they're observers, the freest people in the world because of that. They're above politics." But he eventually adopted a favorite, vaguely reactionary saying, "In the Old West they didn't have food stamps," and expressed pleasure at the controversy *The Wild Bunch* stirred up. "It shocked the hell out of a lot of moralistic weirdo pinko liberals."

But when *The Wild Bunch* became the subject of a protest by Nosotros, a newly formed Latino activist group, Oates was drawn in more intelligently. "I feel that some of the protest by Mexican-American groups is justified, in fact, much of it is justified," he said. "I feel it is the fault of the semi-intellectual community that writes about or makes films about Mexico, or hillbillies, or any specific group of people that does not *belong* to their semi-intellectual community. The clichéd Mexican or the clichéd southerner or the clichéd anyone is not a full man," he said. "We represented these people in some cases as idiots and I don't blame them for protesting." Yet Oates also defended *The Wild Bunch*, which he believed "did *not* misrepresent anybody because many of the scenes were roughly akin to photographs. . . . The women *did* carry guns and they *did* nurse their babies while they were carrying bandoliers across their bodies, with their breasts hanging out between the cross points of the bandoliers."

Meanwhile, Vickery was about to arrive in the United States, and Oates had already told her he expected her to get along with the mother of his children. Fortunately, the young woman from the rainy isle had a sunny disposition. Still, there would be times when she would express, albeit indirectly, that she felt a little like "the second Mrs. DeWinter."

Before Vickery would see Manderley, Oates was off to the Mojave. The night before he was to arrive there on location, Oates was in the Raincheck. Howard Dayton, who had reverted to driving a cab for a living, also stopped in and found his old friend drinking, laughing, and pursuing the ladies. The night wore on, and Oates became worried that he would sleep through any wake-up call. With his arm around a woman, he suggested Dayton drive him in the cab to Indio, and Dayton agreed. Somewhere east of Banning, Dayton heard the unmistakable sounds of amour coming from the backseat of his cab. He dropped Oates and his lover in Indio and then made the drive back to Los Angeles, where Oates's agent paid him two hundred dollars. Dayton promptly gave his dispatcher fifty dollars not to ask why he had not logged any other fares.

In the desert, a four-acre set replete with guards' barracks, warden's office, mess hall, kitchen, hospital, blacksmith shop, mule shed, solitary confinement cell, gallows, and seven guard towers had been built in Joshua Tree National Monument (now a national park), the first development to occur within the park's boundaries. The set, designed by Edward Carrere, included fourteen buildings surrounded by a wall that was twenty feet high and four feet thick. The structures were built to last, to withstand both aerial filming by helicopter and desert storms, the latter of which had obliterated the first attempt at construction. The sprawling complex took seven weeks to build, and because of park restrictions, native sage, ocotillo, Joshua trees, and creosote bushes had to be trucked in to flesh out the scenery. In addition, a large rock pile outside the walls required eighty truckloads of rocks collected from the surrounding desert.

There Was a Crooked Man was the work of producer-director Joe Mankiewicz, and the four-time Academy Award winner was content with the location. "I always said when I got around to a Western, I wanted it to be shot near Palm Springs," he said. The proximity of exaggerated comfort may have affected the project's authenticity, though. Written by David Newman and Robert Benton, who had scripted *Bonnie and Clyde*, this so-called cynical western about a particularly duplicitous prison break gives off a surreal sheen as natural as studio suntans. Oates alone looks real, a flesh-and-blood alien moving among Plasticine androids.

Making his third film in a year for Warner Brothers, Oates was in a good humor for on-site press interviews, buoyed by the knowledge that Vickery would soon be joining him. Alzamora would drive her to the high desert, regaling his passenger with tales of his thwarted acting career. "Things are looking up," he would say. "My agent got a phone." Oates and Vickery were reunited among the desert vegetation, which Oates took to. They counted stars and reveled in the preserve's otherworldly offerings. In the future, they would revisit Joshua Tree in a variety of mind-sets, but one of them would always be love.

Oates was Vickery's man of the hour, although some doubted her motives. Alzamora said, "I think Vickery was impressed with this American actor unlike any other who'd been sent over to England to appear in this film [*Crooks and Coronets*]." He believed that Vickery was acutely aware that Oates could aid her professional pursuits, including providing her with a green card.

At the location, Vickery was understandably captivated. "Henry Fonda was a very elegant, gracious man who painted watercolors," she recalled of one of *Crooked*'s leading men. Of the other, Kirk Douglas, she noted, "The crew had fixed up a white picket fence, artificial turf, and a birdbath around Kirk's trailer. It was a sort of humorous deference to his royalty."

One of the film's attempts to cater to changing tastes was the casting of Michael Blodgett, a young renegade actor who would attempt to increase the film's hipness. Prone to excess, Blodgett made an impression on Vickery. "One night Michael Blodgett went out and had too much of something and ended up bathing naked in Kirk's birdbath," she said.

Blodgett was not alone in his misadventures. One day Vickery and Oates joined an outing in Indio. As they said their goodbyes in an alleyway, police cars appeared, hemming in the entire group. They were all taken to the police station, but Oates and Vickery, innocent bystanders, were released without charge. "Apparently one of the crew had started growing marijuana plants in his motel garden," Vickery explained.

In *There Was a Crooked Man*, captured outlaw Paris Pitman Jr. (Douglas) plots a prison escape to unearth $500,000 in robbery money he has buried in a nest of rattlesnakes. Pitman tells the inmates and anyone else who will listen about his secret stash. Among the incarcerated is Floyd Moon (Oates), whom Pitman befriends and then kills in his breakout. *Films and Filming* liked the movie, noting that "the Arizona Territorial Prison is filled with more characters of variable eccentricity than 'Grand Hotel.' Mankiewicz knows it and hams it up to the highest Arizona heavens." In early scenes, Floyd Moon goes high-desert native in a slightly psychedelic poncho. (Douglas, by contrast, looks as if he has just stepped out of a St. Tropez discotheque.) Moon is mute for the film's first forty minutes. The pseudohip script did not help Oates's performance, and *Crooked*'s mores are outdated. There are a few flashes of appealing ensemble acting, and the leads are reliable, but in terms of writing, it cannot compare to *Bonnie and Clyde*.

After the wrap, Vickery's commitments took her back to England; Oates went to Los Angeles. They spent a brief time together in Oates's new, and first real, home, a converted pool house high atop Briar Knoll off Mulholland Drive. The house at 2961 Briar Knoll Drive was as significant to Oates as the Roach Coach was, and the lot's rustling trees contributed to its sense of languid movement. The house, purchased for thirty thousand dollars, provided a rustic lookout over the San Fernando Valley, and its grounds featured a hillside garden and a pool larger than the floor plan. The wood-framed structure had a small shotgun kitchen that adjoined the living room, one bedroom, and one bath. Part of a larger estate (Robert Vaughn lived in the lower, bigger house and had access to the estate's tennis courts), Oates's secluded dwelling was modest and unassuming, yet it had a quiet, welcoming largesse, and he loved it down to the ground. "The house is modern California—that's the way I describe it," Oates proudly said. There was a fence around its perimeters, and from the road outside, it was difficult to see. He had bought it furnished but had begun to augment the interior in a style that was western, hippie, and eclectic. In the bathroom there was natural (for the time) Neutrogena soap, and in the kitchen there were bottles of booze and vitamins, if not always food.

It was "one of the most beautiful June weddings," columnist Dorothy Manners gushed. "Talk about a romantic setting: all of the 500 guests gathered on a sandy white beach at sunset were laden with garlands of tropical flowers of every hue. Instead of exchanging rings, the [bride and groom] gave each other flowers when it came time to say 'I do.'"

On a beach during the summer solstice at sunset, forty-year-old Warren Oates embraced his twenty-nine-year-old bride, Vickery. Invited guests—apart from the five hundred who were mostly press people on a publicity junket for the Warner Brothers/Seven Arts Film Festival due to begin on June 28—stayed at the Kings Inn Hotel on Grand Bahama Island. Gordon Oates flew in from Kentucky, arriving before his brother did, and took charge of entertaining his future sister-in-law. In a bar Gordon ordered a perfect Rob Roy on the rocks, which captivated Vickery. "I'd never heard of such a fancy title for a drink before," she said. "Gordon was a very conventional older brother, a businessman, quiet and polite, very kind to me."

When the younger Oates brother arrived, he began looking for a maid of honor. He enlisted sexy Stella Stevens, who had recently finished playing the paramour in *The Ballad of Cable Hogue*. "I unfortunately didn't know Warren Oates very well at all when he asked me to be maid of honor," Stevens said. "I would have liked to get to know Warren better, but he was marrying another woman."

The wedding felt entirely cinematic, with Ben Johnson tentatively watching the ceremony over a hedge. Now on his third marriage, Oates had formed a habit of getting married in unusual settings: the quaint and picturesque Duncan Memorial Chapel, the exotic melee of a raucous Mexican border town, and now with the gentle azure surf lapping at his heels. But he had never before wed with a view to his career. "Crook Duo Marries," reported the *Cleveland Plain Dealer*.

A wire service Hollywood reporter, Dick Kleiner, was on the story as well, observing that "Julie Shaw, Louisville TV personality, made a Kentucky toast involving horses, whiskey, and women. I said that it wasn't necessary to toast her [Vickery]—her new initials made her a walking toast." In a lengthy article, Oates turned his thoughts away from his nuptials and told Kleiner, "I would have liked to have lived in the '20s and gone to Paris and hobnobbed with all the American expatriates. I have a yen to write—I did two pages of a novel and started the third, but just stared at that blank piece of paper for three days."

The wedding generated ink, including a glamorous layout in a French fashion magazine. Several papers reported on the couple's eighteen-hour honeymoon, but in fact Oates and Vickery stayed a couple of days on Paradise Island before the film festival began.

On June 28, *The Wild Bunch* was screened in the Bahamas for a coterie of Warner Brothers stars and reviewers. The reaction was electric and diverse. Clint Walker felt the killings were unrealistic. "I've seen people die," the man who had played Yellowstone Kelly said, "and they don't die like that." Kim Novak also had reservations because of the film's perceived cruelty to horses. Bryan Forbes and Danny Kaye, the director and one of the stars of *The Madwoman of Chaillot*, walked out on Peckinpah's masterpiece. "Imagine walking out on that great film," Stella Stevens said, "and then they show a piece of junk like 'Madwoman.'"

Oates said, "The ladies, all these critics and people who'd flown in there for this, half of them booed and stormed and screeched and shouted when 'The Wild Bunch' was on. It pissed Sam off something fierce; he got up and yelled at them, or whatever he did. Essentially, his innocence, his perfection, his attitude toward films and what makes them exciting, got a negative vote that day from all these people. And I think that hurt him deeply. It pissed him off, and it frustrated him."

Critics were largely negative, but crucially, Roger Ebert of the *Chicago Sun-Times* defended the film, giving an impassioned speech about its significance. The *Independent Film Journal* examined *The Wild Bunch* next to a review of *The Maltese Bippy*, a fluff piece spun off from television's Rowan and Martin's *Laugh In*. Of *The Wild Bunch*, the reviewer calmly concluded that "its many merits should ultimately triumph over the roar of controversy."

After the film festival, Warren Oates left the Bahamas in advance of his new bride, who stayed behind for visa reasons. Abe Greenburg of the *Los Angeles Westside Citizen* described the departing groom as "disconsolate." But if he had only newsprint to keep him warm for the next few days, he was considerably better covered than in the past. In early July, as the press had duly noted, he had another movie to make, this time in Colorado. On *Barquero* he would have his new partner along for the ride: the Roach Coach.

Life seemed full as a blue moon when Oates headed east in the Roach Coach, Vickery at his side and Jennifer and Timothy in the back, starting their summer vacation. When they stopped along the way, Oates, with wizened face and grizzly beard, would be complimented on his three adorable children: perky Jennifer, curly-haired Timmy, and pixyish Vickery.

In Colorado, they stayed in a big house in Florence, a former silver mining town, while the remainder of the cast were situated in a motel across town. When her husband was working, Vickery immersed herself in the children's lives, walking them down the street to the public swimming pool and keeping them entertained. The big house with its antique furniture spooked Jennifer. "I was on the third floor, and I saw a giant, giant moth. It was probably a three-inch moth but I was convinced that they grew moths bigger in Colorado," she remembered. Vickery did her best to assuage Jennifer's fears. Timothy and Jennifer took to their stepmother instantly. "She was so young, and very, very sweet. I really liked her," Jennifer said, despite finding it perplexing that Vickery poured ketchup on her eggs.

Armand Alzamora was playing a minor part in the film, which had begun on a tragic note. While scouting locations on July 13, the pilot of the small plane hit a butte, and the plane flipped four times, eventually crashing and killing both the pilot and the director, Gerald Finnerman. Location scout Robert Sparr was hospitalized. The precarious budget meant the film might be axed, but Gordon Douglas was secured as director.

Barquero starred Lee Van Cleef. Mariette Hartley, who worked with Oates in *Stoney Burke* and *Ride the High Country*, also appeared in the film. Her sophisticated yet homespun allure is undeniable, putting her in sharp contrast to costar supervixen Marie Gomez. "Between Marie Gomez and me, it was the concave and the convex," said Hartley, whose bosom Peckinpah had

once ordered to be padded. Hartley did not feel the cast camaraderie. "I drank a little, but I didn't smoke [pot]. I felt very isolated
because I wasn't doing that, or drinking. I wouldn't be invited
because nobody wants somebody around who's not doing it."

John Davis Chandler had driven to Colorado with his new
wife. "It was a wonderful location," Chandler said. "Gordon
Douglas heading up the whole thing, there was never a cross
moment." The movie, oddly, was an exercise in mean-spiritedness,
one part druggy nightmare, another part western.

It also featured Oates's nearest thing to a nude scene, about
which the notoriously bashful actor was not pleased. "They got us
both nude but they'd never dare to photograph it," Oates growled
after the fact. "They never dared to push the camera down." He
continued, "I don't agree with nude pictures. You would think
that America is more advanced than to need dirty films to satiate
perverted desires, but we aren't. We're just like everybody else
only fortunately we don't have any heavy thing saying you can't
make this film and you can't show it. In their minds they're doing
something spicy, and it's just a load of old baloney." Aside from
his reactionary stance, it was also a personal issue. "I'm not that
attractive in the nude," Oates insisted. "And in the second place,
my body is my privacy; it's my blank sheet of paper and it is not
for sale."

Filming took place in a frontier village built at the Brush Hollow Reservoir near Penrose, which became known as Buckskin
Joe's. *Barquero* centers on a gruff bargeman, Travis, played by
Van Cleef, who covets with almost unnatural zeal his river raft
near the Mexican border. The barquero's circumstances in his village, Lonely Dell, are compounded by the arrival of Jake Remy's
(Oates) bandits, who have robbed Buckskin and fled to Lonely
Dell en route to Mexico. The bandits take Travis hostage, but he
is rescued by Mountain Phil (Forrest Tucker), and the two men
kill two of the bandits and take the other, Fair (John Davis Chandler), hostage.

"Oates is a pot-smoking madman haunted by chrome colored dreams and given to shooting up the river for defying him
in another fine, eccentric performance," the *Hollywood Reporter*

said, but his Remy is a man without a single redeeming feature. If Oates made a point of imbuing each performance with morality, with Remy he missed the boat. He takes his villainy to the hilt: it is his meanest hour on-screen, but it is also one of his least interesting. From his entrance—first line, "I need a drink"—to his response to his prostitute's question "Will I see you again?" of "I don't think so" and a gunshot, his performance reflects dissolute nihilism.

During a press junket in El Paso, Oates described *Barquero* as "a little Wild Bunchy with no high degree of think factor," and local reviewer Sam Pendergrast concurred. "It hasn't the cynical honesty or the creative impact of 'The Wild Bunch' but it has some of the new mandatory conventions—the captive dragged by his heels from a horse, the ambivalent sinister hero, the impromptu violence, the catalogue of mayhem techniques. . . . Perhaps the most disturbingly modern aspect of the movie is a scene in which Oates, as the bank-robbing bandit leader, lies around puffing on a suspicious cigarette, starts hallucinating, and ends up trying to shoot the river to death. The closest thing to a pioneer pot party we've seen on the screen." Alain Garel, in the French magazine *Image et Son*, found the scene compelling enough to question Oates about shooting the river for getting in the way of his escape. Oates answered, mistakenly attributing the film to Sam Peckinpah, "Some scenes you pull back from. In 'Barquero' I looked to Sam to do it."

On July 20, in the midst of filming, Oates and his family and friends gathered in the big front room of the rented house to watch the first moon landing. A crowd of people jostled in the large living room, with the televised event flickering in the background like a nagging conscience. A world away, Will Hutchins was in Paris. He and his girlfriend were looking for a particular Spanish movie, but instead they found a double feature: *The Shooting*, which had yet to open in the United States, with *Ride in the Whirlwind*.

As Oates prepared to leave Colorado, an item appeared in the *Hollywood Reporter*. "Warren Oates takes his new bride Vickery Turner on their belated honeymoon as he winds up his Barquero role next month and is seeking a yacht lease for seven months of cruising around the south of France." If the planted plan sounded more European Vickery than domestic Warren, it probably was.

Heading back to California, Vickery drove a car, with Oates bringing up the rear in the RV. They followed one another through coal country, past rivers and red rock canyons, over the Continental Divide and Monarch Pass, and to Soldier Summit, dotted with pines and cottonwoods at 7,477 feet. Outside Helper, Utah, Vickery saw a young Native American man beside his broken-down pickup truck. She pulled in next to him and explained that her husband was two minutes behind in a big RV that could offer a push. "We both waited and waited silently. Forty-five minutes later, Warren appeared," she said. "He had stopped to smoke a joint on a hillside and commune with nature."

Vickery Turner published a novel in 1984. *Focusing* features Leon Pike, an actor turned politician with more than a passing resemblance to Oates. In *Focusing* she transposed the scene of the stranded motorist encounter to New Mexico. "After some prodding it came out that he had seen a most inviting rock jutting out over a canyon and had stopped to play his bongo drums and puff on a weed, 'just for five minutes.'"

Vickery said, "Warren sometimes got stoned. He had a case of hepatitis from eating fish when he filmed *The Return of the Magnificent Seven* and drinking wasn't good for him, although he went on drinking. I think smoking marijuana was easier on his stomach. As he was so shy, I think a little artificial fortification helped him handle social occasions. I didn't drink or smoke, so I was the sober girl from England at many parties."

A few months after they returned to Los Angeles, Oates and Vickery went to a party where John Davis Chandler and his wife Marti were also in attendance. The couple circulated separately until Marti rushed back to her husband.

"I almost had a heart attack!" she announced. "This quirky guy came up to me with this twisted sort of face and this low guttural voice."

The man had said, "Hey sweetheart, why don't you drop that jerk and let's get out of here?"

Marti looked at her pursuer. "Who are you?" she demanded. "I don't know you. Get away from me."

"Marti, Marti, don't you know me?" the man laughed. "I'm Warren Oates from Colorado."

Chandler explained, "He had shaved. Everything was a little lopsided with him."

However off-kilter Oates was, Vickery was exotic for him, and when he flew to the United Kingdom to meet his new in-laws, he made an impression. The Turners lived in a small terraced home above the shop where Mr. Turner ran a picture-framing business in the London suburb of Thornton Heath in Surrey. "Warren looks quite something strolling down Thornton Heath High Street and dropping into the new Wimpy bar for a cup of coffee," Vickery told the British press. The deeply tanned Oates, dressed in what his son Timothy described as "hillbilly redneck done good, fur trimmed jackets and bell-bottoms," cut a lively swath in an English town the likes of which David Jones—before he changed his name to Bowie—had strained to escape.

Then there was the relatively spartan lifestyle of Britain at the time: it took months to get a home telephone; there were three, mostly black-and-white, television stations and very few televisions; and central heating was a rarity. "Leon was never comfortable in my parents' home," says the narrator of *Focusing*. "He felt no need to be reminded of struggle. . . . He would carry my father's battered oil stove into the lavatory and sit there shivering, gazing at the antique rusting chain dangling over his head and dream about a suite at the Dorchester."

When Oates and his wife returned to Los Angeles in late fall, Vickery began to look for work, but her forays were not immediately rewarded. Her husband's experience was different.

The Movie Murderer was a quickie, quixotic television movie that aired on February 2, 1970, as part of NBC's World Premiere movie series. It might not immediately spring to mind as a standout in Oates's career, but his performance in the role of a lonely, fortyish professional arsonist ranks among his finest. Subtle, even sexy, his Alfred Fisher is driven, human, disappointed, and flamboyantly destructive. Arthur Kennedy played an investigator on

Fisher's trail, and although they have no scenes together, the two fine actors play off each other with aplomb in several split-screen moments (for which director Boris Sagal had a penchant). Oates's moments with frustrated, whiskey-soaked hotel owner Norma Crane ooze with happy-hour despondency, and Oates is spared the creaking "freak-out" portions revolving around a cartoonishly Warholesque underground movie director played by Severn Darden. Interestingly, Darden and another *Movie Murderer* player, Robert Webber, would figure in two of Oates's most significant films in the coming decade.

As much as Oates loved the role of Alfred Fisher, he was ultimately disappointed when, as he told Dudley Saunders, "somewhere between conception and final editing, they decided to use it as a pilot for a new TV series, so they built up the young cop and turned it into a detective yarn." The young cop who received the thrust was a clean-shaven unknown named Tom Selleck.

"Oates develops his role step by step with deliberate power," noted *Daily Variety*. Most who have seen the film are admirers, among them Will Hutchins ("My impression was that's how Warren wanted to present himself. That was Warren to a T") and Verna Bloom.

During the transitional year of 1969, the end of the peace-and-love era from which Oates cherry-picked his personal totems—pot, bell-bottoms, printed shirts, beads, and an ethos of possibility, but probably not the prevailing hue of progressive politics—he made a film that summed up his complete openness about his career. Terrence Malick, then a student in the Center for Advanced Film Studies program at the fledgling American Film Institute in Hollywood, was preparing to film his thesis, *Lanton Mills*. Malick enticed Harry Dean Stanton and Oates for a day's filming around several Los Angeles locales. He cobbled together a movie that is as offbeat as the lone man on the dance floor but has just enough style and perverse confidence to carry the viewer along.

In the opening sequence, Lanton Mills (Stanton) rides up on horseback to a house to collect Tilman, played by Malick with pre–John Belushian confidence. Live oaks and sumacs dot the surrounding brown velour hills. "Weren't you supposed to be here yesterday?" Tilman asks. "I'm here now," comes the reply. If "existential" could be spelled out using branding symbols, this script might begin with the Circle E.

Tilman and Mills ride off to meet the old man to finalize plans for a bank robbery. Arriving, they find a boy (Tony Bill) on the porch wearing a placard that reads "Deaf." John Spocks (Oates) sidles into his entrance like a sidewinder, plumbing his *Barquero* depths (and quite possibly Remy's wardrobe). "Have you papers for my arrest?" Spocks asks the dumbfounded pair. "Name is John Spocks and I'm a bumblebee." Revealing that he is the slowest draw in the West—"slow on the draw and fast on the trigger, and there you are"—Spocks also brags that he has killed the boy's father, putting a glitch in Mills and Tilman's foggy plan. Lanton opts to kill Spocks in an attempt to change his luck. "Why?" Spocks pleads, arms outstretched, but Lanton scatter-shoots around him, and he falls to the ground.

Tilman talks to the dying Spocks, relieving him of his pocket watch in the process. He rejoins Mills, who then goes back to Spocks, who is busily trying to get the attention of a very black pig. "You just gonna sit there in the dark in these weeds and die like an old hen?" Mills asks Spocks, who does not have much of a choice. Mills and Tilman mull over the idea of letting the "mute" boy shoot at him, over Spocks's protests. Mills worries that Spocks might feel slighted if they do not drink with him, so Tilman retrieves a flask hidden in his saddlebag and takes it to him. After riding some distance, Tilman does a Big Bird dance to illustrate his exuberance. They ride on, and the scenery jolts into present-day Beverly Hills, with the Beverly Wilshire Hotel visible—suddenly the short film is an Occurrence beneath the Owl Drug Sign. They enter a modern-day bank, and Mills gives the patrons orders. He has acquired a stutter, as if he has not fully caught up with the wrinkle in time. The robbery fails, Tilman is captured, and Mills is fatally shot. Mills tells a police officer he is from Texas during their banal chitchat. "I'm enjoying this conversation but I'm dizzy," Mills tells him. "Maybe I've been getting too much nookie. But that's impossible, ain't it?" The film ends with Tilman being corralled into a police car.

Lanton Mills is a fevered dream filled with inscrutable lyricism, lovely camera work from Caleb Deschanel, and an appealing sound track credited to the Weasel Brothers. Oates, who acted here with his entire being, might not have thought too much about what it all meant—"Surprise me" is one of his lines—but he knew for certain he would work with the wunderkind Malick again in a heartbeat.

As the old year drew in, the third Mrs. Oates might not have gotten her Riviera honeymoon cruise, but the couple certainly took in the bright lights of a nighttime desert sky and the low lights of the old, familiar (to her husband anyway) Raincheck Room. Chris Sanchez, the former wife of Will Hutchins and a veteran of the Great Divorce Dinner, was in the Raincheck one night with a girlfriend visiting from England. They ran into the new couple, who insisted they join them for dinner. They laughed and talked late into the rain-dazzled wee hours.

14

Spread upon the Earth

Warren Oates was a creature of habit, and whenever he could, he slipped into patterns as suited to him as the woven Navajo blankets he cherished. In the late morning ("At six o'clock in the morning I'm just barely alive anyhow"), he would drive down the hill in his red Mazda rotary engine truck to get coffee and pastries. "Warren liked to go meet his men friends for coffee at Pupi's on the Strip in the morning," Vickery said. "Warren was a very shy man and could get tongue-tied around some people, but he loved his friends who he could relax with." The populace of Pupi's qualified: Pernell Roberts, B. J. Merholz, Jack Nicholson, Monte Hellman, Robert Culp. Sometimes he took Timothy, who would play chess with his father on the patisserie's patio. Timothy would read out the daily figures from the newspaper's fine-print stock report to Warren, whose vision was faulty but whose actor's vanity precluded wearing eyeglasses. Oates's dread of doctors also contributed to his reluctance to see an optometrist. He had a magnifying sheet about the size of a sheet of paper that he used in private, but to take this out with him socially would have been unseemly.

"My dad was a procrastinator in certain aspects of his life. His personal life, he would just put it off and put it off," Timothy said. "He wouldn't go to the dentist. He wouldn't go to the doctor. He wouldn't go get his car registered."

Teddy and the two children had moved to a place near Oates and Vickery's Briar Knoll abode. They now lived on Dona Emilia, about eight blocks down Laurel Canyon Boulevard. Soon his children and their neighborhood friends were going up to Briar Knoll to swim. "I'd walk straight up the hill and risk stumbling down or walk up the street, but I always went up to visit," said Timothy. "I probably came up the hill unannounced a couple of times, and he probably scrambled a bit. I know he did smoke here and there, but he never exposed me to that—it was never an open thing."

Oates had a nightly ritual that Vickery fictionalized in her novel: "a few puffs on a weed, a slow stroll around the pool, a conversation with his ancestors." How she was adjusting to her new life, including the proximity of the former Mrs. Oates, is indicated by a term Teddy and Vickery coined for their relationship. The two women were "wives-in-law" and identified themselves thus on the countless occasions they were asked.

For Vickery, the life represented a sudden swerve toward the domestic. For a working actress and writer, the transition had its share of rocky moments. Reluctant to let go of her screen career, the woman who had been called a "fatty turnip" in school was vigilant about her diet, frequently to her husband's dismay. "I ate an apple and my wife ate the peel," Oates would say, but that he was eating fruit at all was the result of Vickery's influence. She also sought out different places to go, one of which was the Aware Inn.

Handily located on the Strip, the Aware Inn, opened in 1957, was California's first organic restaurant (among its reviews is one that proclaims the patrons who care most about organic foods are former drug addicts). But the Aware Inn was far more than a plateful of forlorn sprouts atop sandpaper bread: its upscale ambience, extensive wine cellar, and menu embracing everything from escargot to tofu offered enough to placate Oates, whose palate did not run to the teetotal or the lean. Monte Hellman observed that his friend opted for "gravy on everything, butter piled on, the fattiest cuts of meat."

When Vickery and Oates walked in on a brisk January day, they saw, seated alone, Warren Beatty. "I just got off the phone with Julie [Christie]," Beatty told the couple. "I said, 'Hi, it's Warren,' and she said, 'Warren who? Warren Oates? Warren Berlinger?'" Beatty laughed before telling the two he had been working on a script about the Soviet Union.

Oates and Vickery socialized at the Raincheck, at Sam Peckinpah's Trancas Beach home in Malibu, and at Jack Nicholson's nearby Mulholland pad. 'We bumped into Bill Cosby once and he insisted we go back to his house," Vickery recalled. Another night they were reunited with Telly Savalas, who regaled them in his home by playing his new album.

Vickery's daily routine was considerably more humdrum. The Briar Knoll house did not have a washing machine, and although Oates often took the laundry to a "fluff and fold" place on Sunset Boulevard, "once," Vickery recalled, "we went round the corner to Teddy's house, where I used her washing machine. They chatted while I washed."

Oates had been reading scripts. "'Two-Lane Blacktop,' 'Deadhead Miles,' 'The Hired Hand'—all great and they all came to me in January, February, and March. I just couldn't believe it," he told the *Los Angeles Times*. "How was I gonna do 'em all? Well, they couldn't set up 'Deadhead Miles' at Warners because I wasn't a name, so that was that. Bruce Dern, a good friend of mine, was up for GTO in 'Two-Lane Blacktop' but couldn't do it. So I was back in the race."

The race had begun with *The Hired Hand*, which Peter Fonda and producer William Hayward had acquired in London, where Fonda was doing publicity for *Easy Rider*. He and Hayward had been looking for material to produce for their newly formed Pando Productions and had been going through script after script. "No one's writing the Great American Novel any more," Hayward observed. "Everyone thinks he has produced the Great American Script."

In London, a production company called Lifton Films sent Fonda a packet including *The Hired Hand* script, by Scotsman Alan Sharp, a project they hoped to entice him to star in. Hayward was instantly enthralled, as was Fonda. Hayward explained, "Our image of the west has been conditioned by countless television and motion picture versions—and it just didn't happen that way. In 'The Hired Hand,' we felt we had a story that had more legality in it than any western I had ever read. These characters weren't gunfighters, they were drifters, or as the sheriff calls them, 'travellin' men.' There are strong relevancies to today's troubled times and the people involved."

They bought the script, which Fonda originally envisioned as a vehicle for himself and his father. Henry Fonda eventually backed out, feeling he was too old for the part, and the younger Fonda began to mentally recast the character of Arch Harris. "Peter and his wife, Susan, had watched me on television and I'd done a couple of films with his dad," Oates explained. "I did one character where I had a cowbell around my neck and Peter thought that was just about the grooviest thing going. He had been really working over the problem of who to get to play Arch when Susan said, 'Why don't you get Warren Oates?'"

"I had watched Warren in a couple of films and realized there was something else going on in this man," Fonda said. "When he wasn't playing the assistant sidekick character or the doofus goofus role, he had this quality which in a strange way was dashing— like Bogart. He had to play wisdom and experience and when it came time to cast the role, I didn't even think of anyone else."

Oates read the script and was immediately struck by its power and simplicity. Fonda was offering $25,000 for the role; Oates's agent, Jerry Steiner, asked for twice that. Oates got in his Mazda truck and drove over to Pando's offices with his son Timothy in the passenger seat. Pando occupied a craftsman-style duplex just off Melrose Avenue on Seward Street. Pando's interior was, as Fonda put it, "hand painted and collaged out in a most imaginative way." Outside, twin flagpoles jutted up from its lawn, one flying the black flag of anarchy, the other an upside-down Old Glory, the universal symbol of distress. What Oates, a renegade with a staunchly conservative stripe, made of this counterculture proclamation is unknown, but his dedication to the project in question was its own kind of patriotic zeal.

Two secretaries were inside, big dogs resting by their desks. Oates patted the head of a golden retriever, who thumped her tail against the hardwood floor in appreciation. Then he was shown into Fonda's dining room–cum–office. Timmy took a seat on an overstuffed armchair, fascinated to watch his father at work and to gape at Fonda, whom he considered a real movie star.

"I always take my little boy along to check everybody out," Oates later explained. "Peter asked me, 'What did you think of it [the script]?' Of course I had my little boy there, prompting me. I said 'it's about the responsibilities of love and friendship.' He cracked a big grin and essentially that was the beginning of our relationship." Fonda and Hayward had to give up their $50,000 production fee so they could bring Oates on board.

Over the holiday season, Sam Peckinpah sent Oates and Vickery a Christmas card, and in spring, he had another offering for them. *The Wild Bunch* had been nominated for two Academy Awards: best screenplay (Peckinpah and Walon Green) and best score (Jerry Fielding). Peckinpah campaigned on the film's behalf and was quickly dismayed when Warner Brothers did not support him with the essential trade ads. He and Green were also involved with preproduction for *Straw Dogs* and decided to skip the ceremony. Peckinpah asked Oates to take their places. "If he [Peckinpah] won an award for *The Wild Bunch*, Warren was going to accept," Vickery said.

Vickery spent the day of April 7, 1970, getting ready for the event. She wore a long, cream-colored sleeveless gown with a loose shoulder wrap and left her shiny blonde hair down. Her husband told her he intended to wear his white suit, which was hastily being "washed" in a bucket beside the pool. She was not thrilled. Oates relented and put on the dark suit he had planned to wear all along.

They were driven to the Dorothy Chandler Pavilion in downtown Los Angeles, wearing eveningwear in the afternoon sun. The crowds occupying the bleachers reserved their cheers for stars like John Wayne, who would win the award for best actor for *True Grit*; Cary Grant, who was up for an honorary award; and the deeply tanned Elizabeth Taylor and Richard Burton. The commotion surrounding arriving celebrities competed with a protest by about eighty Latino activists, carrying signs and shouting "Chicano power" on the Flower Street sidewalk. Special targets were *Butch Cassidy and the Sundance Kid* and *The Wild Bunch*, which, according to Tomas Martinez, a sociology professor from Stanford University, depicted Latinos as "inferior, incompetent, worthless, and ignorant."

Oates was never one for shows of protest, but he grasped the deeper issue. "They're gaining attention to their problem, which is their purpose. I agree with them in spirit, because we have too many films that just skirt over life." Yet he felt the protestors were "making demands that are not plausible." His thoughts were a step up from those of the myriad unenlightened pundits, one of whom would describe Raquel Welch as "the girl least likely to be mistaken for the Frito Bandito."

Inside, Oates and Vickery went past the staircase beneath the chandeliers, and eventually the Forty-second Annual Academy Awards got under way. There was no fixed presenter; instead, there were Bob Hope and various actors termed "friends of Oscar" who rotated to give out the awards. A disclaimer before the broadcast reassured viewers that regardless of the films' ratings, all excerpts had been edited. Gregory Peck, academy president, took the podium to announce that Mexico and Brazil had joined the list of countries watching a live broadcast. He introduced the coterie of stars who would be presenting Oscars and yielded the podium to Hope. This year's gathering, Hope suggested, would "separate the men from *The Boys in the Band*," and he noted that "the everyone-who's-anyone in the room" had made "such a crowd that *Bob and Carol and Ted and Alice* all had to sit in the same seat." Pictures had changed, he said, so much that if *High Noon* were made today, it would be about a lunch hour in a junior high school.

If Oates was hoping that Fred Astaire would sing his personal favorite, "One for My Baby," he had to settle for the legendary dancer leaping through a raucous and awkward rock-and-roll orchestra number that was far from classic. B. J. Thomas sang "Raindrops Keep Falling on My Head" and seemed as oblivious of the antics of the cyclists on stage with him as he was of a cutesy child on a tricycle at the number's end.

Two and a half hours had passed. Cary Grant, accepting his honorary award, insisted that movies' best years were still ahead.

A squeaky-clean trio, the Sandpipers, sang "Come Saturday Morning" right before, at the three-hour mark, Ali MacGraw and James Earl Jones announced the screenwriting award. It went to William Goldman for *Butch Cassidy and the Sundance Kid*. However disappointed, now Oates could relax. As the cameras brushed past him and Vickery seated behind Alice Ghostley (the designated accepter for winner Maggie Smith), the well-groomed Oates looked as if he had just taken his pew at the Oak Grove Baptist Church.

At the end of the program, as the X-rated *Midnight Cowboy* took top honors, Bob Hope predicted that movies would "never again reflect a lollipop world." Still, the sugary *Butch Cassidy and the Sundance Kid* had won best screenplay, keeping Oates off the stage and Oscar beyond Peckinpah's reach.

The Governors Ball took place across town at the Beverly Hilton Hotel, where Oates knew Jack Nicholson, Clint Eastwood, and Dennis Hopper, who wore a white Stetson to the glitzy ball (as well as to the ceremony). Michelle Phillips, on Hopper's arm, radiated new Hollywood as much of the fashion refracted the new West. Candice Bergen wore fringe, a squash blossom necklace, and beads, while Dyan Cannon sported Sant'Angelo's Indian princess midi.

In three years, Marlon Brando would decline his Oscar, sending Sacheen Littlefeather to the podium to take a stance for the American Indian. It was not a move Oates would have made. "If I won an Oscar, I wouldn't send some Indian maiden to refuse it for me. I'd break the track record to the stage to get it," Oates said.

In May, Oates went on a publicity tour for *Barquero*. It took him to Abilene, Texas, where the movie was opening in its statewide premiere at the Paramount Theatre on Friday, May 15. Two days prior, Oates was given the key to the city and cheered on by the local citizens, who saved their less restrained response for voluptuous Marie Gomez. Frank Sheffield managed the Paramount, an old-style movie palace that was built in 1930 and seated thirteen hundred. Oates and Gomez stayed at the Downtowner Motor Hotel. "Built in the '60s, it was new and the nicest we had, so that's where we put 'em," Sheffield said. During the day, Sheffield took the visiting celebrities to the country club.

"We're not a very big town, but we've got a country club whose food is really, really superb. They are famous for their stew, and boy, [Oates] really went wild over that stew." Gomez went along as well, turning quite a few heads. "She was very friendly," Sheffield said. "And ol' Warren, boy he was a nice guy. They were different from today's people."

While her husband was in Texas, Vickery went to England to look for a woman director for her project "Trust in God." Asked about her husband, she told the *Times* of London, a bit pejoratively, "He acts in Westerns. Did you see 'The Wild Bunch'?" The reporter concluded that Vickery was "well-versed in the facts and figures of women's liberation (she briefed herself at militant meetings in Los Angeles) but is cheerfully unfrustrated herself."

An actress in living in New York City was awakened by a phone call at three o'clock in the morning. The caller, a little lit, excitedly introduced himself. "I'm Warren Oates, and I understand we'll be working together in *The Hired Hand*." Verna Bloom started to wake up when Oates lavished praise on her work and reiterated his elation that he would be acting with her. Eventually she leaned over her boyfriend to hang up the phone. "Who was that?" he asked, and she tried to explain until the sun's rays peeked through the Manhattan skyline.

Shooting began on May 26. Oates drove his new car, a Ford Capri, from his Briar Knoll home to location near Santa Fe, New Mexico. Oates's two children would soon follow with Vickery in the Roach Coach. The Capri died en route, and Oates drove the remainder in a rental, thinking about the script and its pertinence to his life. "'The Hired Hand' is the America of what Walt Whitman means to me," he later said. "I'd respect Peter for no other reason than showing me the family as an ideal unit. That's very close to me, I've gone through divorce."

Oates met Fonda in Santa Fe and was immediately bundled into Fonda's blue Ford Blazer. To Fonda, Oates "looked kind of like Wile E. Coyote, when he just knows something is going to blow up in front of him. I took him around the state of New Mexico, showing him every single location." Fonda finally asked his passenger, "Are you tired, Warren?"

"Tired?" Oates replied. "I drove fifteen hours to get here, and I haven't stopped."

They headed for Warm Springs, run by hippies, and promptly fell asleep on the cement.

Although *The Hired Hand* was initially slated to film in Italy, Fonda opted to make it in New Mexico because the state's scenic diversity offered both the town Del Norte (filmed in the town of Cabezon and plucked from a book on historical ghost towns) and the Eden-like ranch to which Fonda returns.

The film's lyricism is at its apogee when Oates's character, Arch Harris, reads from the Gospel according to Thomas, something Fonda was unable to do without becoming too emotional. Harris reads, "The kingdom of the Father is spread upon the earth and man does not see it," as the story, sumptuously shot by Vilmos Zsigmond, begins to unfurl like parchment. Almost every cast member was on moviedom's fringe, which may have helped them summon an interpretation of the West less steeped in false history than in possibility, hardship, and subtlety. Writer Alan Sharp, who was not on set, later said that the resultant film "reflected the influences of hallucinogens," and although that point is inarguable, it is equally true that *The Hired Hand* generally avoids self-indulgence.

With a group of novices—Zsigmond had never shot a movie; Lawrence G. Paull was navigating his first assignment as a full-fledged art director; Frank Mazzola (responsible for the ethereal montages) was a relative newcomer; and even Fonda was making his directorial debut—there were blips. Cameras jammed, including during a scene in which Harris jumps over the bar after a patron (Michael McClure) questions Hannah's (Bloom) morality.

Scheduled for eight weeks, *The Hired Hand* ran to ten, not least because Fonda injured his foot. Ted Markland, who played the villainous Luke alongside Owen Orr's Mace, stood in for Fonda in some of the distance scenes. "A lot of those scenes—Warren driving into the sunset with Peter—that was me. And we had a ball. Peter would say, 'Come back!' and we'd just keep riding." Markland had costarred on television's *The High Chaparral* and was a veteran of *Bonanza* while privately pursuing a spiritual quest considerably ahead of the trend toward higher consciousness. "He was actually the ringleader of that entire desert experience," said John Phillip Law. Markland showed the Joshua Tree ropes to Timothy Leary, the Rolling Stones, Gram Parsons, and a reluctant Lenny Bruce, among others. Oates had experienced Joshua Tree while filming *There Was a Crooked Man* and was primed for more. Markland's interest in metaphysics, Native American ritual, and tequila made him a good match for Oates.

In the evenings, they congregated in Santa Fe, where they stayed at the Inn of the Governors in the historic plaza district. (Those who went to Cuba, New Mexico, slid downscale into its Frontier Motel and its brand-new Tastee Freez.) The camaraderie was strong enough that the actors, if not their occasionally hotheaded director, took most problems in stride. When Oates and Bloom were filming the quiet scenes on the porch (an exterior location), a drive-in theater in the valley below was showing *Easy Rider*. Its sound track wafted up, an unwanted contact high. Bloom and Oates were so deep into their characters that they did not notice.

"Warren was the most generous actor I ever worked with, onscreen and off," Bloom said. "He would set up stuff. The scene on the porch, he and I both felt the unwritten subtext. During that scene, he gets a look in his eyes, I can't describe it, and then starts rubbing the tops of my feet. It was the sexiest thing, and it really fed me for sure. Rather than anything in the script—the writer was not around at all so at times we just filled in. We felt that scene set it up for Warren's character to be the one that comes back."

Among the crew was a Kentuckian who grew up fourteen miles from Greenville, where Oates had gone to Saturday matinees as a child. Bob Watkins was from a place near, appropriately enough, Friendship, and he was a tall, soft-spoken, quiet man with a checkered past—rumor had it that he had served time for attempted bank robbery. He was working on *The Hired Hand* with a friend, Anthony Mazzola, who was the prop master. When they were filming near the old courthouse, Mazzola told Watkins he had to meet Oates. "There are not a lot of people in Hollywood from Kentucky, so I went over. Warren was sitting by himself in this rinky-dink trailer," Watkins said. "Anthony introduced us and then ran off, as he was a busy guy in the film, and Warren and I sat and talked. From the moment we met, we were tighter than a frog's ass. We got closer and closer, worked together the rest of the film."

Watkins would work as Oates's driver but would also offer other kinds of directions, introducing him to Zen Buddhism while accompanying him through raucous nights, mellow twilights, tangled romances, and a lot of highways and back roads. "This guy six years my junior, out there in the middle of New Mexico," Oates marveled. "His great uncle lived in my little town. No reason at all to run into a man like that, but we're from the same county and we end up in New Mexico together and we're interested in the same things."

When Vickery arrived, Oates was also reunited with the Roach Coach. Together they would ride, catching Bloom's attention. "Riding in the Land of Enchantment, we'd look over and there on a parallel road, Vickery would be driving the camper and Warren would be on the roof videoing the sunset while the vehicle was *moving*," she marveled.

Oates was later asked how Fonda handled his dual responsibilities of actor and director. "No problem. He separated them, he is organized enough. It was a very difficult thing to do. I never felt he was the director walking in front of the camera. It takes an organized man to lead a bunch of actors."

The Hired Hand opens with a slow-motion montage of sun, river, and sand. Arch Harris (Oates) and Harry Collings (Fonda) are on the shore as young Dan (Robert Pratt) frolics in the water before joining them and regaling the two more seasoned riders with his dream of California. Their reverie is interrupted when a fishing line they have set catches the body of a young girl. Collings cuts the line, and the body drifts on. The men ride to Del Norte, a debauched outpost commandeered by McVey (Severn Darden) and his two henchmen, Luke and Mace. Collings has elected to return to his wife and their young daughter, and Harris comes along. Collings reconciles with his wife, but as David Castell wrote in *Films Illustrated*, "the idyll is doomed, for Fonda is the love object of two contrasting personalities who, by their very natures, will make conflicting demands on him. . . . Warren Oates could not be bettered as the loyal, perceptive Arch. Fonda has created a film of considerable truth and charm, and come up with a new hat for the Western to wear."

When it was released in 1971, *The Hired Hand* received mostly favorable reviews, except in *Time* and *Newsweek*. Molly Haskell noted its "yearnings for a sagebrush 'A Doll's House'"; *Variety* deemed "the most touching scene . . . when Miss Bloom and Fonda resume their married life; the least touching when Fonda dies in Oates's arms." But a premature demise was in store for the innovative work: Universal pulled the film after a one-week run. "The fallout after the film was tragic," Bloom said. Fonda told acquaintance Harry Northup, "All I'd asked is that people sit still for eighty-three minutes." Upon the film's eventual rerelease, Fonda said, "My friend Mr. Oates had such a wonderful romantic presence. He was the perfect actor at the perfect moment to play this part. So handsome, so natural. I'm so proud we were able to get those aspects of him on film."

Much of the cast, including Oates and Vickery, spent the Fourth of July at Larry Hagman's Malibu beach house. The outré and entertaining Hagman had been part of *The Hired Hand*, playing a sheriff, but his part had been cut. Holiday festivities at the beachfront property involved a parade along the shore with the guests flying flags of their own choosing.

By August, Oates would be playing a drifter again, with horsepower gunning in place of a horse's hooves. *Two-Lane Blacktop* had a meandering origin. Its original screenplay, by Will Corry, was the story of two men, one black and one white, who drive across the country with a young girl. Michael Laughlin, one of Hollywood's youngest producers at thirty-two, optioned the script for $100,000 for Cinema Center. Laughlin approached Monte Hellman with Corry's script, which the director told Brad Stevens was "The Gumball Rally." "Only it was a Disney version of that, if you can imagine such a thing. It was the most insipid, silly, sentimental, dumb movie you can imagine."

Hellman was an admirer of a science fiction book called *Nog* by Rudy Wurlitzer, and he tracked down the author, who flitted between Nova Scotia and New York, in San Francisco. Wurlitzer was not intrigued by the assignment—cars left him cold—but he was broke, so he agreed to do it. In four weeks, Wurlitzer rewrote Corry's original script, at one point enlisting the help of his friend Terrence Malick. "I was interested in what happens to love, for one thing," Hellman said. "I wanted to see where the two worlds met, to see how much romance is left in an unromantic world."

In February 1970, while Hellman was scouting locations, Cinema Center abruptly cancelled the project. The director commenced courting almost every major studio. MGM rejected the picture because it offered limited camera angles. Finally, Ned Tanen at Universal, who supervised *The Last Movie*, *The Hired Hand*, and *Diary of a Mad Housewife*, gave Hellman $850,000 to make *Two-Lane Blacktop* with directorial authority from first shot to final cut. The modest budget was further dented by a payment to Cinema Center to release the property.

Filming began in Los Angeles on August 13, a little later than the anticipated May start. It was a postponement that favored Oates, who had not been available for the role of GTO, a teller of tall tales, wearer of V-necked sweaters, and driver of a 1970 Pontiac GTO, "the paralyzing orange of one of those inedible marshmallow peanuts from Woolworth's," Shelley Benoit wrote in *Show* magazine.

"GTO is time," Hellman told Beverly Walker, the film's publicist. "GTO's function is a reference to the process of time. A reminder of mortality. GTO sings 'Time is on My Side.' Well, it's not. The love thing is involved with him, too. The temporal nature of love. At least, of sexual love. He's been through it. He's part of the generation gap." Hellman had thought of Oates early on. "I really cast him in my head as GTO almost before the script was completed," Hellman said. "I'd say maybe halfway through I began to think about Warren. It wasn't really definite in my head until the script was completed and we were doing the casting in Los Angeles. Rudy Wurlitzer came with me to see a screening of 'The Shooting' and about 15 minutes into 'The Shooting' we turned to each other and said simultaneously 'GTO.'"

Hellman asked Oates about his availability with a view to shooting in spring. Oates enthusiastically agreed, but during the interim he became involved with *The Hired Hand*. GTO needed to be recast. Bruce Dern said,

> Roger Corman had a script supervisor named Monte Hellman. By the late '60s, he was carrying around this script. . . . Right about the end of June there were three movies I was up for the lead. All three came to fruition the same day. One was called *The Grissom Gang*, one was called *Two-Lane Blacktop*, and the third was *Deadhead Miles*, a movie that Tony Bill was producing for a director called Henry Zimmerman, about a truck driver who picked up a hitchhiker.
>
> At eleven forty-five on Friday morning, the last Friday in June, Michael Laughlin, who was married at that time to Leslie Caron—she was big stuff—Laughlin called my agent, Ronnie Leif, and offered me the part of GTO for a thousand dollars a week. The billing would be the same as the other three actors.

Leif asked Laughlin, "That's all you're going to offer him, a thousand a week?"

Laughlin replied, "Take it or leave it." Leif said that he would call Dern and get back to Laughlin after lunch.

When he called Laughlin after lunch, however, the producer told him, "We got Warren Oates."

"Bruce Dern, younger than Warren, would have been too young, really," Beverly Walker noted. "It was a youth film à la *Easy Rider*, and we made much of the generational divide."

Oates and Harry Dean Stanton would work together on *Two-Lane*. Firm friends, they had a Raincheck routine. "I was at Warner Brothers today and somebody asked about you," Oates would say. "Who was it?" Stanton asked. "Nobody." When that wore thin, they took to wearing a series of horrible hats and greet-

ing each other by saying, "Nice hat." Critic David Thomson suggested the two men would be ideal in *Waiting for Godot*.

They also often vied for work. "We were up for the same parts
a lot of the times. We didn't have a *rivalry* going," Stanton said,
but Hellman begged to differ. "There was a lot of rivalry between
Harry Dean and Warren. Harry Dean was always complaining,
muttering under his breath about playing second fiddle to Warren
Oates. He felt that he should have been playing Warren's parts."

The role of the driver was proving difficult to cast. "There
weren't any star actors in that age group who were right. I
thought a star from another field might be a possible way to do
it . . . an actor or a singer or anyone who'd experienced some
measure of success and self-confidence," Hellman said. Michael
Laughlin was driving down Sunset Boulevard when he noticed
a billboard for *Sweet Baby James*. Hellman was taken by James
Taylor's gaunt face, straight hair parted in the middle, and high-
beam blue eyes. Laughlin called Hellman and suggested he look
Taylor up and buy an album. "I quickly went out and bought a
couple of albums and I liked his face as well," Hellman said. He
sent the script to Taylor's agent, Peter Asher, who recommended
his client take the role of the driver. "I've always seen The Driver
as the same character as Aznavour in 'Shoot the Piano Player,'"
Hellman said. However, Hellman resisted having Taylor sing,
deeming it "detrimental empathy."

Hellman's casting director, Fred Roos, had worked on *Zabris-
kie Point*, and he complained that his new employer was harder
to please than Michelangelo Antonioni. Three days before shooting, the mechanic had yet to be cast. "The night before, it was
getting so close to the wire I took out a copy of Arthur Hopkins'
Reference Point which is a kind of bible to me," Hellman said.
"He wrote about the Casting Gods and how always at the last
minute the Casting Gods can bring you a Humphrey Bogart or a
Katharine Hepburn. I said, well, now's the time for the Casting
Gods to help me. The next day, Dennis Wilson walked in." Hellman found Wilson "very sensitive, very emotional, and he's tuned
into the character in a funny way: he has built and driven racing cars himself." Hellman's selection of musicians to play both

the driver and the mechanic was "just an accident." However, Hellman realized that "as musicians James and Dennis respect each other in a way that is analogous to the rapport between The Driver and The Mechanic."

The frontispiece of the ninety-five-cent paperback *Two-Lane Blacktop* describes the girl, who would be played in the film by Laurie (née Laurene) Bird: "She is young, slight, dungareed, horny—she has latched on for the ride—or rather the trip." A native of Glen Cove, Long Island, Bird was by far the most "street" of the group. Her mother had died when Bird was three, and she was attending Jamaica High School when her father put her out to fend for herself after she turned fifteen. Bird took the only recourse available, panhandling in New York City, until someone suggested the pretty teen try modeling. Survival was tough, but what did not kill her made her stranger: she had a unique spirit, jaded yet carefree, and was wise beyond her years. She herself sewed the yak-skin purse she brought to the part of the girl, swinging it as carelessly as Julie Christie does her nifty handbag in *Billy Liar*. "I'm doing this for something to do," Bird would say, adding that she was pretty much playing herself.

It was a gamble, but the casting of nonactors James Taylor, Dennis Wilson, and Laurie Bird was also a studied conceit. Bruce Dern had expressed apprehension about working with nonactors, but Oates saw it differently: "It didn't bother me at all. Working with them was a groove, you know?" he said.

Yet the role of GTO caused the veteran actor real anxiety, and the resultant special treatment he received from Hellman drew Taylor's ire. Hellman later decreed the film his most difficult, "grueling due to the nature of the way we had to shoot it, which was across the country so we'd drive a bit, shoot a bit." Publicist Walker ran interference with Taylor's managers, who were worried that their client—fresh out of rehab—would relapse. "Warren was the sanest person of anyone in the cast," Walker insisted.

Oates drove the Roach Coach, which Hellman described as being "equipped with a stereo system, his stash of pot," ahead to Arizona, while Vickery stayed home, finding life on the road "dreary."

Like *The Shooting*, *Two-Lane Blacktop* was filmed in sequence. A company of thirty-four, plus three 1955 Chevy sedans and two 1970 Pontiac GTOs, traversed Needles, California; Flagstaff, Arizona; Santa Fe and Tucumcari, New Mexico; Boswell, Oklahoma; Little Rock, Arkansas; and Memphis, Tennessee. Walker wrote, "Hellman frequently scheduled filming between sunset and dawn in motel interiors, diners, and gas stations. Daylight sequences were sometimes shot on lonely country roads or against the backgrounds of sleepy hamlets. By the time the company rolled into Marysville, TN at the foot of the Smokey Mountains for the final day of shooting, Hellman had achieved his purpose of affecting every member of the cast and crew with the feeling of having moved across a vast expanse of the United States."

Most of them felt the wear and tear. But for Oates, the road was his lair, and the hours between sunset and dawn, prime time. From Flagstaff, he called Bob Watkins in Taos and asked him to join him in Arizona. Oates and Watkins hoped to witness a snake dance on the Hopi reservation, and James Taylor and his girlfriend, singer Joni Mitchell, were interested in coming along as well. In the morning, Oates, Watkins, Mitchell and Taylor plus guitars, and Timothy and Jennifer packed into the Roach Coach. Oates drove the incomparably beautiful road from Flagstaff's altitudinal greenery to the Hopi mesa. Their dream of seeing a snake dance was a long shot. "It's almost magic if it works," Watkins said. "You either get stopped by weather or the Hopi." But they were able to see the dangerous—poisonous snakes are involved—and sacred ceremony, performed to invite rain. On the walk back to the motor home, they met a Hopi woman carrying a bucket of tamales for sale.

In the Roach Coach, Oates tuned to a radio station in Flagstaff, which reported that the only place it was raining was in Walpi, on the Hopi reservation. For the adults, it was a perfect day. Taylor and Mitchell played guitars and sang together. "It was like the line from his song, 'I've seen sunny days that I thought would never end,'" Watkins said. "It was such a beautiful day."

But it was harder for Jennifer and Timothy. "You couldn't

point or take any pictures of the ceremony, and Timothy and I had to sit on our hands because we wanted to point," Jennifer said. Before they began the return trip to Flagstaff, Jennifer begged her father not to smoke pot on the way. "I knew he was driving us; he's going to sit in the front seat, and they're going to pass the joint across, and he's going to hit it, and he's going to be stoned while he's driving me and my brother and all these other people." Despite promising his daughter he would abstain, "he did it anyway," she said. "I was mad. Even though I didn't see him, I know that he did. So I felt on the edge of my seat all the way, and I also had to watch the road the entire time. And it was nighttime as well. Not only that but he picked up a hitchhiker—he would always pick up hitchhikers."

Back on the set, by the time they moved on to Santa Fe, the highly strung Taylor was in mental overdrive. He told the *Los Angeles Times*, "I'm not an actor. I'll never do this again. If I ever did another film I'd have to be the director and writer, I'd have to be in control." What was stressing out the twenty-two-year-old singer-songwriter was Hellman's refusal to let his actors see the script, a ploy Hellman intended to be beneficial. "I thought there would be an advantage in not knowing what happened beyond the point of the story we were shooting," Hellman said. "If they know what's going to happen, particularly without experience, they were going to be affected."

But Oates was having none of it either. He was due to film the next morning, talking specifics about cars, a world beyond his remit. Oates had read the screenplay several months before, but he had not seen the shooting script, so in desperation, he went to Hellman and said, "I gotta have my pages. I gotta understand what the hell . . ."

In GTO's first scene, he picks up a Texas hitchhiker (Bill Keller) whose natty suit and string tie indicate that he is a regional businessman. GTO's V-neck sweater and trousers with flares like car fins suggest a lifestyle at odds with that of the street racers, but one that is also distinct from any conventional careerism. Oates loved playing a compulsive liar, but GTO's toolbox lexicon was a challenge. Oates said,

That was a gruesome day. First of all I had to learn a lot of nomenclature to understand about the automobile that I'm not familiar with, even though I served time in the US Marine Corps as an aviation mechanic. I'd closed out that aspect of my life and I didn't understand it at all so I had to learn that dialog first and it was brutal.

I think that day we began to understand something. . . . We determined that GTO was not lying. I believe everything I say and I carry it through each character I meet. That's how I worked the first day and that's how I got into it really.

The scene contains a moment that made it into the final cut "by the skin of its teeth," the director explained. "Warren at one point near the end of the scene looks over and does a kind of comic take, reacting to the character and in a sense you might think it's too big, it's larger than life. But we felt that it was right, it was in character. It's a very funny scene anyway and a funny reaction. Warren . . . is aware of his ability to make people laugh. I don't think it was ever out of hand or to the point of being unbelievable." GTO, Oates said, "represents a comic and tragic figure; you have to walk a very tight line to achieve this. So if I got a little large in one area, Monte pulled me back. If I went the other way, Monte pulled me back. Sometimes Monte thought I was too funny and sometimes I thought he held me back. Maybe I'd pout a little, he'd clear his throat and we'd get it done. Monte and I knew each other."

The screenplay describes GTO as wearing a "light, very expensive cashmere sweater. His blond hair is neither long nor short. He looks like an aging fraternity boy or slightly spaced young executive who has been seized by some mysterious and unconscious trauma." His opening diatribe, "When the 455 came out with the Mach IV Ram-Air with tunnel-port heads, beefed lower end and a Holley high-riser set-up, I was on line—390 hp and 500 foot-pounds of torque," was indeed an ordeal. But when his passenger asks him, "How come you ain't in Bakersfield?" GTO's response, "Because I'm in the Southwest," is pure Oates. His matter-of-fact nature also helped him identify Taylor's source of conflict.

"The difference between me and Jimmy is that he's a corporal and I'm just a soldier," Oates told Kevin Thomas. "I like a strong director—I need one. I work better that way. I keep telling my agent I'd rather have a director be mean to me. If he's in full command of the ship we'll make the film work. If the strength isn't there, then there are arguments." Hellman's strength was deceptive, however, and his style could easily be mistaken as weak. At one point Oates accused him of inaccessibility as Taylor continued his rants. A crewmember said, "If it wasn't for Warren, we'd wonder if we were really making a movie," but Oates had faced a series of struggles. "I complained bitterly to Rudy Wurlitzer, the writer, and finally got a script—but only my dialog!" Oates said. "I couldn't believe Monte would do it that way. The script is a road map for the actor. See, Monte didn't want us to know what the end was. I didn't care how it ended! I just wanted to know what I was supposed to be doing." But Oates continued, "In defense of him, he thought he'd get something fresh and brand new from the kids that way. I'm not talking out of turn when I say Jimmy Taylor had terrible struggles relinquishing control to Monte. And Laurie Bird was new, too, and defending herself. Monte would say, 'Talk low' and they just didn't want to do it."

After Santa Fe, the company moved on to Tucumcari, a small town on Route 66 in eastern New Mexico. There they set up camp at the Pow Wow Motel. Vickery joined Oates.

Michael Goodwin wrote in *Rolling Stone*, "The film company tends to segregate a little, the split being a matter of age, length of hair, and state of consciousness more than anything else. The old trip. For the straighter members of the crew, evenings that aren't spent shooting are for television in the motel room, movie rap, or an endless poker game. For the others there is James, music, and the usual state-of-the-universe rap." Harry Dean Stanton could cross party lines, traveling between the camps. Oates kept his usual perspective from his motor home perched just away from the fray. Taylor broke ranks and visited him now and again, pronouncing him "a real endearing cat." Jennifer and Timothy, along with Monte Hellman's children and other kids, made good use of the Pow Wow's swimming pool, where Dennis Wilson held court

when he was not in his room, where he had had the motel's cocktail lounge piano transplanted. "Dennis Wilson was always in the
pool, and he was great with all of us kids," Jennifer said. "He'd
throw us all over the pool."

By now, all actors had copies of the script, but Joni Mitchell insisted that once Taylor got it, he never really read it. One
cold night at half-past midnight, a dinner was served: pork chops,
home fries, asparagus, bread pudding, baked apples, fruit cocktail, strong coffee. The next morning, they would be shooting
the scene in which GTO and the two young men agree to race
for pink slips. The screenplay indicates that the pinks were never
mailed, but this detail was omitted from the final version of the
film. At six o'clock the next morning the weather was clear. The
race would begin in earnest two miles outside Tucumcari, at a Ute
gas station. The sequence would take two twelve-hour days to
complete and compose ten crucial minutes of the film.

The film was being shot in Techniscope, a more affordable,
half-frame version of the widescreen Cinemascope process. It
utilized eighteen possible camera angles—but no process shots.
"You have a slight loss in quality in terms of grain, but a slight
gain in the amount of light, brightness," Hellman explained. "We
wanted to be close in the cars but still keep three people in the
shot. We had a platform set up around the car while it was moving and the camera could be slid in any direction on the pipes but
not when the car was moving. We never had any moving shots
through the windshield because I thought I wanted the illusion of
being inside the car."

Hellman said, "My favorite scene is [the] one [in which Oates]
gets soaked in the rain at the gas station. He's waiting by the Coke
machine . . . and he has a lot of time there where, you know,
his thoughts are racing but . . . he's not acting out any particular action. And it's a ballet. I mean he's really doing everything
while he's doing nothing. He was always doing something. He
was never at rest."

The next afternoon, the company drove into Texas because
Hellman wanted to use Texas Rangers in the scene in which GTO
is pulled over for speeding. Then they were back outside Tucum-

cari, where water rushed in an irrigation ditch and a rooster crowed, causing sound problems. GTO stops again at the side of the road to tell off the other three for interfering with his story to the police. They then form an uneasy alliance, swapping tea, sharing a flask of liquor, and eating hardboiled eggs. "The normally reliable Warren is blowing it from agitation; James repeatedly breaks up laughing, Dennis is nodding out," writer Shelley Benoit observed. Oates remembered shooting the scene. "If he [Hellman] likes it, we print it," Oates said, "and if he doesn't, we go. I will ultimately do what he says because he just says 'Once again please,' quietly and firmly and that's the way we do it. I eat another egg. *Eighteen* eggs."

More problems followed. The Pontiac GTO broke down, and the spare one had no plates, so it could not be used. The ever-present wind blew over a light, which broke when it hit the ground. A window fell out of the 1955 Chevy. The hour grew later, and Benoit began to view the proceedings differently. "Laurie is really Dorothy with James and Dennis the Scarecrow and the Tin Woodman; Warren the Cowardly Lion." Dawn started to break.

Saturday was the cast and crew's last night in Tucumcari before they moved on to Durant, Oklahoma. They had chateaubriand for dinner, seated at long tables in hard folding chairs. The next morning, Jennifer and her brother slept in the motor home while their father joined the others for breakfast. All of a sudden, the vehicle started moving, and Jennifer was shocked to see a strange man at the wheel. "Luckily he was driving us to the next location, but it would have been *nice* if maybe Dad had come by or somebody had come by and said, 'You're not being kidnapped.' I was on alert that entire trip. I thought, 'Is this for real? Who knows?' It could have been anybody. But this man gets into the motor home with me and Timothy and starts driving."

In Little Rock, Oates spent time with a reporter from the *Los Angeles Herald-Examiner*. Winfred Blevins told the actor he had fished nearby Lake Ouachita as a boy, and that was enough for Oates to insist Blevins show him the way. "Warren Oates eases his camper over a rise, and we can see Lake Ouachita. 'A slow pan from left to right,' Oates shouts grandly, sweeping his arm

180 degrees to indicate the camera movement. . . . It is all so idyllic and beautiful that it seems unreal," Blevins wrote. "In 1970 such places exist only in the movies. As Oates makes his pretend pan shot, his tape cartridge stereo booms the final measures of Tchaikovsky's 'Romeo and Juliet.'" Oates said, "The only thing I am committed to, I mean REALLY committed to, is combining music with this kind of scenery." He told Blevins how much he loved traveling in his camper and playing the music of Vivaldi, Beethoven, and other composers at full volume. Blevins concluded, "He is the kind of man who gives the phrase 'lust for life' a charged meaning."

Blevins then visited the film set and quickly became aware of the charged atmosphere. He went to dinner with Oates, Vickery, and James Taylor. "Oates and Taylor drink," Blevins noted. "Taylor begins to open up about Hellman."

Taylor told Blevins, "I've been used and abused. Monte is USING me." Oates stepped in, assuring Taylor he would be very good in the film. "I've been strung out on a lot of things, man," Taylor continued. "I've been on the juice. I've been in and out of a couple of nuthouses. Monte's doing the right thing but it hurts."

As late as 1993, Taylor was still smarting. In *TV Guide*'s What I Watch column, he said, "I only watch about an hour a day, which may have something to do with the fact that I made a movie in 1971 [*sic*] that went very badly. Occasionally it [*Two-Lane Blacktop*] turns up on TV at 3 A.M. and I think the fear of seeing it may be why I'm so cautious of watching TV today." The writer asked Taylor when he had last seen the film. "Never," he replied. "I've never seen it." But in the South, in 1970, Taylor's nightmare and Oates's groove were about to wrap.

The film's final moments belong to Taylor and his car. Hellman said, "The film slows down in the projector presumably and then the film stops and the frame burns. It was an intellectual decision and I'm always suspicious of intellectual decisions. I felt I wanted to bring the audience out of the film, to make some other statement about speed; in this case, the speed of film going through a projector, to suddenly shift from the film back to the audience."

GTO is last seen with two more hitchhikers, spinning a yarn

as colorful as his sweaters. "GTO has been picking up hitchhikers on the road forever and will go on doing so," Oates said. "This man would never mature even though he was trying to, he'd hang on to the fringe of every fad that's happening in society." Hellman said of Oates's performance, "I think he identified with the tragedy of that character."

Like *The Hired Hand*, *Two-Lane Blacktop* was in for a bumpy ride. But Hellman received immense gratification when it premiered in London. "My agent in London came and he couldn't get in because the house was filled, and there were people standing. And to have your agent turned away at the opening of your movie is one of those great joys that as Warren said at the end of 'Two-Lane,' 'Those satisfactions are permanent.'"

Before the end of 1970, Oates would pay a visit to Ted Markland in Joshua Tree National Monument. "I sang some modern Buddhist songs up on the mountain, and Warren banged a drum," Markland said. But he got a jolt when he woke up the next morning. Oates was out in front of the Roach Coach, dressed in overalls and a hat. "C'mon, Teddy, have some breakfast," he said. Out in the middle of nowhere, he was rustling up bacon and eggs.

"I would have given you a candy bar," Markland told him.

The Year of Warren Oates

When Peter Fonda proclaimed 1971 "the year of Warren Oates," in critical terms he was not far off. The reviews Oates received were ecstatic. "Warren Oates is a total smash as another drifter whose insecurities are no different than those of his younger companions. Much of the story's import is on his back and he carries it like a champion in an outstanding performance," raved *Daily Variety* of Oates in *Two-Lane Blacktop*. Kevin Thomas insisted Oates "has what it takes to hold the center of attention in the big leagues." By the end of the year, he would be hailed as the successor to Humphrey Bogart and one of the nation's finest actors. Critic Charles Champlin would rate him a double Oscar contender for *Two-Lane Blacktop* and *The Hired Hand*.

The attention did not translate into excess press, although Oates did a rare television interview on *The Virginia Graham Show* in mid-October. Never a fan of talk shows, Oates said elsewhere, "I don't see where it would benefit me in any way whatsoever to walk onto a talk show and discuss something. So if I came on the talk show, I would probably be acting because I'm scared to death in the first place. If you walk out there as Warren Oates, dummy actor, sitting there, a schlump, what the hell is interesting about that?" But he was advised to take exposure where he could get it. "I don't think I set up a single interview for Warren, and he had a right to feel angry about that. That couldn't have made him happy," Beverly Walker said of her efforts with

Two-Lane Blacktop. "We were operating under the biases of the 1960s—they were in full sway."

What did make Oates happy was the Yale Law School Film Society's Warren Oates Film Festival, held on February 23 and 24. There Oates told the audience that his purpose in life was "to watch the Fords go by and play chess." His acting skills he attributed to a new source. "Anything I need to know about acting is in 'Zen Mind, Beginner's Mind,'" Oates told the crowd. Bob Watkins, who had given Oates the book by Shunryu Suzuki, was touched and a bit startled. "I gave Warren the book and one of Suzuki Roshi's teachings is to always keep a beginner's mind as opposed to an expert's mind. I knew he was impressed with it, but more than that, he really loved it."

Oates's Zen would help him during the next two nights in Dallas and then in El Paso, where *The Shooting* was being shown. Last seen on television and then tabled by distributor Walter Reade as too difficult to place, it and companion *Ride in the Whirlwind* had been bought by producer Jack Harris, fueled by the strength of Jack Nicholson's mounting fame from *Easy Rider* and *Five Easy Pieces.* Nicholson met Oates and Will Hutchins in Dallas but would not continue to El Paso with his costars. As the *El Paso Times* noted on February 24, "The appearance of Jack Nicholson in El Paso Thursday for the opening of 'The Shooting' at the Plaza and Cinema Park was cancelled Monday after his nomination for the Academy Award of best actor in 'Five Easy Pieces' was announced."

El Pasoans would have to content themselves with Oates, Hutchins, Harris, and Hellman (who later begged off because of a bout with the flu). A separate story in the local paper informed its readers that the touring party would arrive at El Paso International Airport via Continental Airlines at 9:20 a.m. Thursday. The newspaper also ran an advertisement promoting the event. "In person tomorrow! Will Hutchins, Warren Oates, 7.30 p.m. Plaza Theatre, 8:15 p.m. Cinema Park. Suspenseful Desert Pursuit in the 'High Noon' Tradition. Unequalled climax which we urge you not to reveal. Free Pop Guns for the Kiddies While They Last!"

Thursday started with a luncheon at the El Paso Club, where Oates and Hutchins were guests of honor. Jack Harris took the opportunity to proclaim *The Shooting* a precursor to movies such as *Bonnie and Clyde* and other plot-driven low-budget movies before ducking out to return to Los Angeles. Hutchins, described by a reporter as "a tall and handsome actor with a flair for conversation," spoke next. Then Oates said that although the film had been made with love, "you may like it or you may hate it. It is that type of picture." After appearing before a sizable throng at the ornate Plaza Theatre downtown, Oates and Hutchins were whisked away to Cinema Park, a drive-in where they were introduced by Howell Eurich. Hutchins joked, "Honk if you think I'm funny" to the crowd tucked up tight inside their automobiles. The next day, they went to the Juarez dog track. The featured race was named "The Shooting."

After returning from Texas, Oates would be home for a while. Emboldened by the recent work he had done, he took a more serious approach to his career. "I've got to make sure the next thing I do is as good as the last one," he said. "I don't sleep well and I don't breathe deeply."

Friends noticed his absence at the usual watering holes: the Raincheck, Barney's Beanery, Dan Tana's, Schwab's, Pupi's. "He started to move into a slightly better career position so that he wasn't that much of a hanger-out," B. J. Merholz related. "He had too many irons in the fire, and he was going to meetings with a suit on. He took his career and work very seriously and would play the game of meetings." No longer would Oates, in his own words, "pick up a beer bottle and clear the table with it" or chase a fellow out of the Raincheck "like a raving banshee wielding a knife."

Oates's relationship with Teddy, maintained primarily because of the children, was complicated. One night, after he heard gunshots in their hilltop neighborhood, he drove by his wife and children's house a few blocks away. Oates spotted a car belonging to Teddy's new boyfriend, Bill, and when he called the next morning, Jennifer answered.

"I know Bill stayed over last night!" her father charged.

"That's none of your business if Bill stays over," his precocious preteen daughter fired back. "You need to step back in line because this isn't fair. Mom gets to have a boyfriend considering you have a wife, OK?"

Terrence Malick had given Oates a script he and Brian Kalin had written. "The Land of the Prickly Pear" haunted Oates and gave him a focus that enabled him to shake off GTO, who had been clinging pretty tightly. Malick initially hoped Oates would play one of the parts, but Oates wanted to direct it, and he convinced Malick to play the role intended for him. "Terry is playing the part they wanted me to play and I assure you it's a great part," Oates told an audience at the American Film Institute (AFI). "I think Terry is absolutely perfect for it. So you see, I've cast a non-actor, following in Monte's footsteps." George Stevens Jr., who moderated the AFI panel, referenced Malick's *Lanton Mills* and the element of reciprocity in Oates's decision.

Bruce Dern was also recruited early on, while Oates was still considering acting in the film. Dern remembered,

Terry Malick had a project that was absolutely as fascinating a project as I'd ever seen. He called me up and asked if I'd come over to his house that night for sandwiches and would I read a script with Warren Oates and him and Jeff Bridges. And I went over to his house and it was the first time I'd seen Warren in maybe five years. We'd done a *Gunsmoke* together where we kidnapped Miss Kitty and it's called "The Jailer" or something like that. And we did all kinds of nasty shit to Miss Kitty before the sheriff came and blew us all away. It was fun.

We sat down and read this script and I was blown away by it. In a nutshell this was the story: I was a farmer and Warren was my friend and he had the next farm. And we were like late thirties guys. And a young kid had written me a letter and he was in his last year at Yale. It was 1928 and we were in Wyoming. He wanted to come out. He was a photography major and he wanted to be a *Time-Life* photographer, and he wanted to spend the summer on a ranch and take pictures. So I agreed to have him come out.

About the second day he's here, we hear this enormously loud crash in the mountains. We find this plane crash and in it, there's no one except one dead man, and out of the woods stumbles this kind of flapper woman who's totally out of it but very good with language. She says that her name is Zelda and her husband is F. Scott.

It gets more and more twisted and bizarre and she lies to us a number of times. We're country people that take things very simply. At the end of it, she's got to be taken down off the mountain, but we leave her there. And we never know what happens to her. It's typical Terry Malick.

The project captivated Oates, who harbored a fascination for the Jazz Age, and the script would become one of a handful of pet projects he would try to shepherd over the next few years. In September he told *Newsweek* he wanted to direct a series of films about American history, "great sweeping things," as he described them, and "The Land of the Prickly Pear" was at the top of his list. In July, speaking at the AFI, he talked about his yearning to direct. "I'm not tired of acting, but I've learned a lot as an actor and I feel that I can try it as a director." A fellow panelist asked whether it was a case of quitting while he was ahead. "No, you're never ahead!" Oates vehemently responded. He began to explain the film's plot before thinking better of it. "If you've got about 12 hours I'll tell it to you," he said.

By August, he had condensed the synopsis to under twelve hours, but his enthusiasm for the project was undiminished. "It's a collage of the 20s," he told Kevin Thomas. "It suggested to me how America expanded at that time. It's about the impact of Eastern morality on Western Puritanism. There's this couple—F. Scott Fitzgerald and Zelda is the image—who engage a pilot to fly them to San Francisco or wherever but have to land in a blue-stemmed grass field in Wyoming owned by this Puritan beet farmer. Then there's this kind of Johnny Appleseed, a poor man's Walt Whitman. And then they try to fly over the mountains." He persuaded Peter Fonda to buy "The Land of the Prickly Pear," and Fonda earmarked the project specifically for his friend Oates to direct.

Soon after working with Oates on *Two-Lane Blacktop*, producer Michael Laughlin signed him to a multipicture deal, the first of which would be a film noir homage called, alternatively, "Open Shadow" and "Chandler," the latter being a nod to mystery writer Raymond. Oates would play a private eye in the project, which would costar Laughlin's wife, Leslie Caron. Filming was to begin on May 22 in California.

Before he left for the central coast, he and Monte Hellman drove down to Anaheim to visit a factory that manufactured exquisitely designed magnetic chess pieces. After placing their orders, they had dinner at Belisle's on Harbor Boulevard. Housed in a pink stucco building, the diner-style restaurant specialized in down-market southern cooking, serving possum, grits, pig's feet, and other delicacies. Oates was in hog heaven.

California's Monterey Peninsula was another kind of heaven, and Oates, who had driven up in the Roach Coach, stayed at the Highlands Inn, a luxury hotel that afforded an unparalleled view of the Pacific Ocean. It was the kind of elegance that befitted Leslie Caron, who was to play a gangster's mistress reluctantly falling for Oates, a detective with an impossibly strict code of honor. On paper, Oates and Caron may not seem the most obvious on-screen duo. As for their chemistry? "Zero," said Mitch Ryan, who was also in the film, along with another name from Oates's Louisville past, Royal Dano.

Despite their lack of chemistry on-screen and her bemusement at the Roach Coach, Caron and Oates got along very well. "We didn't have all that much in common—he was from a very different world from me and lived a different life. He was terribly sweet and a very nice person, a very, very good actor, excellent. He was quite, I don't mean this the wrong way, but he was quite wild. I think he lived in a caravan; he definitely lived in a trailer," Caron said. They did not socialize much. "I was quite disciplined about getting up early, and he probably went to another kind of watering hole," Caron admitted. That assumption was also held by Ryan, who was having his own tussles with the bottle. "I was in as bad a shape as Warren at that time," Ryan said. "Warren was not a happy man [during the filming], although he did a job and worked hard, and was great. *Chandler* was a very difficult movie, and I remember it sort of fondly," Ryan said.

Its fate was equally split. But in the publicity interludes during filming, Oates said, "I'm trying to live down the cattle rustlers and outlaws of my movie past, and live on the right side of the law." He also talked up Laughlin and his peers. "A whole new breed of people have survived the last two years in Hollywood," he observed. "These survivors do several things well, one at a time. Young writers want to direct, directors want to act, actors want to do both. Several team up to make a picture, and next time the line-up changes. You need a scorecard, but it's more exciting to work with the rising generation. At a time when major studios are afraid, young filmmakers are breaking old rules, making new ones. Which is why, I suppose, I throw my lot with the Peter Fondas and the Mike Laughlins."

He used the platform to promote "Prickly Pear," stressing he wanted to direct and not act, insisting that to do both at once was like rigging a camera on skis. "It's *intime* all right, but it sure lacks objectivity. The idea that it's genius to direct yourself as an actor is part of the Hollywood myth. For every Chaplin 'City Lights' or an Orson Welles 'Citizen Kane,' there are a dozen flops we'll tactfully skip," he said.

Much of *Chandler*'s action took place on a train, and Caron used her press interviews to further her passion. "I've always been mad for trains, American trains, French trains, English trains, and it's been marvelous to be paid for enjoying a train ride," she said. "Hollywood has always had a love affair with trains."

As affairs went, Hollywood was about to do *Chandler* wrong. Early reviews found that the Oates and Caron pairing "play[ed] as if this couple is speaking a foreign language that neither of them felt too secure with" and noted that they "walk dazedly through confused plotting. . . . At 85 minutes the film still seems interminable." For once, Oates played older than he was. His character was described as "50, bone-weary and passed by," and a weathered Oates looked every bit of it.

From the outset, there were problems with MGM. Caron said later, "My husband has a great deal of instinct about good properties, and he absolutely adored Chandler as a writer, and he proposed to do this film and the studio wouldn't give him free hand. . . . The studio really treated the film very badly." Caron, in whose Spanish-style Los Angeles home part of the movie was filmed, had a very informed idea why. "I suspect it's because it didn't cost enough money. If a film didn't cost enough, it could easily be shelved. I think the film had that problem." Eventually, Caron sued MGM to get equal billing with Oates, and on December 29, she and Laughlin filed a $9.5 million lawsuit over subsequent editing and release.

Oates told Kevin Thomas the film was "an attempt to do a 1946, '47 or '48 Sam Spade story. It's today but Leslie and I are still living in that era. I'm worried. I hope Leslie, fantastic lady and actress that she is, saves me." Oates later called *Chandler* "a horrible film. It was an exciting concept, but the writing and directing were bad. Three days after we started it, I told a friend it was a loser. I saw it crumble for eight weeks on location and then it crumbled some more in the cutting room." He thought its fate would be the lower depths of a drive-in double bill, where it might one day surface above its meager budget, but *Chandler* left no shadow, open or otherwise. For better or for worse, the case was closed.

Oates turned forty-three on July 5, and on July 7, he and Monte Hellman went to the AFI, then located in Beverly Hills' Greystone Mansion, to talk about *Two-Lane Blacktop*. The campus was a good venue for a screening of the film *Esquire* magazine had giddily deemed its movie of the year, only to retract its position. "On the strength of the screenplay, which we read with avidity and delight, 'Two-Lane Blacktop' was billed on April's cover as our nomination for movie of the year. . . . We now withdraw our nomination. The screenplay was wonderful—an account of a cross-country drag race in which a '55 Chevrolet serves as a metaphor for the human condition—but the film is vapid," its editors wrote.

The turnaround flummoxed Oates. "'Esquire' magazine said something about this, 'it's not the script we read.' Well, it couldn't be, because of the time. . . . I think that the mood of the script is there and the mood of the people and what Rudy [Wurlitzer] intended to convey is there in the script," he explained to the AFI audience. Introduced by George Stevens Jr. as "an actor who's described in this week's 'Time' magazine as 'among the finest actors in American motion pictures' which is no news to those of us who saw 'Private Property' about ten to 12 years ago," Oates was dressed for the occasion in a tweed suit jacket and equally natty beard.

In advance of its opening in Hollywood on July 14 at Hollywood Pacific Theatre, the *Chicago Sun-Times*' Roger Ebert wrote, "What I liked about 'Two-Lane Blacktop' was the sense of life that occasionally sneaked through, particularly in the character of GTO (Warren Oates). He is the only character who is fully occupied with being himself (rather than the instrument of a metaphor), and so we get the sense we've met somebody."

Editorial writer Ernest B. Furgurson took a different tack in an article titled "Filmmaker Shows What's Wrong in U.S.—Unwittingly," beginning with the observation that beleaguered President Richard Nixon's trip to China distracted a nation that then "shrugs off that sleight of hand and returns to its bemusement with hamburger prices and job prospects. . . . A comparative study of national attitudes in 1964 and this year [1971] finds 77% of Americans wanting now for the country to concentrate harder on domestic problems and less on what happens abroad." Prompted by positive notices in the *New York Times* that compared the tempo of *Two-Lane Blacktop* to good rock music, Furgurson had agreed to see the film. "Despite two warning signals, I responded to this plug. The red lights were the word 'filmmaker' and the comparison to 'good rock.' . . . The overall impact, however, is that if this empty film 'vividly captures the tempo and rhythm of American life,' then America is in far worse shape than Eugene McCarthy ever told us it was . . . worse than even Arthur Burns, the chairman of the Federal Reserve Board, was saying just last week."

At the AFI, Oates expressed surprise at having been cast in *Two-Lane Blacktop* based on *The Shooting*, unable to see any similarity between the characters other than "maybe as being the leading man, the straight-on, over the horizon leading man." But he championed the film's editing:

> I saw the longer version and it caused you to slow down. It gave you time to get out. What the cut did was make it a tight, entertaining film and that's what we're about. We're not here to hang it up. As "Two-Lane" is now, it's going to appeal to audiences.
>
> The amazing thing to me is that people in our own industry go to see rough cuts, agents and the like, and they come out of the rough cut saying "wow, what a terrible film," fully understanding that a film is not a film until perhaps somebody has finally closed the door and said you've got to release it. Terrible judgments are made and gossip is passed back and forth. It's incredible to me, you know?

But the word was not getting out about the movie. "Nobody's spending any money on advertising!" Hellman exclaimed. "We had a quarter page in the 'New York Times' on Sunday and we open [in New York] today. Not today when George C. Scott's new movie has half a page. Somebody's spending money but we're not."

Hellman outlined his next project, Wurlitzer's *Pat Garrett and Billy the Kid*, which would star Jon Voight as Billy. But the work would go awry, ending Hellman's relationship with Wurlitzer. The film would eventually be made by Sam Peckinpah with Kris Kristofferson in the title role.

In a few weeks, on August 13, *The Hired Hand* would make a quiet bow at Regent Theatre in Westwood. "As he did in 'Two-Lane Blacktop,' Oates comes to dominate the movie by natural energy and credibility of his performance," Charles Champlin noted. "He creates a character who is not a clownish sidekick but a tramp cowboy, wise but not bright, kindly, not a hero." Champlin was ultimately at odds with the picture, however. "There are moments of considerable if irrelevant beauty, but there are other moments when 'The Hired Hand' begins to feel like the only feature ever made entirely in slow motion. It is cinematography gone mad, an endless succession of double and triple images gauzily superimposed and shifting and fading and lingering."

In a feature article about Oates, Kevin Thomas began, "The reviews for 'Two-Lane Blacktop,' Monte Hellman's enigmatic street-racing odyssey, have been mixed, but praise for Warren Oates has been universally unanimous." Indeed, the accolades were pouring in like gravy. Both *Time* and *Newsweek* also ran features, each with photographs depicting a lived-in Oates with a fetching and youthful Vickery.

Oates described GTO as "a guy in the corner of a bar always looking to buy someone a drink and in comes the guy who wants someone to buy him that drink." He told *Newsweek*, "I had to go into GTO as if I had no morality." Weldon Stone's favorite word—"morality"—was very much with him, as was loyalty to his friends. "Nicholson and Hellman, the people I've worked with, have come to the front. We're all the same, the tail end of the Beat Generation. The whole group has an enormous tenacity and individualism." He continued, "I'd like to do something about self-exiled Americans today, men who have run off because they can't maintain their dignity where they are. I'd love to play Daniel Ellsberg. He had a moral stance, a valid one, and they're trying to ruin his life." It was against this backdrop that he would leave the country, albeit for a short time.

Peter Fonda had been sailing his boat, the *Tatoosh*, and was making noises to the press about leaving the mainland for Maui to avoid impending ecological disaster. The hurtful treatment of his film was cause enough for retreat. But before any new Eden could be attempted, there was Europe to consider.

Returning after Labor Day, Fonda prepared to go abroad with *The Hired Hand*, and Oates would be along for the journey. On the way, after hearing mention of *The Trip*, Oates would quip, "That's the one we've been on, right?"

"No, that's Fritz the Cat," retorted Fonda, whom Oates called Flyer after the popular tennis shoes, PF Flyers.

Before he left, Oates whisked son Timothy away for a camping trip at Joshua Tree National Monument. Evenings in the desert were notoriously cold, and as night fell, Oates took out one match, pointed toward a fire pit, and told his eight-year-old son, "Timmy, if you don't get this fire going with one match, it's going to be cold tonight." His son lit the parched wood and trembled as it sparked, leapt, and soon went out. It got cold, and then colder. His father had a solution. "He brought out the old Bic lighter," Timothy recalled. They fell asleep under a sky as star studded as a Nudie suit.

Oates flew to Europe alone. Conducted at high speed—"Flyer" did not do slow—the publicity trip was a wild one. Fonda wrote extensively about it in his autobiography. Oates went ahead to Stockholm and later met Fonda at the airport. "After four days of publicity and promotion . . . Mr. Oates and I were ready to party a little. Horny Warts [Fonda had a cockeyed thesaurus of endearments for his friend] had latched onto a lovely Swede and was ready to club hop." They all hopped to a sequence of jazz clubs, where they were rewarded with drinks, and Fonda shared his stash of grass. Later in the evening, Fonda reported, Oates retired to their hotel suite with his date.

The next morning, the two men flew to Copenhagen, where Fonda explained the necessity of booking a suite, which would allow them to bring back female guests. In Hamburg they drank and took turns carrying each other back to hotel rooms. "For twenty feet I'd carry Warren, and so forth until we finally made it up to our suite. We kind of traded who was going to be the big brother–father figure back and forth, back and forth until we both collapsed in hysterics . . . the last line being 'I wonder what the maids are going to think when they open the door in the morning?' because we didn't put the No Disturb on. We just crashed out on the floor with smiles on our faces," Fonda said.

In the airport in Stuttgart, Fonda drew the ire of filmmakers who noticed him taking delivery of a Mercedes 300 SEL 6.3. The crew recorded the event and chided the actor for purchasing such an establishment car. Local news crews were also there for the stars' arrival, and they chased Fonda and Oates, who sped off in a flurry of flashbulbs. Oates told the press in London, "A German television interviewer asked Peter why he was getting a Mercedes Benz and did he not think that this was not what people would expect of him, and was he therefore not trying to change his image? Well, I can tell you, Peter had a few unkind things to say to him on the air about that. And he was right."

A screening of *The Hired Hand* at Paris's Cinémathèque Française did not go smoothly. During the question-and-answer session, Fonda defended the film's pace and numerous dissolves to the cineastes. "It only hurt for a short time," Fonda wrote, "for we had a case of Dom and some touch."

In Italy, Oates begged Fonda to stop by an olive grove. He bounded out and began gobbling olives off the tree. "No, Warren!" Fonda shouted as Oates's face turned various shades of green. Near Genoa, Fonda threw a coin in the Po River, prompting Oates to ask whether the implied luck was for the river or for them. They could have used it in Milan, where the film's third reel, pressed at the Technicolor lab in London, was woefully out of focus, eliminating the film's chances of being included in the Circa de Stampa competition. In Rome, at a screening for the David de Donatello committee, the same thing happened. These experiences were so dispiriting that Fonda used press interviews to despair over the state of the environment rather than talk about his seemingly sabotaged film. Some thought he had deliberately shot the third reel out of focus.

In London, it was hard to be optimistic as they checked into the Dorchester, where Vickery would soon arrive. Oates suggested Fonda stay in the hotel while he attended a prescreening; he returned, by Fonda's watch, far too early. Fonda was afraid his friend had watched the movie at high speed, and he frantically explained he could not check for focus at high speed. Oates assumed the fatherly role and calmed Fonda down. "Bubba Bear," Oates told him, "it is no longer a question of focus. The entire third reel has been printed so light that the only way I could tell it was our movie was the soundtrack, which was perfect." The next morning's press screening was postponed until the afternoon, when fortunately a better print was shown.

In London Fonda and Oates appeared at the South Bank's National Film Theatre. "I've done my share of, if I may say so, shit-kickers," Oates told the audience. "I enjoyed being in each one because each one was different. If it wasn't, I tried to bring some distance to it. I had a chance in 'The Hired Hand' and 'Two-Lane Blacktop' to stretch my legs a little bit."

Oates was in a playful mood, asking "everyone to wake up and move over two seats because it gives a different perspective." He pointed out, "There's a gentleman way back there who's been waving his hand for a long time. He may want to talk to Peter."

"How'd you spot that?" Fonda asked.

"I don't know, man," Oates replied.

When Fonda spoke of his friendship with Hopper and, by extension, Oates, Oates clarified the concept. "It's about tribalism," he said softly.

Reunited with his wife, Oates obviously had to curtail his philandering, if not his drinking. One reporter from the *Evening Standard* came across his subject nursing a glass of milk after he had been turned away from the Dorchester's grillroom, which had required that he change out of his alpaca jacket into something more formal. Fonda and Oates had adjoining suites and a shared "drawing room," the writer explained. "The obligatory guitar was against a sofa and the room looked untidy." Oates corralled his smaller segment of the press into his bedroom, as he held on tight to his glass of milk.

Vickery, described as a tiny blonde who came up to her husband's shoulder, was a hit with the British press. "She is cheerfully, engagingly irreverent about her husband, definitely not in his shadow," the *Evening Standard* observed. Oates again spoke about "Prickly Pear," with its F. Scott and Zelda prototypes. "The Puritanism of America could not catch up with the technological advances of the time. And it is the same now, everything is accelerating in America except a morality." Of *The Hired Hand*, he noted, "Peter was trying to show that the words of St. Thomas refer to how little man cares for his environment, that passing through on earth he does not pay attention to the pollution of the rivers or the air we breathe. That man considers he is more important than the tree next to him."

John Sandilands from the British glossy *Honey* met Oates minus the milk but still with the jacket in the Dorchester's cocktail bar. "He was wearing a large, shapeless cardigan made from the wool of a yak or some animal equally unkempt, tight pants and high-heeled boots and the slightly defiant air of one feeling fairly out of place in those surroundings," Sandilands noted. "He is much closer to the new style of Hollywood actor than the old."

"I've never tuned into the Hollywood circuit," Oates told him. "I still don't understand most of those dudes who run big studios. You can't get through to them that you'd be happy to take a film camera and a sleeping bag and go out on the road and make the goddamn thing yourself." He then turned his attention to politics. "Governments are so wrapped up in their own goddamn power trips that they forget about the people. They lose sight of the dignity of men."

Writer and actor moved into the dining room, where, using his steak as a prop, Oates demonstrated how a villain stabs an adversary. "You have to turn the wrist a little as the blade goes in, and while you're doing it, you have to grunt in a very *nasty* way." Fortunately, his wife came to the rescue.

"Will you tell this guy what you call me, honey?" Oates asked her.

"An inspirational genius," Vickery gushed.

Oates told *Films Illustrated*, "Up until this year, there was some danger that I would become the all-time heavy in westerns. Michael Winner has now offered me parts in two westerns, both of them heavies, because that's what he sees me as and that's what I'm known for. Luckily I have been able to say no gracefully on each occasion, but I really cannot do that sort of thing any more. I *will* not." He had recently turned down another western that would have afforded him the opportunity to play against Jean-Louis Trintignant, one of his favorite actors. Then he talked about cars. "The automobile has created a health hazard and a life hazard. It's drifted down to one's own identity being snuffed up by this little box you insulate yourself in every morning." He explained, "In America people have been rebuilding junk automobiles for a long time, trying to beat Detroit, to make a better, faster, safer machine than Detroit can make. And Detroit goes on making longer, wider, broader, more powerful automobiles so that every little American can have his big image."

He spoke about his and his contemporaries' place in filmmaking. "We are all rather rebellious and, if I can be vain, we are all relatively honest people and have this desire to beat the enormous cost of making films."

Enormous cost had plagued Dennis Hopper's *The Last Movie*, and it was Hopper whom Oates would be joining in Mexico in November, having signed to appear in "Dime Box" (which would become *Kid Blue*) on September 2. Earlier in the year, Oates had done a quickie for Aaron Spelling Productions called *The Reluctant Heroes*, which aired on ABC on November 23. *Los Angeles Times* critic Jerry Beigel dismissed the effort as "'The Dirty Half Dozen,' or as it is set in the safely distant Korean War, perhaps 'H*A*S*H.'" Oates played good ol' boy Leroy Sprague in a rather simplistic tale with mediocre action sequences and an obtrusive score. The actors playing the protagonists, including Ken Berry, Jim Hutton, and Don Marshall, are far too old to be soldiers, but the story of a maverick unit prevailing against the odds suffices. *Daily Variety* decided that "Warren Oates as the redneck does a fine job of conniving us."

If, on flying out of London, he had left behind journeys akin to *Fritz the Cat*, what Oates was about to encounter in the Mexican desert would make those exploits seem tame. The famously X-rated feline was about to come face-to-face with a pack of Mad Dogs.

16

Secrets and Strengths

On the flight from London to Chupaderos in the state of Durango, Mexico, Oates was unaware that a sultry, auburn-haired young beauty was about to make virtually the same semiarduous trek. He probably did not give his transgressions against married life much thought on the long ride. After all, he had always had an eye for the ladies; in New York City women and drinking were nearly all he and Howard Dayton had lived for. And his age, forty-three, resoundingly late midlife in 1971 terms, had done nothing to abate his ability to fall for a pretty face, regardless of the fact that he had left his very sexy young wife with her family in England. In Mexico he would soon forget, and he would have all kinds of help.

Lee Purcell, a magnificently attractive young actress from Cherry Point, North Carolina, had no idea what she was getting into. She had previously worked on *Dirty Little Billy*, a warts-and-all account of Billy the Kid that was too much for its time. "Billy the Kid was a punk," ran its tagline. Short years later, it might have played better.

Purcell arrived with miles of luggage at the same time director James Frawley and his girlfriend appeared. "Frawley's lady had this huge blue suitcase, and when she unzipped it, one hundred heads of lettuce fell out," said Purcell incredulously. Over the next three days, cast and crew ate lots of lettuce, the last outpost of health they would see for some time. "I can't imagine a film set like that again, never again," Purcell said. "It was like being thrown into a Cirque de Soleil. People leaping out of second-story windows, people with blood running down them. I don't know how a foot of that film ever got shot. There was certainly acid, incredible amounts of drinking, incredible amounts of insanity. I'm surprised everybody didn't have a heart attack. I'm surprised I didn't. I'm surprised the craft service guy didn't have a heart attack. I doubt there has ever been a film that crazy."

The movie she was talking about was *Kid Blue*, and its producer was a man named Marvin Schwartz. When filming was over, a traumatized Schwartz joined a monastery. "He went off to India after this and became known as Brother Jon!" Dennis Hopper explained.

Edwin "Bud" Shrake and his Lone Star compatriot, Gary Cartwright, were journalists and writers. Shrake had a tidy sideline in screenwriting, edited *Sports Illustrated*, and was working on a novel about Dallas in the years just before the Kennedy assassination. Cartwright wrote for *Life*, the *New York Times Magazine*, *Sport*, and, eventually, *Texas Monthly*. He would dabble less frequently after writing *Confessions of a Washed-Up Sportswriter*, in which he bade farewell to the genre. The men represented the time-honored and often perilous intersection of sports writing, political commentary, and just plain excess. Shrake, Cartwright, and friends named their collective, which they minted in Austin, Texas, Mad Dog Inc., and now the Mad Dogs set their sights on Durango. "More than two dozen hallucinogenic plants grow wild in the states of Chihuahua and Torreon, and most of them appeared at one time or another in the Mad Dog Winnebago," Cartwright wrote. The Roach Coach might have been home in California, but its driver would be game.

Dime Box, the setting of *Kid Blue*, is a Texas town that takes its name from a local custom of leaving a coin in the mailbox for the postman to put toward a stamp. *Kid Blue* (named after Hopper's character, whose real name is Bickford Waner) sought to capitalize on Hopper's fame. Director James Frawley was attracted to the script and to Shrake's unusual style. He explained,

Bud (Edwin) Shrake, apart from being a sportswriter, was

a classical scholar. The theme evolves much more from Bud Shrake's experience of living in Texas. I mean, here's this long-haired, weirdo writer—and there's a whole group of them in Texas now—living in the most reactionary, most fascist section of the country, so they are really living a Kid Blue existence in Dime Box . . . smoking dope and knowing you could get twenty years in prison for doing it, and at the same time feeling a certain responsibility to that particular community because of the assassination of Kennedy. There's a whole band of artists and writers in Texas and [they] are there because they feel responsible. . . . Larry McMurtry is one of them, and a guy named Pete Gent. . . . "Kid Blue" grew out of that as well as our own general feeling.

"Durango represented the peak of Mad Dog debauchery," Steven L. Davis writes in *Texas Literary Outlaws*. Hopper was the first to become an official member, with Peter Boyle, Howard Hesseman, and Oates not far behind. Ben Johnson, around whom Oates always tried to appear straight, was playing a sheriff in the film, and he naturally abstained from joining the Mad Dog pack.

The men quickly formed mischievous plans to restage the scenes without informing the director or camera operators. "The longer we were in Durango, the crazier it got," Cartwright said, "until there was virtually no separation between the movie that Schwartz was producing and the one we were living." To say nothing of the movie-within-a-movie the Mad Dogs were filming with their Super 8 cameras. *The Congressman's Carrot* probably did not have much of a plot and, as Hopper noted, "was not much of a movie," but it consumed a certain amount of the cast's energy.

Hopper and Oates had met when they made appearances on different episodes of *The Rifleman*, and they ran into each other a lot, at the Raincheck and in Sam Peckinpah's office and trailer. "Sam was one of the few guys in the studio who smoked grass. We could always go into his office and smoke a joint," Hopper said. "Sam was cool."

Oates spent time near Hopper's Taos enclave, the Mud Palace, which the locals, many of whom were not pleased with Hopper's residence, knew as the Mabel Dodge Luhan House. Less than comfortable with the longhaired communal vibe, Oates preferred to stay on Hopper's property outside Taos, 360 acres that Bob Watkins alerted Hopper to when the former was working on *The Hired Hand*. "He found this incredible little corner, and I bought some land [that is] a little like Bryce Canyon," Hopper said. "It has a log cabin on it, and Warren stayed up there. He just came to camp." The two men were also among Ted Markland's Joshua Tree mystics. "We all went up there and took acid with Warren. Gram Parsons was around, Steve McQueen, and Owen Orr. Going out to Joshua Tree, those were some strange nights. We'd go to a spot that Ted Markland had put a chair of his father's. . . . I think Warren was involved in stealing Gram Parsons's body at the airport."

Country-rock singer Parsons overdosed at the Joshua Tree Inn on September 19, 1973, and his body was being shipped from LAX to Louisiana for burial when Parsons's road manager and a friend hijacked the body and took it to Joshua Tree National Monument and burned it, according to the singer's wishes. That Oates played a role in the madcap thievery is highly unlikely. As Gordon Dawson put it, "He [Hopper] may have such good memories of Warren that he imagines him where he wasn't."

The Joshua Tree pilgrimages and Oates's recent European jaunt laid a good foundation for the rigors of *Kid Blue*. Hopper had just completed the wildly excessive *The Last Movie*, and Lee Purcell observed, "I think he'd built up his immunity by the time of *Kid Blue*." The carousel of carousing would begin each evening, if it had not been revolving all day. "I wouldn't say everybody was entirely professional while shooting, but I would say most were," Purcell said. She added, "Not all. I won't name names." But one thing was certain: "Afterwards, we would party." The rabble-rousing was not all sweetness and light. "People got hurt, got in fights," Purcell said. "Warren was like, 'Oh, stop.' He was very cool. He did not fight," she insisted.

Shortly after Purcell arrived, she and the other women in the cast and crew were gathered together for a briefing. The jet-lagged Purcell listened with increasing anxiety as she and the others were told, "Whatever you do, don't go out alone after dark unless you have a large man, preferably armed, with you. It's very dangerous. Don't go to the hotel. The only place to go to eat is the hotel, but don't go to the hotel. Have your housekeepers prepare food because last night a woman was at the hotel and her husband came in with a machete and decapitated her." Purcell had no appetite for tacos de cabeza. "The whole three months, I never set foot in that hotel. It was a very scary location, very unsafe."

The situation meant that the company passed the time in other ways. "Whose house do you want to go to?" became a frequent refrain. Purcell explained, "At night, maybe because there was no place to go—the choice was the hotel where you could get decapitated or you could walk the streets and get shot at; they shot at people in the streets—we became, more so than on most films, very insular in each other's houses. A lot of things happened that I don't think normally happen."

Once the lettuce was gone, local residents showed up with little burners on which they would cook food. "It was severely cooked, and I can tell you," recalled Purcell, "it was the most amazing food." Sooner or later, though, everybody got sick.

In the Winnebago, Oates came up with a spur-of-the-moment recipe for his fellow Mad Dogs: magic mushrooms on toast, followed by crushed-up Dexedrine flambéed in brandy. The snack was rounded out with spoonfuls of vanilla-flavored LSD. A few days later, two tanks of nitrous oxide, ordered from Mexico City, arrived.

Somehow, a movie was getting made, with some of the cast working twenty-four hours straight. Purcell would fall asleep and be brought oxygen, "and then I would wake up and they'd shoot me. I'd start fading again and they'd bring me more oxygen."

Purcell and Oates played Molly and Reese Ford. Reese was a man out of time, perversely fascinated by the ancient Greeks and man love and inattentive to his sexy wife. In almost every way, Reese was in diametric opposition to the actor who played him, but Oates's performance is heartfelt, more tragic than camp, and

Warren Oates (first row, fifth from right) next to his friend Bobby Coleman, in Depoy, Kentucky, 1934. Courtesy of Gordon Oates.

The wrong side of the tracks, 1931. Courtesy of Timothy Oates.

"That, or jail": Oates (first row, center) in the U.S. Marine Corps, 1946. Courtesy of Timothy Oates.

"Acting gave me an identity": University of Louisville, circa 1949–1952. Courtesy of Timothy Oates.

Bring me the head shots of Warren Oates, early 1960s. Courtesy of Timothy Oates.

Trackdown with Robert and Nancy Culp, 1959. Courtesy of Timothy Oates.

The Playgoer.
the magazine in the theatre

"ONE FLEW OVER THE CUCKOO'S NEST"

One Flew over the Cuckoo's Nest with Priscilla Morrill, 1965. Courtesy of Warren Miller.

Teddy and Warren with Jennifer, center, and friends, ca. 1965. Courtesy of Timothy Oates.

One Flew over the Cuckoo's Nest, 1965. Courtesy of Timothy Oates.

Oates, Ben Johnson, and Edmond O'Brien during the filming of *The Wild Bunch,* 1968. Courtesy of Timothy Oates.

On the *Yonder*, 1969. Courtesy of Timothy Oates.

The conservative anarchist as flower child, 1968. Courtesy of Timothy Oates.

An ice cream break with Vickery Turner, 1970. Courtesy of Timothy Oates.

Blissed out in Joshua Tree National Monument, 1971. Courtesy of Timothy Oates.

Oates and friend Armand Alzamora, 1974. Courtesy of Armand Alzamora.

Oates and Jack (Daniels), 1978. Courtesy of Timothy Oates.

With son Timothy, during the filming of *Tom Sawyer*, 1972. Courtesy of Timothy Oates.

Checkmates: chess with Harry Dean Stanton during a *Dillinger* off moment, 1972. Courtesy of Timothy Oates.

With John Milius and J.D., 1972. Courtesy of Timothy Oates.

Bring Me the Head of Alfredo Garcia: Sam Peckinpah, Isela Vega, and Oates, 1973.
Courtesy of Timothy Oates.

A Sunset Boulevard marquee, 1974. Photograph by Armand Alzamora. Courtesy of Armand Alzamora.

L. Dean Jones, Peter Fonda, Steven Lim, Bob Watkins, and Oates finding their tribe during the making of *Race with the Devil*, 1975. Courtesy of L. Dean Jones.

Lonesome Car-boy ad campaign for Pioneer Stereo Japan, circa 1976. Courtesy of Timothy Oates.

Oates and Judy in Montana, 1978. Photograph by L. Dean Jones. Courtesy of Torrey Oates.

Oates with Becky McGuane Fonda and Timothy, 1976. Courtesy of Timothy Oates.

Oates and Judy, Montana interior, 1977. Photograph by L. Dean Jones. Courtesy of L. Dean Jones.

Oates, Judy, Torrey, cigarettes, and alcohol, 1980.
Photograph by L. Dean Jones. Courtesy of Torrey Oates.

"Kiss me, you fool," circa 1977. Photograph by L. Dean Jones. Courtesy of L. Dean Jones.

Oates with bandaged hands atop Emigrant Peak, 1978. Photograph by L. Dean Jones. Courtesy of L. Dean Jones.

Timothy, his friend John Robinson, and Oates in Los Feliz, 1982. Courtesy of Timothy Oates.

"Compassionate mind pervades the universe": Oates with Bob and Sandy Watkins, 1981. Courtesy of Bob Watkins.

gently understated, particularly considering the excess enveloping him. But he had help, as Hopper recalled. "Warren couldn't remember lines, and he used to have them written everywhere, on his cup, on his hand, under the table. Unless you were close and realized it, you would never know it, that he was reading them. He had this whole thing devised. He didn't ask people to put cards out or anything; he did it himself. It took me a while to figure it out. He was writing on his hands, but he was really a genius with it."

Crib notes or not, Hopper was impressed by Oates's skill. "He was a trained actor; he knew what he was doing. It wasn't like he was just some guy that had the talent and waltzed through it." He added, "I don't remember ever seeing Warren lose it, no matter what kind of narcotic he'd ingested. We didn't do heroin, but there was certainly a lot of cocaine and a lot of LSD. He used that quite a bit, and grass." And it was no secret what Oates stored in the pouch his character wore. The pipe Reese Ford puffed on was stuffed not with Old Gold but with Oates's favorite stash.

Purcell had been carrying her script around in a folder instead of a three-ring binder, and it was as cumbersome as it was inefficient. Oates noticed. "You know," he told her, "that's not a very good script cover." The next day he brought her a new three-ring binder. Purcell was touched by this simple thoughtfulness. She always used the Spanish pronunciation of his last name. "We'd met in Mexico and people screwed up our names, so he was always and forever to me 'Señor Oh-wat-ehz.' I never called him Warren."

Soon, Señor Oh-wat-ehz and the dark-haired young woman were spending time together. They went shopping, and he bought Purcell a shirt. They both purchased several pairs of boots, the Mexican leather goods being both attractive and wildly affordable. But it was more than simple shopping sprees. "Warren was very protective of me, and Ben [Johnson] was protective of me for other reasons. Ben looked at me as a child," she said, while Oates did not. "Warren was very slight. He was tall, taller than I am." He was about five feet, eleven inches, to Purcell's leggy five feet, seven inches, so boots also raised him in her estimation. "Yeah," she sighed, "he was real hot, incredibly attractive, incredibly nice." She continued, "I don't know if he was married. Warren never spoke of a wife or girlfriend at all. I don't recall any women visiting him on the set. I would definitely have noticed."

Oates was set to appear in a supposedly nude bathtub scene with Hopper in which Purcell soaped them down. "The funniest thing was this bathing scene," Hopper said, "and he wore these big long trunks. The whole gay thing just drove him crazy—he couldn't hack it. So he wore these long trunks, and we had to get bubbles to cover these black pants he wore in the bath! It was unbelievable; it was way beyond anything." Purcell did not recall Oates's being awkward, but the scene did involve some difficult logistics. "They were in the bathtub, and they had this enema-thing, some kind of personal item that they took the long tubing to get the water out the window that way. If he was uncomfortable, I certainly didn't know it. It was different for him. Warren's greatest strength was his vulnerability. Warren always had what the best actors had: Warren always had a secret."

The company spent the holidays together, having turkey tacos on Thanksgiving and exchanging gifts on Christmas. On New Year's Eve, the Mad Dog catering service served several batches of pot brownies.

Ben Johnson remained in the background. "Ben Johnson was 'No cusswords on the set,' 'Don't say that in front of a lady,' while we were just totally insane around him," Hopper said. Purcell, who had rodeoed with Johnson, was talking to the actor between takes when a guy walked by and swore, "and not even particularly foul," she said. "Ben grabs him by the neck. . . . I bet that guy never swore again!"

"I recall a conversation between John Wayne and Ben Johnson on a street in Durango," Oates told a symposium on western movies held in 1976.

We were shooting a film down there and it ended up being called "Kid Blue" and John was down there looking for locations or not looking for them—hell, he built the place. So, Ben and Mr. Wayne have this shootout on the street and I was there to witness it in real life. John says, "Well, Ben, I see that little picture you did [*The Last Picture Show*] and it's doing all right now." Ben says, "Yep, yeah it's doing okay. It's kinda surprised everybody." And John says, "Yeah, it was kind of a dirty film, though." Ben says, "Yeah, I turned the damned thing down once but they just kept right on insistin' and it had some ugly scenes in there I didn't like." And it wasn't long until they were cussin' about how they weren't going to do a dirty picture ever again.

On the same set Ben's mother and Ben's wife were working in the picture because Ben wanted them down there with him. Our leading lady, Janice Page [*sic*], had a scene in a buggy and during the rehearsal she came in improvising with a lot of vulgar words. And it was a large sort of picnic setting and Ben stood up and said "Listen, I don't want to hear any more talk like that in front of my mother and in front of my wife and I'm going to go home if you say anything like that again." And actually he got up and left.

Hopalong Cassidy and Ben Johnson have rubbed off on my life. That's about all I have to say.

Johnson himself said about *Kid Blue*, "We had a lot of problems on that movie. We had some people that weren't too capable as actors because of what they were doing, and, you know, it just—it held us up a lot of times. Warren wasn't one of those, but we did have a lot of problems on that show."

Into the Durango fray flew journalist Dudley Saunders, wearing a pressed shirt and a crisp suit and prepared to write a newspaper story about Oates. Arriving for the last four days of filming, Saunders was immediately aware this was no usual shoot. He also noticed that Oates seemed happy; his sentences ran dizzily toward rambling. "Sometimes Oates talks in agonizingly slow and disconnected phrases, changing the subject repeatedly, backtracking until neither you nor he is really sure what he is talking about. He frequently becomes bored, distracted, his mind elsewhere. At other times, he breaks loose in a torrent of words, constructing complex Faulknerian sentences. His diatribes against selfish politicians are endless general attacks against greed and corruption and self-interest."

Oates peppered his speeches with favorite sayings like "When it's there, it's there," "When it's right, it's right," and the contemporary "When you're hot, you're hot." He told Saunders, "When you're there, you're there, and right now I'm there," while lighting one of the two dozen cigarettes he would smoke during their three-hour interview. He complained about career problems, lousy scripts, and the difficulty in finding good roles, but Saunders's presence also put him in mind of home. "I'm not as consumed with acting as many others. I'd be just as happy and fulfilled writing and directing. That's what I'm into now. . . . I want to make a film set in the 1930s about a boy living in Depoy, Kentucky, and firing up the church stove on cold mornings and ringing the bell and hearing the older people talking about the shooting down at the coal mines and listening to stories about wars on the radio."

He also suddenly remembered he had a wife.

> My wife says I change metabolically when I start a role. If I start reading a script and like the part, I start changing right then, becoming that person whether I get the part or not. I'm not easy to live with when I'm working because I'm here and yet I'm not here. I'm partly that other person.
>
> In "Dime Box" I'm having trouble becoming that other person. The part hasn't consumed me the way most parts do. It's a weak character and at this time I don't feel weak in my life. I have great strength right now because of my age and the time gone by and the things I learned. . . . I'm not particularly fond of the character because he runs away. I ran away from something years ago, but I don't run away any more.

The flight he referred to could have been from his first wife, Bobbie, and their troubled young marriage. If, as Oates told Teddy, he left her after finding out that she had had an abortion, the abandonment would not have left him.

On the last day, cast, crew, and critic went to a chilly auditorium of a local school to watch a dozen reels of rushes. "Everyone laughed uproariously as they viewed take after take of several comedy sequences, congratulating each other for good bits. The word 'beautiful' must have been repeated 30 times," Saunders reported. "Their enthusiasm gradually faded, however, as they watched several of the dull, trite scenes."

Oates felt that the movie would have a negative effect on his career only "if it really loses big money or if I'm bad. It won't hurt me because I won't be the reason it failed. I'm not the dominant figure. People usually blame failure on the dominant figure in a film, whether it is an actor or a director."

Before Oates flew back to Los Angeles with Saunders, he had to say goodbye to Lee Purcell, who was sad to part. "We had a nice time," said Purcell, who would see Oates one more time in her life. "I never had a bad time with Señor Oates ever."

On the plane trip home, Oates confessed that much of the filming had been "a harrowing experience." He also geared up to see Vickery, boasting that she took good care of him and kept him stocked with vitamins. She also, he said, encouraged him to write. Vickery was waiting for her husband at LAX. When he saw her, "Oates's scowling face 'youthened' a decade," Saunders noted. He described Vickery as "a cute, bubbly, sexy, British actress." She was wearing a short, Edwardian, baby doll dress with an elaborately outsized, leafy collar that she had purchased in London. Once Oates had time to assess the outfit, he snarled, "What the hell are you wearing?" Vickery had a right to pout, but she also had good news. She had signed to appear with Richard Chamberlain in Jonathan Miller's production of *Richard II* at the Ahmanson Theatre in Los Angeles. Her unfulfilling days as a Hollywood housewife had ended.

Kid Blue had been completed on January 13, 1972. Amazingly, it ran only a couple days past schedule and cost $2 million. As with the last three projects Oates had made, it had a patchy outcome, starting with the change of its name, which *Variety* reported on March 9, 1973. Frawley said, "It was changed for the same reason that the film was incorrectly sold by Fox. I think they wanted 'Cat Ballou' and when they got something closer to 'McCabe and Mrs. Miller,' they were confused and a little angry."

Kid Blue pioneered negative advertising. "The first movie in history to admit it's a box office failure. . . . Maybe he should blame the whole damned thing on Watergate," ran dunderheaded copy. "It's no 'Deep Throat,'" another advertisement incomprehensibly read.

The film was shot with two fairly wide-angle lenses, with a long one reserved for capturing stunts. The set that had been built in Mexico was left standing to take advantage of Mexican incentives, Frawley explained. He added that Hopper had previously been to Durango for *True Grit* with John Wayne, "and it blew his mind that these people who lived on three cents a year in this small town were invaded by a company making a million-dollar picture, putting up these incredible buildings, and leaving." Frawley continued, "Every part in the film was cast from my first choice. I wanted Warren and I wanted Ben Johnson." For Oates's role as Reese Ford, Richard Chamberlain and Donald Sutherland had been suggested. "They were looking for a kind of foppish thing. And it isn't that at all. Because Reese Ford, in a different age, might have been a homosexual. In a different context he might have felt that he could allow these feelings to extend to a physical thing. But in Dime Box there were no gay bars for him to relate to; in that framework, if he had that impulse, it was driven out of his mind."

When the film was released in mid-1973, it gathered a wide swath of reviews. "Rotten," assessed the *New Republic*. Rex Reed deemed it "one of the nicer surprises of the season." Jon Landau in *Rolling Stone* lamented that Hopper was not at the helm. "I for one wish that he was still directing," Landau wrote. "'Kid Blue' just passes the time for all concerned, especially the audience." The *Hollywood Reporter* felt it "manages to be both a counterculture protest movie and an amusing, comic western," and the reviewer singled out Oates as giving "a very solid performance. The Hopper-Oates relationship is handled with humor and real emotion. It's one of the fresher elements in 'Kid Blue.'" Kevin Thomas in the *Los Angeles Times* was less sure. While praising Oates's performance, he found Reese Ford to be "a sweet, naïve man whose adored but bored young wife (well played by Lee Purcell) throws herself at Hopper. . . . Oates is heartbreakingly good in a role that is actually frustratingly sketchy." *Newsweek* concluded, "Oates oscillates between admirable generosity and just plain foolishness."

The film all but disappeared, despite being picked up by the New York Film Festival and having a gala screening in Dallas on June 19, 1973, with Frawley in attendance. When, in August 2006, *Kid Blue* reemerged in New York City as part of a Warren Oates series, the *Village Voice* praised its "honest hatred of work." "When it comes to the sub-genre of Pothead Westerns, this is at the top of a very short list," Harry Knowles wrote, before guffawing at Hopper's thirty-seven-year-old "kid." *Kid Blue* is more than the sum of the products the Great American Ceramic Novelty Company spews out, but it struggles with manic busyness and a dizzying array of characters, many of whom are not very interestingly drawn. The Indians are as cringe-worthy as they were in 1959's *Yellowstone Kelly*, and many of the jokes fall flatter than a panhandle pancake. But Oates's role, played with assorted prompts and a pipe barrel full of pot, never meets the hysteria of his environs, and when he walks off into the desert, the loss is heartfelt.

Dudley Saunders's lengthy story "Wandering Warren Oates" appeared in the *Louisville Times*' Sunday magazine on February 20, 1972. "The restless, enigmatic Kentuckian has been hailed by some movie critics as 'the new Bogart,'" a photo caption raved, and Saunders explained that Oates would "teach young Ryan O'Neal how to act" in his next project. Saunders asked Oates to describe himself and received "a capsule self-description that would drive a semanticist mad." "I am a conformist," Oates said. "I conform to my understanding of the world in which I live. I am a survivalist. That's all. When you are there, everything else is there. Everything is created at once." Saunders unwittingly created a little enmity between himself and the actor by describing him as "monkey-faced." Fellow Kentuckian Ned Beatty soon told Saunders that Oates did not like that one bit.

The past year had found Oates at the center of the Hollywood hippie counterculture, yet nobody ever shouted at him to get a haircut. He embraced Zen but, as friends put it, wasn't much of a joiner, grasped the mystical underpinnings of collage and tribalism, and eagerly ingested relevant substances. Yet he also smoked cigarettes and drank martinis in a manner more applicable to the madmen of Madison Avenue than the pioneers and no-accounts in Taos and Marin. He still had his flower child's soul, although the breed was as thin on the ground as blades of grass at the corner of Haight and Ashbury. But beneath his alpaca coat and leather vest, augmented by a string of beads, beat the unsteady, frequently racing heart of a dues-paying member of the establishment.

In his next film, he would play it straight while his wife stayed in Los Angeles to tread the boards in *Richard II*. Vickery's notices were not stellar, but once she was acting again, she grew increasingly wary of traipsing across the country after her husband. Her husband, when pressed about it, felt she should enjoy the perks of being Mrs. Warren Oates. And there were pluses: She loved her husband's sense of humor, especially when he pretended he was a grasshopper clinging to a tall marijuana plant in a garden on a windy night. "He would roll his eyes, like a nervous and stoned grasshopper would, and cling terrified to the imaginary plant as he was buffeted by the wind," said Vickery, who would roar with laughter.

Vickery also loved it when new friends Verna Bloom and her partner, film critic Jay Cocks, came by the Briar Knoll house, where they had been ordered to avail themselves of whatever was in the kitchen and to lounge by the pool whether their hosts were there or not. When Bloom and Cocks married, Oates sent the new couple three leather items as a wedding gift: a tall container for fireplace matches, a small square box, and a round jewelry box.

Oates and Vickery went to parties at Jack Nicholson's house on Mulholland and at Sam Peckinpah's home on Trancas Beach. Although Vickery's abstinence from smoking and drinking did not bother Oates, he was unnerved by how little she ate. He would call Armand Alzamora and say, "I can't take this any more! You know what my wife had to eat today? One pea and one piece of lettuce!" Vickery never ordered dessert but would take spoonfuls of Oates's. Eventually he learned to eat his piece of pie or crème caramel guardedly, with his arm around it. Vickery was a hit with his children, especially after she wrote a ten-page script that starred daughter Jennifer and her friends. The delighted kids took to it with glee.

Vickery's American stage debut at the Ahmanson Theatre was a high-profile event, largely because of the presence of Jonathan Miller and Richard Chamberlain. Vickery was overshadowed, possibly for the best. "Vickery Turner, for example, doesn't really tell us that Richard's queen hasn't seen much of life; what she tells us is that Vickery Turner hasn't done a lot of Shakespeare," wrote Dan Sullivan in the *Los Angeles Times*. Oates was on location in Houston when she was replaced in the play. After she was cut, she joined her husband, who had driven the Roach Coach to Houston.

The Thief Who Came to Dinner was written by Walter Hill and directed and coproduced by Bud Yorkin. It starred Ryan O'Neal as Webster McGee, a nascent techie who yearns for the challenges posed by high-end crime. Charlotte Rampling was set to play opposite O'Neal but bowed out because she was pregnant. She was replaced by Jacqueline Bisset as Laura Keaton. The substitution did not bother Oates (investigator Dave Reilly) and Ned Beatty. "We never had a scene together, but we spent some time around the pool together in Houston, Texas," Beatty said. "And one of the great moments of our experience together was when Jackie Bisset came and sat down by the pool in her swimming attire. It was two real happy Kentucky boys, I'll tell you."

Beatty and Oates spent a lot of time poolside, talking about women and politics. "Warren, you know, our backgrounds are pretty similar. How would you describe your politics?" Beatty asked him. "He just screwed up that face, man. You know, it was a small face anyway, and when he pulled down on it, it just became mock orange . . . this thing that's just got little doodles all over it. And he thought for a second and he said, 'You know, I'm a by-god constitutional anarchist.' I thought that was the best description of a certain kind of politics which I suspect a lot of Kentuckians fall into," he concluded. Beatty was equally tickled by the Roach Coach and the fact that when Oates decided he wanted to go out to dinner, he drove through downtown Houston in the hulking, rambling vehicle.

Thief is uneven and unremarkable. Oates ran himself ragged and served up what little was asked of him. "This type of comedy is not his forte," observed the *QP Herald*, but Alan Eyles in *Focus on Film* felt the film's greatest pleasure lay in Oates's "performance typically keyed to facial expressions, ranging from premature glee to subsequent hurt, frustration . . . his voice remaining low key and monotonous." Kevin Thomas again lauded the actor. "Oates lends the film some much-needed wry edges," he wrote in the *Los Angeles Times*. Doubtless the plot's association with chess pleased the fanatical Oates, but *Thief*'s editing favored O'Neal, and the film ended up sloppy and disjointed. Oates's frenetic driving scenes, had he been behind the wheel and not in a process shot, would have truly tied him up in knots.

One night in early summer, Oates was whiling away the hours in the Raincheck, an option Vickery was often able to decline. Teddy was at the bar too, and she introduced her ex-husband to her new acquaintance, a Brooklyn native named Warren Miller. Miller had come west for the movies and taken the fork in the road that led to the Raincheck. Nine years Oates's junior, and nine times the talker, Miller shared Oates's penchant for a spiritual quest, which sometimes doubled as a good night out. Oates immediately took to the man who lived around the corner from the Raincheck in a courtyard bungalow complex called Windsor Gardens, which would be home to characters such as Bruce Weintraub, Paul Jabara, Hiram Keller, Sally Kirkland, and Jennifer Lee, a beautiful model who would eventually wed Richard Pryor.

Miller, partly fictionalized in Vickery's novel *Focusing* as Michael Paderoski, talked a blue streak, but he was also a beloved sidekick for Oates, who admired his spark, his sensibility ("Miller, you're wiser than a treeful of owls," Oates told him on the sidewalk outside Dan Tana's), and—crucially—his acting advice. By the time the night was over, the two men had forged a production company, W2 Productions, which they documented on a cocktail napkin accompanied by the blurry date, June 1, 1972. And they had a property in mind, a story of a western loner that was owned by Miller. True to his word, Oates announced his intention to direct "Harry Weill and the Red Sioux Indian" in the *Hollywood Reporter* on November 28.

Miller also became part of the traveling team in the Roach Coach, keeping a loaded backpack by his door in case they were off and running. He sometimes drew Oates's wrath for leaving around the vehicle's interior his smelly socks, the odor of which would rise above the ham hock stew Oates often had simmering on the stove.

Oates would soon be off to play a small but weighty part in Terrence Malick's first feature film, *Badlands*. Miller house-sat and drove Oates's yellow Opel, filling it up using his friend's credit card. Their signatures, it seemed, were virtually identical. When Oates began writing poetry—an introspective commitment many of his friends never knew he undertook—it was often Miller he shared it with, telling him, "I focus on the last raindrop that falls."

It was not raining when Oates and Vickery left in the Roach Coach for Colorado locations, which would stand in for South Dakota in *Badlands*. They made a few stops on the way, especially as Oates loved to park the RV in the middle of a field at the end of the day and watch the sunset.

Sargis, the father of Holly (Sissy Spacek), was a role that did not largely impact Oates's life. Oates is on-screen for a scant two minutes and thirty-five seconds, but he lends gravitas and anger to his scenes with Holly and Kit (Martin Sheen) and provides the foundation from which they head off on their crime spree, based on the 1958 exploits of Charles Starkweather and Caril Fugate. "A fine, wily turn from Warren Oates as her doomed father," Janet Maslin wrote in the *New York Times*, and the haunting dream that is *Badlands* is all the better for that turn.

"Oates encapsulates whole social or cultural histories in a single instant of presence," James Morrison and Thomas Schur write in *The Films of Terrence Malick*. "A walking sign-system, he does not so much *be* as *mean*, signifying lanky taciturnity and tight-lipped menace, coiled anger that never really explodes." Film critic David Thomson said, "I have this image from *Badlands* of him up on a chair, on a platform, painting this sign. And there's just something wondrously dark and comic when he turns to look at the characters who are looking at him; it was a sublime image. He isn't in the film very long, because he's burned to a crisp very quickly, but I love that image."

It was so quiet on the prairie—the film was shot entirely on location, with some 70 percent of its dialogue looped—that the whir of the camera was audible. Off camera, in a soft conversation on the quieter plains, Vickery asked Terrence Malick if he thought she should go to Oxford, England, where she had been offered the role of Celemine in *The Misanthrope*. Malick, who had studied at Oxford as a Rhodes Scholar (he later dropped out), encouraged her to accept the part, a vote of confidence that improved her life but helped end her marriage.

"Times apart were a great strain," she acknowledged. "The long separations were a problem. I would rush back to different locations, the Arctic where he was filming 'The White Dawn' and the Midwest where he was filming 'Tom Sawyer.'" But it would prove to be too much. By the time Vickery was doing a version of *Love Story* for Britain's ATV, her husband was headed east to Missouri, and their relationship was going south.

Oates agreed to play Mark Twain's circumspect drunkard Muff Potter in a musical adaptation of *Tom Sawyer* on one condition: he wanted to sing rather than be dubbed. Producer Arthur P. Jacobs and associate producer Frank Capra Jr. agreed and gave Oates two numbers. In the final film, however, "The River Song" is sung by country and western star Charley Pride, and Oates hops and grins his way through—but does not sing—Potter's signature tune, "A Man's Gotta Be (What He's Born to Be)." The promotion of the *Tom Sawyer* score by Richard and Robert Sherman, who also penned the screenplay, was forefront, and the release of the official sound track, with Oates's name in place of Pride's, followed the movie's nationwide opening in May 1973.

The Sherman brothers had learned their craft at Disney and had won Academy Awards for *Mary Poppins*. The score and screenplay they wrote for *Tom Sawyer* had been intended for Warner

Brothers/Seven Arts, but it was shelved when Kinney Corporation bought the studio. At one time, *Tom Sawyer* was going to be filmed in Cinerama; then that most American of stories was set to be made in Europe. Eventually a buyer stepped in, claiming the project for its inaugural foray into film. The musical adaptation of *Tom Sawyer* would be the first-ever movie from *Reader's Digest*. The flag-waving, family-oriented compendium provided its rationale in its July 1973 issue. "Why has the Reader's Digest ventured into drama in reel life?" the editors asked. "Quite frankly, our motives contain more than a trace of missionary zeal. For years, the Digest has been outspoken in its criticism of the movie industry's lapses into violence and pornography. The time had come to put some money where our mouth was." The editors' tastes ran to a collaboration with United Artists in "a $2.5 million musical adaptation of Mark Twain's 'Tom Sawyer.'"

Richard Sherman had long been aware of Oates's work, going back to his appearance as a Civil War soldier in *Studio One*. "That's when I first took notice of Warren," Sherman said. "When we were talking about who could play Muff Potter, it just sprang into my mind: my god, he'd be perfect."

Oates had often referred to his Tom Sawyeresque childhood, and he threw himself into the role of Muff Potter feetfirst. On arriving in Arrow Rock, Missouri, a tiny town of eighty-one that would serve as now hopelessly modernized Hannibal, Oates characteristically befriended the locals, inviting many of them to share a Coke or two. His children were with him, and both appeared as extras in the movie. Timothy, now nine, mirrors his father's running style in the opening credits, and Jennifer, twelve, is in several crowd scenes. It is as wholesome as *Kid Blue* is wild.

There were children aplenty in Arrow Rock, blissful in their disregard of the frequent 120-degree temperatures. There were also teenagers, including fourteen-year-old Kansas City native Jeff East, who was cast as Huck Finn despite his having no previous acting experience other than appearing in a meatpacking commercial. The ninth grader caught the eye of Oates's preteen daughter, who, years later, was slightly crestfallen when she opened her Hollywood door to find East delivering the pizza she had ordered.

Tom Sawyer was directed by Don Taylor, who loved the locale Frank Capra Jr. had scouted. On July 19 and 20, Oates performed Muff's song, at the apex of which he "flings bottle and himself into water," according to the production notes. "The way he played Muff Potter, to me that's Warren," Teddy Oates said. "The song, 'A Man's Gotta Be (What He's Born to Be),' when they ask him, 'Why do you drink, Muff Potter?' that's his philosophy, you know. A man's gotta be what he's born to be."

Although she may have recognized his essence, she did not hear his singing voice. "Warren did not sing well. It's as simple as that," Richard Sherman said. "We got a fellow named Billy Strange, a wonderful country singer, to imitate exactly the way Warren sang it, in the same way, the same style. It was Warren's performance done by a professional singer. That's the reason he was in tune, he held his notes, and he did all the things a non-trained singer can't do on a sound track." Oates was not happy. Sherman explained,

> I don't think Warren liked that too much—he didn't like the idea that he had been looped. But that happens many times. I mean, it happened in *The Sound of Music* when Christopher Plummer was convinced he'd sung *Edelweiss* when it was actually Bill Lee. We never credited the looper, the other voice, so it remained Warren Oates singing it. He styled the song; he set the style, the mood, the breathing, the whole tone. It was actually Warren's performance. When he's loping along, singing that song, scratching himself and jumping over a hedge, his breathing, and his giggling, and his tripping, it's all stuff that Warren did. There was nobody else who could do what we wanted him to do—a lovable drunk like that, a lovable guy with a heart of gold, but he had a weakness, and he'd bury his bottles every which way in town. His timing was great. He wasn't just a personality; he was a craftsman.

Tom Sawyer wrapped in late August. When it was released a year later, the *Los Angeles Herald-Examiner* reported, "Warren Oates is charming, quietly complex as Muff Potter, the town drunk, avoiding the pitfalls of a broad characterization in which a lesser actor would have wallowed." The *Los Angeles Times* took a responsible tack. "Warren Oates is sympathetic and colorful as Muff Potter although the handling curiously finds more sport than anguish in his drunkenness." *Variety* felt that Oates and Celeste Holm kept the film together for older audiences while noting Oates was "the most authentic person in the film."

Oates loved the film. Sherman said,

> Warren was very, very happy with this picture. He liked the people he was working with. He liked the director, and he liked Jeff East and Johnny Whittaker very much. They sort of bonded; they really did. In the end, when Muff Potter is going to leave town and Johnny Whittaker was saying goodbye to him, he really was crying. It was one of the last shots in the picture, and they both were all weepy. . . . Everybody on the set was crying because Muff was going away. He just wanders out there. Warren was one of a kind, like Bogart, like Cagney. He was a special guy.

Vickery visited Missouri briefly. Her visit was cut short because her mother was in the hospital fighting cancer, a battle she soon lost. Her bereaved daughter returned to south London as her husband and his two children drove the southern route back to Los Angeles. After settling in, they went for a family dinner with Teddy, who told her ex she and her friend Carole Ginter had spent a midsummer day sailing out at Marina del Rey. Also onboard was a handsome Hispanic man with "a blonde hussy in the cabin," as Teddy put it. She had seen him somewhere before.

Finally, she asked, "Is your name Jose Ramon Tirado?"

"Sí!" came the reply.

"I couldn't believe it," Teddy told Oates. "There was our favorite bullfighter."

Her husband laughed and was certain the breeze caused by the fanning red cape from their Tijuana past called for a toast. After several shots of tequila, they took the kids home and swiftly headed for the Raincheck.

In some ways, Teddy still occupied the role of wife to Oates, with Vickery a kind of fleeting and fleeing girlfriend. "I'm not sure about the marriage to Vickery, because Warren never made much of it. She wanted to come to the United States, and he said OK," Teddy said.

The Raincheck was as hopping as ever. Harry Dean Stanton was in, and Warren Miller was eating a steak sandwich at a table next to Marni Nixon, who was dining with her maid. Teddy and Oates went to the bar—not Warren's usual "scouting" stool at the end, but a midzone buffered by bodies. Stanton and Oates did their "nice hat" bit and then spoke about the next film they would be doing together, in Oklahoma. Oates returned to where Teddy was sitting, and she told him she had been thinking about taking a job in Atlanta. That did not go down well with her ex-husband, who liked having her and his children nearby. Then Oates saw Bo Hopkins and excused himself.

After greeting Hopkins, he commenced to harangue him for not taking the part of Pretty Boy Floyd in Oates's next—and biggest—picture. But Hopkins was committed to another film. "Damn it, get out of it!" Oates said. "Goddamn it, I want you to be in this one." He sat down with Hopkins and tried to convince him long after Teddy called it a night.

17

Three White Suits

Warren Oates had a surprise for his wife. As she entered LAX upon return from London, the grieving woman with a faltering marriage was met by her husband, his press agent Stan Moress, a photographer, a brass band, and three giggling, screaming girls holding balloons and a "Welcome Home" banner. "I was very embarrassed," Vickery said. In her fictional version, the narrator was far more charitable about the misfiring welcome wagon. "Leon looked quite heroic in a white suit. . . . Behind them was a small brass band that struck up a tuneless rendition of 'Rule Britannia' as soon as I walked out of Customs."

At their home, Warren Miller had left a recording of Mozart's Quintet for Clarinet and Strings, K. 581, on the turntable with the guide pushed to the side, so it would play over and over. Miller sought to remove himself, but the reunited couple insisted he stay, talk, have a meal, have a drink. It did not augur well that they needed someone else around to shore up their relationship.

Oates would be home for a month, and he was consumed by his next role to an extent that was obsessive, even for him. When their marriage ended, Vickery would blame it on time spent apart, while Oates would name John Dillinger as a corespondent. Oates would study his script and lapse into silence, which he valued and courted. Bob Watkins said, "If he smoked, maybe he'd philosophize a little bit, but Warren was a lot like my second teacher, Suzuki Roshi, who had a saying, 'One word and already you've gone astray.'"

Oates intended to play public enemy number one, he said, "like the Indiana farm boy he was." His next director would be a whiz kid straight out of the University of Southern California's film school. John Milius was making his feature debut after writing the original screenplay for *The Life and Times of Judge Roy Bean*.

In fall 1972, Oates left for Oklahoma, and his wife had little inclination to follow. Instead she went back to England, this time for five months, to play Charlotte Brontë in a television serial about the famous Yorkshire family. She told the English press, "In many respects Charlotte was more liberated than a lot of women are today. She wasn't encumbered by many domestic chores. She had practically the whole day in which to exercise her mental faculties and, in a practical sense, was more liberated than I am." The reporter cited similarities between actor and role. "Charlotte Brontë and Vickery Turner were born in April, married in June, and both their mothers died of cancer. Both are small. . . . 'And we both,' says Vickery, 'share a big jaw and a squashy nose.'"

Self-image was also on her husband's mind during the filming of *Dillinger*. In fact, the press made much of the actor's physical resemblance to the gangster. That did not mean that Oates was not having a great deal of difficulty with the role. In early October, he called Warren Miller from Oklahoma several times to voice his distress. The opening sequence was filmed first, showing a bank robbery culminating with the gangster saying he would like to withdraw his entire account. "You're being robbed by the Dillinger gang. That's the best there is. This could be one of the big moments in your life. Don't make it your last," went the dialogue. Oates phoned Miller upon its conclusion. "I'm not happy," he told his friend. "I don't have the character." When Miller eventually saw the finished product, he was flabbergasted Oates had felt that way. On another occasion Oates phoned, upset that the bunting in the hoedown scene was plastic and not paper, which he felt would have been more historically accurate.

Oates felt his mind-set was not good during the making of *Dillinger*. In part, he was certain they were not given enough time to film. But *Dillinger* represented the first "quality" film from B-movie stalwarts American International Pictures, which had given it a $1 million budget—a large amount for the company. Oates's angst was not evident among his fellow actors, however, and he caroused (and played chess) with Harry Dean Stanton, made friends with the Oklahoma extras, and dined with Ben Johnson.

He also took time to help a novice actor; no doubt it helped that she was devastatingly attractive. "I was lucky to be put opposite Warren. He'd put in extra time to help me with my lines," said Michelle Phillips, who played Dillinger's moll, Billie Frechette. "He was a very professional person and the sweetest man alive, so dear and helpful. I was making the transition from singer to actress, and it is very difficult, so it was really good I had Warren." Phillips, who was dating Jack Nicholson during filming, said, "Warren was not a womanizer. But that didn't mean he didn't flirt. And women flirted with him because he was adorable." She also took note of Oates's ease with the movie's extras. "Milius did a smart thing in that he hired a lot of locals, and Warren was very generous with them too. He was a kind of hillbilly; the people were a little like that too, and they loved him."

To aid her character's transformation from seized to besotted, Oates scared and then calmed her, "making my reaction so vivid." And if he had problems with his character, she was unaware. "Dillinger never killed anyone, and Warren liked that very much. He wasn't Clyde [Barrow]." (After the film's release, *New Republic* observed, "Warren Oates, the Dillinger, can't hold the screen like Warren Beatty.")

During downtime, they would repair to hotel bars. "He had true American values, was a total gentleman, and had nothing to go out and prove," Phillips said. "We had such a good time while Richard Dreyfuss [who played Baby Face Nelson] was off reading Nietzsche." During the company move between Ardmore and Enid, "we all piled into Warren's motor home. Harry Dean Stanton and I had our guitars, and we played and sang, and passed the bottle around," Phillips said.

Oates's smoking in the film was the subject of an aside in Mary Murphy's *Los Angeles Times* column. Oates, she wrote, "smokes filter-tipped cigarettes which didn't exist in 1933, so cameramen have to be sure not to show the cigarettes or the package which sometimes bulges in Oates's pocket."

In the early 1970s, Enid, like Ardmore, appeared remarkably unaltered since the Depression. "We were really transported back," Phillips said. "The scenery hadn't changed." The sound crew had a happy accident too: a local train passed through the town several times a day, sounding as mournful as it had during a desperate decade.

On November 13 and 14, cast and crew were in Oklahoma City to film the scene outside the Biograph Theater in which Dillinger is shot to death after being betrayed by the lady in red. Milius had located two FBI agents who were close to Dillinger when he was killed on July 22, 1934, and Charles Batsell Winstead and Clarence Hurt appeared in the reenactment.

Oates claimed he had not thoroughly researched the role of Dillinger. "I didn't read lots of books about him, but I looked at all the pictures available. He was polite, well mannered, and got along with everyone, he had a country business manner, which was not a city man, very much the romanticist." In his portrayal, he explained, "I copied the way Dillinger held his chin tucked in and the way he always stood with his left foot forward and his hand in his left pocket, and the manner in which I felt he laid back watching others and then took his own course." Oates also drew from the writer-director's idea of the character. "Milius has conceived [Dillinger] as a Robin Hood, symbol of a last desperate attempt at heroism. His gang was never part of the Mob. He had a very meteoric career, just three or four years as a bank robber before he was killed at 33. One of the reasons many saw him as a hero, and the decade adored him was because during the Depression the banks were considered adversaries," Oates said.

Ben Johnson said in 1992, "I think *Dillinger* is one of the best pictures ever made, and I thought Warren did a great job in it. I don't know who they could have picked to [do] a better job. I think he had an opportunity to show people what he could do." Of his own role as Melvin Purvis, he continued, "That was kind of a different role for me, but after we got started into the thing, I kind of enjoyed doing it, you know. But it was pretty tough some-

times. I'd asked Milius, 'How do you want me to play this?' and
he'd always say, 'Well, how would Ben Johnson play it?' So as far
as getting help from the director, I didn't get much help."

Reviews in major publications were mixed, leaning toward the
downside. Eight were negative, four were neutral, and three—
those in the *Daily News*, *Newsday*, and the *San Francisco Chronicle*—were positive. "Warren Oates has never had a better chance
to show his folksy humor within the context of a leading man
role," wrote Joseph Gelmis in *Newsday*. "He's magnificent, precisely the right mixture of American brashness and know-how
and plain good looks and common sense. . . . Michael Pollard
was good for some laughs in 'Bonnie and Clyde' but everybody
is funny in 'Dillinger.'" *Time* found the movie "slack and derivative," and Kevin Thomas, always in Oates's corner, noted in the
Los Angeles Times that he was "masterful" but that the movie was
"as well-made as it is trite and hollow." The *New Yorker* felt Oates
portrayed Dillinger as "more huckster than villain . . . a crooked
sort of charm and a smile that looks fixed by Novocain."

Dillinger received an R rating despite the absence of explicit
sex scenes. Still, it managed to prompt *Product Digest* to say it
provided "one more tarnish on the good name of the industry."
Milius was quickly portrayed as an über-Peckinpah, as in Linda
Strawn's *Los Angeles Times* profile. "I like Kurosawa violence
. . . John Ford violence," Milius told Strawn. "Violence that takes
place within a code. I am Japanese at heart. I live by the Kendo
code of bushido. Honor and skill. All my characters have their
codes. I mean, Dillinger probably had no code. He was probably
just a common criminal—a hood, you know. And the FBI probably had no code. But in my 'Dillinger' there is a whole chivalric
code of the hunter and the hunted."

Oates was, to the *Village Voice*, "a B-movie heavy with A
movie (as in artiness and atmosphere) ambition." The reviewer
concluded that he did not "have enough magnetism to galva-
nize the audience." But the *Hollywood Reporter* begged to differ: "Warren Oates's excellence as a character actor steadies the
movie; he is charming, funny, and sympathetic."

The heart of the matter was that Oates, at this point in his career, was a leading man still burdened with the character actor tag. Howard Dayton liked his old friend's performance in *Dillinger* but had one crucial reservation. "He wasn't mean enough," Dayton said. "The original version with Lawrence Tierney . . . Now, he was *mean*."

Oates was about to join Vickery in London, where he would take time to consider making a film in Mexico with Sergio Leone. "I've had the flu and I'm very tired," he told Bridget Byrne. "I made four films last year [he was not counting *Badlands*] and I need mental rest." He would be leaving a new member of the rambling family. During the filming of *Dillinger*, a stray dog, a collie mix, wandered onto the set and into his new owner's heart. Oates named him J.D., evoking the role he was playing but probably unaware it also reflected his walk-on television debut.

If *Dillinger* did not hold the film world hostage, it did revive the "new Bogart" tag to the degree that England's *Daily Mirror* ran pictures of the actors side by side, at a time most papers were comparing Oates's mug to that of John Dillinger. He also turned up in an Earl Wilson article titled "Are Mustached Men Sexy?" alongside Robert Redford, swimmer Mark Spitz, Charles Bronson, Marcello Mastroanni, Franco Nero, Jack Nicholson, Richard Benjamin, Gene Kelly, and Richard Roundtree, who was then appearing in *Shaft in Africa*.

At the end of 1972, *The Hired Hand* was shown on NBC, and Charles Champlin cited it as the most interesting movie of the week, although he had problems with its "intensely poetic style." Also on offer for the first week in December were *The African Queen*, "which has lately been making more crossings than the Catalina ferry," Champlin chided, and 1936's *The Petrified Forest*. Both films, of course, starred Humphrey Bogart.

Of the five films Oates had made in 1972, *The Thief Who Came to Dinner* was the first out of the gate. Its premiere in Texas benefited the Children's Mental Health Services of Houston. Ryan O'Neal was otherwise occupied, but Oates, Jacqueline Bisset, and director Bud Yorkin came to Houston, where the movie was set, "a city of oil millionaires, astronauts, and poor Chicanos." Yorkin called to the stage Oates, who had roared with laughter during the film's screening, and Bisset, who protested, "I really have nothing to say." Yorkin assured her, "You don't have to say anything. Just stand there and look beautiful." Feminists everywhere, including Mrs. Warren Oates, would have been shocked. Mr. Oates, however, continued with his best belly laugh.

The White Dawn is spoken of in extremes, even if it is not the best or worst picture ever made. It is fascinating, if underwritten, with a quiet pace and sense of place more akin to Terrence Malick's *The New World* than to blockbusters. But the superlatives tied to the film have almost everything to do with the conditions under which it was made, some sixteen hundred miles due north of Montreal in the Arctic community of Frobisher Bay (now Iqaluit), on Canada's Baffin Island. Philip Kaufman's adaptation of the novel by outdoorsman James Houston would test his limits and those of his actors and his crew. Certain members of Oates's camp would insist it so hampered his health that he never really recovered, but although the actor complained bitterly throughout the four-month ordeal, he would not have missed it for the world. He used his resources to find ways to cope, and his interests in shamanism and indigenous communities buoyed him.

Oates played Billy, one of three whalers marooned in the Arctic in the late nineteenth century. The other two roles were filled by Lou Gossett and Timothy Bottoms, with Inuits taking on the parts of native people. Oates got along with Gossett and Bottoms as well as the native players, although during one scene he grumbled, "How do you upstage a tit?" in response to a young woman's partial nudity.

With Kaufman, Oates was less enchanted. The director had attended the University of Chicago and then Harvard Law School before going to Europe, where he decided he wanted to make films. His style ranged far from Oates territory. Actor Harry Northup ran into Oates in Schwab's just after *The White Dawn* wrapped, and he said Oates told him Kaufman wanted to make the film as if he were John Ford and Oates were John Wayne. "You aren't John Ford and I sure as hell ain't John Wayne" was Oates's acerbic reply.

Before filming began, Oates broke a tooth and decided to leave it that way, playing the role of Billy with a space between his teeth. He was not a man who had a good relationship with his teeth, but the gap worked well on film and spared him a hated trip to the dentist.

Oates arrived in Frobisher Bay during Arctic spring, May 1973. The town, four hundred miles above the tree line, was in one of the least populous areas on earth, and the minimal crew (mainly Canadians who spoke French) and actors would either snowmobile or dogsled to location, regardless of the weather. A meager $1.7 million budget meant filming continued in temperatures that could reach 52 degrees below zero. Food was flown in from Montreal, but bad water on-site meant everyone got sick.

They stayed at a hunting lodge and used an old army encampment's meat locker as a screening room. There cast and crew would sit, shivering, as they watched the dailies. Of the three main actors, Timothy Bottoms, much like the character he played, took to the life best, going so far as to sleep in an igloo. Oates took many photos and employed his video camera, and he was generally intrigued, if testier than usual. "Warren was very much like the character in the movie," Kaufman said. "I think he was living the character, Billy, a little bit while he was there. It was a balance of Warren's creative spirit and his ornery side—the ornery side often because it was pretty desolate, cold, lonely."

A polar bear brought in from the Seattle zoo was overjoyed to see snow. Anxious to assure animal lovers that the bear was not hurt, Kaufman insisted later that he was actually pampered, returning "with black shades and an ascot on his neck." Other creatures, including walruses and seals, were killed and eaten by the Inuits, who hunted them as a matter of course. Ravens, however, were not included in the prey because the native people regarded them as messengers.

Oates had signed on for the project almost immediately. "I knew this character as soon as I read the first few pages of the script," he claimed, though he was unaware of what he was getting himself into. "Everybody was pushed to the limit," Kaufman said. "Everyone was sick. I had dysentery the whole time. When the ice melted, you could see that the water supply was just murky rust."

There was a bar—welcoming for the actors but a divisive issue for the Inuits. "A lot of people who cared about the Inuit didn't want alcohol to be legal for them because there's something to do with Vitamin C and the liver. They weren't able to hold it in a way, say, a Warren Oates would hold it, *to a point*," Kaufman said. Shortly after the film wrapped, a young Inuit actress wandered off into the snow after drinking and was later found frozen to death.

There was initially tension between the actors and the indigenous people, heightened when a knife Oates threw during a scene bounced off a rock and hit a woman above the eye, causing profuse bleeding. "There was a lot of hostility for a while," Kaufman said of the incident. But it was smoothed over so well that the Inuits put together an impromptu Warren Oates film festival, featuring *The Wild Bunch*, *The Hired Hand*, and *Two-Lane Blacktop* in the meat locker turned screening room.

Oates gave his director a rough time. "He was a very bright guy, gregarious, but I also think he had dark periods and seemed to be looking for trouble and causing trouble. There was a lot of over-the-top fighting. I think he was subject to black moods," Kaufman said. In the interest of keeping a tenuous peace, Kaufman overlooked Oates's predilections. "In the supplies it was rumored that there was, along with the dailies, a little acid dropped in there. I can see Warren sitting there reading the *Wall Street Journal* on acid, birds flying around his head. Even though he wasn't a hippie, he was sort of in touch with the culture of the time, except that at the same time Warren was very conservative, sort of a right-winger in a way."

Oates was undeniably fascinated by the indigenous culture. "Warren [was] excited about the Eskimos and the shamanistic themes and all that," Kaufman said. "He had some connection with the Indians, conversations with the shaman."

Warren Miller, who had sent Oates care packages of windowpane acid, got a call one night. "I'm standing on my head playing cards with Eskimos," Oates announced giddily. Then Vickery arrived, as welcome as the thaw. "He was on his best behavior when she was there," Kaufman noted. "She was really nice and warm. We all wanted to get together a pool to keep her there! Warren was on such good behavior when she was there, but once she was gone . . . At the time, she was very stabilizing for him. I wish she'd been there the whole time. It would have been easier on us all." Kaufman explained, "Everybody loved Warren, but at the same time . . . In retrospect we can sort of laugh at what he was doing. He just needed to create a little emotion. A lot of actors know how to run and look scared, but Warren had that hair-trigger, dangerous quality that could explode at any point. That was both the fun and pain of being around him."

The White Dawn, hampered by an R rating caused by six seconds of exposed thigh flesh, did not fare well on release, but it is infinitely watchable and intriguing, with awe-inspiring cinematography from Michael Chapman and an icy Henry Mancini score. Its account, from a true story, of three nineteenth-century whalers marooned on Baffin Island who are tended to and then, a year later, murdered by the native population is haunting and never grandiose, and its exploration of several culture clashes is far from cursory. "If the movie had been more successful, there would have been cultural exchanges, and the filmmaking business would have happened there because they were wonderful, natural actors," Kaufman lamented. "It was one of those movies that was released and, for whatever reason, didn't catch on, wasn't pushed commercially, and our blood, sweat, and chilblains didn't amount to what we hoped they would. I doubt that Warren had any further contact [with the Inuits], but I know he liked the spiritual context."

In the fall, Vickery was preparing to appear in a play in Los Angeles that had been previewed in Denver. *A Day after the Fair* starred Deborah Kerr and was due for a run at the Shubert Theater in Century City. After that, it would go on the road, and Oates was considering going with her, although he did not want to be perceived as Mr. Vickery Turner. As it happened, he did not go with her or change his name: a part he was unable to pass up appeared. It was a lead role, it was in Mexico, and it was for Sam Peckinpah. For Oates, that represented the holy trinity.

By the end of September, Oates and Vickery were formally separated. In November, he was deep in Mexico while his wife was in Chicago touring with the play. She was woken up in her room at the Hotel Chicago on Rush Street and served with divorce papers at 9:45 a.m. on November 16. Vickery's future husband, Michael Shannon, who lived in New York, was also touring with the play; they had met in Los Angeles.

An early November piece by Sidney Skolsky looked at Oates in a terse, personal way.

He has a bad temper. It shows suddenly.

He hasn't a special hobby, unless it is playing chess. He tries to find an actor, between set-ups, to play chess with him. ("I always try to win as I do at everything.")

He is straightforward. ("None of that Hollywood put-on for me.") He looks for straightforwardness in friends.

He has a cat and a dog for pets. The dog is named J.D. I don't have to tell you who it's named after. He loves horses and takes jobs in pictures where he can ride one. ("When I get rich I'm going to buy me a few horses for pets.")

He is not a good handyman around the house. He is untidy.

He hasn't any favorite dishes. ("When I'm hungry I'll eat whatever is set before me.") He is a big eater. He likes a drink.

He sleeps in anything from a sleeping bag to a king-size bed. He wears his clothes in the bag. He sleeps with Vickery in the king-size bed. He usually wears pajamas. The color of his pajamas is green and that's also the color of the bed sheets.

Green—even the jealous stripe—was not the color of divorce, as Oates and Vickery split cleanly. Eventually Oates said, "I hope Vickery has found herself a young man in New York who will give her the time and attention she deserves." For her part, Vickery said at the marriage's end, "He told a friend of mine, after I'd left him, 'Perhaps now I'll get a good meal for a change.'"

Oates's marriage to Vickery lasted four years, two months, and nine days, but in terms of the time they spent together, it was closer to a summer romance with occasional rain clouds. Although his infidelities had slowed down, they still occurred, and that was like being a little bit pregnant. One night in the Raincheck, a woman had danced her way down the bar and cozied up to Oates. He asked her if she wanted to go skiing. "When?" she asked. "Right now," came the reply. They got up and left the bar, waltzed into a waiting cab bound for LAX, and flew to Aspen. They would buy what equipment they needed when they got there.

Oates had his wild streak and his demons, but they were underpinned by a very real shyness. Coupled with a propensity toward drinking, the result could be destructive and deceptively volatile, an internal combustion of the soul.

His interest in the universe was steadfast, and Oates became a disciple of *Worlds in Collision* by Immanuel Velikovsky. First published in 1950, the tome is a cosmic stew with a cataclysmic chaser, mixing biblical and indigenous beliefs—part Nostradamus and part Carlos Castaneda. The planet Mars is given a starring role. Reading *Worlds in Collision* enhanced by certain substances might make it all seem as compelling as gravity. "*Worlds in Collision* and *Zen Mind* give a pretty good idea of what he believed in," said Bob Watkins. "He got a lot out of *Worlds in Collision* and wrote poetry out of that book."

"Worlds in Collision" could almost serve as an alternate title for Oates's next film, although his and Sam Peckinpah's worlds did not so much collide as collude, and the dark depths would seem like a tourist destination compared to where they would go together. As Bennie, Oates would go deep, and then come up with someone else.

Bring Me the Head of Alfredo Garcia, based on an idea by Frank Kowalski, had been knocking around for some time. Originally, after writing a twenty-page treatment with Kowalski, Peckinpah thought of it as a project for Lee Marvin and Jane Fonda. That Marvin was considered might have rankled Oates. "When you get around to Marvin, then you're beginning to reach into my backyard," he had said.

Peckinpah employed a scriptwriter named Walter Kelley to do

the screenplay. Kelley wrote the first half before being unceremoniously relieved of his duties, and Peckinpah finished the 105-page script with Gordon Dawson, who had moved up from his wardrobe responsibilities and was now a working writer. Dawson explained,

> Kowalski had the idea, and he laid it on Sam when they were driving in his Porsche to Vegas. He really liked it. Kowalski couldn't crack the screenplay for some reason, so Sam sent it to me over here. I wrote it. It was so easy: I just wrote tongue-in-cheek Peckinpah. I wrote Sam. How can I drag this guy through every toilet in Mexico? I knew Mexico and I knew Sam, and I knew how much Sam loved Mexico. And I knew what Sam liked about Mexico, so I just put it all in there.
>
> At first I thought it was a joke. I never thought it would get made because it was such a down and dirty picture.

Peckinpah, in the aftermath of *Pat Garrett and Billy the Kid* and *The Getaway*, must have felt empowered to even consider such an undertaking. "But instead of the new life promised by the end of 'The Getaway' Bennie seems to have found the purgatory foretold in 'Pat Garrett,'" Richard Combs wrote in *Sight and Sound*. "The script deals with female vengeance," Peckinpah said. The story still shocks years later. He showed the script, about a man who is sent to retrieve the head of an already dead man to collect a bounty, to James Coburn and Peter Falk. Both men, neither of whom qualifies as a shrinking violet, recoiled. Then Peckinpah thought of Oates, to whom he still felt indebted for having brought to him *The Ballad of Cable Hogue*. Peckinpah then gave the lead to Jason Robards.

"Dillinger was a populist hero in the same way that Bennie is. They ride on the fringes of society. It was the kind of character he gravitated towards," said Garner Simmons, who also played a small role in the film. Oates was never, ever going to say no. "If a director like Peckinpah offers me a film tomorrow, I'm not going to read the script," he told *Image et Son*. "I wouldn't know how to stop myself. There aren't many people I'd say that about."

Filming was set to begin in early September, but Oates was ill (the expiration of his marriage could not have helped). The start of production was delayed for a couple of weeks, and Mort Sahl then had to pull out of his role because of a lecturing commitment. With Sahl's departure, Oates lost a chess partner, and the part of Quill went to Gig Young.

In hopes of securing a PG rating for his project, Peckinpah wrote a letter to the MPAA. "I am moving ahead but walking backwards," the director wrote. "We tested 11 people yesterday and surprisingly enough, they were all superb. Warren Oates, I feel, will give his best performance in the part of Bennie." In terms of ratings, however, Peckinpah's hopes were dashed by a reply from Richard M. Mathison. "There are certain elements in this story which may go beyond the R category and lead to an X rating," the official explained.

In the film, Bennie would get ten thousand dollars for Alfredo's head. Oates would be paid fifty thousand dollars to portray Bennie, but some primping was necessary: In the production notes for September 19, Peckinpah wrote, "Call Warren Oates and get him to Max Factor for hairpiece as soon as possible." Five days later, he dictated, "Try and obtain some turkeys." And then back to Oates: "White hush puppy shoes ok but get some matching brown ones. Get Warren's saddlebag, age it down and cover his initials with something and use it in the picture." The notes continued, "Buy some neck scarves for Bennie. 'Charro' costume for Warren Oates. 3 white suits."

There was also a reminder to contact Harry Dean Stanton at a Ramada Inn. Peckinpah planned to offer him the part of Paco, if Kris Kristofferson was not available. "I don't know if I would have taken it," Stanton said cryptically. Before the cast flew down to Mexico City, an interesting interlude occurred. Garner Simmons, working on his Peckinpah treatise, arranged to meet Oates in Hollywood. He had been down with *Alfredo Garcia* during preproduction, and then called Oates and told him what he was doing. The two men met at the Brasserie in Sunset Plaza on Wednesday, September 3, the same day the requiem funeral mass for John Ford was being held at the Blessed Sacrament Church with some eight hundred people in attendance. "Many who came into the restaurant had been to the funeral," Simmons said. Over dinner and drinks, Oates told him that acting was a kind of personal therapy. "He was able to express all the feelings he had, to dig inside himself to find the truth."

Also returning to work with Peckinpah, against his better judgment, was Chalo Gonzalez, who would be paid two hundred dollars a week for his role as, well, Chalo. "Sam had such a strange power over all of us. I don't know why. Sometimes I think we were masochists," Gonzalez said. "With *Alfredo Garcia* I was working at Paramount, and he called me up and said, 'Listen, you promised to do a picture with me. Warren Oates was there and Gordie Dawson was there and they overheard you saying that you would do the part. I even wrote the part for you.'"

"I knew he was lying," Gonzalez explained, "but I said, 'OK, I'll do it. Last time.'" When Gonzalez ran into Warren Oates, he asked if Peckinpah's story was true. "Warren, did I say that?"

"Oh yeah," Oates told him.

Alfredo Garcia would be shot in Mexico City and Cuernavaca and would feature "a pop and beer tie-up," a first for a Mexican production. Oates's initial address was Adolfo Prieto 1207, floor 5, a domicile eventually shared by his costar, Mexican screen actress Isela Vega, who got the part of Elita in early September and would receive seven thousand dollars for her efforts.

Vega, the Sonora Señora, was a native beauty who had been photographed by Tom Kelley, famous for his nude shots of Marilyn Monroe. Extremely comfortable in her own skin, Vega would show a lot of it while quietly decrying how little the role gave her to do. "Isela Vega did a lot of nude scenes," said Gonzalez. "This was nothing new for her. She was a wild girl. She didn't mind taking her clothes off. "

When Gonzalez arrived in Mexico City, Peckinpah told him, "Go to wardrobe; Isela Vega is there."

"You look a little burned," Gonzalez said to Vega.

"This is nothing," Vega replied, lifting up her skirt. "I went to sleep in the sun and I burned my ass."

"She was a pistol," Dawson said. "She came out on the first

day on the set, and she was dressed in something a little low cut. She looked around and everyone was trying to get an angle to look down her cleavage."

"All right boys, everybody gather round. Stop what you're doing. C'mere," Vega said.

"She just stripped away and said, 'Here, take a good look at 'em. From now on, stop staring at them.' She had more balls than a lot of guys, I'll tell ya," Dawson said. "She was a great broad; she'd just stand there and do it, just walk naked through the crew, the toughest broad you could ever want. You couldn't ask for a better one. She's a hoot to be around, and so was Warren. And you've got characters like Gig Young and Bob Webber . . . Holy cow. You had to work them all with a butterfly net."

There were no butterflies in the film, but there were flies—and a fly wrangler. Rumors that cockroaches were brought in were unfounded, but fights came with the scenery. "They had arguments, Sam and Warren shouting," Gonzalez said. "Once they started doing the film it was OK, but before that you could hear the arguments in the trailer. They were shouting a lot, but you know, sometimes they shout because they are happy; sometimes they are mad. You don't pay attention to these guys anymore. You say, the hell with it."

Before Vega was cast, Oates had tested with eleven actresses and one newscaster from the Los Angeles market. Oates told Garner Simmons,

> I went down to Mexico to do the tests for the picture, and I was a little jumpy. But Sam has a way of directing you that's like shorthand. I went through this one scene with the first actress, and Sam comes up to me and says, "Don't screw around with it. Right there is where it's at, so don't screw around with it." Then with another girl he comes up to me and says, "Who do you think you are, John Dillinger?" Or with another girl, "Who do you think you're doing, Warren Oates? You had it, so don't screw around with it."

Shooting was set to begin on October 1 but was again delayed because of makeup problems related to Vega's sunburn. The next couple of days were hampered by smoke coming from the Chevrolet. "Lessons learned from the making of the film," Peckinpah wrote: "Carefully check the cars; the Mexican mechanical problems were great." "The old Chevy we had," Dawson said, "it couldn't make it up the hill, and we all had to get together and push it." On October 5 they could not shoot at all. The road they were using had to stay open all day in readiness for the Mexican president's wife to use.

Oates was finding it a challenge to get into the character of Bennie, a disheveled expatriate living on the rough edges of Mexico, making a living playing piano for tourists in a bar that is not so much seedy as downright abject. His marginal existence is made divine only by his love for Elita, a prostitute who returns his affection but also is adamant that he not desecrate the grave of her former flame, Alfredo Garcia. To Elita, no payoff is great enough. For Bennie, the money he is offered for Garcia's head is a last, desperate grasp at salvation.

The sad sack was a stretch for him, and he called Warren Miller for advice. "Sometimes," Miller told him, "you feel so at odds with yourself, you're sitting up wearing sunglasses in bed. It's a way of not facing the world." Oates appropriated an oversize pair of mirrored spectacles from Sam Peckinpah. Oates said, "I really tried to do Sam Peckinpah, as much as I knew about him, his mannerisms, and everything he did. I've had infinite opportunities to study him. When you work for a director, if he's a very impressive person you try to steal from him anyhow; if he's an animated fellow with a passion, like Sam. I tried to say it all, what I knew about Sam and his love for Mexico." Dawson explained, "I was writing Sam, and I think I shared that with Warren. Certainly, if you're looking for someone to look at, you can just look across the camera and see Sam sitting there, and it would be very easy to get into that character."

Garner Simmons said, "In 'Alfredo Garcia' Warren Oates is playing Sam and for Sam to vest that, there was something very special there. They were very much kindred spirits. Sam saw himself as a kind of outlaw and so did Warren. They were outsiders and they'd grown up in the business together, starting out when Sam was a writer. When he got the chance to direct, he used Warren the first chance he got."

Warren Miller asked Oates if he could fly down to Mexico City for a visit, and Oates was rarely one to refuse. After he got there, the full-bearded Miller wrangled his way into a screen test with his friend. "I got into the Chevy with him, and I was terrified. All traces of Oates had disappeared—he was that mean." Miller was not cast, but in terms of Bennie, Oates never looked in the rearview mirror again. "He was really into the character," Dawson said, "and I think the dialogue would have come out of him naturally. There were some very poignant scenes with him and Isela, and those were very poignant to watch him do."

Indeed, when Bennie proposes to Elita during a picnic, there were tears from onlookers and actors. "I just knew there was no place to hide in that scene," Oates told Donnie Fritts, who played a biker in the film. "She had me, and I was cryin' too."

Alfredo Garcia was not shot in sequence, and the weather, plus Oates's singular performances in which he did something new in every take, made matching a nightmare. Then there was the problem of getting three cars that looked alike. But nothing compared to the whirlwind being evoked by Peckinpah. "I just hated it with Sam when he was going to do a picture in Mexico," Dawson said. "You just knew he was going to be out of control."

Peckinpah played with actors as if they were sparrows on string. "He loved to mess with actors' minds so Warren could think he was pissed off with him just to get Warren really edgy and red-eyed for a scene," Dawson recalled. "He had a game called Rope, and he would just string people out on rope and yank it every now and then, and really get them rattled. He thought that was how he got the best out of people. He was so insecure that the only way he could have control of a set was to make sure everyone was more insecure than he was. He really kept everybody on edge." Simmons said, "Sam had the uncanny ability to keep all the actors off balance because that's the way he saw the world: there were no absolutes."

Drinking and drugs held unusual sway. Oates might have been

swigging vodka and tequila, but Peckinpah was swinging head-long into cocaine. Dawson said,

> Sam did fall apart during the shooting of the film, no doubt about it. But just because he fell apart didn't mean that we could take it easy. It didn't make it any easier on anybody. Sam falling apart meant you had to be even more on your toes. You sit around and wait for him—he was supposed to be there at six o'clock and he wasn't there till ten. We all sat on our asses, but that doesn't mean he didn't get out of the car spitting and snorting and finding blame everywhere. *He* certainly wasn't faulted for the late start.

Beneath his tanned and tough exterior, Oates could be very fragile. "Oates was a coiled spring," said Dawson. "He was on his game, no doubt about it. When you're part of a big ensemble cast like *Major Dundee* or *The Wild Bunch*, you can sit around and play poker and grab ass and not think about it much. But this was him, and he was on his game completely. He was 100 percent. But it was also incredibly invigorating for him too. He was really coming up with the goods, and that always feels good. He certainly did the film justice."

Several bars were scouted for the Mexico City one where Bennie plays the sticky ivories: El Reno, Los Mangos, the Panama Club ("genuine drinks"), the Fulstos Club, and the Florida Club. Los Mangos was in the lead for a while—"few gringos, Mexican bartender," went the production notes. But the Tlaquepaque Bar in Mexico City got the nod as the lair in which Bennie appears. He was going to play "I Remember April," but the filmmakers found they would have to pay six thousand dollars for the song. "Guantanamera" was substituted, with Oates asking for earplugs so he could listen to his preferred Pete Seeger version of the song while miming his piano playing. In the scene, Katy Haber, Peckinpah's assistant and lover, is seated in the audience wearing blood-red beads around her neck.

The Tlaquepaque was where Stanley Meisler from the *Los Angeles Times* interviewed Peckinpah and producer Martin Baum for a piece on the new phenomenon of runaway productions. In October, the National Conference of Motion Picture and Television unions passed a resolution against Peckinpah, declaring that *Alfredo Garcia* could have been filmed in the United States and threatening to picket when it appeared in theaters.

"I don't think these people can read," Peckinpah responded, while tucking into a goat shank sopped up by corn tortillas. "This is a story about contemporary Mexico and it couldn't be made anywhere else. According to them, I probably should have made 'Straw Dogs' in Arizona and 'The Wild Bunch' in Cucamonga." Meisler wrote that the Tlaquepaque "was a bar that tried to cater to American tourists and therefore represented what Mexicans believe Americans want in an authentic Mexican cantina. Once shooting was at an end, and Gig Young picked his way through American tourists toward Warren Oates playing the cantina piano, an observer had the strange feeling that here was Mexico trying to look like Hollywood. Yet this was Mexico and could not have been duplicated with any sense of reality anywhere else."

Baum defended Peckinpah to Meisler. "I think that the unions have a good case with the wrong picture. I think they picked on Sam Peckinpah because he is a colorful man. It guarantees their getting into the papers. There's been more written on this picture than on Watergate."

"Not quite," Peckinpah said.

"Well, there's been more written in 'Variety,' in the trade papers."

"I'm delighted to make pictures in the United States," Peckinpah concluded. "I think the crews there are great—just as I think Mexican crews are great."

Clearly the food agreed with the irascible director. The bar did not with Dawson. "It was an ugly, crappy, down and dirty place. You could smell the urinal from the fucking bar. If every trumpet didn't sound like it was full of spit, it wasn't Mexican."

Joining Gordon Dawson for dinner one night, Oates was not happy to be the butt of an unintentional joke. "The housekeeper asked us what he drank and we said he drinks vodka," Dawson said. "We're all sitting down to dinner and there was a big glass of what Warren thought was water. He was thirsty and he took a big drink of water. . . . Oh my god, he spit it all over us. He was jumping around saying, 'You son of a bitch, Dawson!'"

Gonzalez was along on another night. "One day we went to a restaurant, and El Indio [Emilio Fernandez] had six girls with him."

"Pass one of the girls to Warren so he can have fun," Fernandez ordered.

"Warren wasn't having too much fun because he couldn't speak Spanish, and then Emilio Fernandez got pissed off and left, and then Warren and Isela went together, Sam and Katy [Haber] had gone together, and left the poor girl there. I took the girl in my car to Emilio Fernandez's house, but he wouldn't open the door. He was crazy. And Warren and him got along together fantastically."

Peckinpah threw a cast party in the Tlaquepaque. Amid the shouting, the merriment, and the sometimes mournful mariachi music, Isela Vega took to the stage in attempts to subdue the revelers. "I will show them my ass," she pronounced.

"Isela, goddamn it, put your clothes on," Peckinpah growled.

"They will never listen unless I do something like this."

The announcements that followed were trivial but peppered with expletives. Vega was urged to shed more "ropa" before she began singing "Guantanamera," lustily at first, and then woefully off-key. "What you see is what you get," she announced before retrieving her pantalones and going to sit with Peckinpah and Oates.

"I love your nipples," Peckinpah said, and then suggested a salacious act he wished upon her. "Warren will be there," he added.

Oates gasped slightly but recovered and laughed. "When your neck gets tired," he said to Peckinpah.

A raffle was organized—the prize might have been just about anything—but by the time the night was over, no one remembered to draw the winning ticket.

In the midst of filming, Peckinpah decided he wanted to go to Acapulco. Gonzalez said, "We rented a van, a motor home, and

Warren and myself and Sam took off. During the whole drive to Acapulco, Warren was picking up marijuana seeds and throwing them out on both sides of the highway."

"I want Mexico to be a paradise!" Oates exclaimed.

When they got to Acapulco, Oates was placed on the fourteenth floor of a hotel, but because of a recent earthquake, the elevator was inoperable. "If you think I am going to walk fourteen [sic] flights of stairs, you're crazy," Oates said. Peckinpah suggested they go to the beach and stay there, but Oates elected to find another hotel, and the getaway proceeded as planned. "We had drinks; he was a joy to be with. He was not a belligerent guy like Sam. This guy, he got along with anybody," said Gonzalez.

But there was a movie to be made. An early scene in which Bennie finds he has crabs had upset the sporadically prissy Oates, but later that evening, he grew even more antsy when he found out that his Trans World Airlines stock had started to slide. Warren Miller was staying with him at the time. "We were in Mexico City, in two little beds, and Warren's got a calculator trying to figure out what to do about his TWA stock, which was slipping to $2 a share."

"You can see how a person could become a fascist when they got older," Oates ranted.

If the crabs incident and his stock's nosedive disturbed Oates, his character was about to become inconsolable. After the picnic at which Bennie declares his love for Elita, they pull over to have dinner and spend the night out under the sky. But two interlopers appear. For their roles as Paco and John, Kris Kristofferson and musician Donnie Fritts were paid $433 a day. Paco plays guitar—Kristofferson had wanted to sing the Mexican standard "Cielito Lindo," which Vega sang—and then at gunpoint orders Elita away from the campfire. Bennie is left helpless with John as Elita is made almost complicit in the rape scene.

"'Alfredo' has basic dramatic weaknesses," Oates said in 1974. "It's structured around a Rita Hayworth figure and a down-and-out piano player. They're in love and trying to survive, two classic dramatic figures. But the crab scene and the rape scene destroy the idealistic relationship between these people; it shatters their harmony, the dramatic logic. It was the most difficult thing for me to adjust to. It hurt the story and I never understood it. I challenged Sam on it."

The graveyard where Alfredo is buried had to be changed. The same rains that delayed production had rendered the chosen location too verdant. The furniture store where Elita reluctantly asks after the body was in Huitzilac, a village that had a tiny, whitewashed burial ground that would serve. The light in the cemetery—as often in the film—was wavering day for night, and the demand on Oates to portray a grave robber who would in turn be buried and then discover that his lover, Elita, had been murdered, was gargantuan. Oates played it to the depths. Garner Simmons observed, "Put a man on a journey like this, it's the heart of darkness, the darkest part of the soul and it's a very tragic story because he [Bennie] gives away the one thing he cares about without realizing it. It costs him the woman he loves. Sam respected Warren's willingness to go to the deepest, darkest parts of himself."

To reach that core, Oates had a little help. "We did mushrooms together the morning of the scene where he had to come out of the grave," Dawson revealed. "He was totally on mushrooms for that whole scene. I was like his wingman just off camera, the one spraying him down and doing all the stuff. He and I had the communication on that so he could block everything else out."

It worked, but it also wrenched Oates's soul. With Elita dead, Oates the actor mourned the end of his efforts as a romantic lead. "Warren was very much in tune," Simmons said. "He responded to things. He was an actor who would internalize whatever the external elements were and then find the truth in that, get it on the screen. Despite his ability to be raucous, he could really underplay things and play the emotion in his face. He was a very emotional actor."

Peckinpah was elated with Oates's performance. But he was angry again with Chalo Gonzalez. "Sam got pissed with me," Gonzalez remembered. "Through the whole picture, I am drinking, and the other guy [Esteban, played by Enrique Lucero] is singing and not doing anything. Then we have a flat tire, and the other guy is drinking. There was no dialogue, and then it just came out of me, 'How come I'm doing all the work and you're doing all the drinking?'"

"Cut! What did you say?" Peckinpah asked Gonzalez. "Son of a bitch, that's great! Thank you." An uneasy truce prevailed, but for a variety of reasons Gonzalez—and Oates—never worked for Sam Peckinpah again.

With Elita gone, Bennie shifts to a relationship with Alfredo's head, by turns tender and truly, unsteadily insane. "We took a cast of a Latin-looking extra's head in L.A. and took his picture to be in the locket," Dawson said. "We cast his head, so that it was a head when he pulled it out of the bag. It may have been a ball—one or two rubber balls—for rolling around in the car. And it wasn't cockroaches we brought in; it was flies. We brought in a guy from the University of Texas to breed flies because flies have a one-day lifespan. Bringing flies to Mexico is a bit like bringing grass to Mexico," he concluded. The flies that buzzed around the head were attracted by drubbing the ball with grease and then sprinkling sugar on it. Another scene called for the flies to bite Bennie's legs, and they did. "I think because they were sterilized, they bit harder," Oates said. "They were very angry."

On a road trip with Alfredo's head, Bennie stops to get ice to preserve his bounty. Dawson recalled,

We were all set up to film, and a light plane came over us and dropped just out of sight at the tree line. Then we heard a crash. Right after it, almost, came these Suburbans with these guys in shades and suits and machine guns, and they went off into the forest and came back with these two really badly injured people and two duffel bags. They asked us if we could use our company doctor to tend to the injured people and we said yeah. They cleared out the school and took in the two people and the two duffel bags. Emilio Fernandez went with them, and he came out a little while later with one of the duffel bags. It was full of kilos of dope, and it was passed around.

It was a defining moment for the entire experience of *Alfredo Garcia.*

At one point, Oates felt so wounded by Peckinpah's treatment that he enlisted Fernandez to join him in writing a wine-soaked plea to their director.

Dear Sam: Warren Oates and Emilo [*sic*] F. have been gifted by representatives of God Bacchus limitenos with four cases of nectar of the grapes and we have been palating its products that have filtered in perfumes going out from our stomachs to our hearts, to name of Sam Peckinpah. Sam, there is no doubt of our gratitude to you for incorporating us to do the picture in this significant film, so important a task of yours. Sam, nobody is more capable than you to fulfill manifest of this new cycle. This new cycle demands rhythms, dynamics but the Indio cannot forget you being close to your cameraman not only to impose but to search beauty, good taste and being you personally, Peckinpah. Sam, the greatest gift ever given to man for expressing himself is the medium of motion pictures. All the arts, the trades, the life of this world and the unconquered mysteries of the planetary system. . . . Sam, you have been given an arm of two edges, to do good or bad: you must think that pictures, which you are involved as a business . . . to guide, educate, elevate . . . and never to degenerate the younger generations. Sam, control your temper, never use vial [*sic*] language, because the people who work for you, work for you unconditionally as slaves. Sam, forget all the bitter and unsatisfactory incidence [*sic*] of a day and start the next day with love and gratitude. Sam, love your people and come close to them and they will give you without fright the best that you need. Sam we love you and are gratefully to you and please forget this letter.

In early December, Oates decided to drive the company RV from Huitzilac up to the tip of Mount Popo, Mexico's second-highest mountain. En route, a fire broke out in the dressing room. He swerved to the side of the road, grabbed some of his wardrobe and other valuables, and, with the help of passing motorists, fought the blaze. He was treated for second-degree burns.

"'Alfredo Garcia' was a real torturous ride," Garner Simmons summed up. "I was one of the guards in the film during the final shootout. Warren kills me and then I laid there for a day and a half while people walked over me so Sam could get what he wanted on film."

"We had a couple of endings to *Alfredo Garcia*, and I finally said, 'Do we kill him or does he drive away?'" Dawson said.

"Fuck it," came Peckinpah's reply. "Kill him."

Peckinpah said, "I was playing cards with Helmut [Dantine] and I said to him, 'You know, Bennie can't get away alive.'" Dantine agreed. All that was left was for Katy Haber to type the final script change.

After *Alfredo Garcia*, Oates would often be associated both with excess and with white suits. "The white suit was a natural because it would show all the aging and all the blood," Dawson explained. "It would start out clean and it would be cheesy enough for him, and it would really be in shitty condition by the time the picture was over. And it was. And he was."

Oates did not wait for the aftermath of or fallout from *Alfredo Garcia*. He quickly told Teddy, "Don't ever go see this!" When she finally did, she suspected he had warned her off because of the nude scenes.

After insisting that Isela Vega visit him in Los Angeles, Oates threw himself into his next movie. When he ran into Harry Northup in Schwab's, Northup, who would write a poem called "The Ragged Vertical" with the line "Handsome as Warren Oates / in a white suit," asked him how he handled his role, particularly when delivering Bennie's head to El Jefe. "I just used my Zen," Oates said with his most beguiling smile.

"I never heard him say he used his Zen," Dawson laughed. "I know he used his mushrooms and his hangover." Whatever he used, it worked well enough that his tour de force overshadowed Vega's quiet power. But the quality of her performance streams through like Alfredo's visage in the burlap bag.

"If you look at a film like *High Sierra*, *Alfredo Garcia* is almost an echo of that," Simmons said. "A star-crossed love affair set against some pretty tough odds. In Warren's playing of Bennie, he allows himself to experience all the shades of gray from black to white. In the end he's ennobled by what he does."

If Oates was able to see it that way, it must have been a huge comfort. But critical and public reaction would have to wait. If it seemed a little bit outré to make a film about a grave-robbing, homicidal, tequila-drinking madman with a foul mouth, why speak at all in your next film? And if a litter of human corpses is untidy, how about a bathtub full of dead roosters?

18

Family Style

"Some things didn't jibe, maybe, in there but as far as my personal gratification, I got more out of 'Alfredo Garcia,'" Oates said. "But as a human being, I get more out of 'The Wild Bunch.'"

Oates would be home in Los Angeles briefly at the beginning of 1974, long enough to see Teddy and his two children make their move to Atlanta. Teddy, who had been working for NBC, would eventually join the growing Turner Broadcasting Network. Her ex-husband had told her he would stake her three months on the road as she went around the United States to find out where she wanted to live. "When you find the place, I will have the furniture sent," he said.

She decided on Atlanta. Their new location would prove handy, although the kids had to start new schools and deal with all the issues that stirred up. "Atlanta was different," Timothy said. "It was the South. And no one knew who Dad was." The schooling they had received in California was superior, Timothy thought. "I felt like a very smart kid when we moved to Atlanta." He also played sports, especially soccer. "I was a wing and a forward, very fast. I could run forever." Oates instructed his kids not to follow in his footsteps. "Do not get into this business," he would say. But it was falling on fallow ears, as Timothy noted. "When your dad's an actor and he takes you to the sets, it's all like a circus, with all the trucks and all the people and all the energy. And you kinda had fun on the sets. You're nine years old and you're in *Tom Sawyer*."

As they were settling in to Atlanta, where Jennifer started Sequoyah High School, Oates called Teddy. "Guess where my next location is, Teddy? Right where you are, honey!"

"Oh goody," she teased. "I thought I got away from you."

When *Alfredo Garcia* was released, Oates toured in support while trying to distance himself from the film, which drew intensely negative criticism in most places. But first he found a couple of escape routes, the first of which involved a trip to Georgia, where he shook off the ghost of Bennie as he retreated into mute-by-choice Frank Mansfield.

Cockfighter was a novel by Charles Willeford. An early edition featured a blurb from another outsider author, Harry Crews, and noted that Willeford lived in Miami "because the crime rate—the highest in the nation—provides a writer with an exciting environment." As a property, *Cockfighter* came to the attention of Roger Corman, who at one point intended to direct the film himself and hoped to place Steve McQueen in the role of Frank Mansfield. "The story of a Southern man who has a stable of fighting cocks, I thought, would provide a rich visual context for a solid film," Corman said. The prospect delighted Willeford. "For several years now I have been showing some of his genre films to my cinema appreciation classes," Willeford wrote. To supplement his writing, Willeford taught at Miami-Dade Community College, and he was overjoyed when Corman's purchase came to fruition.

There was a change of director, with Corman calling in Monte Hellman. Hellman was unaware of Willeford's reputation as an author, but he liked what he saw. Willeford did not know Hellman from mayonnaise, but he was familiar with Oates's work, and he professed admiration for the actor's performance in *Major Dundee*. Willeford finished the final draft in his adoptive home of Florida and waited a year before a production date was scheduled in Georgia.

On December 13, 1973, Corman contacted Hellman, who asked Earl Mac Rauch, a friend of Terrence Malick's, to work with him on the rewrite, for which Corman gave them a week. With so little time, they did what they could, concentrating on the love story between Frank Mansfield and Mary Elizabeth (who would be played by Patricia Pearcy). Hellman felt the movie needed more such material. He penned the film's last line, "She loves me, Omar," and sent the decidedly unsentimental Corman into convulsions.

"The worst thing you can do is work for Roger Corman," Oates said later. "He would want to make 'Gone With The Wind' for $50,000." Corman wanted to make *Cockfighter* for $450,000, and over a four-week period, he did.

In "*Cockfighter*, I think [Frank Mansfield is] a part you could not imagine anyone else doing," David Thomson said, and it is difficult to quibble. Willeford was pleased to have Oates as his lead character, and the feeling was mutual. "Warren Oates, who plays Frank Mansfield in the film, was delighted with the non-speaking role," Willeford noted. "He is in every scene, because the work is from the protagonist's point-of-view, but without lines to learn he had ample time to experiment with body language, movement, and acting techniques he rarely had the opportunity to try in his earlier films."

The cast included Harry Dean Stanton (whose black-and-white shoes were meant to suggest ambivalence), Troy Donahue, Laurie Bird, Patricia Pearcy, and Millie Perkins. Oates suggested Donnie Fritts for the small role of a masked gunman, and his *Alfredo Garcia* coplayer was delighted. "Oates was funky," said Fritts, "and I had to get next to that. He was a gentleman with an edge." It was a bit of casting that likewise pleased Willeford, who pronounced Fritts a much better actor than his cohort Kris Kristofferson.

Oates drove to location with Bob Watkins and J.D., stopping at every opportune family-style restaurant along the way and waving off Alamogordo, which they christened "Out of My Gordo." Always on their days off from filming, they would research where to eat family style, "biscuits and grits, real southern stuff," Watkins said. "They'd bring a bowl of green beans and a bowl of mashed potatoes, and a plate of meat, and when they were low they'd bring more out." Waylon Jennings ("He was our age; he dressed our way," said Watkins) vied for airtime with classical symphonies, and stoned silence was as comfortable as moccasins. Oates peppered his conversation with his laugh, his favorite phrase, "wooly booger," and his frequent assertion, "I don't give a damn as long as they pay me."

"Warren was not all that interested in other people's dramas," Watkins said (and they would live on the fringes of several). "If I'd tell him something bizarre about someone, he would just laugh. That's one of the reasons we were good friends: he wasn't one to make judgments. And he was a loner, but not just a loner. He could be sociable, but he didn't have to have something going on all the time."

They also detoured for hot springs, which Oates could find just about anywhere. In Atlanta, they checked in to the Holiday Inn and readied themselves to work twelve to sixteen hours a day.

The cinematographer on *Cockfighter* was Spanish-born Nestor Almendros, who had worked for François Truffaut and later filmed *Days of Heaven*. "Nestor Almendros is a genius; I am convinced of it," Willeford said. "He is usually on the lookout for something typically American, primarily to put it down, I think, but he is also genuinely curious. He believes, for example, that the Holiday Inn is pure Americana." Almendros had been a fan of Hellman's *The Shooting* and *Two-Lane Blacktop*, and he took the assignment on which he was given a "non-union crew made up of young beginners with more enthusiasm than skill," he wrote in his memoir, *A Man with a Camera*. "I found myself again facing the rather tacky but extraordinarily photogenic image of contemporary America: billboards, gas stations, cafeterias, etc; to say nothing of those small Roman circuses, the cockpits."

The backwoods—and, in some states, illegal—sport of cock-fighting was a subculture choice for Hellman and an exploitation circuit gambit for Corman. Although Corman would eventually insist that Hellman was repulsed by the gore and violence (an assertion Hellman denied), Oates had only slight qualms. Watkins explained, "We were from the country, man. Your grandmother wrung the chicken's neck every Sunday." Watkins played a Miami gambler in one of the film's hotel scenes in which a fight is held right in the room.

Much of *Cockfighter*'s action is captured in Willeford's *Cock-fighter Journal: The Story of a Shooting*, which was published in a limited set of three hundred copies. Printed on Warren Old Style paper, the remarkable treatise is droll, biting, and incisive. That Oates and Willeford got along is evidenced by a trip the two men took in the Roach Coach between locations. On the jaunt, Willeford told Oates about his new project, a novel (never finished) called "The First Five in Line," in which game show contestants sacrifice various body parts to compete for prizes. Willeford pumped Oates for his assessment of its potential as a real television game show. It is possible, but not very likely, that Oates remained as mute as Mansfield. Willeford eventually recounted this mini–road trip in an all but lost memoir called *Remembering Warren Oates; or, The Demise of "The First Five in Line,"* according to Willeford's biographer, Don Herron.

But the rare *Cockfighter Journal* remains. Opening on April 6, 1974, at the Holiday Inn in Atlanta, Willeford reported that in the film the actors wore their own clothes, apart from Oates. The rest of the costumes came from the Goodwill store in Atlanta and a couple other thrift stores. "Laurie Bird, who went shopping in Atlanta for her own costumes, was forced to return most of them because they were too expensive (and she's the director's girlfriend)," he observed. He expressed dismay that Hellman and Bird ate off the same plate and that she got all the tomatoes. But he had reason for optimism regarding the 1959 Cadillac that Oates would be driving. The gray and black tail-finned beauty was exactly what the author ordered.

Willeford was happy to be cast as Ed Middleton. On April 9 he and Oates filmed a scene in which Middleton brings Frank to his house and another in which he buys the rooster, White Lightning. It rained off and on that day, and filming ended after nine o'clock, at which time Hellman told Willeford he was tremendous. The writer took this to mean "'adequate' in film parlance." But Willeford did not downsize Oates's contribution. "Working with Warren Oates was great, and we had good rapport. He has perfect timing, sharp reflexive reactions, and in a least two scenes there were a couple of takes where there was a warm feeling between us that should come over on the screen." Oates praised Willeford's performance, employing his personal superlative. "Warren was nice enough to say that I was a lot like Ben Johnson, in that I repeat my lines exactly right each time. That was a nice compliment and I felt good about it, which he intended."

Everyone, Willeford felt, was scared of Roger Corman. This confounded the writer, who found Corman easygoing. But there was a very real problem on the set: smoking. Oates, Willeford, and Corman's British assistant Frances Kimbrough were the only smokers working on the film, and Laurie Bird was their primary adversary. "She turns white with self-righteous anger when you light one up," Willeford said. "The words 'please' and 'thank you' are not in her vocabulary, so it is easy enough to ignore her commands."

But on April 10, Willeford had kind words for Bird, who he felt was just right for Dody White, Frank's girlfriend. Frank trades her to Jack Burke (Stanton) in a lost wager, and Dody reacts suitably. "She is from Queens," Willeford noted, "and she has managed, by study, to eliminate most of her New York accent, substituting, instead, a pseudo-British accent. But when she says 'Fuck you!' to Frank, as she does in the trailer scene, she reverts to pure Queens."

None of the actors wore makeup on the film, apart from the women who applied their own, mindful of the story. Oates was tan from *Alfredo Garcia*, which he told Willeford he had hated making. "Warren said he had scenes where he had to kick the severed head . . . and even talk to it. There is little or no plot to 'Bring Me . . . ' Warren said, but there is so much action that he doesn't think anyone will notice it. In the picture, he also picks up a case of crabs from a prostitute and tells her: 'Either change your sheets or get a new occupation!' We agreed, both of us, that this was a memorable line."

On Easter Sunday, April 14, Oates and Stanton traveled to Atlanta to join Teddy and their children for dinner. By the time they returned to the location in Toccoa, Ed Begley Jr. had arrived, and coproducer Sam Gelfman ordered three carloads of cast and crew to drive some thirty miles to the middle of nowhere—

between Toccoa and Lavonia—for dinner. "We ate family style," Willeford recorded, "and all we could possibly eat. The full dishes kept coming: fried chicken, country ham, fried catfish, hush puppies, hot biscuits, fried fish, string beans, and fried potatoes. There were great jars of black sorghum molasses, and platters of tub butter for the biscuits." The price for the feast was three dollars per person.

It was just as well they were fortified: Oates and Begley were to film a fight scene in which Begley would end up in a trough of murky green water. Fortunately, the temperature climbed to the mid-sixties, but Begley, playing Tom Peeples, was stressed. "I was very new to stunt work," he said, "and I'm not certain that there was a stunt coordinator on the set. Warren called a halt to the sequence for a while until they made the ax safer with some tape. I believe he had cut his hand on it." Indeed, Oates had gotten cut: the prop man had used a sharp-edged rather than a dull ax.

The accident eluded Willeford's watchful eye. He was occupied with concerns that the proceedings made Frank "seem like a very hard man indeed. Ed Begley, Jr. is so good in this scene that he, not Frank, will have the audience's sympathy. Warren, a true professional, is precise in his movements, and never makes an unnecessary gesture. He has handled enough gamecocks by now that handling seems natural to him."

Oates and Willeford rode together from Toccoa to Atlanta, pulling into a truck stop for cornbread and steak and talking about *Alfredo Garcia* and "The First Five in Line." Oates's dog was along. "J.D.," Willeford wrote, "is half-husky, part-Collie, and something else that is undefinable. He is only a year old and I can't tell whether he is stupid or merely young." After reaching their destination at eleven that night, they headed straight to the bar without checking in, to drink with Stanton and Begley and two Treasury agents. Well after two o'clock in the morning, the eclectic gathering called it a night.

Frank's farm was a working game farm, replete with thirty roosters, owned by a man named A. B. Greeson. It was used for the montage shots at the beginning of the film as well as the place where Frank chops off the head of a black rooster, which horrifically did not go according to plan. The head came only partially off, and Almendros ran out of film. Fortunately, because two cameras were used, they did not need to film it again. "Warren, who had a difficult time psyching himself up to chop off the head, wouldn't have wanted to kill another rooster," Willeford said.

Then Willeford started to worry that lines like "Frank was bragging about his cock" would get unintentional laughs, but he soon came to terms with that. "If the audience is going to laugh every time the word is mentioned, my undeserved reputation as a comedy writer will be enhanced." If he only knew what fate awaited the film: in its rerelease as *Born to Kill*, Jon Davison would write copy for the trailer that included the line "Frank Mansfield strolled into town with his cock in his hand. And what he did was illegal in 47 states!" A loftier ad campaign aimed at the art house cinema crowd used a puzzle motif and the words "love, courage, manhood, heart," but it too missed its target.

The interior shots of Frank's house were also filmed at Greeson's farm. Frank writes a letter to Mary Elizabeth, and Hellman requested that Oates actually pen it. He shot the scene from several different angles. Because Oates's handwriting was nearly illegible, it was still necessary to add a voice-over, a narration Oates wrote himself. "We had done a number of interviews with some of the cockfighters that were playing peripheral roles in the movie, talking to them about why they liked the sport, why they were so obsessed with it," Hellman said. "And Warren got very close to these guys and listened in on a lot of the discussions. Then he basically wrote his own narration. He also wrote some stuff that didn't necessarily get into the movie but expressed his interest in homely philosophy." One of the lines Hellman thought he might have written was "Beauty is only skin-deep, but ugly goes clean to the bone," but that fine line belonged to Dorothy Parker.

During the various cockfighting scenes, locals were used as extras, including one hippie whom Oates and Watkins took under their wing. "Warren and I took a fancy to him because he was a dark horse," Watkins noted. At Allmont Pit, the Allman Brothers Band came by. "They all look sinister except Dickie Betts,"

Willeford felt. Hellman, to keep the extras natural, did not yell "Action!" when they were present.

On April 22, cast and crew were in Sandy Springs, Georgia, where they watched the rushes. Willeford was particularly happy with a scene in which Harry Dean Stanton's Burke tells Frank he is now married to Dody, the girlfriend he traded. However, Willeford noted, "Their fight on-screen is not as amusing as it was when it was actually filmed. That's because of the silence. The audience, which was not informed of the impending fight, went wild when Dody climbed over the pit rail and began to flail at Frank with her handbag."

The next day, weather permitting, Willeford was to film a porch scene with Oates. If it rained, the hotel robbery scene would be shot instead. With twenty-some dead chickens in plastic bags, bought at a country cockfight, being kept for the latter's hotel bathtub, it was wise to pray for rain.

But the weather held, and the Foxhall mansion and tournament scenes were shot at Bulloch Hall, a restored antebellum structure that is now a museum. Conveniently, a cockpit was about one hundred yards downwind. When another drag pit scene was shot, a surprise visitor arrived. "Governor Jimmy Carter, to my astonishment, visited the set this afternoon," Willeford wrote. "He only stayed a few minutes, introduced himself, shook hands with some of us, and then departed. Governor Carter didn't hang around the set for more than ten minutes. . . . This was enough; his tacit approval of the film and our work offset the complaining interview with the Humane Society official about the film in the 'Atlanta Constitution.'" Carter told Hellman his family had been cockfighters for generations.

On April 25, Sam Gelfman announced that *Cockfighter* would open in Atlanta in July. "I worry constantly that Frank won't come off sympathetically," Willeford wrote in his journal. "A hell of a lot is riding on the charm of Oates's smile. Luckily, no one has ever smiled more engagingly than Warren Oates."

Shooting was drawing to a close on the last day of April at Rooster City, outside Atlanta, which would be filmed as the farm of Mansfield's sidekick Omar Baradinsky (Richard B. Shull).

Baradinsky and Mansfield are set to become partners, contingent on Mansfield's being named cockfighter of the year, and they celebrate with champagne, a moment Willeford insisted he modeled on the works of Ernst Lubitsch. The day before, the main ballroom scene had been filmed at the Georgian Terrace Hotel in Atlanta—the same setting that stood in for the entrance hall and ballroom in *Gone with the Wind*.

All that remained to be filmed was a swimming scene with Frank and Mary Elizabeth. Oates had told Willeford he was reluctant to do the partly nude sequence, and he claimed Pearcy was nervous about it as well. The scene was delayed when the CECO-mobile (a camera truck) turned over and got stuck in a ditch. The crew unsuccessfully enlisted a farmer to pull it out with a tractor. Finally a wrecker driver arrived. "Shit," he said. "I thought you was stuck." He righted the vehicle and got it back on the road in two minutes flat.

Oates repeatedly told Hellman that the dialogue-free Mansfield was the easiest part he had ever played. Hellman said,

> That was one of the grossest understatements of all time. He gives one of the great movie performances in *Cockfighter*. There were two really fascinating scenes. One is the scene by the river, with Mary Elizabeth. That was probably the biggest challenge to him as a silent actor. And the scene is something like, hell, I think it approached seven minutes. And it was all one shot, without a cut. He just showed every color in that scene and I think it was an extraordinary achievement for an actor to be able to do what he did without the use of language.
>
> The other scene, where he steps on the head of the rooster. . . . It was unique, in this power of it and emotion of it and what he brought to it. It wasn't so much the fact that it was wordless. If there had been dialogue, that scene would have been just as powerful.

Willeford prepared to take his leave, feeling that *Cockfighter* would do well. "Frank's stubbornness will appeal to anyone who talks too much, which includes writers like myself," he wrote. Friday, he noted, "is the first day of the spring semester, and I'll be back in the classroom, back to mundane reality, teaching D. H. Lawrence to bewildered strangers."

At the airport he met Millie Perkins, who he had initially thought was too pretty and slight to play Frances Mansfield, Frank's sister-in-law. Frances is married to the dissolute Randall Mansfield, played to the hilt by Troy Donahue. Perkins informed Willeford that her line "Randy's such a snob. He's never forgiven my father for being a dentist" was cut because both Hellman and Sam Gelfman had relatives who were dentists. Perkins and Donahue both begged for the line to remain, but their protests went unheeded.

"I took *Cockfighter* because of Monte," Perkins said. "When I met up with Warren in *Cockfighter*, it was a distant friendship. We didn't get together again emotionally, as much as we loved each other. If I hadn't been married, I probably would have been one of his wives. But life had changed. It had passed us by."

Cockfighter had a trajectory as scattershot as its multiple titles, among them *Born to Kill*, *Wild Drifter*, and *Gamblin' Man*, but Oates prevailed as "a master portrayer of canny underdogs," in Kevin Thomas's words. "The extra demands on Oates's capacity for expressiveness show up his talent all the more. It's a tribute to Oates that he could find some scrappy bedrock dignity in his cockfighter, just as he did in so many men living on the margin of his existence." *Variety* deemed the film "not for sensitive film-goers" and described Oates's silence as a "heavy burden" under which he managed to deliver "an okay performance." The reviewer pointed out that the cockfighting theme was dealt with responsibly and was far less sensational than in John Schlesinger's *Day of the Locust*. *Films International* looked a little deeper, finding Hellman "eliciting an extraordinary performance from perennial folk-myth player Warren Oates. With the merest smile or inclination of the head, he manages to convey more meaning than most actors employing a full range of voice and gesture. [Scenes are] presented with humor and economy, marred only occasionally by irritatingly prolonged dissolves."

Cockfighter fared well at the Edinburgh International Film Festival (from which it would be banned during a later run in 2007), and Britain's *Sight and Sound* put it on its ten best list for 1974. When Willeford, who had been dismayed that his was the only Roger Corman film not to turn a profit, got wind of that, he went "out into the night and drank without economy."

But Corman's claws were inescapable, and they marred the film. He thought the film suffered from Hellman's squeamishness, that the director had "pulled away from the bloody stuff," and so he dispatched editor Lewis Teague to Arizona to film several more gruesome fighting sequences. Then he called in Joe Dante to make a trailer. "I've got Warren doing sign language, a bunch of chickens, no action, what am I gonna do?" Dante pondered. He made a zippy trailer for the film's opening in Georgia, but the film still flopped like a rubber chicken.

However, Corman was not finished. He instructed Dante to intercut the film with a dynamite truck chase scene from *Night Call Nurses* and a bedroom scene from *Private Duty Nurses*. Spliced together as a one-minute montage, they could be used as a dream sequence, Corman suggested. "To Roger's credit, he tried to save it," Dante said. "But in saving it, he lost some of the best scenes, the more thoughtful ones." But time has prevailed: the movie that survived is *Cockfighter*, and it is Hellman to the hilt.

After it was finished, Oates said, "'Cockfighter' is about a guy who raises and trains cockfighters. It's a big, brawling story with 25 characters in it and he [Corman] gives Monte a four-week shooting schedule. He wouldn't pay a second unit to pick up some traveling stuff and inserts. And the music was wrong; it should have been low-down guitar picking. I don't care if they release it or not. It ain't bitterness but just an insight. I've had the experience many times," he concluded wearily.

Jack Nicholson reportedly said, "*Cockfighter* is as good as any actor is ever allowed to be." With *The White Dawn*, *Bring Me the Head of Alfredo Garcia*, and *Cockfighter*, Oates had made a trinity of extraordinary and extreme films. If he was having trouble deciding what to do next, it was understandable. But he had a cure for that.

"I've given up my wives for girls," Oates admitted. He told British journalist Jack Bentley that his marriage to Vickery had fallen apart because of a job. "I blame it almost entirely on my role in 'Dillinger.' Or maybe on myself for taking the part. Not because as some friends imagined, I was living the role at home and giving Vickery the horrors. The truth is, I was never at home for her to notice it. That's when being married to me must have seemed like a waste of time. I haven't stopped working for more than a few days in the last four years, and last year I made four films."

But the incessant work had its financial rewards, and for the first time in a long while, Oates was comfortable. "Ironically enough I've now made enough money not to have to work so hard," he said. "I've just finished a film called 'Cockfighter' and I'll just loaf around and go where the fancy takes me. Now I've got plenty of time to spend with a wife, I haven't got one." Not that he was complaining. "You'd be surprised at the female affection I get along the highways," he said. "And thanks to 'Dillinger,' a lot of fan worship."

Oates was also, before *Alfredo Garcia*'s release, getting a lot of good press, which he shrugged off. "Critics! I don't pay any attention to them, no matter what they say. I take notice of people—people along the highways who pay to see my films. They're my only true critics."

After *Cockfighter*, he clocked more highway miles, driving in the Roach Coach with Bob Watkins from Georgia to Montana. When he arrived in Livingston, near the northern gate of Yellowstone National Park, Oates effectively traversed a personal continental divide. He celebrated a birthday, his forty-sixth, there, and it would not be the last time he commemorated his life in Montana.

19

The Grand Experiment

In 1974, Livingston, Montana, and nearby Paradise Valley were as pretty and remote as could be reached by RV or four-wheel drive. "The Montana mountains . . . are more beautiful than any woman ever born," Oates exclaimed. "Mountains and their snowcaps are breathtaking in their grandeur." He said he was writing a film about them.

In cognoscenti terms, the area had been homesteaded by Tom McGuane, Peter Fonda, and William "Gatz" Hjorstberg. Oates would join their group, which was sometimes referred to as the Montana Mafia. Livingston and its environs would provide Oates with a community and a fly-fishing cast of friends that also included Russell Chatham, Jim Harrison, Richard Brautigan, and eventually Sam Peckinpah.

The Great Plains town of Livingston and its environs are ruggedly western, wide open yet close knit. Indigenous peoples have lived there for thousands of years, and the archaeological site at Wilsall holds the oldest Native American burial ground on the continent. On July 15, 1806, explorer William Clark came to the area and rested himself, his group, and their tired horses. "Many of them Can Scercely proceed over the Stone and gravel," Clark wrote. Little matter: a Crow raiding party appropriated all fifty horses the next day.

The Northern Pacific Railroad is really what made Livingston, and a huge depot was built in the foothills of the Rocky Mountains, halfway between terminal points. With the railroad came jobs: dispatchers, switchmen, telegraph and repair crews, and workers in the service industries that supported them. Cut sandstone buildings appeared, shops sprang up, bar doors swung open, and a red-light district prospered on South B Street, where "soiled doves" made a living near the railroad's hub just far enough from the affluent houses along Main Street.

Calamity Jane, the six-foot-tall markswoman, bought and sold cattle to ranchers in the sixty-mile stretch known as Paradise Valley. She also benefited from the proceeds of her biography, which she made sure was available for purchase in Yellowstone National Park. Jane liked this part of Montana, and her way of life was subsidized by her popularity with the public. The same formula still worked a century later.

Tom McGuane, a Wyandotte, Michigan, native, had spent time in Wyoming and felt at home in the West. He had married Portia Rebecca Crockett. Becky was a diminutive, pretty-as-Montana blonde well loved for her personal warmth, magnetism, and vibrancy. She met Oates when he and Watkins appeared on the McGuanes' doorstep.

In the summer of 1974, Frank Perry was filming McGuane's *Rancho Deluxe* in Livingston. *Rancho Deluxe* was a posthippie, postironic western featuring Jeff Bridges and Sam Waterston as hapless cattle rustlers. In the film, rusty pickup trucks have replaced trusty steeds, and beer comes with chasers other than just whiskey.

Oates had made the trip partly because he was interested in what would be McGuane's directorial debut, a movie based on his novel *92 in the Shade*. The author had wrangled both screenwriting duty and directorship—an impressive coup for novice or seasoned pro. It was also one of the few times a writer had filmed his own novel. Whether Oates had his eye on the role of Tom Skelton (which went to Peter Fonda) or Nichol Dance is the subject of some dispute. Regardless, the way he got the latter only reinforced his conviction that he was in the right place.

Peter Fonda explained,

Warren knew that Jimmy Buffett was in this film, *Rancho Deluxe*, whose screenplay was written by Tom McGuane. And he drove up just to screw around with his friends in the movies, as it were, and play a little scene in a bar band. I was calling Tom McGuane almost daily from Hawaii, suggesting I was the right person to play in *92 in the Shade*. I did not know Warren was here [in Montana]. I knew that Jeff Bridges was here and that Sam Waterston was here. They were both in *Rancho Deluxe*, and they wanted to play the role that I was speaking about. . . . Becky would answer the calls, sometimes at three in the morning, and tell me, "Oh, Tom's at the Guest House." I always thought that meant a cabin outside the ranch, but it was actually a motel in town.

Fonda had been given a copy of *92 in the Shade* and was keen to acquire it, only to find that producer Elliott Kastner had purchased the rights. "I was upset I didn't get the property. But I was damned if I was going to give up the part. I knew Warren was perfect for Nichol Dance. And I knew I was perfect for Tom Skelton."

Fonda remembered, "I must have made two dozen calls to McGuane at his ranch. And finally I called him and I said, 'Tom, maybe you don't like how I act, maybe you don't like my look, or maybe you find I'm not right for the part for other reasons, and I can understand that. But I'll tell you something—if you don't get Warren Oates to play Nichol Dance, you don't understand your own book.' And McGuane says, 'Here, why don't you talk to him? Warren is sitting here right across the coffee table from me.'"

McGuane denied that he had to be cajoled into casting Oates; he insisted he required no persuasion. "I thought I was lucky to have him. I was elated to have him. Warren had a special kind of bemused quality when he really played his cards close to his chest. You could see him in all kinds of circumstances and he wasn't going to let on if things were not to his liking. He had a way of shining it on that was pretty clever."

The primary thing that would be shining in Oates's appear-

ance in *Rancho Deluxe* was his sateen cowboy shirt, straight from
the set of *Cockfighter*. He would also wear it as he started to hit
the town. "I met Warren and Bob at the same moment, down at
the Emigrant Saloon, during the filming of *Rancho Deluxe*," said
William Hjortsberg, a novelist, screenwriter, and transplanted
New Yorker. That summer, Hjortsberg was hanging around and
working as Sam Waterston's stand-in. Many of Livingston's residents were in the film in some way. "It was such a kind of hippie
event, and I think if you were walking around town that day and
wanted to be in a movie . . ." McGuane explained. "Warren just
kind of hung around, got in it."

"I think they had just finished *Cockfighter* and came up in the
Roach Coach from Georgia," Hjortsberg continued. "It was Bob
who struck up the conversation, but Warren was so affable. We
were in there doing what made the Roach Coach memorable, and
Bob said he was a great fan of my book, *Gray Matters*. I was so
pleased because not that many people knew about that book."

Watkins said, "Yeah, I probably read it four times."

"What? I haven't even read Hemingway four times. Why?"

"Well," Watkins replied, "when you're in the joint and you
find a book you like, you tend to go back to it."

"He was a real outlaw," Hjortsberg said, "where Warren was
just a pretend outlaw."

Oates's cameo in the film, as a harmonica player in a band
playing "Livingston Saturday Night," was filmed at the Wrangler Bar. Hjortsberg explained, "The two great bars we all went
to, there was a shit-kicker cowboy bar called the Longbranch
Saloon and right next door—they even cut through so you could
go back and forth—was the Wrangler. 'Hippie' is probably not
the right idea because the long-hairs, they were all the blue-
collar guys. They worked for the railroad or did stuff like that.
Then there were the rancher guys. They would have country
bands in the Longbranch and they'd have rock and roll bands
in the Wrangler."

"Livingston Saturday Night" was written by Jimmy Buffett,
and Oates gave a gusto performance miming his harmonica playing to the crowd's raucousness. He had recently sung backup

vocals on Kris Kristofferson's "Rocket to Stardom," but this was the closest he would get to the live rock star experience. In terms of exuberance, it echoed his manic process-shot driving, and the crowd's rowdiness kept pace in an atmosphere where two-steps could not begin to be enough.

Oates already knew Buffett, but many more Montana transplants would become close friends. It was in the cards—the same ones he played close to his chest—that he would buy a place there. "It just seemed like a natural thing," Becky McGuane (now Fonda) said, adding that "Warren was very astute about his investments, so he was smart about buying land." When Tom McGuane offered him a handful of acres that abutted a national forest, he did not think twice. "I thought he was here on a visit," McGuane said, "but he took hold of Montana the minute he saw it."

Chico Hot Springs would become Oates's home away from wherever home might be. Located in Pray, a town with a post office, a church, a bar, and a handful of cabins in various states of disrepair, Chico's sulfur pots, watering holes, and owner Mike Art's hospitable largesse were made to order.

Meanwhile, *Rancho Deluxe* had hit a snag. One of the actors, Richard Bright, was refusing to come out of his room at the Guest House motel. Bright had been an underground actor in San Francisco and played Billy the Kid in Michael McClure's controversial play *The Beard*.

"I can get him out of there," Bob Watkins told the police who had arrived on scene. "Give me half an hour."

"Watkins went in alone and unarmed and sat for about an hour and then came out with his arm around a sobbing Richard Bright," Hjortsberg related. "Walked him out, walked him around, sobered him up, and sent him back to work."

Oates and Watkins then headed back to L.A.—Peter Fonda called it "Smell A"—but Oates knew he had found a place where he wanted to hang his hat. "Our little wave of immigrants, nobody made any waves [in Montana]," Hjortsberg said. "No one built big houses. Except for Warren, nobody built any houses at all. McGuane bought an old ranch house and just fixed it up inside. The whole tendency was not to stand out. We just wanted to blend in and pretend we were ranchers."

A press release for *The White Dawn* incorrectly credited Oates with a role in *Huckleberry Finn* and described his Hollywood home as being filled with "memorabilia, guns, Eskimo sculpture, film posters, guitars, autographed photos of lissome misses—the house is small, only a stopping-off place between location trips for the actor, who seems never ever to make a film in Hollywood proper."

In terms of lissome misses, Oates could not have missed the one who now lived at the foot of the hill, Judy Jones. But in Montana, Becky McGuane had asked him who the woman was in the photos he carried in his wallet. "Michelle Phillips," he told her. Phillips had been ending her relationship with Jack Nicholson at the time she and Oates filmed *Dillinger*, but the extraordinary beauty obviously made an impression on him. What Oates had for his *Dillinger* costar certainly qualified as a crush. What his neighbor fostered was, according to his second ex-wife, something a bit more permanent. "One time he called me and said, 'Teddy, you've got to come back to me. The girl down below me, she's got her eye on me, and I'm going to give in one of these days, I'm afraid.'"

Dan Tana's is located a stone's throw from the Troubadour, on Santa Monica Boulevard near Doheny Drive and the beginning of Beverly Hills. Cozy and quaint, with a bar as tight as its patrons, it tended toward a celebrity clientele rather than the country-rock or pop-rock crowd that hit the Troubadour. Oates went; Harry Dean Stanton went; Ed Begley Jr. went. Tom McGuane eventually found his way.

Dana Ruscha, then separated from her artist husband, Ed Ruscha, was at Dan Tana's one night when she ran into Oates. She had met him before, at a party at Nicholson's house. "Jack used to have a lot of parties at that time, and everybody passed through. I had actually seen Warren onstage in *Cuckoo's Nest* at the Players' Ring down on Santa Monica, and I was so blown away," Ruscha said. She told Oates as much at the party, and he was thrilled. It transpired that they were also neighbors. "I lived in Laurel Canyon and he lived up on Briar Knoll, and I gave him my address. The next morning I found this envelope in my mailbox that had this really washed piece of beautiful green glass in it, and a note from him. So sweet."

Ruscha had become friends with Warren Miller's neighbor Jennifer Lee, who had not yet begun her stormy relationship with Richard Pryor. Curiously, her future husband's shorthand for making a move was an Oates line from *The Wild Bunch*. "Roll the ball, Tector," Pryor would say, when he wanted to roll.

"It was fun back in the day," Jennifer Lee said.

> Good drugs, good sex. We all walked that fine line. Some of us fell over, and some of us made it back. [Warren] was a hard-drinking, hard-smoking, hard-living guy and self-punishing. Warren was some sort of vulnerable machismo, a very tender man. His sadness was palpable. There was something defeated about him, melancholy yet very heroic. That's really the energy he put out . . . hunched over, shoulders sloped, smoking a cigarette, and looking at the camera like, "Hello, I'm here, but I don't really care if you take a picture or if you're not going to take a picture." There was never this incredible high energy. But boy, was he a smoker.

Both Lee and Ruscha took lots of photos, but it is doubtful anyone minded. "We were young, hot babes," Lee said. She and Oates had a chemistry, but now it was tempered by his own circumstances. "Obviously Warren was an alcoholic, and if nobody used that word, allow me to use it," Lee said.

His drinking did not bother Lee, who had her own battle with addiction. But what mutual attraction they had was tested when Lee accompanied Oates on a press trip in the summer. Until then they had seen each other often at Dan Tana's, Petit Patisserie, Pupi's, the Brasserie, and, of course, the Raincheck. "I know every turn of Laurel Canyon from Dan Tana's," Lee's friend Ruscha said, and Oates surely did too.

Oates began the barrage of press for three films with practically simultaneous releases by speaking with Alain Garel from *Image et Son*. With depth and candor, he looked back on his career. Of his early success, he said, "Maybe I was an actor able to be employed at a reasonable price." Then he raved about Peckinpah, allowed that he learned much from Joseph Mankiewicz, and insisted that he had no interest in alternative films. "I don't want to do experimental cinema. I'm not interested in doing a film with John Cassavetes."

He told Ray Loynd of the *Los Angeles Herald-Examiner*, "What I really want to do is write and direct and act in only those films I feel very strong about. Bertolucci wanted me for his new film, '1900' but I can't play an Italian." Oates, whom Loynd found "almost boyishly shy in manner," lost the part to the bigger name of Burt Lancaster.

In July, Isela Vega arrived in Los Angeles. She took two trips with Oates: one to Catalina (Sam Peckinpah came along) and the other to Joshua Tree National Monument. The sea cruise came first, on Peckinpah's new Fuji 35 diesel ketch. Vega, who had a tantalizing way with words, later reported that Oates "saved my life. We were on a boat together and I was drunk. I fell off the boat and went down to the bottom. I realized I couldn't breathe very well. Fortunately there was Warren on top and he pulled me out." On terra firma, she needed a car to get around the Los Angeles metropolis, so Oates sold her his yellow Opel Capri. Then they took the Roach Coach to Joshua Tree for a sojourn with Ted Markland and his mountain. Markland told Oates that he and Peter Fonda had attended a screening of *Alfredo Garcia* in Los Angeles. "Peter and I were laughing in places no one else was. Warren said, 'You should laugh. I almost killed Sam. I had a gun pointed at him.'"

Whatever Oates and Vega's relationship was, to onlookers it seemed pretty tight. Vega, however, remained characteristically coy. "He was one of the ones who said no," she told Earl Wilson. "He was separating, I was separating at the time of the film. He's my ideal. I love him for his soul, for his sweetness as a man. He's not selfish, he's warm. But he got away."

On July 25, Jennifer Lee flew with Oates to Ottawa for the

premiere of *The White Dawn* at the Place de Ville Cinemas. At the reception, Oates wore a tuxedo and Lee a black formal dress as they met the Canadian prime minister, Pierre Trudeau, and his wife, Margaret, and spoke with the other guests, including many of the Inuit actors. When the night was over, he and Lee went back to the hotel.

"I did not sleep with him, and I slept with everybody," Lee said. "He never made a pass like some men do and you don't want it. He was pretty passive, kind of checked out in that area, at least for me. I was running with big macho motherfuckers, so anything less than . . . I never saw him in that sexual way. He was not a sexual being. I think the women in his life pursued him."

Lee enjoyed *The White Dawn*, but the next Oates film on their itinerary did not have the same effect. "We hit New York and saw 'Bring Me the Head of Alfredo Garcia' and I got really upset because I thought that movie was awful. We said our goodbyes and then I went upstate to see my parents, and all I could talk about was this horrible movie."

Saying that *Alfredo Garcia* was polarizing is like saying that filming *The White Dawn* was a little uncomfortable. Oates's publicity tour was for three brave and challenging films, and although none of them would yield good box office receipts, Oates was particularly hurt by the failure of *The White Dawn*. "It was a beautiful picture," he said, "different and meaningful and fascinating. But the distributors got worried about 'The Great Gatsby's' slow start and started spending all their money to promote it. They simply dropped 'The White Dawn' and some other big pictures to try to protect their big investment in 'Gatsby.'"

In the case of *Alfredo Garcia*, Peckinpah did what he could. While Oates was filming *Cockfighter*, the director sent Fred Goldberg and Buddy Young at United Artists some copy for *Alfredo Garcia*'s advertising campaign. Among his suggestions:

This is a true story. If you don't like it, forget it.
    One thing else is true: Two New Stars, Warren Oates and Tough Crazy Mexicana named Isela Vega.

Don't Laugh "What did you do today, baby?"
Don't Laugh "How do you structure your day?"

He signed off, "I don't know if these are any good or are of any value, but somebody might be able to use them 'somehow, somewhere along the way.'" Buddy Young returned a letter with faint praise; Peckinpah's suggestions indicated he was a few notches down from the top of his game. When he was sent the artwork in London, he fired back a telegram: "SAW THE ART WORK TODAY VOMITED REFUSE TO HAVE MY NAME CONNECTED WITH THIS TYPE OF SHABBY SUB ALLIED ARTIST EXPLOITATION SAM BECKINBAH [*sic*]."

Alfredo Garcia had two previews: One was July 6 at the Warfield Theater on Market Street in San Francisco, where it played with *S.P.Y.S.* The other was the next night, July 7, in Long Beach at the Town Theater on Atlantic Boulevard. There it shared the bill with *Thunderbolt and Lightfoot*, and Gordon Dawson was in the audience. "We met in Long Beach, and we had all the marketing people. They passed out [response] cards to the audience, and they were just terrible. I remember sitting in the trailer with Sam and all these people saying, 'Jesus Christ, what are we going to do with this?' It was one really awful evening."

If audiences were perplexed, many critics were aghast. *Alfredo Garcia* was confiscated in Munich and banned in Sweden and in Buenos Aires. Helmut Dantine leapt to its defense, writing a lengthy article for Germany's *Der Spiegel* magazine. "While I was distressed at my own country's suppression of artistic and valid truths, I had become proud of Germany with its introspection and liberality. I fervently hope I will not have to evaluate my thoughts," the actor wrote.

Peckinpah became a member of the Chicano activist group Nosotros, who were unhappy with the film's depiction of Mexicans. The organization privately announced it did not want to boycott the picture because that would only make people want to see it more.

Product Digest fretted, "What in the world are unsuspecting audiences going to make of this bizarre new movie from the brilliant Sam Peckinpah?" *Newsweek* saw Oates and Vega as "two middle-aged roughed up losers" and described the plot as a "necrophiliac and nonsensical struggle for the love of a woman" during which Oates flashes "his mirthless corncob smile." Vega's performance was alternately called "warmly played," possessing the "warmth and sincerity of Moreau and Mercouri," and "an exercise in wood." *Los Angeles* magazine posited, "instead of Chanel No. 5, this girl should wear Black Flag," before adding, "to be fair, Oates is excellent." Vincent Canby in the *New York Times* thought the film worked as a parable of Peckinpah as an innocent in Hollywood but "doesn't make a great deal of sense read any other way." "The second half of the film belongs entirely to Oates and his tour de force monologues over Alfredo's fly-ridden head," wrote John H. Dorr in the *Hollywood Reporter*. Charles Champlin's unfavorable critique in the *Los Angeles Times* prompted a defense from a couple in Orange County. Almer John Davis and Alicia Carol Hill told Champlain, "We wish to reward you with an empty tequila bottle and a one-way ticket to tenderness."

There were plenty of empty bottles in the suites at the Sherry-Netherland in New York where Peckinpah and Oates were staying. John Bryson, writing and photographing a piece for *New York* magazine, and Tom Topor of the *New York Post* witnessed the action. Bryson reported that Oates greeted Peckinpah with "Up yours" and that Peckinpah in turn said Oates was "a poet, a singer, and a piss-poor actor. For some reason I keep using him all the time."

Bryson trailed after Peckinpah and Oates between July 27 and 30 and produced a shell-shocked article accompanied by a disturbing photograph of Oates, Vega, and Peckinpah sprawled and soused outside the Russian Tea Room just after two o'clock in the morning. On the afternoon of July 29, Topor went to the Sherry-Netherland to interview Oates. Jennifer Lee was still around, and Topor noted,

> When the girlfriend of the actor came to the suite to pick him up, the director, who had never met her, began kissing her neck . . . and the girl, not quite sure how to respond, played

along, smiling, feminine, the perfect Peckinpah heroine to the ultimate Peckinpah hero.

"I love this movie," Peckinpah said. "I cry. I cry. The only reason I'm here is because of you, baby."

"Ding hao [very good]," Oates responded. Peckinpah rubbed Oates's head. "Ding hao."

Topor characterized the exchange as Oates's "docile acting in the hands of an authoritarian director."

"All of us worked for scale because we wanted to make the picture," Peckinpah told Bryson, "so if it doesn't make any money, we're dead. I live in an apartment on the Fox lot and I have a palatial estate at Paradise Cove in Malibu, almost 30 feet long and nine feet wide. It's a trailer."

On July 30, Oates and Peckinpah left for Chicago. There the film would be well received, enabling Oates to leave on a high for Atlanta, where he would attend the premiere of *Cockfighter*. Held at Roswell Village Twin Cinemas, the event—understandably picketed by the ASPCA—was, perversely, a benefit for the Roswell High School Boosters Club. The boosters made two thousand dollars for their cause, and *Box Office* reported that "Warren Oates, star of the film which was made in the Roswell vicinity, was a popular figure at the premiere as were associate producer Samuel Gelfman and Charles Willeford, the University of Miami professor who wrote the film's script." Roger Corman was unable to attend.

Oates told the press, "I'm not going to run after things I can't tackle. This [success] all happened quite by accident and I'm going to keep it that way. I'm not going to be pushing to play F. Scott Fitzgerald, Ernest Hemingway, Hitler, or anything like that." Then he left for Texas to join Isela Vega.

At the Whitehall Hotel in Houston, Vega posed poolside and caused, according to the *Post*'s Marge Crumbaker, a traffic jam. The item was indicative of the kind of press *Alfredo Garcia* would receive there, centered on the sexy star currently appearing in the July issue of *Playboy*. In Dallas–Fort Worth, columnists Jack Gordon, Elston Brooks, and Perry Stewart all referred to the map of

Texas T-shirt that Vega wore, which, they quipped, significantly altered the topography of the Lone Star State.

Fort Worth's Petroleum Club at 777 Main Street was established in 1953 for Texas oilmen and similarly money-drenched businessmen. Outfitted with dark wood paneling, myriad chandeliers, and panoramic views, the Petroleum Club also had a busboy named Alfredo, who waited on Vega, Oates, and his son, now eleven. Journalist Elston Brooks of the *Fort Worth Star-Telegram* described Oates as twice divorced and reported him as saying, "There are a lot of pictures I don't want Tim to see until he's older. I took him to 'The White Dawn' but not this one." Oates ordered cornbread at the fancy club before holding forth about his next projects. "I'd like to play Howard Hughes," he told the assembled, although he had said in Georgia that he would avoid high-profile leads. "He's a man who did it all by himself. He didn't ask anybody else to take up that big plane of his that crashed: he was the one at the controls. I'd also like to do a story about a returning POW from Vietnam who everyone thought was dead. He comes back to find his wife remarried and all his friends divided into two camps about what's right and what's wrong." Although Vega insisted the relationship was platonic, Brooks observed, "Miss Vega entwined her fingers around Oates's hand throughout lunch. The 'look' was unmistakable."

In Dallas, the venue was Brennan's, an offshoot of the famed New Orleans eatery, and Timothy was again in tow when Oates met the *Dallas Times-Herald's* Don Safran for dinner. Safran complimented Oates's white suit and cool green tie. "It's not a suit at all," Oates told him. "Just a pair of white pants that don't match this white sport coat." Oates was tired and reflective while he battled to persuade Timothy to eat his dinner.

"I think I have the record for worst locations," he said. "I spent four months in the Antarctic [*sic*] doing 'White Dawn' and then had to report to the interior of Mexico for this film." He sighed, "It's just my job. Sometimes when I see the movies it is hard for me to believe I was actually there in the middle of it." He waxed philosophical. "What I'm beginning to wonder about myself is—have I removed myself from society? Have I been away too long on all of my location trips? Do I read enough? Do I question enough? My reason for being an actor, like most any other actor, is to really nail something important down, to really find something to say in my work. And I tell myself that if I am sincere about my work, I should understand the time I live in."

But he was exhausted as he regaled Safran with an anecdote from *The Wild Bunch*. "In that scene with the scorpions and the ants, the scorpions never stood a chance," he said. It was hard to know who he was rooting for, but it is very likely he had a soft spot for the scorpions.

Oates would alternately defend and play down his role in *Alfredo Garcia*, but he was undeniably proud of it. "It was a very unusual character to get to play," he said later. "It had a beginning, a middle, and an end: it started at the beginning of the picture and ended at the end of the picture. A lot of my roles start somewhere else."

"We had a couple of fans. Roger Ebert was a big fan," Gordon Dawson said. "Maybe [Oates's attitude] was a self-preservation issue, who knows. If you're in a picture that's really getting slammed and panned, you might say, 'Goddamn director, he didn't know what he was doing.'" Garner Simmons added, "I saw Sam and Warren in Chicago, one of the only towns it got good reviews in. I walked into a hotel suite where they were. Warren was a very physical guy and he was really pleased; he had a great time and laughed. It was a very upbeat press junket in Chicago, and at that time Warren was not apologizing for his work. And of course he shouldn't be. The performance he gave was extraordinary. But purely out of concern for the need to work, if the film is not doing well, you're going to distance yourself from it."

"It was a lousy movie," Robert Culp insisted. "There's no excuse for it. Sam was high on cocaine and it shows. I always wondered why Sam cast Warren in *Bring Me the Head of Alfredo Garcia* for the simple reason that I thought that the image of that character was kind of the antithesis of Warren. But Sam saw something else, and he wanted to play that part himself—and he thought he could elicit that performance out of Warren."

Ben Johnson said, "I don't think that was the property to move him over the top. He was a better actor than a lot of us was, you know, and I think if Peckinpah was going to really help him, he should have done it like in *The Wild Bunch* or something with that magnitude. That was too controversial to make a big star out of somebody, I think. Some people loved the movie. Some people hated it. There's not much in between." Oates would certainly have taken heed of his idol, Johnson.

Alfredo Garcia managed to land on several ten best lists (but not as many as *Badlands*, which wound up on at least eight major critics' favorites of 1974), as well as earning a place in the book *The 50 Worst Films of All Time*. By 1980, it made back its costs, and by 1981 it had obtained a paltry worldwide gross of $2,676,864.10. In 2006, it easily wormed its way into *1001 Movies You Must See Before You Die*.

"I'm getting out of violence," Oates told Ray Loynd in Los Angeles. "There seems to be a growing reaction to it. People's outcry about violent films is well-deserved although Peckinpah's films, constructively speaking, may have caused some revulsion to the violence in our lives." If he was down on *Alfredo Garcia* with Loynd, he was digging his way out of a grave with Dudley Saunders. "It was too violent. It was a downer. I loved the way the character started . . . but how can an actor or an audience care about people who do so many senseless, disgusting things? I'll undoubtedly do other films that involve violence, but I'm through with violence for violence's sake. That picture turned me off. I can work without having to do that kind of film."

92 in the Shade was definitely not that kind of film, and its location, Key West, was a welcome destination for a man who had spent portions of the previous year in the frozen tundra, probing the depths of Mexico, and hitting the high points of the southern cockfighting circuit. He was optimistic, too, about *92 in the Shade*, for himself and for Peter Fonda. "This will really turn it for Peter Fonda," Oates said, "and he deserves it. It's essentially about a young man who comes back home to Key West. I play an older fishing guide whose territory is threatened." Oates also had high praise for the thirty-four-year-old McGuane. "It's the best script I've read in years. The talent is super. McGuane has everybody so excited they are working for a pittance just to be part of it. He's got it all together."

However positive Oates was about Tom McGuane, Fonda came from a different place. McGuane would lose his wife to Fonda—only after she had a deep dalliance with Oates—and Fonda would deride his director's abilities. "McGuane cut short every scene we had," Fonda lamented. "Warren and I were just so upset because we loved this film so much and Tom . . . just did not know enough about directing."

Oates and Watkins drove all the way from Hollywood to Key West in the Roach Coach. "We'd stop at coffee stops to get coffee and sandwiches, and he had the old Stetson hat, and he'd put that on, and shades. But woe if anybody recognized him, they'd talk to him, ask him to sign things. He'd hide out beforehand, but if he got caught, he'd be gracious about it." The two men talked and smoked their way across the country, discussing politics ("He felt we don't have as much input as we're led to believe") and religion. Watkins said,

> We never got into the Christian aspect at all. Buddhists don't think much about afterlife. Life is suffering, but there's a way around it, and it's important what you do now. I think that's what Warren came to believe. From my perspective, there wasn't a mean bone in the guy's body. I never heard him put anybody down heavily. I never heard him being overtly critical. He'd bullshit a little bit, but that's all. It wasn't cool to wax philosophical. Warren was that way around me. He was always, "It's good and it's bad, but the way you get through it is to be lighthearted. To be heavy is like picking up rocks."

They talked about music, and they talked about women. Watkins said Oates had perfected a look for getting the girl. "Can'tcha love me?" his eyes would say.

And there were women on *92 in the Shade*. Margot Kidder and Elizabeth Ashley were at the pinnacle of 1970s chic: platform shoes, tube tops, feathered haircuts. Cute as they were, they did not hold a candle to Becky McGuane. Warm, ready with a hug, and recently embarked on an open relationship with her husband, she was a dream walking. Becky was ethereal whereas Isela Vega was earthy, and if Oates had been "checked out," where Jennifer Lee was concerned, he would be returned to the sexual library not particularly overdue.

Oates checked in—in the traditional sense—to the Pier House motel in Key West. Its most famous resident was Tennessee Williams, who could often be seen having lunch several tables away from Truman Capote, who was spending his first Key West winter at the establishment. Key West was a world unto itself, with its literary cache also including Hemingway, Wallace Stevens, Hart Crane, Robert Frost, and now Tom McGuane, plus his wife and his young son. "I'd admired it from afar," he told the *Los Angeles Times'* Jerry Parker. "There was a literary aura of which I was very conscious. Also I was a dirty hippie and it was a good dirty hippie town at that time."

Robert Altman was set to direct *92 in the Shade* at one point, but Nicholas Roeg refused, telling McGuane, "No one should do it but you." He received similar encouragement from Bob Rafelson and Peckinpah, but his friend the writer Fred Exley told him the film was a total waste of time. "I hope you'll get back to your serious work soon," the author of *A Fan's Notes* said. Financing came from Britain's Sir Lew Grade, who provided $1 million for the film, which had no distribution deal at the time it was being made. The actors worked for subpar pay—Margot Kidder told Parker she received $4,000 less than what she received for her last picture—and Fonda said he turned down half a million elsewhere. Fonda, Oates, and McGuane would share in the film's profits, if any.

The story of the somewhat starry-eyed fishing boat guide, Tom Skelton (Fonda), and his nemesis, rough-neck Nichol Dance (Oates), is surreal and captivating, but its array of characters—Skelton's ruthless grandfather, his bedridden-by-choice father, and a baton twirler named Jennie (Elizabeth Ashley)—could do with a strong dose of Charles Willeford realism. Harry Dean Stanton as Jennie's cowed husband and Margot Kidder as Skelton's liberated girlfriend Miranda are fine as supporting players: you can taste the saltwater on their skin. Oates and Fonda sail through, but the story suffers from a confusing confluence of factors that could prompt a mini-hurricane.

Elizabeth Ashley had met McGuane during the filming of *Rancho Deluxe* and was smitten enough to take a week's vacation from her Broadway appearance in *Cat on a Hot Tin Roof* to play the sexually charged baton twirler. "He's one of those men," she said of McGuane, "who if he passed through your life, it's a privilege; you just got lucky." "Lucky" is how many publications took her remarks, quickly reporting that Ashley and McGuane were an item. "We are not lovers," McGuane insisted. "Elizabeth is my friend but she is an even better friend of my wife's."

McGuane was happy with Oates's performance. "He was so easygoing in life, in the day-to-day world, that it was startling how loaded for bear he was when he came to work. I had to get used to it," he said. "I'd come to the set and I'd get ready to shoot something, and I'd continue communicating with him as we had informally before we were actually working. And I would find a very driven, highly focused, and somewhat inflexible person to work with, which was fine with me because he brought a lot of force to it. But the idea that he was lighthearted or casual went right out the window."

At one point, Harry Dean Stanton was having some difficulty with his scene. He finally said to Oates, "Warren, I don't know what to do in the scene."

"Harry Dean," Oates replied, "whatever you do is right."

Using his Zen, Oates would have been hard pressed to define "right" as it pertained to romantic entanglements, for which Key West was proving a breeding ground. Fonda, however, denied this in a manner that suggested things must have changed since he and Oates took a wild ride through Europe. "There's been stuff written about how we were real crazed and were playing musical beds down in Key West," Fonda said. "It's because Key West has that reputation for oddness and weirdness. But to tell you the truth, Warren, myself, and at least I know Michael Butler, the cameraman, we were all very straight. It was Mr. McGuane himself who was going around hitting all the flowers he could find, a Mr. Bumblebee. . . . He was being such a bad boy."

But in her book *Actress: Postcards from the Road*, Elizabeth Ashley writes that she, Becky, and Tom reached an early understanding. "We decided that the three of us were going to be pioneers on the frontier of a Brave New World, guinea pigs in a Grand Experiment in breaking the rules and expanding the boundaries. We would follow our sexual instincts wherever they led us, tell each other the truth, and see where the lines actually were." Bob Watkins added, "None of us speculated about it; we all had respect for each other. If somebody showed up with somebody else in the morning, no one was going to say anything about it." And so Oates and Becky McGuane began an affair in Key West. "They were cool, Humphrey and Lauren," Watkins said. "I was rooting for them."

The wrap party for *92 in the Shade* was held at Louie's Backyard, a cavernous restaurant on the waterfront. Tennessee Williams, Truman Capote, James Kirkwood, and James Lee Herlihy joined McGuane and his troupe, who whooped it up with abandon. It was an apt ending for a film that would struggle to find one.

Oates told Dudley Saunders, "A lot of films look good on paper, but fall apart when the cameras start rolling. But I can't see how that could happen to '92.' The script is beautiful. The characters are well-developed, and everything seems to be falling into place. Even the crew is excited, and they are always the first to sense if a picture is going right or wrong."

He did not foresee dueling endings. Fonda said,

When we were coming to do the ending of *92 in the Shade*, Warren and I tried to figure out what was going to happen, because the beginning didn't start off properly. McGuane had written it very specifically, where I get shot. I get the surprise of my life. And Warren didn't want to shoot me because he liked me too much. I said, 'Warren, that's offscreen. This is onscreen.' We ended up shooting two [actually three] endings, one where we struggle for the gun, and we throw it in the water, and we end up hugging each other and laughing and laughing. And another one where he shoots me, and I die in the boat, and he gets out of the boat and walks ashore. And the third one, we both look at the gun, we throw the gun away, both of us get out of the boat and walk to shore.

Initial bookings contained the ending with a freeze-frame of the gun's explosion. Cable and theatrical versions showed Dance and Skelton laughing together and agreeing not to fight over water rights. "What the hell, all it is is ocean," Dance pronounces.

When the filming was over, Tom McGuane and Elizabeth Ashley went to Connecticut, and Oates took Becky McGuane to Los Angeles. "Almost every man who met Becky fell in love with her and maybe she'd had one or two minor affairs in the 15 years she and McGuane had been married, but this was the first time she had actually fallen in love with someone else," Ashley attested. She described an unhappy McGuane who leapt to the phone the morning his wife called from the Hollywood Hills. Ashley availed herself of the bedroom extension. "Warren got on the phone. He thought we were all crazy and couldn't understand why Becky was putting up with any of it."

"Look, it's real simple," Oates said. "Becky and I love each other. You and McGuane love each other. Fine. Becky moves in with me. You move in with McGuane. Each of us has a civilized, sane relationship and we all live happily ever after. What's the matter with that?"

Ashley explained her grand experiment. "Warren listened quietly for a minute, then summed up his response in a word."

"Bullshit."

"Warren would say it like that," Watkins said, "but not with anger. He would say it with enthusiasm."

Becky McGuane eventually rejoined her husband and his girlfriend in Connecticut. The next day, the married couple flew home to Montana.

20

Another Wilderness

Rebecca Crockett McGuane—both Bob Watkins and Oates refused to call her Portia—had meant something big to Oates. "I know he was crazy about her," said Dana Ruscha. "I would know. I was very interested in it all." She added, "He liked Isela Vega too."

Vickery Turner had since married the actor Michael Shannon, prompting one witness to say she had left her husband for a younger man. Whether or not that was the case, "Vickery was good for Warren," Verna Bloom insisted. "Warren's darker and crazier side got the better of her." "I met Vickery once at an audition," said Michael Anderson Jr., "and she mentioned she was married to Warren." His assessment? "She adored him." Ruscha disagreed: "Vickery, I couldn't see anything they had. Zilch. I don't think he ever found his soul mate. The women he found were women he thought were a step up, or possessed some quality that eluded him. He could have met someone if he wanted to. He just had some other idea in his head."

Then there was Teddy. "My parents almost got remarried," Timothy Oates said. "My mom asked us, and we said we didn't want to go back to L.A., so she said no. She probably knew it wasn't a wise move and that Dad was probably just lonely."

Any loneliness was not for want of romantic chops, if Millie Perkins, Lee Purcell, Becky McGuane, and Dana Ruscha were anything to go by. Maybe he just was not applying himself, as Jennifer Lee had intimated. "The love of nature is what I remember most about him," Ruscha concluded. "He loved the outdoors, loved to see sunsets, really in tune with nature and kind of humble for an actor. I remember one time we stopped along the road to get some food, and there was a long line. He just stood in this long line waiting for his turn. And he was pretty recognizable in the '70s. I can't imagine anyone doing that today."

Oates's annual earnings in the first half of the 1970s ran about $150,000. For his last picture, *92 in the Shade,* he had taken a pay cut, something he and Peter Fonda were looking to redress by doing a movie that would be a sure-fire moneymaker. Fonda said, "Warren and I had to make some money after we broke from McGuane because McGuane didn't pay us anything. So we did another film, 'Race with the Dickens,' 'Race with the Devil,' 'Driving Witchcraft,' 'Mobile Madness,' [for] which we got paid a lot of money."

Another title for what would become *Race with the Devil* was the almost inscrutable "So Mote It Be." At fifteen, Oates's daughter Jennifer was smart enough not to be thrown by the arcane verbiage, and when her father handed her the script, she gave it her enthusiastic stamp of approval. "I was sitting in the living room at the little house on Briar Knoll, and my dad shows me this script, and he goes, 'Jennifer, I want you to read this. Peter Fonda and I are thinking about doing it, but I'm not going to do it unless you say we should.' I read it, and I said, 'Definitely do it!'"

"I'm going to see if I can get a motor home out of them too," her father replied.

"Do that too!" Jennifer insisted.

"I felt very important that he really wanted my opinion. I'm sure they would have done it anyway, but it was cute that he did that."

Oates had recently been disappointed when he did not get the role of Randle P. McMurphy in Milos Forman's screen adaptation of *One Flew over the Cuckoo's Nest.* Preproduction on that film, which would star Jack Nicholson, began at the same time that Oates was announced for *92 in the Shade.* (Interestingly, Verna Bloom tested for the part of Nurse Ratched and was convinced she blew her chances when she said she did not think the filmmakers should change the point of view that enabled the Indian to speak.) It is intriguing to think what Ken Kesey might have made of an Oates performance. "Kesey never liked the movie," said Dale Wasserman, who wrote the play adaptation. "I think he once referred to Nicholson as 'that grinning dwarf.'"

Instead Oates signed to play Frank Stewart, a motorcycle shop owner, in *Race with the Devil*, as announced in the trades on December 13, 1974. He would be working with friends and driving a motor home, about as close to a busman's holiday as he could get.

Before Oates took the wheel of the beleaguered vehicle in the film, the Roach Coach would be pressed into service for a couple of trips. The first was a New Year's Eve excursion to Joshua Tree National Monument, where it snowed in some portions. There was the usual craziness, but this time two new recruits were along for the ride. Oates had occasionally dated a former model named Judy Jones, who lived next door, and her younger brother, Dean, sometimes walked up to visit Warren in his house, where he had recently put up a poster from *Bring Me the Head of Alfredo Garcia*. Dean asked him what he thought of the film.

"I don't think it's too good," Oates told him.

Judy and her brother traveled in the motor home with Oates and Bob Watkins, and they headed out to stay with Ted Markland. "Both Bob and Warren could function while they were high," L. Dean Jones (known as "the kid" to his cohorts) noted. Markland held his guitar to the wind as it blew the strings. "Listen to the wind," he said to the group huddled by the fire, warding off the cold night with something like fortitude. "We called Ted 'Captain Sunshine,'" Watkins said. "So much of what we did borders on being illegal."

At the campsite, Judy took a quarter hit of LSD and promptly went to bed for the first four days of 1975. Others with stronger or more tailored constitutions were able to stay up, and up, and up. "There were these white lights in the sky," Dean recalled. "Oates shouted, 'Did anybody else see that?'" Watkins rationalized, "The UFOs in Joshua Tree were mostly LSD. If you take LSD and go to Joshua Tree, you're going to see a world of stuff.

It's going to be hallucinogenic. We'd see planes going across the sky and two or three people would see a flying saucer and others would say it's a plane. They'd say, 'Did you see it? It was going this way and this way!' Well, their eyes were going this way and this way!"

But the cool-headed Watkins was flummoxed by what they all saw on the road to San Antonio. Oates, Watkins, Warren Miller, L. Dean Jones, and Harry Dean Stanton made the journey on which they became convinced they were not alone. Versions differed, but the first thing that happened was that the Roach Coach broke down in Arizona, and Oates took it to a gas station to have it repaired. Jones was convinced that the price he was being charged was exorbitant, but Oates did not care. "Just pay it," Oates growled. Watkins advised Jones not to argue.

"That was one crazed drive," Jones said. "On the road to San Antonio, we all saw a UFO, and by the time we got to the Holiday Inn, we just pulled into the lot and watched the neon sign blinking on and off. After about four hours, Warren needed a drink, so he went inside and got our rooms."

Watkins remembered it this way:

We drove from Warren's house to San Antonio for *Race with the Devil*. Just before the suburbia of San Antonio, the whole left side of the landscape lit up like a meteor had hit. Warren did a double [take]. But it stayed that way—it stayed lit up. He pulled onto the island of the highway, and we scrambled out of the motor home and climbed up the ladder to the top, but we couldn't see anything. We scratched our heads and then finally drove into downtown San Antonio and found the Holiday Inn, pulled into the parking lot. Warren ran inside and checked to see if anyone from the crew saw anything about a plane crash or a flying saucer landing. Nobody knew anything!

We were hallucinating to some extent, but we all saw it, and it lasted a while, for us to go up on the roof.

Warren Miller's account is the most cinematic.

We were in the Roach Coach, near the Mexican border, and we decided to take half a dose of LSD. We stopped and looked at all the lightning, eventually falling back into a pile of what turned out to be a dung heap. But we kept staring at the sky. Warren would say, "Miller, the sky!" and there would be a blast of light. Then we began to attempt to head to San Antonio, but cars started to appear. I realized that if we kept at least five feet away from any other vehicle on all sides, we would be OK. Suddenly Warren turns off the highway, makes a wild left turn, and there below was the Holiday Inn where we'd booked. Oates turns off the ignition, grabs his white jacket . . .

"I'll get the room," he said.

Race with the Devil would be similarly charmed, with one major blip. Oates's friend and fellow zany Lee Frost had been hired to direct his and Wes Bishop's "*Deliverance*-inspired" story of Texan Satanists chasing two happy couples—Oates and Loretta Swit (Hot Lips from television's popular show *M*A*S*H* in a role Oates had hoped would be played by Madeline Kahn) and Fonda and Lara Parker (icily pretty Angelique from the daytime soap opera *Dark Shadows*)—after the vacationers witness a human sacrifice. Bishop had also signed on to the Twentieth Century–Fox production, which began filming on Friday, January 13, 1975.

L. Dean Jones had come to San Antonio with Oates and crew, despite Oates's having suspended his involvement with Judy. "I'm not going out with your sister any more, but I'm not sending you home," Oates told the kid. "Relative to us, he was [a kid]," Bob Watkins explained, "and it must have really made an indelible imprint on his life to be subjected to us at a young age."

Once everyone was on set, a pattern formed. Jones explained,

Warren was very close with Wes Bishop. They had a *Race with the Devil* routine. They would drive to the set, Bob would roll joints, and Peter and Warren would sit around and work on dialogue, as they didn't like the script. Peter and Warren made up their own dialogue, and Wes Bishop didn't care. In the hotel, Warren had a double suite—he'd sleep in one of the rooms, and Bob and I slept in the other. Peter was listening to the Eric Clapton album *461 Ocean Boulevard*, and they'd order everything from room service and sit around and talk about *The Hired Hand*, especially the sound track, and stuff like movie groupies.

The makeshift dialogue worried cinematographer Robert Jessup. "Everyone was just making it up themselves and nothing made sense." Studio bosses elected to make a change. Alan Ladd Jr., then president of Twentieth Century–Fox, wanted Paul Maslansky to produce. Ladd assured Maslansky that Frost and Bishop were aware they had been axed.

Then Jack Starrett, a Texas actor and former quarterback who had played the blabbering Gabby in *Blazing Saddles* before directing *Cleopatra Jones* and a couple other quickies, got a visit from his agent. Starrett had been hired by Frost and Bishop to play the good ol' bad boy sheriff in *Race*, but, he explained, "My agent burst in and said, 'Come on, we have to get you over to Fox, there's been a change in your role.' I said, 'What do they want me to play?' and he said, 'The director.'"

Starrett met Maslansky for drinks, and then they boarded the plane for San Antonio. When they got there, they were told that Fonda and Oates had barricaded themselves in their hotel rooms to protest the sacking of Frost. The two men finally agreed to meet with the new team, but not before Oates had told Fonda, "Now listen, Flyer, I don't want you to get mad now. We go down for this meeting, I want you to keep your mouth shut, and don't say anything dirty. Let me do the talking." In the meeting room were a couch, a glass coffee table, and an air conditioner, on which Fonda perched.

"Maybe you shouldn't just fire a director," Oates told Maslansky and Starrett. "Maybe you should consider what's going on and see if you can help the director instead of just . . ." Having run out of words, he picked up the coffee table and flipped it in the air, where it did a complete somersault and landed on its feet. Its contents went flying, but the glass table performed like an Olympic gymnast. Maslansky was not rattled. "We had a couple of drinks," he said, "and the next thing you know, they were saying, 'Well, okay, let's give it hell.'"

Starrett, who would not have been out of place on *Kid Blue*, eventually fit like kid gloves, but it took some time. "It's very difficult coming in a week into shooting like that," Starrett said. "I had to start again from scratch. I adopted an Italian accent and wore a Fellini hat, and gradually loosened up with the crew and the actors." They reembarked on what Maslansky called "a movie of the week schedule," working fifteen hours a day. "We'd work nice long days and at night, well, all of us would end up getting pretty drunk, I guess."

Oates and Fonda carefully assembled their tribe around them. First, writer Jim Harrison came down, asking to borrow money while Fonda and Oates encouraged him to write a screenplay. Steve Lim, who was working as an assistant director on the film, was immediately drawn to the group. A young searcher, Lim referred to the time as "my Ken Kesey period," not missing the irony that he, a Chinese American, was being introduced to Buddhism by a Kentucky hillbilly named Bob Watkins. "Peter Fonda, Dan Gerber, Warren Oates, Bob—I was lost and then I was found by those guys. You find your tribe," said Lim, who would soon join the exodus to Montana. "It was a confluence of film and letters, a magic period. Warren made an enduring impression on me. I knew Warren as not only as a man of great talent, warmth, and light, but one among a special group of teachers and fellow travelers."

Oates had introduced Becky McGuane to Peter Fonda in Florida. Fonda engraved the date, January 19, in his mind, unable to forget the blonde beauty standing at the bar with Oates. Aware that Fonda was sprung for Becky, Oates did a strange—possibly gallant, possibly opportune—thing. He not only stepped away from his relationship with her but cleared the way for Fonda to swoop in.

"Flyer," Oates told him, "you know Becky and Tom are getting a divorce."

"What?" Fonda ran to the phone and called Becky, whose estranged husband was in London, and insisted she come to San Antonio. "I want you to come down here and join us. Jim Harrison is here, Dan Gerber will be here, Warren, of course, is here with me." By the time she arrived, he had arranged to have her suite filled with yellow roses. "I proposed marriage to her that night and every other night, and every other day until she finally gave up on Armistice Day," Fonda said.

Whatever heartbreak Oates felt he chose to bury by having an affair with a comely stand-in. She was not, however, the young lovely who played the (nude) human sacrifice. That role went to Peggy Kokernot, a former Miss Texas, who Starrett noticed "disappeared pretty quickly back to the safety of her home in Austin after she finished filming the scene."

The realistic extras were no accident. Maslansky had placed an ad in local newspapers calling for "Satanists and black magic experts," and what responses he received both pleased and alarmed him. The eight-week shoot in San Antonio and surrounding south Texas towns also called for a lot of stunts, one of which featured Joie Chitwood Jr. driving a pickup truck as it balanced on two wheels. In another, a car was propelled five feet off the ground and into a midair spin. The effect was a success although the stuntman sustained minor injuries.

The stuntmen took it in their stride. The actors, when faced with rattlesnakes, were not as calm. "The snakes were Texas rattlers," Fonda said, "but in the crazy illogic of the movie business, they were imported from California. Naturally they had a handler with them. But when it came down to the nitty, Warren, Loretta, Lara and I were pretty much on our own while the cameras were turning and we weren't too happy about that at all." Indeed Oates was not. The rattlers were especially unruly, he noted, "because they didn't know they couldn't bite, so they just kept striking anyway, and if they hit your hand or arm, it just about scared you to death. Those weren't easy scenes. I think everybody had nightmares after that."

In a drunken chat between Roger March and Frank Stewart, Fonda and Oates ad-libbed about their friendship as they sat outside the RV. The mutual affection seeps through the scene. "I looked at Warren [as someone] who was just ten years older than I was," Fonda said. "Ten years and six months. We'd talk about things in the world. He wasn't really a father figure to me, nor an older brother, but a concerned friend and somebody that I trusted completely, a really true friend."

As with many Oates films, the ending was proving problematic. Lara Parker said, "They came up with the ring of fire idea which is spooky but not really tied in at all with the story. It's just more meanness." She offered a suggestion, that the focus be on the sacrifice's shed garments, but the ring of fire won out. "The ending just sucked," Paul Maslansky asserted. Oates said nothing. "If Warren didn't like something, he would say it," Watkins said. "He was not the type to go on and on. He would give his opinion, and if you didn't like it, that was your problem."

Race with the Devil was a crowd pleaser, one of the few films from which Oates would receive handsome residuals. Reviews were mixed. *Variety* found that "Oates does his usual believably gritty job with the meager character material here. Fonda is less dreary than usual." *Time*'s Jay Cocks was less taken. "AAA might use 'Race With the Devil' to illustrate the perils of driving off the interstate. It seems of little use for any other purpose." *Cinema Retro* looked back: "Everyone does a great job but Oates is clearly the standout," it said.

"We drove back from Texas, never stopping," L. Dean Jones said. "We got home to the house on Briar Knoll, and the first thing, Warren wanted to go back out for coffee." He went to Pupi's. The other travelers went to sleep.

A few years later, Jones drove to Montana with Oates, and they stopped in a couple of diners. In one, Oates delivered the elaborate *Five Easy Pieces* monologue, asking for an omelet and toast and holding the chicken salad. In another, *Race with the Devil* was on the television. The waitresses were looking from the television to him, and finally one said, "Is that you?" "Yes, ma'am, it is," Oates replied. On the way back, they tried another diner, where Oates ordered biscuits and gravy but could not get them. Jones watched quietly as Oates went a little berserk. "He had a real thing about biscuits and gravy."

Early 1975 marked a critical time in Oates's career and led into a wilderness year. George Pappas, who had served as producer on *92 in the Shade*, said,

> The critics and people in the business haven't been predicting great things for him just to be nice. They've all recognized the man's quality. One of these days the right role and the right director will come along and everything will click. Then they'll be offering him the kind of roles they send to Jack Nicholson and Gene Hackman now. He's the same rough-cut, one of a kind type, embodying a lot of qualities most men wish they had. And it's to his advantage that he isn't handsome, that he looks like an ordinary man. But there isn't anything ordinary about him. You see that face once and you remember it. You hear him say a line and you know that he is saying that line the only possible way that line could be said. The right way.

Montana took up a major share of Oates's focus, but a serious relationship had also been building over his yard fence. Judy Jones, born on July 17, 1943, was in astrological terms a Cancer, like Oates and Monte Hellman. In iconic terms, she was the ultimate California girl. Jones had grown up coastal, primarily in the pristine storybook community of Corona del Mar. On the portion of the Pacific Coast Highway that passes through Corona del Mar was a restaurant called The Quiet Woman. Its shingle depicted a headless torso in a corset. The representation—which would draw feminists' ire—in no way reflected the teenage Jones, who could do wonders for a bustier but had a head on her shoulders she intended to use.

She enrolled in the University of Southern California majoring in public relations but was quick to realize she was more likely to end up typing press releases than writing them. After friends kept telling her she should consider modeling, she was signed by the Nina Blanchard Agency. One of her assignments was modeling leopard-print Catalina swimsuits with a real leopard. During the shoot, the animal went for her hands and then grabbed her legs, which were in its mouth for some nine minutes. "It was excruciating," Judy said. "I had an out-of-body experience. When I finally returned home, I was in a wheelchair." The accident was life changing in other than the obvious ways. "I grew up," she said. "I began reading, and working with animals."

Judy married a wealthy businessman, and they moved to a house in the Hollywood Hills, off Laurel Canyon Boulevard and on Robert Vaughn's estate. They were not happy, and her husband embarked on a series of affairs almost immediately. She spent a lot of time in her yard, walking around and chatting to her neighbor, whom she would see when she was out looking for raccoons or climbing a tree.

"Did you see the stars last night?" the man in the Mexican sombrero would ask her.

"At first we were platonic neighbors," Judy said. When Oates told her about making *The White Dawn*, she said she would love to go to the Arctic. She asked, somewhat naively, whether she could take her dogs. Oates gave her a resounding no, adding, "The way they treat sled dogs, Judy, you could never take it."

"Warren's pool house was basically put together by hookers and bartenders," she colorfully commented. "It had a huge fig tree in the back." She was drawn to the man fifteen years her senior, whom she viewed as "a loner, a lone wolf, a mystery, a total enigma." She and Oates would talk over the fence, and she learned he was looking to start another family. "I was getting close to thirty—my modeling career would end then—and I wanted a family too. My husband did not. Warren disdained my husband. I think he knew what kind of man he was."

One night her husband came home late, and Judy's Samoyed dog lunged at him. He shot the dog, and Oates came running over, thinking Judy had been shot. "He took my husband to the hospital, but that was it, that was the catalyst. My marriage was over."

She began seeing Oates more seriously, and immediately, there were changes. "At USC, I drank for one year, but I did not smoke or swear," she said. "After I met Warren, I started to drink, smoke, and swear."

Across the west side and on up to Malibu, another neighborly conversation took place. Bruce Dern had moved into Malibu Colony, across the street from Frank Capra. "My next-door neighbor was Sam Peckinpah, who was renting a house and now just moving. I didn't know him at all, but I talked to him because I loved *Ride the High Country*." Dern asked why he had not gotten a read for that film.

"Nobody called me about you," Peckinpah answered. "I saw *Wild River*. You were good in *Wild River*. I didn't think you were particularly western."

"Was Warren Oates western?"

"He sure as hell is!"

Dern proceeded to tell him a story.

"Oh my god, that's a movie, Bruce. That's a movie."

"Yeah, but you'd give the lead to Warren Oates," Dern said.

They started to dissect Oates's career, and Peckinpah told him, "They don't appreciate what Warren does because Warren is every western man and he's a real man. In a way, he's kind of the last cowboy. He's a modern version of what cowboys who gave up being cowboys wanted to do with their lives. He doesn't fit in in Hollywood. And Warren's trouble is, he hasn't really found a place where he fits yet."

Over the past two years, Oates had worked consistently and hard, with little time for repose. Montana added some balance to his life—for a while. Even an idyll has a tipping point, and the time would come when some of those closest to him felt he was healthier in the traps of Tinseltown than in Big Sky Country. The conviction would divide friends into two camps.

In the summer of 1975, with little else to do, Oates took his son to Livingston, headed south to the McGuanes' ranch, near Emigrant, and began to survey the initial 6 acres he bought at Gold Prize Creek. The acreage, sometimes called Six-Mile, would expand to 640 and then 1,280 and eventually double again.

The land had a series of primitive cabins with no electricity or facilities, and Timothy and his father camped indoors for a while, listening to the scratch of pack rats scurrying across the warped wood floor. When that proved too much, they moved to the Wan-

I-Gan, owned by Bill and Doris Whithorn, who had purchased the trading post–cum–general store and its twelve cabins in 1948. A character in her own right, Doris Whithorn pioneered the selling of offbeat souvenirs: antler key chains, bottled spring water, and rattlesnake wallets and hatbands culled from the unfortunate snakes rounded up in the observation pit outside. But her pièce de résistance was the Turd Bird, a novelty item made from porcupine quills and horse feces, with pipe cleaners for spindly legs. "The Wan-I-Gan has everything," its slogan trumpeted, and it served as a general store for fishermen, hunters, cowboys, hikers, and tourists.

Near Billings, *The Missouri Breaks* was being filmed. The role McGuane wrote for Oates went to the exponentially larger figure of Marlon Brando, who would play opposite Jack Nicholson. "I foresaw *The Missouri Breaks* as a kind of modest, moderate-budget movie," McGuane said. "It was very kind of hard-edge, thoroughly gritty, and hopefully authentic western. When it got inflated with all the *Paint Your Wagon* elements, and got kind of baroque, it was distinctly going in a different direction than the one I had in mind."

The film's talking point was Brando's bizarre performance, in which he elected to wear a dress, shared a carrot with his horse, and changed his accent with the variable prairie winds. "There were lots of exciting things about the flamboyant stuff that Brando brought to it," McGuane allowed, "but I think the movie would have been better if Warren had been cast in the role. I wanted the audience to feel close up to what it was like to be in that world. Warren would have been a great help in that sense because he always had an authenticity that reminded me of what harder-bitten types on the actual frontier might have been like."

Friends passed through Montana during the making of the film. Dana Ruscha came by and went for a ride in Oates's new four-wheel drive. Steve McQueen phoned, saying he and Ali Mac-Graw wanted to visit and that they would be landing in a helicopter. "Warren decided to scare the hell out of them, so he grabbed a sawed-off shotgun," said Bob Watkins, now acting as caretaker of the property. As Oates took aim for the chopper, the pilot beat a hasty retreat. They turned around, doubled back, and eventually got the joke.

In Billings Oates met a young man who had come up to see his brother, Randy, who was acting in the film. Dennis Quaid made friends with Oates and fell in love with Montana. "I'm from Houston, Texas," Quaid explained, "and I guess this is what every kid thinks Texas looks like, so maybe this is what Warren wanted Kentucky to look like." The two men went to dinner, where Oates ordered steak, only to cut off the meat and eat the fat, and smoked constantly. Despite his worrying health habits, the older man would become a kind of mentor to the young actor. "I think my dad was to Dennis Quaid as Ben Johnson was to my dad," Timothy noted. Timothy had celebrated his twelfth birthday that August by going fly-fishing in the Yellowstone River with his father, who had given him a fly rod, waders, and all the fittings.

That Oates was on good terms with McGuane illustrated that there were no hard feelings over Oates's involvement with Becky, who was now with Peter Fonda. "Warren had a kind of skittishness to his personality, and he was not the kind of person you would have arguments with. I don't remember him having an argument with anyone," McGuane said. "Part of it was that he had a sort of conciliatory nature, but part of it was that he really avoided conflict."

While *The Missouri Breaks* was being completed, both *92 in the Shade* and *Race with the Devil* opened. *92*, despite a glowing review in the *New York Times*, was neglected by the studio, prompting the reviewer to comment, "United Artists dropped a good one."

"I never really wanted that job much in the first place," McGuane said in hindsight. "In some ways I'm glad it wasn't successful enough to keep me doing it." L. Dean Jones remembered, "I went to the *92* premiere in Westwood with Warren Oates and Tom McGuane. There were only about twenty-five people there. It was sad."

Race with the Devil was another matter, opening strong and earning money for its principals. Oates had been shrewd to take points.

That fall, he went back to stay at Chico, where proprietor Mike Art talked him into going elk hunting. Oates, Art, and Watkins loaded packhorses and, early in the morning, rode off to make camp. Art said,

> We went up the gulch, up an old sheepherders' trail to the top of Emigrant, Chico Peak. We got up around 6 p.m. Bunch of deer running around. We make camp, build a fire, started cooking steaks. Oates pulled out a bottle of brandy, and we started swapping war stories. Around 9 p.m., we'd finished a couple of bottles of brandy and were feeling pretty good. So we started singing. About 1 a.m., the fire started to go out, and we thought we better get to sleep. But the stories kept going on and the singing kept going on. Pretty soon, it was dawn, 5 a.m. We thought, OK, let's go hunting.

After breakfast, the men grabbed their guns and stalked off, looking for elk, only to find their plans had hit a snag. "There wasn't an elk within a hundred miles after all that singing and yelling. We'd scared them off," Art said.

The men would meet in Chico's restaurant bar, Oates drinking "anything too loose to chew," as Art put it. "He was into tequila a lot, vodka, vodka and tequila. He'd never turn down a drink." On occasion Oates would hop over the counter and serve as bartender for the evening, pouring strong drinks for the patrons. From his safari jacket's pockets, Oates would take out a different brand of cigarette—Lucky Strike, Kool, Camel, Marlboro, Kent, Viceroy—line them up on the table, and go down the row, smoking from each pack as he went along. "I couldn't say Warren was ever the picture of health," Dennis Quaid related. "He was always kind of scrawny, and he had his wild ways. He never took care of himself."

Before he went home, Oates spent a lively Halloween in Montana with Becky McGuane, who, after separating from her husband, had bought a ranch there. Fonda had already moved in, along with his children, but he was away making a movie. "Meet me in town and we'll just mess around," Oates told her on the phone. They met at the Longbranch, Becky adorable in a dress and fancy shoes and Oates in jeans and a plaid hunting jacket. But they were stopped at the bar's entrance. "You don't have costumes on," the doorman explained. "I think we do," Oates replied. "We're deer hunters."

The doorman relented, and Oates and Becky danced, witnessing painter Russell Chatham win first prize dressed as, Becky insisted, "a gorgeous drag queen." Several hours passed before Becky said, "Warren, I've got to make tracks because I've got to get the kids up for school." As she drove home, she realized there had been a major snowstorm. "There must have been three feet of snow, especially in my driveway. I had to run a mile up the driveway in my party shoes, and that was the last time I would ever not be prepared for winter." Safely inside, she called the Longbranch and asked for Oates, insisting that he stay in town because it was too dangerous to drive. He took her advice, sleeping it off at Chatham's. Whether he dreamed of drag queens, of stalking deer, or of dancing, one thing was certain. As Mike Art put it, "He had the hots for Becky Fonda. Even after she married Peter, they were very, very close."

On New Year's Day, 1976, there was something strange about the Hollywood sign. "HOLLYWEED" read the letters, a nod to the fact that as of that date, marijuana possession was no longer a criminal offense in the state of California.

Oates spent time with Judy Jones, and her brother Dean was often over, watching television and talking. Dean had heard gravelly-voiced singer Tom Waits's song "The Piano Has Been Drinking," and on February 3, he called Oates's attention to the television screen, where Waits was an incongruous guest along with Joey Bishop, Marissa Berenson, and game show host Bert Convy on the homey *Dinah's Place*. "Warren, you've got to see this guy," Dean insisted. Waits fumbled through his interview, erratically searching his pockets for his lighter. Oates took one look at the disheveled singer's predicament and pronounced, "That guy stole my act."

Late one night, Peter Fonda and Dean Jones were visiting Oates while *Dillinger* was on. The film abruptly cut out as the station went off the air to the strains of the national anthem. Oates immediately went to the phone and called the station, impersonating an irate viewer who had planned his evening around watching the movie. Jones and Fonda fell over laughing.

By May, Oates would be working. In a profile of him for the *Los Angeles Herald-Examiner*, Dorothy Manners wrote, "His status professionally in Hollywood is that of a very fine actor, in the star category actually, who has not yet come up with a film to put him over the top as a household name as have Al Pacino, Robert De Niro, and one or two others in his age bracket." She had kindly shaved a few years off the older Oates.

His current project, *Drum*, the tawdry sequel to blaxploitation potboiler *Mandingo*, was not likely to be the film to work the magic. But Oates put on a brave face, using the interview to attempt to make a progressive point. "Is it a good time for riots in Boston over busing black and white children to school?" he asked. "How far have we come away from what was going on in 1850, the time of the film? It was called slavery then, one of the ugliest words in human experience. It's called 'rights' today. But the immoral problem is with us more than one hundred years later. All 'Drum' asks is that we REMEMBER how it all started. Is that enticing? It should be inspirational to us to examine our hearts rather than dragging our feet."

His enthusiasm for one of his costars was evident. "Wait till you see Ken Norton," Oates exclaimed. "This big guy is terrific both as an actor and a prize fighter. He's going to take on Muhammad Ali you know—and soon. Ken is the fighter who almost put Ali down for the count and broke his jaw as well. Can you imagine what it will mean for the picture if Norton does beat Ali? I think he will. What do you think about that!"

Oates concluded the interview by insisting he was probably the only person who ever drove up to the Beverly Hills Hotel "in an unwashed station wagon with a big bag of laundry on the seat. Jean said as long as I was coming into town, I might as well drop it off."

Manners asked whether Jean—actually Judy Jones—was his wife. "Not per se," came the canny answer. He changed the topic to his place in Montana. "It really isn't an operating ranch, just a lot of land with a brook running through and a lot of trees and a great deal of quietness. It's where I'm heading when I'm through."

Dino de Laurentiis was executive producer for *Drum*. De Laurentiis—whose name does not appear in the credits—replaced director Burt Kennedy with Steve Carver, who worked with only four days' preparation. The film also featured Isela Vega as a New Orleans madam (on set, she was up to her old antics, assuming suggestive positions in the buff and teasing the crew by asking, "Is this enough? Want to see more?") and Pam Grier as breeder slave Drum's lover. Adapted from Kyle Onstott's southern graphic novel, *Drum* is corn on the cob. As Kevin Thomas observed, "In 'Drum' virtually all the white Southerners are stupid, sex-crazed sadists."

When Thomas called Oates's character "an engagingly funny villain," this time he was being too kind. *Drum* is grim, difficult to watch—even for laughs—and sadly squanders the talents of Oates, Lucien Ballard, Vega, Grier, and Norton. But it made money, and producer Ralph Serpe was honored by the Los Angeles City Council for hiring minorities. Originally X rated, *Drum* was financially successful among the lowest common denominator after being downgraded to an R. But whatever the rating, *Variety*'s reviewer did not mince words. Oates was "rarely seen to such disadvantage."

Walking across the lot at MGM, Bo Hopkins came across a downcast-looking Oates. Upon seeing his friend and *Wild Bunch* cohort, Hopkins greeted him with a hug. "Hell, we're shooting this thing," Oates began telling him, before disparaging *Drum*. But he reiterated his philosophy of not turning anything down. "If you pass buildings when you're going into town, look over at a few of them, because those are movies that I didn't turn down. I own those buildings." Oates owned none of the skyscrapers of 1976 Los Angeles, but Hopkins took his point. "I don't trust any of these sons of bitches," Oates continued. "Goddamn it, I wish to hell I hadn't gotten into some of this shit."

Hopkins brought up a Phil Feldman script about two ski bums

that Feldman wanted Hopkins and Oates for. Oates prevaricated, aware he was up for a potentially big payday working for William Friedkin. When he was with Sam Peckinpah, Oates ran into Hopkins once more, this time at the Goldwyn lot on Santa Monica Boulevard. The men went across the street to the Pullman car bar, the Formosa Café. "We had a couple of beers. . . . We had a lot of beers," Hopkins said. Among the topics they mulled over were old times spent at the River Bottom Bar in Burbank, which was owned by Tom Simcox. After a western at Warner Brothers wrapped, they would decamp and drink to the sounds of the fights that would inevitably break out among the extras and spill over into the stars.

Oates was not one to reminisce much, relying instead on a mix of lay Buddhism and cosmic consciousness. Now he was also moving toward psychic phenomena. With the influence of Judy Jones, he began to read Rudolph Steiner and Joseph Campbell, whose *Hero with a Thousand Faces* Oates took to heart. "Warren was on a quest spiritually," Judy said, and the two would spend hours in the prototypical New Age bookstore Bodhi Tree in Los Angeles. "Warren lived in the future," she continued. "He was in the present, but his thoughts and inner dialogue were always about the future. He was searching for answers, very metaphysical. He was looking for 'Why are we here?' That was a major part of his life."

Judy also had a different bead on why he initially chose to retreat to Montana. "Everyone thought it was because it was western or whatever, but Warren really felt that something very big was coming as far as changes, what would now be referred to as global warming. He felt that huge revolutions were coming. Warren felt that Montana was going to be a safety zone—there was even a group there called the Ascended Masters—he felt that Paradise Valley was going to be a refuge."

Oates made a forgettable movie called *Dixie Dynamite* largely because of his camaraderie with producer Wes Bishop and director Lee Frost, who also cowrote the script. The film targeted the big-screen circuit of drive-ins and sensational double bills, and the men who conceived it made no apologies for content.

Dixie's script is vastly inferior to that of *Race with the Devil*, but it is harmless enough, a brainless tale of two shapely, leggy backwoods gals, Dixie (Jane Anne Johnstone) and Patsy (Kathy McHaley), out for revenge. Christopher George is a sheriff with a heart, while Oates is nonthreatening family friend Mack, who has a sideline as a motocross racer. Oates wears a lime green Kawasaki shirt recycled from *Race*, but he left the real riding to Steve McQueen, who is discernible, if you squint, taking over for Oates in the motorcycle sequences.

21

Dog Days

W arren would give you the character you wanted," Judy Jones said. Although she was speaking in personal rather than professional terms, the statement was equally applicable. Bob Watkins agreed. "Everybody puts on a different face," he said. "Everyone who knows you sees a different you. I think about Judy and Teddy, they knew a different Warren. The wives were married to him at different times, professionally, economically, maturity, all those factors. Everybody had a different idea of who he was. Warren had many facets." It is doubtful that Oates's public would have thought of the rabble-rousing tough guy as someone who considered himself a Buddhist practitioner or a writer of poetry, which he had begun to pursue avidly.

His position as a highly regarded actor did not preclude his admiring others. On one plane trip, Joan Kennedy was also onboard, and Oates asked her to sign his copy of *Newsweek*, which featured her on the cover. He was generous in his praise of peers and encouraging to those who needed it, but in private he could be moody, ornery, and stubborn.

As a parent, he often accepted film assignments on the basis of whether his children could join him, but other times he was absent or out of touch. For her birthday, he gave Jennifer a copy of a book about Thomas Jefferson, unlikely to engage a teenage mind. Another year she received a thick, full-color atlas. "Now, that was a nice gift," she said. "But Dad, Thomas Jefferson? I'm really busy, I've got to go." She explained, "When we saw him, it was an event, and we were happy." But the girl who was his apple cheeks, the little hand to his big hand, was growing up, and he was not thrilled with associated milestones such as makeup. "It's hardly like I was wearing too much makeup, but any makeup, basically he'd come up and wipe my cheek because I might have too much blush on. And I'm telling you, I did not wear that much makeup."

Through Jennifer Lee, Oates had met musician John Prine at Dan Tana's. Oates was a great fan of Prine's song "Paradise," about a disappeared town in Muhlenberg County, and he invited Prine up to Briar Knoll. When Bob Watkins came by, he also expressed admiration for the song about their neck of the woods. "Man, I gotta tell ya," Prine said, "I'm from Chicago. I wrote that song for my grandfather."

Oates had a script by Walon Green that he wanted to make, about a man who drives through Mexico showing outdoor movies, and he had also taken several stabs at writing. "He was very good at scenes and had great tempo, but maybe not the writing," L. Dean Jones said. Of his often expressed desire to direct, Jones added, "I don't think he'd be that good, but he'd be great at getting his friends and cronies together!"

An unexpected guest also arrived at Briar Knoll: the stand-in with whom Oates had had a fling during *Race with the Devil*. It was a bit awkward when his girlfriend Judy casually walked in and saw Oates with someone else.

At Six-Mile, construction was under way. By the bicentennial summer of 1976, Oates hoped for livable cabins, a structure over the root cellar, and a place for guests in the converted bathhouse. He had been promised a part in William Friedkin's adventure thriller *Sorcerer*, after Steve McQueen turned it down. When he shared the news with Harry Dean Stanton, Stanton was nonplussed: he had been promised the same role. *Sorcerer* went into production, and with subsequent delays, overruns, and exorbitant costs, soon enough Oates was replaced by Roy Scheider.

Oates lamented, "I started building a house and barn up there with the money I thought I was going to make for 'Sorcerer.' Bill Friedkin wanted me for the part, but he likes to spend lots of money on his pictures. By the time the budget had grown beyond the $10 million mark, Universal decided my name wasn't big enough to carry that big a picture. So he hired Roy Scheider. That meant I had to get busy and make the money I had already spent for the house and the barn."

Oates had been trying to interest Sam Peckinpah in joining him in Montana, and on June 1, 1976, Peckinpah made an initial payment of $26,000 for half interest in the six hundred acres, and he would own a small chunk of the upper portion. The agreement was based on a verbal understanding—Sam's sister, Fern Lea Peter, suspected a few drinks had passed between friends— but Peckinpah would not spend substantial amounts of time in Montana until he completed *Convoy* in 1977, at which time the property would be valued at $600,000.

In late June and on into the Fourth of July in 1976, the Sun Valley Center for the Arts and Humanities hosted a conference, Western Movies: Myths and Images. It brought together an array of western personalities past and present, including Buster Crabbe, Blanche Sweet, Tim McCoy, Chief Dan George, Clint Eastwood, writer Arthur Knight, and Oates, McGuane, and Peter Fonda. Oates participated in two panels, "The Paradox of the Western Hero" and "Picture Cowboys: The Star, the Posse, and the Reel West." In the first, he told the audience he had been reading *Journal of a Trapper* by Osborne Russell, and he related how the western genre had impacted his life. "When I was living in Kentucky, as a child I began to hitchhike to the movies in Greenville, Kentucky, and my first movies were Tom Mix and Gene Autry et al. The morality that's presented in the western theme is a morality that we try, or want to try to live up to, and simply by association to me some of that has been a parallel in my own life. I view it all very spiritually."

Audience questions soon moved on to the topic of violence. Oates said,

When we were making a promotional tour for "The Hired Hand," strangely in Germany they thought "The Hired Hand" was a farmer picture. And here, there was violent objection to the severing of—not only the severing of my finger but simply to deliver the finger in a wrapped-up piece of cloth. Now, it seems to me that on the one hand someone might think it's a farmer picture and on the other hand we start talking about violence to the point that it becomes so exasperating to try to determine really what the hell kind of movie we can make and deal with dramatic structures and present them so they're entertaining. You get forced into all kinds of situations.

When I take a script up to read it, I don't read it as a script. I try to read it as a novel, as a great yarn, as a great fable because it isn't real; it's a representation of something. I try to find the good in it, the good in the man I'm playing and the bad because there's good and bad in everyone and there's certainly good and bad in every western character. And I try to find that quality that's going to explain him as a human being and his ethics because the hero has to have a code of ethics that we admire. And, that to me is the basis of a western movie or the basis of "Baretta."

There's someone singularly attacking something with a code of ethics that is immediately identifiable to all of us in the society regardless of whether we are men or women, regardless of whether there is violence or non-violence, or food stamps or out working on your own because a code of ethics does not involve food stamps. A code of ethics involves going to work and doing something for yourself and that's what the western hero did. He didn't take any crap off anybody.

Clint Eastwood added, "The basis of drama is conflict and that has been since time began and since drama was first invented. And, you look back in Shakespearean plays, they were pretty tough stuff and a lot tougher than some of the stuff we're doing now." Oates concurred. "The conflict was in the things they didn't talk about. That's what they want to see, that's what the western movie came to. It's the things we didn't want to talk about."

In the next panel, Oates was both lyrical and prosaic. After talking about the knights of the Holy Grail, he concluded, "As far as me being a star, I just can't accept that. I think I'm more an actor and a lucky man who's been able to live out a fantasy of his life. That's about all I have to say." Writer Arthur Knight confessed, "I was afraid and almost certain that I was going to be the one chosen to follow Warren Oates."

From Idaho Oates went to Montana for the national birthday celebration. Livingston made much of the Fourth of July, with a parade—more of a small procession—on July 2, and a rodeo and cookout where corn on the cob and Coors Light were the staples. He had arrived in time to catch the tail end of the festivities, but he was just as interested in settling into his home. He drove past the Wan-I-Gan, turned, and opened the first of a series of gates to the property, driving parallel to the winding Gold Prize Creek, past the bathhouse with its picture windows offering views of Emigrant Peak. "It always reminded me of the peak in the Paramount movies with the little halo of stars over the top," Gatz Hjorstberg said of the mountain in the Absaroka chain that would draw Oates's awe.

He drove past a small pond with a large boulder in the center, by Bob Watkins's cabin that he shared with his wife, Sandy, past a small well, and up to his A-frame home perched over a root cellar—soon to become a wine cellar—and attached barn. Farther along was a one-room cabin with a built-in bed and an iron woodstove that had belonged to McGuane. At the upper reaches that border on the national forest, Sam Peckinpah would build a cabin with a fireplace but no electricity that his sister, Fern Lea, doubted he ever spent a night in. He favored first the Yellowstone Lodge, then the Murray Hotel, interspersed with stays at Chico.

There was a Jacuzzi adjacent to Oates's house, but he soon learned that some of his structures impinged on a neighbor's property. "He didn't sell at a bargain rate," Joe Swindlehurst, Oates's friend and attorney, wryly noted.

Oates's cabin was small. The entrance was on the ground floor, where there was a small kitchen. Up a treacherous flight of stairs was an open space, doorless except for one to a tiny bathroom. The front room had high ceilings and a couch and desk. In the back was a sleeping space.

"Back when it was a root cellar," L. Dean Jones said, "there was a marmot living in there, and this drove Warren crazy. One day we were sitting around, and we hear a bang. Warren comes staggering out of the cellar with his six-gun."

"I got the son of a bitch," he said, cartoonishly wobbling, stunned by the loud sound.

Oates set about a routine, toting his six-gun and sometimes even wearing a badge, hopefully not in town, where residents were likely to view such a costume with the derision they reserved for the smog device on Warren Miller's California car. Oates would drive the short distance to the post office in Pray, where he would pick up his mail, and into town to shop at Sax and Fryer, a dry goods store and Livingston's oldest continuously operating business. There he would converse with its elegant owner, John Fryer.

Oates would also go to Chico, where he gathered for dinner with Judy and her brother Dean, Bob Watkins and Sandy, Warren Miller, Mike Art and his wife, Gatz Hjortsberg, Russell Chatham, Timothy and Jennifer, Jimmy Buffett and his sister Lori, and Richard Brautigan. Things were looking up for Chico, which had been in dusty disarray when Art purchased it in 1973. As Timothy Oates observed, "Chico was going through a transition, and now they started having prime rib and king crab as opposed to a sit-down dinner of a cold ham steak, a baked potato that was so hard, and a roll you couldn't spread butter on." Now there were aperitifs, wine with the meal, brandy after, and stories long into the starlit night.

Oates regaled the group with a tale about *The Wild Bunch*. Peckinpah, Oates said, came onto the set with a brutal hangover. The scene to be filmed was one with a lot of banditos. Peckinpah walked through their ranks and then finally commanded one bandito, "Take off your pants." The man resisted, but he soon complied. He was wearing nude-colored boxer shorts. "He's out of wardrobe," Peckinpah sneered. "I can't work like this." And that was it for the day.

As dinner's end, some of the group returned to Six-Mile, where other friends were already staying. The acreage suddenly felt densely populated, catching Judy by surprise the next morning. "The kitchen was so small that we had to have people for breakfast in two servings, lunch two servings, and dinner two servings. The refrigerator was incapable, so we kept things cold in the creek. People were sleeping in the bathhouse; people were sleeping in the barn," she said.

Gordon Oates had been an early visitor to Six-Mile, and he was puzzled as to why his brother would want to be so far out in the sticks. For Judy, disenchantment was already beginning to bite. "I loved Montana because it's a natural pathway for the migration of animals," she said. "But the syndrome of socialization and the perpetual drop-ins, 'Hi, we're friends of so-and-so,' I just couldn't adjust to that friendliness, so to speak."

Social historian Toby Thompson, who wrote about Livingston, Paradise Valley, Oates, and McGuane in the "Arts" chapter of *The '60s Report*, recalled, "I had to drive across Warren's land, and I spotted him fishing in the creek. He had caught a small trout." Thompson explained he was a friend of McGuane's and offered him some nuts he was eating from a jar. "I had to pour them into his hand, and he sort of turned his hand around in this odd way that was quite formal, almost like the way you'd turn your hand if you were tipping up a jar of moonshine," Thompson said. "I poured them into this oddly cupped hand that was extended to me, we chatted for a second, and then I drove on up to where I was going to hike. He was very affable and polite, and had this sort of working-class courtliness to him." It would not be long before they crossed paths again.

Jimmy Buffett was also staying at McGuane's, where Thompson was hanging out a lot. One Saturday night, he came back into town from hiking and went to the Wrangler Bar around nine, where he met Buffett. They went on to the Emigrant Saloon. McGuane arrived with a friend, and they all decamped to the wild bar of the region, the Two-Bit Saloon in Gardiner. After a trip to the natural hot springs, they returned to the Two-Bit at four on Sunday morning. "Hell, I'll just open the bar back up," the owner said, and Buffett played a new song he had written called "Margaritaville."

At seven, McGuane went home as it dawned on Buffett and

Thompson and two other cohorts that they did not have enough gas to make it back to Livingston. Suddenly, Thompson had an idea. "Let's go see Warren!" Buffett enthusiastically agreed. "We pulled into Warren's driveway, went up the path, knocked on the door," Thompson said. "Warren comes down straight out of bed, takes one look at us, and gets this enormous grin on his face. His wife is making sort of complaining noises and his son, maybe about thirteen and a little bit irritated."

Oates invited them in and made them coffee. Then he noticed Thompson's Nocona cowboy boots. "Where'd you get those boots?" Oates asked. "Man, those are beautiful boots."

Thompson, worse for wear, sat on the floor and struggled to pull them off. "Warren, if you can get those on, you can have 'em," knowing, even in his inebriated state, that they would not fit Oates.

"Well, I guess they don't fit," Thompson laughed.

"Wait a minute, wait a minute," Oates insisted. He went into the bathroom and got talcum powder, which he shook into the boots. "He did everything, about three or four different tries to get these boots on. He couldn't get them on his feet. He's hopping around on one leg trying to get the boots on. Everyone's laughing."

About a week later, Thompson saw Oates at a party at Richard Brautigan's house. "Good god, Warren, you tried to beat me out of my boots. I was drunk on the floor, Jesus, I was incapacitated!"

"Well, you told me I could have 'em if I got 'em on," Oates replied. "Be careful what you say."

Zak Zakovi, an artist and contractor who worked on the cabin, was less enamored of Oates's antics. "One day the business manager was coming to town, so we bust a gut to get the cedar floor finished," Zakovi said. "Warren was intent on getting a new pair of boots—he was the big shot—and he did get some, not cowboy boots but thick-soled Montana boots that collect all sorts of rocks in their tread. So Warren wears these boots on the floor, unaware that the rocks are destroying the pristine cedar floor. Whatever happened during that two- to three-day party, they trashed our floor, the walls. In terms of fixing it, I told him, 'Forget it.'"

Judy Jones and Warren Oates were as different as their dogs: J.D. was mixed-breed, impetuous, and wily, and Judy's canines were pampered and elegant. "Judy had an elegance and a chicness about her," Jennifer Lee said. Steve Lim, who would spend time as part of the Montana tribe, added, "Judy was a kind of lily."

There were those who considered Judy more "Hollywood" than Vickery and Teddy, some who viewed her cautiously, more still who found her all wrong for Oates, and a majority of old friends who never met her. But as their romance took shape, there was little doubt that an era of sorts was coming to a close in the Hollywood Hills. Dana Ruscha stopped coming by to watch the sunsets as her young son cavorted in the pool; Verna Bloom and her husband had drifted away after Vickery was out of the picture; and others did not feel welcome. Gordon Dawson and his wife came by and smoked a joint or two. But by and large, the age of hanging out and dropping in at Briar Knoll ended a lot more hastily than it had begun.

In its place were visits with psychics, who would ask Oates to lead because he had six planets in Cancer, and intensely private moments during which he would light a fire, brush his girlfriend's long brown hair, then sing her a song or read a poem he had written.

That Christmas, he went to Louisville, but before he left, he did an interview with the *Hollywood Press* in which he reflected on his career. The role of GTO, he said, was "a pivotal part for me. It was something I'd wanted all along, I guess. I always knew I could bring off a leading role and do it well, but until 'Two-Lane Blacktop' it seemed like nobody was willing to take that kind of chance with me." His remarks, even with their trademark qualifiers, represented a switch from his usual "I'm happy as I am" stance, but by now big-screen leads were retreating into the past. There was, however, one person who wanted Oates to portray him on film if his life were ever dramatized. Gary Gilmore told Norman Mailer that Warren Oates would be his first choice.

The *Hollywood Press* piece, which misidentified Oates as a native of Tennessee, observed that he held close to his rural roots. "He frequently returns to his home state but it is more like a war campaign than a homecoming. He's taken a stance in protesting the strip mining that has ruined much of his native countryside." It is not clear whether this stance went beyond singing along to John Prine's "Paradise." But when he returned to western Kentucky that summer, it would be anything but a war campaign.

Oates's agent at the time was Wilt Melnick, who also represented Debbie Reynolds, Kim Novak, Rod Taylor, Margot Kidder, and a young actor named Timothy Hutton. When a young Australian photographer turned filmmaker, Roger Donaldson, began to put together what would be his first film, he purchased the rights to *Smith's Dream* by C. K. Stead for $5,000. Then he scraped together the $450,000 budget. The story concerned a young man who flees after being framed as a terrorist by a government creating its own disaster scenarios to impose restrictive policies on the populace. Donaldson, with longish hair and sail-like flared jeans, was aware his budget was modest, but he thought he had a reasonable amount of money to offer the one name he knew he needed to make the film viable. For the part of Colonel Willoughby, he set his sights on Jack Nicholson. He contacted Nicholson's agent, Sandy Bresler, who promptly replied that his client would not be going anywhere for $5,000. But then Bresler thought for a moment. "I know this actor who loves fishing," he said, and he gave Donaldson Wilt Melnick's contact information. Melnick was not sure Oates would do it, but he would ask.

"My agent had been to New Zealand a year before, he and his wife," Oates said, "and they really loved New Zealand. He said, 'This is a great opportunity, a young film company. It's not the kind of remuneration you normally receive but you'll get more than that by going.'" Oates had another reason for agreeing: he wanted to outdo his friend Dennis Hopper, who had recently gone to the Philippines for Philippe Mora's *Mad Dog Morgan*.

So for $5,000 plus airfare and expenses for him and Judy, Oates went to New Zealand. The documentary *The Making of "Sleeping Dogs"* shows the couple arriving at Auckland Airport.

Oates looks happy, if tired compared to Judy's radiance. In the next clip he is tanned, relaxed, and, despite the fourteen-hour days and bare-bones production, content. "We have the same technique, the same implements to do the job," he said. "[Acting is] the biggest common denominator in the world. There's no metric system to deal with. There's no emotional conflicts. We are sort of a unit—wherever we go, you'll not be a stranger. If you didn't understand the language, it wouldn't matter. I know the talk: that'd be acting, right? It's a remarkable occupation we're all in."

The movie's antihero, Smith, was played by a young unknown named Sam Neill. Much of the forty-day shoot took place in and around Coromandel and Herne Bay. Crew members performed multiple jobs on New Zealand's first ever 33 mm independent film.

Oates soon gave the director a scare. Donaldson remembered,

When Warren turned up, I was intimidated by this very experienced American actor, to be telling [him] what to do. The very first shot of the film is him driving in one of these jeeps and getting out at the side of the pool, and walking towards Sam, who is seeing him for the first time. And he has in his hand a piece of white paper and in the other, a bottle of beer. Somebody leaned over and whispered in my ear, "That's the script he's holding!"

Warren played it as though "This is the address I'm looking for," but in fact he was reading the lines he was about to say in the scene!

After calming down, Donaldson remembered, "We were paying him the grand total of five thousand bucks to come out from the States and do this role. I didn't think we could afford to be cheeky. He walked in the door and started saying his lines," Donaldson said. "We had to say 'Roll it.'"

"Oates wasn't there to carry a weak cast," Howard Willis wrote in the *New Zealand Report*. Ian Mune, Nevan Rowe, Neill, and cinematographer Michael Seresin were all strong. Oates's small but important part was not always easy for him—he was thrown into an unheated pool (the weather was often cold during filming), and he protested about wearing a fez during a party scene. But nothing prepared him for the shock he had when he learned about the gun he would use. Machine and repeating guns were illegal in New Zealand, and they could not be imported for use in a movie. The guns in the film were made of wood, with cables running up the actors' arms. Oates was dumbfounded when he was told he would have to shake his gun to make it look convincing.

The resultant film was one Donaldson insisted was not as much antiwar as "a warning to authority." *Sleeping Dogs* is confusing at times, but it is never dull, and it is chillingly prescient. It became all the more powerful in 1981, when there were riots in New Zealand, and is certainly cautionary worldwide three decades hence.

Sleeping Dogs was the first New Zealand–produced feature to be distributed in the United States, although it would take some time. When it opened at the D. W. Griffith Theatre in New York on February 28, 1982, Janet Maslin wrote in the *New York Times*, "Mr. Oates seems larger and livelier than anyone else in the movie—perhaps because he's so assured as an actor; perhaps because he's virtually the only person on screen who ever laughs." In fact, at one point, Colonel Willoughby advises Smith to "lighten up." It was a phrase that would come back to Oates.

Next he finally had a shot at being the new Bogart, even if it was in an endeavor that television critic Cecil Smith deemed "maybe the silliest in the history of the medium." A television version of *The African Queen* went into production in the Florida Everglades. Directed by Richard Sarafian as a potential series, the pilot reunited Oates with Mariette Hartley, who had worked with him in *Stoney Burke, Barquero,* and *Ride the High Country*. The two established a camaraderie absent on the earlier endeavors, maybe because present circumstances were unexpectedly harsh, as Hartley related.

There were viciously biting bugs, and Oates and Hartley were pulled through a swamp with no thought for snakes, which were in evidence. "Warren and I tried to talk to Dick, saying, 'You can't do this. If we're going to do this series, you'll have to surround us by netting,'" Hartley said. Inadvertently, they may have been wishing the project toward failure. During filming, Hartley kept up her tendency to "swear like a truck driver, and look like Katharine Hepburn. And Warren was a prude, absolutely a prude. If there were kids around, and I ended up saying 'shit' or something like that, he'd say, 'You can't say that around kids!'" But they were good together, she in the Hepburn-originated part of Rose Sayer and Oates as iconic riverboat skipper Charlie Allnut. "We weren't unlike the two people that did it," Hartley said. Cecil Smith agreed, adding, "They seem at times to be doing imitations rather than giving performances." *Variety* made it three. "Both turn in pro jobs but are necessarily haunted by their predecessors." When it aired on March 18, 1977, *The African Queen* did not get a large viewership, and Oates and Hartley were spared further travails.

Oates made a quickie movie, *Prime Time*, playing a sports announcer. The hodgepodge film from director Bradley Swirnoff had a fifty-thousand-dollar budget and attempted to satirize television in the style of *Kentucky Fried Movie*. Despite his being essentially a day player, Oates got lead billing, and the *Los Angeles Times* thought the whole affair represented the "punk rock of the film industry."

In June, Jennifer graduated from high school in Atlanta, and Oates was there with plans for his daughter that did not necessarily jibe with her own. He wanted her to attend the University of Virginia, where she might "become a lady, learn manners, and the proper way to dress," Jennifer said. "He probably wanted me to join a sorority, but it wasn't for me."

"OK, Dad, fine," she protested, "but I want to go to the University of Georgia." Oates was not thrilled, but he agreed.

"My dad made it OK for me to stay in Georgia," Jennifer said. Teddy, now living in Phoenix, where Timothy went to Apollo High School, wanted her daughter to join them in Arizona. But, Jennifer said, "I had my boyfriend and friends, and I wanted to stay in Georgia. Dad helped me out monetarily so I could live with friends of mine."

In Phoenix, Timothy and his friends started a high school soccer program at a time when the sport was marginalized and the image of a soccer mom was two decades away. Oates encouraged his son, bought the team uniforms, and lent the game legitimacy with his infusion of capital. Soon, the Apollo High School Hawks were able to replace their gym shorts and white T-shirts ("We looked pretty sad," Timothy admitted) with a proper blue and gold kit.

Oates went to Lexington, Kentucky, with Judy for his role in a television miniseries, *Black Beauty*, in which he played kindly horse trainer Jerry Barker. "I never knew a better man than my new master," the horse recounted. The program, which began airing on January 31, 1978, was deemed "acceptable children's fare" by *TV Guide*, but when it premiered opposite *Happy Days*, "*Black Beauty* exactly as you remember it" was no match for the pressing question, "Can the Fonz pull off a miracle for Richie?"

While they were in Lexington, Judy told Oates that at some point in her life she wanted to make a journey into her past and thank everyone who had been helpful to her. Oates took this idea to heart and ran with it, driving his girlfriend to western Kentucky. He asked Judy to marry him in Depoy, and she agreed. In the tiny town, he surprised his childhood friend Bobby Coleman by knocking on his back door and then asking him to be his best man. That afternoon the couple went to Greenville. The Palace Theater had been closed since the late 1960s, but Oates knew that. They visited relatives—Oateses, Mercers, and Earles—with whom they shucked corn and baked cornbread. Then Judy and Oates checked into a mottled motel with a kicked-in door and worn carpet. The marriage papers were on the rickety bureau by the bolted-down television.

On August 24, 1977, in Oak Grove Baptist Church, he married Judy Jones, with Bobby Coleman as best man and Coleman's wife Melva as matron of honor. At forty-nine, Oates, his trimmed beard streaked with gray, wore a white suit with multiple safari pockets; thirty-four-year-old Judy had her hair pulled back and wore a long-sleeved white top and matching skirt. Minister Ora Morgan read them their vows. On the marriage certificate, Oates listed his home as Emigrant, Montana, while Judy opted for Los Angeles. Afterward, because Muhlenberg County was dry, they drove like the wind to get a cocktail and brought back a bottle or two to their makeshift honeymoon suite.

Oates would refer to the circumstances of his marriage as "a sentimental journey." Bob Watkins said, "At a certain age, your life can get overly romantic. I think that's why Warren married Judy in Depoy. 'Here is this young lady and she really cares about me.' He wasn't that impressed with himself, but she was." Oates referred to his new bride—whom Dudley Saunders described as "a slender, soft-spoken, strikingly beautiful brunette in her early 30s"—as his third wife, overlooking Bobbie, as was his wont.

While she was in Kentucky, Judy bought an antique sofa, which she had delivered to the cabin in Montana. Coming in one day, she found Timothy and his teenage friends, who had been fly-fishing, carelessly draped over it, their wet boots nearby.

"Don't sit on that!" she exclaimed.

Oates was not happy. "What the hell's this shit doing here?" he asked her. "This is a place for my kids to enjoy themselves."

"It became a conflict, and I can understand Judy's point," Timothy said. "But you have to let a person have a bit of fun. Judy was very *correct*."

Judy felt uncomfortable in the role of Oates's straight woman. "I drank rum and Coke, but I didn't believe in wife-swapping or putting acid in the punch when you've got twenty kids running around," she said. "There are certain lines of decorum that I thought were basic." It did not help that Peckinpah was around now: Judy quickly determined that his presence was not good for Oates. Often she would stay behind in Los Angeles while her husband called Teddy, who started coming up periodically. "When I'd go to Montana," Teddy said, "no offense, Judy, but if he was there in Montana when I was, he treated me like I was his wife, and everybody accepted me like I was his wife, even though it had been ten years or more. And I liked it."

A note Oates left for Timothy on the tiny kitchen table could not have been homier. "We'll be eating at Bob's tonight," it read. "I'll be back for you and Jennifer. The hot dogs are for J.D.—Dad."

In the fall, the newlyweds traveled to Spain and Italy, where Oates would make his last project with Monte Hellman. *China 9, Liberty 37*, which took its title from a road sign, was a long way from Kanab, Utah, and Oates and Hellman were far from the youthful idealists who had made *The Shooting* together. That filming had been like an energetic and not always comfortable party where guests balanced their paper plates on their knees. By comparison, *China 9* was a middle-aged dinner consumed in leather banquettes. Oates described the film as "a taco western because it isn't in quite the same mold as the Italian spaghetti westerns," and the food analogy was apt, since eating was central to off-camera socializing.

It was a very happy time. "Monte Hellman was very close to Warren. He paralleled his personal and professional life," said Judy. "Except," she added haltingly, "he wasn't in the drug culture." Hellman liked Oates's new wife as well; he was not one of those who found her too Hollywood. He even incorporated one of her jokes—its punch line was "Show him your nuts"—into the script.

"*China 9* was the best time we had working together," Hellman said. "We were staying at a pensione across from the Haster Hotel at the top of the Spanish steppes [in Almería], and we had an Italian camera crew. In the nights we'd take over the entire hotel, including the kitchen, and make pasta. It was a little beach hotel that was normally closed that time of year, and they kept it open for us. It became like a real family." Hellman remembered, "Warren and Giuseppe Rotunno [the cameraman] really developed a tremendous rapport. There was a time when I walked on to the set and they were both down on their hands and knees in a powwow. It was the funniest thing; here are these guys a foot off the ground with their heads together, talking about the scene. They both had a tremendous sense of humor."

The film began shooting on November 2, and in its last week it moved to Rome, where Sam Peckinpah came to act in a brief scene, playing a writer named Wilbur Olsen who was interested in acquiring gunman Drumm's story. "I wasn't part of their relationship," Hellman said. "I had a separate relationship with

Warren and a separate one with Sam. I know it was a love-hate relationship. I know that at times Warren was ready to kill Sam and almost did."

Oates was not the only one with murderous thoughts toward Peckinpah. In Rome, Judy was barely speaking to him, seething from a time in Montana when he had approached her in an aggressive way. "Sam's just an asshole," Oates dismissed, adding that he was trying to get a rise out of her.

Peckinpah filmed with a young English actress named Jenny Agutter, who had been in *Logan's Run* and Nicholas Roeg's cult film *Walkabout*. In *China 9*, Agutter played Oates's wife, who falls for Clayton Drumm (Fabio Testi). Drumm, a nod to a character in *The Shooting*, has been hired to kill Matthew Sebanek (Oates), a grizzled ex-gunman. Sebanek is not without honor, but he is hotheaded, and at one point he shoots bullets into the water, recalling Oates's *Barquero* character. "We could have set this love story in any age," Hellman said in 1977. "But we chose the west since the past seems to have a romantic edge over the present."

Oates and his wife were abroad into the new year. On a side trip to Paris, he bought a heavy black seal coat after giving the rabbit one he was wearing to a homeless person asking for money on a chilly November night. In Spain, Oates delighted in eating tubs full of baby eels, but on Christmas Day Judy conjured up a real holiday meal, making mayonnaise from scratch and cooking a turkey. The night before, screenwriter Jerry Harvey, who would create the Z Channel, a groundbreaking cable television station that showed rare and influential films, had acquired tickets to midnight Mass at the Vatican. As they all sat in the fifth row, the faltering Pope Paul VI said Mass while Harvey muttered under his breath about the sinister and hidden imagery he felt was inherent in Catholicism.

In January, the couple went to Montana, where Judy was reunited with the many orphaned raccoons on the property, which had earned her the nickname "the Coon Queen" from some of her detractors. Gatz Hjortsberg was not in their number. "I quite liked her," he said, and he added, "Warren seemed to have liked her, so that's what's most important. I thought he and Judy were pretty tight. I never saw them fight, and I was a guest there a lot. She'd cook a great meal, and we'd all sit around and get high after dinner and drink tea or talk, ramble around."

That season, a meal gone awry entered their collective vernacular, as Bob Watkins recalled. "Judy had a big meal planned, with salmon in the oven. We sat down, had some food and some wine, and had just about finished when we remembered the fish."

"Forget the fish!" Oates said.

They did, and "Forget the fish" became a gentle in-joke, applied when somebody goofed up.

A Montana teenager named Robert Story, whose forebears were part of the basis for Larry McMurtry's epic *Lonesome Dove*, was hanging around. Oates urged the young man, who was having problems in military school, to come visit him in Los Angeles. "I'll pretend I'm a big movie star," Oates laughed. Within weeks, Story hitchhiked to Hollywood, where Oates welcomed him and gave him a bomber jacket from a recent *Police Story*. With Oates's help, Story began working in Hollywood. "I got kicked out of military school for a drug offense, and I figured politics was out, and Hollywood was in," Story said.

The *Police Story* episode represented the kind of quality television Oates would do for a while. If *The African Queen* was an attempt to cash in on a known quantity, his particular episode of the sporadic cop show was inventive and brave. Originally titled "The Mouth Marines," what became "Day of Terror, Night of Fear" was the story of two bank robbers, one young (Bruce Davison) and one old (Oates). Cecil Smith noted, "In this drama, tautly written and directed by E. Arthur Kean, Oates and his long-haired punk buddy Davison are interrupted robbing a bank and flee up the elevator to the 12th floor office of a travel agency holding its staff and customers hostage." A mousy travel agent, played by Sandy Dennis, is drawn to the old renegade Richey Neptune, and Davison, Smith said, "must compete for attention with such masters as Oates and Sandy Dennis."

Bo Hopkins had said that as a child he sat through double features several times, thinking that if he watched them again, something might change. For Oates, the second half of the bill would play as written.

"We spend every spare moment in Montana," Oates told the press. "It's incredibly beautiful and uncomplicated. We don't go near L.A. unless we have to. Nothing wrong with L.A. We just like it better in Montana."

When he was in Los Angeles, Oates would occasionally hit the old haunts like the Raincheck, Schwab's, and Dan Tana's, but with none of the voracity of before. "Now and then he would call me," Howard Dayton said, "and we would go to the Raincheck Room. He was in Montana; he was working. . . . Every now and then he'd come into Schwab's. I don't think he changed at all. He ran away from it all. I knew he would do that; he went to Montana with his dogs." Harry Northup also saw Oates in Schwab's. "I told him I'd got the role of Carmine in *Used Cars*," Northup said. "It was not much work for some money."

"I turned that role down. I guess you did it for the money," Oates growled gracelessly. Oates, said Northup, was "beautiful but ornery."

In 1978, Oates would turn in what he considered to be his best performance and also labor through another re-creation of a famous role. "Only I could play John Wayne," he facetiously told Dean Jones. The two projects, a television pilot based on *True Grit* and William Friedkin's reworking of an infamous 1950 robbery, *The Brink's Job*, commenced filming almost simultaneously. Oates insisted his biggest problem was not commuting between Boston and Canon City, Colorado. Instead, it was a question of grooming. "I had to be clean-shaven with a 1950s haircut for 'Brink's' and really woolly for 'True Grit.'"

Oates was happy to be in Colorado, where he rekindled an old friendship. "I got to ride Ash, the old horse I rode several times in 'Gunsmoke,'" he said. "He's 26 years old and I really think he recognized me." Oates may have felt empathetic toward the veteran equine, but he himself was not feeling well, racked by a bad cough that cropped up periodically, sounding like an icy wind rattling through a drafty old shack. In one *True Grit* scene, Oates drives a buckboard wagon, which he was capable of doing. On the day of filming, however, he was very sick. He came out of his room and told the assembled camera crew, "I'll just do this once. Have everything in focus." They did, and he did.

Like *The African Queen*, *True Grit* did not rope in the viewers. "A picture has got to be pretty lifeless for a colorful, resourceful actor like Warren Oates, the new [Rooster] Cogburn, to come across badly," Kevin Thomas wrote, but *TV Guide* provided a cheer. "Oates does a good job of filling Wayne's boots. Where Wayne swaggered, Oates ambles." The *Hollywood Reporter* found the balance. "Oates scales his interpretation down to human size although the actor's own brand of orneriness is given scant freedom for expression," Earl Davis observed.

A decade before, when Oates began his retreat from television, he said that he would do another series if the right one came along, and that movies were the capper to the work he did for the small screen. He also expressed concern for the "point of saturation"—his term for overexposure on what would be increasingly referred to as the boob tube. Ten years later, television columnists' titling of their comprehensive reviews simply as "Watchables" did not exactly inspire confidence.

22

Something Incredible

It probably was not a guilty conscience that prompted William Friedkin to cast Warren Oates in his next movie. Instead, when Friedkin began assembling a group of middle-aged ruffians, Oates fit the bill. It was fortunate: Oates turned in a performance that became his favorite. It was playing an unstable safecracker, not a head-hunting piano player, that Oates believed to be his finest hour.

Or half-hour: Specs O'Keefe was not the dominant role in *The Brink's Job*. That went to Peter Falk, who played Tony Pino, mastermind of a $2.7 million robbery of the Brink's vault in Boston's North End in 1950. The five-minute job made folk heroes out of the eleven men who took part, and only $50,000 of their takings were ever recovered by the FBI.

What netted the thieves $2.7 million cost $12.5 million to make. The story had been made before, in 1955, as *Six Bridges to Cross*, and when producer Dino De Laurentiis wanted to retell it, he went to John Frankenheimer. The director turned in a hard-boiled treatment that De Laurentiis hated, so he approached Friedkin. Friedkin would cite as his motivation the half-million-dollar payday, but that was not the only factor. "I made 'The Brink's Job' for a number of reasons, not the least of which was to come to Boston during basketball season," he said.

Friedkin asked Walon Green to write the script because he had liked the honor-among-thieves ethic he had tested to such great effect in *The Wild Bunch*. Green said he based *Brink's* on

The Threepenny Opera, and its occasional romp and caper feel, mixed in with some very real grit, would not have been lost on the Rat Pack. The faces in *The Brink's Job*, however, were not Vegas handsome: Along with Falk and Oates were Peter Boyle, Paul Sorvino, and Allen Goorwitz. Someone who was not in the film was Alex Rocco, the actor who had moonlighted as a bartender in the Raincheck Room. "I was hired by Frankenheimer for *Brink's*, and then I went to Boston, and Friedkin had hired Paul Sorvino. We had a big fight—I called Friedkin every name. He did me wrong, as they say," Rocco explained.

Meanwhile, Oates put aside his own disappointment over losing out to Roy Scheider in Friedkin's *Sorcerer* and went from Colorado to Boston. He praised the volatile director. "His attention to detail is incredible," Oates said. "He plots every little detail. Nothing is left to chance. He rehearses everything until he gets it exactly the way he wants it."

And *Brink's* was detailed. Boston was carefully retrofitted by several decades, with forty-year-old street lamps replacing modern ones, parking meters and traffic lights removed, and cable television antennas dismantled. Set designer Dean Tavoularis, who had worked on *Bonnie and Clyde* and the *Godfather* films, as well as the upcoming *Apocalypse Now*, studied photos of Boston and ordered billboards repainted with replica signs. Producer Ralph Serpe located the three-foot-thick safe the robbers had cracked and had it shipped from Idaho to Boston. Then he scoured museums for vintage Brink's trucks.

The Brink's Job wasn't cheap. A thousand extras were hired at one hundred dollars a day each, and the residents of Boston's tough North End also received payment plus the installation of cable television. The *New York Times* noted, "This was sufficient for most North Enders, who habitually spend their summer evenings leaning on window sills and who were thrilled to see 'Columbo' in their front yard." Oates's role as the thief who squeals on his mates caused him to be a target of hostility and "bad words'" from some Bostonians still incensed over O'Keefe's betrayal. Oates shook it off as part of the job.

More difficult was climbing a chain-link fence inside an office.

But the heavy smoker who was nearing fifty would not give up; eventually he fell and loosened a few already unstable teeth and bloodied his nose. "I'm ready to go back to the Navy," Oates laughed. Later, the rotund Allen Goorwitz likewise took a tumble. "Must be the curse of Old Man Brink," Oates muttered.

Timothy and Jennifer arrived in Boston to join their father and Judy, all staying at a summer estate at Swampscott. Oates enrolled them and Jennifer's boyfriend Mark in sailing lessons and found time for an impromptu game of soccer with his son. "He was watching soccer on PBS with Toby Charles announcing," Timothy said. "A friend and I were kicking the ball around and he took it from us. And we could not get it from him! Two sixteen-year-old prime-shape young kids, and my old man just laughing. He might have had a little artificial happiness going on, but I couldn't believe it."

Oates called Mike Art in Montana late one night. "Mike, Mike," Oates said, "I saw this place out here; it's a run-down old inn right on the sea. I'm going to buy it. . . . You and I are going to buy it, and I'm going to run it."

"Thanks, Warren," Art dismissed. "That's just what I need to do."

In *The Brink's Job*, the moment when O'Keefe rolls over on his cohorts is the erratic film's most memorable and, Dean Jones said, the only time he saw his brother-in-law rehearse. When O'Keefe finally breaks down and confesses to the FBI, the entire crew watching Oates burst into spontaneous applause, prompting Friedkin to say that Oates was "one of the most brilliant actors I've ever had the pleasure of working with."

Oates gave every bit of himself in that scene and in its precursor, when he begins to intimate that he cannot stay locked up much longer. Rarely an actor with vanity, he is a ruined human being, his red eyes teary and raw. David Thomson said, "In *The Brink's Job* he's one of the gang who presents himself as the most expert. And gradually as this goes along, you realize it's bogus. And when he's taken in, you suddenly realize that this tight-lipped guy who keeps telling the cops he's not going to say a word is going to say everything. The film, I think, has some problems overall, but none of them are to do with Oates. He's tremendous in it, and that interrogation scene is both hilarious and tragic at the same time."

Thomas D. Clagett, who has written about Friedkin's films, attested to the brand of "helpless heroism" Oates conjured in O'Keefe's breakdown, and although *Brink's* did not succeed, it was a triumph for the actor. The *Los Angeles Herald-Examiner* noted, "Warren Oates is the biggest surprise. He conducts a resurrection of his own career before your very eyes." Preview audiences applauded his performance. Frank Rich wrote in *Time*, "Oates has a hell of a fine time. Throughout the film he launches into deliriously obsessive speeches about imagined World War II combat adventures."

After *Brink's*, Oates spoke about Montana and his career. "It's a beautiful, quiet existence, and although I enjoy being asked to work, I must admit it takes an effort to say yes and give up my contentment for the hustle and bustle of movie-making. But I love that world too. I've been damned lucky. No complaints at this end." In part, he was being diplomatic, but he was also being disingenuous. The 1978 summer in Montana would have its share of fireworks in various forms, many of which were engineered by Sam Peckinpah.

As summer loomed, Oates had a box office success to his name. *Drum* had made $5.5 million, and there was talk of a sequel to the dubious masterwork. It helped pay the rent at Six-Mile, where Peckinpah was spending increasing amounts of time at—but never sleeping in—the remote cabin on the adjoining property. To commemorate their joint venture, Oates had some of the washers he had saved from *The Wild Bunch* dipped in gold leaf, and he presented them to his friend.

Steve McQueen and Ali MacGraw also drove up to Paradise Valley, attempting to steady their unstable relationship. McQueen, who was investigating making Tom McGuane's *Tom Horn*, spent time at Chico Hot Springs. Sprouting a big beard that almost deflected attention from his piercing blue eyes, McQueen checked in as Harvey Schultz, seeking anonymity. "We hear that at this place, people leave you alone, no one fusses over you," he told

Mike Art. "Two days later, he's in the dining room, waiting to get a cocktail," Art said. "A cowboy walks in and says, 'Hi, I'm Andy Anderson, who are you?' He says, 'I'm Steve McQueen.' Guy says, 'Pleased to meet you, Steve. What do you do?' I was walking by and kind of said, 'See?' [McQueen] was a good guy, too; he wasn't as warm as Warren, but I liked him. He wanted to buy Chico and put in a motorcycle rink."

A group of two dozen people signed on to join Oates for a celebratory birthday hike up Emigrant Peak on July 5. Judy was back in Los Angeles; big, riotous group hikes were not to her taste. Gatz Hjortsberg came along, as did Bob Watkins, Steve Lim, Timothy and Jennifer, L. Dean Jones, Becky and Peter Fonda, and assorted others. "I only hiked Emigrant once," Becky said. "It was so way scary because of all the scree that was up there. You had to really kick back a few gulps of tequila."

Hjortsberg said, "We all went up there. There was booze packed in, of course, and all the elements for a good time. It's not like rock climbing, but it's steep and it's a long haul, a ten-mile walk." Hjortsberg was accompanied by his wife at the time, Marian, and their four-year-old son, Max. Because Max was too little to make the trek on foot, they had brought along a pony named King that was notorious for biting people. "I got a miniature pack saddle and saddle bags, and we packed King in."

The troupe was two-thirds of the way up on the rocky ridge when a storm kicked up, and they skidded down a slope. About four hundred feet below the summit was a little cirque with trees, grass, and flat enough terrain to pitch their regiment of tents. As they began to settle, McGuane tied King to a tree using a double-diamond hitch he had learned at a nearby packing school.

The rain continued to pour down but then slowed to become drizzly and cloudy. "We were in the clouds around a big bonfire," Hjortsberg said, "passing the whiskey bottle and the joints." Suddenly, Peter Fonda blasted some fireworks up in the clouds. They lit up the surrounding clouds. "Warren just loved that," said Hjortsberg. "He was in heaven."

Guitars were brought out, and people sang until they fell asleep. An enormous thunderstorm came, rain hitting the tents.

But the next day was clear, and after a late lunch, several people indulged in a few lines of cocaine. Oates, ecstatic after a toot, ran off down the mountainside and severely gashed his hand. He had barely made it up the mountain, Dean Jones recalled, and in coming down, his ill-advised act of exuberance hurt him.

Bandaged and bowed, he and the others started the hike down. When they got to the tree where King had been tied, only the tiny saddle remained. "Somehow this smart little bastard got loose and ran off," Hjortsberg said. People took turns carrying four-year-old Max, and Hjortsberg took the saddle. They found King at the farthest fenced corner at the foot of the mountain.

Peckinpah's precarious health had precluded his taking the hike up Emigrant Peak. He was staying at the Yellowstone Lodge but would move on to the Murray Hotel, where his upstairs enclave would come to be known as Peck's Place. The Murray became a major hub of activity, not least because it was so cheap. It had eleven-dollar rooms and a lobby divided in half: On one side was a luncheonette frying up burgers and breakfasts. On the other side was a bar. You could drink and then check into a room so small you could open the door and fall face-forward in your boots on the bed. The next morning, there would be fried eggs and ham in the lobby.

Before Peckinpah arrived, Oates and Watkins sometimes rearranged rocks in Gold Prize Creek to alter the sound of the rushing water. With Peckinpah, Oates took to blowing up beaver dams to change the creek's course, a practice to which Judy soon furiously put a stop.

Judy, trying to keep Oates away from Peckinpah, had installed a sturdy gate. One night Peckinpah was driving a pickup at about seventy miles per hour, and he ran right through the gate, knocking it straight up into the air. As it pinwheeled down, Oates, who was on the porch, threw his hat in the air. The hat and the gate hit the ground at the same time.

As cinematic as it was, it did not thrill Judy Oates, who had had a similar episode when she was alone on the ranch. Peckinpah sped up the drive, then screeched to a stop outside the house. "I lost it," Judy said. "I grabbed him by the neck—he was scrawny and diminutive—and told him we had animals on the property, cats, dogs, raccoons. I wasn't going to stand for it." Peckinpah, she said, made muttering noises, attempted to apologize, and then came on to her. It did not work.

His presence, however physically small, made a large impression on a scene that was, as Jennifer Lee put it, "a whole conundrum. Serious, sophisticated . . . I think some very deep shit went on up there, they were all switching back and forth, all of it." Peckinpah and Oates were "both good and bad for each other," Garner Simmons observed. "I'm sure Judy didn't want Warren to come apart at the seams. It rejuvenated both Warren and Sam, all the beauty up there, and you start to feel that life is renewing itself. I always thought Warren's willingness to give Sam a place up there was enormously reaffirming and certainly an act of great kindness because Sam was in a bad place at the time."

"We share a place, it's our heaven," Oates said. "We'd always dreamed of a little ranch somewhere and now, this year, he came in on it with me. He's built himself a beautiful house, lovely old log place, waaaaay in the back, it's four and a half miles from the front of my property to the back, and he's in the very back. And he's going to find solace there, and he's going to start writing, and putting down all of his fury. Something incredible is going to come out of it, I know. Something incredible."

"Incredible" might have been the word his wife would choose too, but the intonation and meaning would have diverged 180 degrees. At one point that summer, they had seventeen people staying with them, friends of friends who had asked to sleep in the barn. There was incessant partying: "Montana was very much the fraternity phase Warren never had," Judy said. "There were no rules; there were crazy amounts of drugs. Warren became very much a guy when he was there, hanging out with the bad boys. It became a midlife crisis, no doubt about it." She would occasionally run interference. "Protect me from them," Oates would plead. Judy explained, "I was the bad guy so he'd still be on the good guy list. We didn't have to play that game anywhere else but Montana."

In particular, she was unhappy with Becky McGuane Fonda,

who she knew harbored deep feelings for her husband. It only added to her discomfort. Mike Art said, "Judy was sweet and always nice to me, a beautiful girl. I think Judy resented all of his friends and all of his buddies. We were all kind of raucous guys, including me. She was envious of the fact that he had so many friends, and she really didn't have that many out here. But she didn't try."

Judy's rivalry with Becky was understandable, and she was unable to apply the "wives-in-law" operating system the other Oates women worked. "Judy was always in a daze. She really was," Becky said. "She had a different perspective on how everything was in this world. She was very into Edgar Cayce and all that 'The world is coming to an end' kind of stuff."

The larger world aside, Judy Oates's summers in Montana were over. She confronted her husband and told him, "I'm not coming here again during the summer. No one participates. I can't be the cook and the cleaner, and the whatever." She also knew they would never have a moment's peace alone together. "He could go along with that, but I couldn't. So I took the dogs and I left the orphaned raccoons for them to take care of." What she did not know at the time was that she was pregnant.

Before he rejoined his wife in the Hollywood Hills, Oates would have some unwelcome guests at Six-Mile. There was a group called the Sportsmen that was dedicated to keeping open abandoned public roads. One of the ways they achieved this was to maintain or restore the road—with or without the owner's permission. One day Gatz Hjorstberg and Oates were having cocktails when a Caterpillar D9 drove right through Oates's fence. Men carrying guns on their shoulders drove the huge vehicle. They paralleled Gold Prize Creek, shouting out that they would be doing a little roadwork.

"Warren, rather than jump up and grab his gun like an outlaw, just grabbed a camera," Hjortsberg said. "And he just followed them all the way, snapping photos. We were taken utterly by surprise—they came rumbling up the private road with their bulldozers. There was a sign McGuane had put in that said 'Anyone is welcome on horse or on foot,' but these guys, weekend sportsmen, wanted to take their four-wheelers up there. Warren never even said anything to them. He just followed them along, snapping pictures."

The resultant lawsuit, which Joe Swindlehurst brought on Oates's behalf, took about a year to be decided. "When the Montana judge saw pictures of an armed mob with a bulldozer driving through fences and driving through a creek, they [the sportsmen] lost the whole deal," Hjortsberg said. "There was a road through the property, and the public used it," Swindlehurst explained. "But the sportsmen went up there with a bulldozer and started conducting bulldozer activities on the road, and Warren went berserk. We sued the sportsmen, and it was determined it was not for the sportsmen." The case continued past 1979, with Oates insisting on allowing only foot and horse travel in that part of the property. Judy furthered the cause, saying she had seen black bears, fish, mink, beavers, and bobcats there, all of which would be impacted by motorized access. After the case was won, Swindlehurst sent Oates a bill, prompting Oates to tell everyone in town he had to do a television movie to pay it. "That was a great exaggeration, because the bill was really rather modest. But he thought that was funny," Swindlehurst said.

Despite Oates's generosity and willingness to pick up the tab, Tom McGuane perceived Oates as "kind of tight. He counted his pennies. It came from his background. I think he knew that the income in this slightly frivolous trade could stop at any time," McGuane said. "There's a saying in our business called 'staying with the money,'" Ned Beatty said. "It really means if you have a question about whether or not you should follow one actor or one actress in a particular scene, you figure out which one's making the most money. And if you stay with the money, you're going to have to do some junk. Warren and I were both in a film that turned out to be kind of an embarrassment."

The movie Beatty referred to was *1941*, and Oates's payment, he told Howard Dayton, was a new fishing pole. He was being playful with his old friend, but Steven Spielberg's comic tale about an enemy invasion following the nation's attack at Pearl Harbor was peculiar. Written by Robert Zemeckis and Bob Gale, with

John Milius as executive producer, the film represented the new guard of Hollywood, and its costs ran as high as $40 million.

Spielberg cast old and new actors: on the one hand, Beatty, Oates, Christopher Lee, and Robert Stack, and on the other, Dan Aykroyd, Penny Marshall, and John Belushi. It was a move that tickled Oates. "It's astounding to me that I keep getting work from young, bright, jumping filmmakers," he said. "I've lasted from the Peter Fonda–Dennis Hopper era into the *Saturday Night Live* era."

Oates's character, "Madman" Maddox, was described as "a gung-ho soldier who rambunctiously defends the Pomona alfalfa fields from unsuspected infiltration by the unseen enemy." Oates saw him as "a career soldier with a childlike enthusiasm to hear those guns again. He can't wait to jump into this idealistic struggle." He said Maddox reminded him of his old drill instructor at Cherry Point, North Carolina. He was thinking of Sergeant Goodwin, the man who carried around his pet raccoon and perched the animal on the shoulder of any underperforming recruit.

Chris Soldo was second assistant director on the film, and he laughed off Oates's assertion that he was compensated only by a fishing pole. "He would have had to legally get some money," he said, adding that his checks were made out to the Muhlenberg County Investment Company. "But that stuff happens." Soldo continued, "*1941* was a very lengthy shoot and a very interesting movie to work on. It was a visual-effects movie without the current computer tools. It made use of old but very interesting visual effects like miniatures and glass paintings."

Filming began without actors during September 1978 at MGM. Oates's first day of work was November 20 at Indian Dunes, a motion picture ranch that held a variety of terrains and landscape possibilities. He worked the first eight days of shooting there—night work, with time off for the Thanksgiving holiday. "The area he worked was a flat airstrip. It actually had a runway on it," Soldo said. "He worked long hours into the night, and it was very, very cold. We were all bundled up in Eddie Bauer jackets and stuff. He had prop glasses with frayed, broken glass, and the prop master worked with Spielberg getting those glasses the way Spielberg wanted them."

They shot well over one hundred days, but Oates worked only the first eight. "We had such a great group of actors on that movie; we had all those crazy *Saturday Night Live* people. Warren was equally as enjoyable, but there was something almost religious about him, something very spiritual," Soldo said. "I don't know if it was an awareness of his own mortality, but there was a very spiritual quality being around him that put everybody at ease."

Oates sang to the assembled and also brought in some of his poetry to hand out. At home he was happy. Judy was expecting a baby, and Oates was thrilled. Complications surrounding her pregnancy required that she stay in bed, but her husband cooked for her and carried her up and down the stairs. Isela Vega and Judy had become friends, and Vega was a frequent visitor who would stride in, pull back the covers where Judy lay naked, and announce, "Let's see what's going on with this baby." Then she would pick up her guitar and serenade mother and unborn child.

John Belushi's bad behavior during the filming of *1941* is well documented, and various books and articles speculate about the number of cast members snorting cocaine—one account lists twenty-five—but this time Oates was not along for the ride. The baby brought about a sea change in him. His new daughter, Torrey, was born at the UCLA hospital on January 7, 1979. Oates was there for the birth, and the emergent life prompted him to give up hunting.

Oates and his wife attended a gala premiere of *1941* at Hollywood's Cinerama Dome in November 1979, but disastrous previews precluded the film's high-profile reveal in the rest of the country. The movie that sought to be *"Animal House* Goes to War" had neither its jokes nor its heart. But as Tom Milne observed in *Sight and Sound*, "One man's banana skin may be someone else's sliced onion. '1941' is perhaps one of those films that should be seen twice so that disappointed expectations over the wayward behavior of the slapstick no longer gets in the way of pleasure over what goes on alongside it." Despite the avalanche of bad reviews, *1941* earned $90 million by 1980, assuaging any studio fears of financial catastrophe.

Mike Art went to Los Angeles and met Oates at chic eatery Ma Maison. "He was a completely different guy," Art observed. "He was, I don't want to say on edge, but he wasn't the same. Not that he was unfriendly or cold or anything, but I could just tell . . . always on the phone. Out here [in Montana] he was just loose." Art knew Oates as a man who was "comfortable in his own skin. He wasn't a multimillionaire, but he was happy. He was on call; everybody wanted him because he was so adaptable."

At the end of the 1970s, however, there was not a deluge of offers. One assignment Oates took was for the religious television program *Insight*. The long-running Paulist program produced both comedies and dramas, and "The Man Who Mugged God," which was broadcast on April 21, 1979, fell into the latter category. "The mugger is a desperate and despairing junkie who demands the beggar's wallet. A colorful parable of the power of God's love," went the description.

In June Oates made another television movie, filmed entirely in Saratoga Springs, New York. *My Old Man* was based on an Ernest Hemingway story about a horse trainer named Frank Butler and his wayward daughter, played by everygirl teenage phenomenon Kristy McNichol. It was directed by John Erman, who had worked with Oates in *Stoney Burke* and *One Flew over the Cuckoo's Nest*. "Warren didn't want to do it at all," Erman said. "Warren was *very* reticent about doing it, and I sort of had to talk him into doing it, the same way I had with *Cuckoo's Nest*." This time Erman encountered a man who "wasn't at his happiest. He had some demons, but never with me and never with the other actors." His moods certainly did not affect his relationship with his on-screen daughter. "Kristy and Warren got along. She was mad about him," Erman related. "He and Kristy were tight." Oates's fondness for the young McNichol is alive in the film, and the dynamic between hard-bitten but softhearted Butler and his love interest, played by Eileen Brennan, is life affirming and never smarmy. "Warren found a way to make that part his own and bring a dimension to it that was very special," Erman said.

Oates might not have agreed, but his family felt that Frank Butler was the nearest approximation of him. "He was very Dad-like," Jennifer said. "The way he dealt with Kristy McNichol's character, very Dad-like. It makes me cry every time, but that's OK. That's the one." Gordon Oates agreed, "That's the role that was closest to Warren himself."

The critics also liked what they saw. "What a pleasure it always is to watch Warren Oates and Eileen Brennan," Kevin Thomas raved. In the *Washington Post*, Tom Shales commented on the actor's "haunting, crusty world-weariness." But Gail Williams in the *Hollywood Reporter* was not smitten, finding Oates's performance merely "technically competent. Still Oates has played this kind of part so many times before, no matter how excellent he is, it seems a stereotype."

The new father was headed for his traditional birthday party in Montana. Judy, at home with their infant daughter, resolutely stayed away, still seething from another encounter she had had with Peckinpah during which he had told her that Oates was just another character actor, never leading man material. Furious, she told Peckinpah she would never forgive him, and she emphasized her point by pushing him against a car. As barbs went, it was one that was always in the cards, and Oates would soon receive a similar slur from Peckinpah.

That July, Oates had a blowout cookout at Pine Creek, five cabins and a general store near Pray. The party started out raucous and then turned surreal, as Timothy explained. "There's my dad and there's all these Hollywood folks. Then the grownups disappear." Emerging to sneak a beer or two from the cooler for his friends, Timothy soon had his eyes opened. "I see people dressed up like *Sgt. Pepper's Lonely Hearts Club Band*. My dad has a rubber chicken and a cowboy hat." Once he detected his son, Oates collected a relative amount of sensibility, and he and Timothy drove to the Murray Hotel to visit Peckinpah, who had recently had a pacemaker inserted. It is doubtful that the atmosphere was much saner there, where Peckinpah had repeatedly been warned against firing guns in the hotel rooms and on the roof. In one incident, he had decided he wanted a resident cat to be a Manx.

That weekend Zak Zakovi saw Oates walking around Livingston, clutching his liver and kidneys. "People would always worry about Warren the next day, but not while he was out partying."

As a parent, Oates was sketchy in many ways. But that he loved all his children was set in stone. And although he was not thrilled that his next assignment was yet another television movie, the plot of *And Baby Makes Six* resonated. A pilot for a potential series, the story revolved around a middle-aged couple, Anna and Michael Cramer (Colleen Dewhurst and Oates). He is the cello-playing owner of an upscale antique store, and his happy-to-stay-at-home wife gleefully admits that "women's lib" has passed her by. They are looking forward to retirement after raising a family, only to learn that Anna is expecting a baby. Michael is against her having the child; he utters the word "abortion" often and with vehemence. One of their sons agrees with him, but their sixteen-year-old daughter (Maggie Cooper) sides with her mother. Anna opts to keep the baby, even as she periodically knocks back glasses of wine—it is the end of the 1970s. After the child is born, the family undergoes a change of heart to embrace the infant, although various problems ensue.

Timothy Hutton played the Cramers' offbeat son Jason with effortless charm and even grace, and Oates proudly beams in their scenes together. There is a good chance he saw something of his young self in the new actor's kooky and endearing performance. In fact, he told L. Dean Jones about Hutton. "This kid is really good," Oates said. *And Baby Makes Six* aired a couple of days before Halloween, and it garnered respectable enough ratings to merit a sequel.

A month later, on the evening of November 30, Oates and Judy went to Burbank Studios for an eight o'clock screening of *My Old Man*, which would run a few days later, on December 7. As they sat in room six, they watched Oates as a curmudgeon with very black hair and a very gray beard, as a rascal and a romantic, before going over to the dimly lit Smoke House Restaurant for a few drinks.

Caring for a new baby in the Briar Knoll home was like running a nursery in a tree house, and Judy began to lobby to move to a bigger space on somewhat lower ground. She had her eye on Los Feliz, the area beneath the Griffith Park Observatory. In Hollywood's younger days, Los Feliz had its share of celebrities in the large houses, and Frank Lloyd Wright's fortress-like Ennis House was there, but it always lacked the woolly wilderness of L.A.'s canyons and tottering hillsides. It would not be easy for Oates to leave Briar Knoll, with its sweeping vistas and red-eyed sunsets, wild animals, plants, and a garden he tended with increasing attention. Nor was he going to do it in a hurry. But early in the new year, his hand was forced: Like Michael Cramer, he was going to be a father again. Two infants in the tiny house, with its pool larger than its floor plan, would be insanity.

That they would move was no longer a source of conflict. Oates's career course, however, was. Werner Herzog was casting his next movie, to be filmed in the Amazon jungle. *Fitzcarraldo* was about rubber baron Brian Sweeney Fitzgerald, and the director had initially considered Jack Nicholson for the role, but he was also interested in Oates. To that end, he had dinner with Oates and Judy. "Warren really wanted to go, thinking it would be one last adventure," Judy said. "I said no. We fought tooth and nail." Judy thought that Oates's health could not withstand the rigors of the remote location. Oates believed otherwise, and his spirit took a hit. The part went to Jason Robards.

His wife's second pregnancy was almost as difficult as the first, and Oates was trying hard to be responsible. For the large part, he was succeeding: he did not spend much time in Montana; he reined in his nightlife, doted on Torrey, and cooked for Judy. He even turned down an offer to be grand marshal of the Kentucky Derby because of his next child's impending birth. The rejection, however, prompted even confirmed family man Gordon Oates to question his brother's sanity.

The last week in April, Oates got a call from L. Q. Jones. A friend of Jones's was studying at the University of Southern California's cinema school, and one of the professors was going to show *The Wild Bunch* to his students on May 1. Jones said he and Strother Martin planned to go along and answer questions, as did Garner Simmons, who had written a biography of Sam Peckinpah for which he had interviewed Oates a few years before. Oates said he would enjoy seeing the film again and fielding students' questions afterward.

Professor Rick Jewell explained, "Another student, Ricardo Méndez Matta, had gotten his master's at Ohio State, writing a thesis on Peckinpah. He finds out that these members of *The Wild Bunch* are coming to my screening and found out from the trades that Peckinpah was in town—he was living in Montana at that point, but he was in town. On the day of the screening, Ricardo starts calling all the hotels in Beverly Hills and asking for Sam Peckinpah. The second or third one, they put him through."

"Oh yeah, Ricardo," the director said as the student explained about the reunion and screening. "I'd love to come, but I don't have a car." Méndez Matta did not either, but his professor did. Jewell agreed to lend the student his car to collect Peckinpah at the Beverly Hills Hotel.

"We're starting the screening," Jewell continued. "L. Q. didn't show; neither did Strother Martin. But Warren came. I met him briefly beforehand, and then I introduced him before the screening, and I told everybody Peckinpah was coming." The excitement was palpable.

Midway through the movie, someone came to tell Jewell he had an important phone call. It was Méndez Matta, who hastily explained that Peckinpah had not understood that he would have to get up and speak before a crowd, having thought it was just a screening. "As soon as I told him, he said, 'Take me to the nearest bar,'" Méndez Matta said.

"Sam is having a few, and I'm thinking, 'Uh-oh,'" Jewell said. "He'd already had a heart attack, and they told him to lay off the booze and the drugs, but he was Sam. The screening's over; everybody's taking a break. In comes Peckinpah; he's walking OK; he looks OK; but I could tell he'd had several."

Jewell motioned for Peckinpah to come onstage with Simmons, Oates, and Peckinpah scholar Paul Seydor for the question-and-answer session. "Warren is a dream, an absolute dream, incredibly wonderful with the students, very articulate. He just oozed enthusiasm for young people, and wanted to communicate with them," Jewell said. Sam, on the other hand, "is OK, if you ask him a question that he thinks is a good question." Jewell got him started by asking about Don Siegel, and Peckinpah responded with depth and intelligence.

One student asked, "What is your favorite film?"

"*Deep Throat*," the director snapped. It did not bode well.

"Somebody else asked something that Peckinpah thought was stupid, so Peckinpah literally got up out of his seat and started walking—we're up on a lifted stage—started walking down toward this kid, shaking his fist. I am thinking, 'Oh my god.' I got up because I thought he might actually assault the kid, and I was going to have to tackle him," Jewell explained, "but he didn't. He stopped short, but he was so belligerent and so angry that it closed off the students. They would not ask him any more questions, and unfortunately they wouldn't ask Warren any more questions because they were so shocked anybody would act like that. Paul was no help, so I had to carry it from that point on. We got through it."

Afterward, Jewell took Oates aside. "I can't thank you enough for coming. You were wonderful, and I'd like to get you back down here when it's just the two of us." Oates said he would like that, and he appeared unfazed by Peckinpah's bad behavior.

Peckinpah then approached the two men. "Is there a place we can get something to eat, and particularly something to drink around here?" Jewell responded that there was, across the street at the 32nd Street Café. "We went over, Sam, Warren, Garner, Paul, myself, and three or four of my more enterprising students, Kirk Ellis among them," said Jewell. Over drinks—Peckinpah had double martinis and laughed that he should not be drinking, while Oates drank margaritas with Mexican beer chasers—Peckinpah laughed and then got mad, and he continually kept Oates from departing. "My wife is about to have a baby. It could happen any time!" Oates pleaded, to no avail. Eventually the astronomical bill arrived. Peckinpah picked it up. Oates drove him back to the hotel and finally went home.

Cody Oates, a son, was born on May 3, 1980. Shortly before

his birth, Oates did a phone interview with Dudley Saunders, saying that the past few years had been his happiest and that being a father enriched his life "beyond belief."

"From what I know of the two mothers, the children have to be different as black and white," Bob Watkins observed. "His age and career between the ladies was totally different." And the times, too, had changed, as the children's names reflected: traditionally named Jennifer and Timothy made way for Torrey and Cody, mimicking the tone of the fledgling decade.

Oates might have been more mature, but that did not mean he was reliable. "The one thing I wanted from Warren was constancy, and this was something he could not give," Judy said. "He was totally unstable, a flight to the moon. I'd send Warren out to pick up a prescription for the kids, something that should take five minutes. Five hours later, he'd return, with the story of the most interesting person he'd met in a bar. He was always looking for innocence."

Oates happily accepted a role in Tony Richardson's movie *The Border*, which would star Jack Nicholson. Judy could have no argument with its location, Texas. Before filming began in early August 1980, Oates completed the sequel to *And Baby Makes Six*, called *Baby Comes Home*. The CBS pilot was almost entirely recast, with only Oates and Dewhurst repeating their roles as surprised midlife parents. The second attempt was better received by the critics, who found Oates's performance "credibly and affectionately played" and "absolutely superb as a patient, loving husband who finally has to explain he's getting on in years, too." Although *Baby Comes Home* would be nominated for an Emmy, its merits were not enough to secure it a spot on the network schedule.

The Border was put on hold when the actors' strike began in August. When it ended after eleven weeks, Oates put in a quick appearance in a four-part television miniseries, *East of Eden*, in which he played one-legged, villainous Cyrus Trask. The adaptation of John Steinbeck's novel also starred Timothy Bottoms and Jane Seymour, and when it debuted in February 1981, this "TV trash-lover's delight" topped the ratings, although it eventually lost out to *Dallas*. Cyrus Trask was gone by that time, but as James Wolcott wrote in the *Village Voice*, "Oates had the smell and grit of the old world in his pores. Even after Trask has been unmasked as a sham, Oates haunted the screen with his brooding, baleful sense of ache and ruin." Richard Corliss in *Time* was more succinct. Even in this potboiler, Oates was "a crafty scene-stealer."

The miniseries was a comfortable format for Oates, who could saunter through his performances with commitment but no real ardor. Meanwhile, at home, he was preparing to move. From the hilltop roost on Briar Knoll, the family was moving to a large, split-level home at 4800 Bonvue Avenue in Los Feliz. Although the new home's manicured perfection did not reflect his taste, it also did not scream "movie star." "Judy chose that house, and he just went along with it," Teddy said. "The house wasn't Warren at all. Tons of stairs, that's not him, and the property was all downhill. That's not him." Becky McGuane Fonda agreed. "The housing difference was very dramatic. It didn't feel right to him. Sometimes love, you know, you do different things. Maybe it was more suited to Judy and the children, who were babies then. They were adorable babies, and Judy, she was spectacular."

As he drove down the hill one of the last times, Oates ran smack into a former flame. "I was driving up Laurel Canyon to the top, and here came Warren down in an open Jeep," said Lee Purcell. "I was, 'Oh my god, Warren.' He pulled over, and we had a really nice talk. That was the last time I ever saw him." She still called him Señor Oh-wat-ehz, and he smiled with a pinch of chagrin.

The Border, based on a series of articles by Evan Maxwell, was British director Tony Richardson's first foray into American cinema, and the topical story of immigration, babies for purchase, police corruption, and love was a natural for a man who delved into human drama. It represented the first joint venture of RKO and Universal. Its script, by David Freeman, Walon Green, and Deric Washburn, concerns border guard Charlie Smith, a role originally intended for Robert Blake but reassigned to the bigger name of Jack Nicholson. Smith has been running drugs across the

Rio Grande, but he undergoes a change of heart when he attempts to reunite an undocumented woman (Elpedia Carrillo) with her kidnapped infant. His shift in conscience causes problems with his materialistic wife (Valerie Perrine) and attracts the snooping of an opportunistic neighbor (Harvey Keitel).

As Red, Oates is Smith's boss, a viciously corrupt border patrol officer. If the portrayal fell into his usual type, Oates said he did not mind. "It's been wonderful for me to be a character actor because I have no fixed concept of myself," he said. "As I've changed physically, my attitudes have changed. I've suddenly gotten the parts that fitted my new physical and emotional self. So each thing I do is different. I feel always in motion."

Filming began in El Paso in late October, and the actors were put up in a Ramada Inn. Cinematographer Vilmos Zsigmond worked on some of the film before decamping to do Brian De Palma's *Blow Out*. The director's daughter, actress Natasha Richardson, was seventeen years old at the time she served as a special production assistant. (Her work was interrupted when she was accepted at the Central School of Speech and Drama in London.) Richardson offered a youthful assessment of the film: "'The Border' is basically the story of two people who escape the smog of Los Angeles and he falls in love with a Mexican girl. It's the 'Dr. Zhivago' of El Paso."

Oates said he was drawn to the weighty subject matter. "It's a film I thought ought to be made," he insisted. "The material, the characters, the relationships between them, all so rich. Charlie was the perfect part for Jack Nicholson. And it was wonderful working with Tony Richardson. I see myself as a collaborator with my director when the director allows it. And Tony evokes just that."

At the start of 1981, filming wrapped. Oates had already made another film by then, and the seemingly throwaway part in a little film would gain him a whole new—and much younger—audience.

While he was working on *The Border*, an item appeared in *People* magazine, which was not usual Oates territory. It read, "Vacant for now is Warren Oates's 900-acre ranch, part of which is co-owned by Sam Peckinpah. Oates bought the property primarily to keep out developers and lets it lie fallow, though he permits neighbors to graze horses and cattle there. 'Everybody needs a little piece of Paradise, but they're not going to get close to me,' says the actor, now filming in Texas with Jack Nicholson. 'I'm sure people kind of resented it when we first moved in here but I think they accept us now. God knows I'm not going to worry about it.'"

The item ran on November 3, 1980. Four days later, Oates suffered a big loss. Steve McQueen, whom he had once jokingly warded off his property with a shotgun, was dead.

23

Kettledrums Roll

Ted Strong, who has a loving, lively, arch, and hip Web site filled with material essential and frivolous about Warren Oates, says that for the *Saturday Night Live* generation, Oates is best known as Sergeant Hulka, the end-of-his-tether military man who makes life difficult for Bill Murray and Harold Ramis in *Stripes*. Hulka the drill instructor, and the three-word, five-syllable retort he dispensed to a strung-out recruit, entered the American lexicon.

The recruit introduces himself. "Name's Francis Sawyer. Everybody calls me Psycho. Any of you guys call me Francis, and I'll kill ya."

"Lighten up, Francis!" Hulka tells him.

The simple, shop-weary delivery to the nervy young man struck a chord with viewers old and young. Lyle Gorch's "Why not?" could not hold a candle to it. Bennie's irreverent dialogue with Alfredo's head was as stuffy as Hamlet's soliloquizing with a skull. Frank Mansfield was intentionally mute. And John Dillinger was just talking to himself. "Lighten up, Francis," was part of the zeitgeist.

Stripes was conceived as a vehicle for comedy duo Cheech and Chong, but Ivan Reitman, who had directed *National Lampoon's Animal House* and *Meatballs*, instead cast actor-comedians Bill Murray and Harold Ramis in the zany tale of two unemployable no-accounts, John Winger and his pal, Russell, who decide to join the U.S. Army. With Oates onboard, it was, said cast member

Judge Reinhold, the sound of "the *Animal House* era and *The Wild Bunch* era clashing."

The forty-two-day shoot of the $9 million Columbia movie enabled Oates to go to Louisville, where filming commenced on November 15; it continued at Fort Knox on November 25. "The Defense Department liked the script and gave us a lot of access, rolled out the tanks, let Ivan command the troops wherever he needed extras," Harold Ramis said. "And they're the greatest extras in the world 'cause they jog back into place, they don't need any breaks, they're real versatile."

The wily, geeky Ramis found Oates "a cool, hip guy. I was in awe of Warren Oates." Reitman's assertion that the actor was "loved, respected, not to be trifled with" was tested when Ramis and company pulled him into a muddy pool after Hulka sends the platoon through the obstacle course at Fort Knox. "Ivan thought it would be funny if we pulled Warren into the mud hole," Ramis said. "So on our last take we pulled Warren into the mud hole."

Oates was livid. "Never do anything to an actor unexpected like that!" he seethed.

"He got really mad. Really mad. It was embarrassing," Ramis cringed.

"He didn't know anything about it [being thrown in the mud]," said Timothy, who was visiting the set with his sister. "That's when he cracked a tooth and his face got so swollen. As professional as my dad is, he thought they could shoot him from another side." As his children waited with him in the trailer, "John Candy parades in the motor home, Bill Murray comes in, here comes Ivan Reitman," Timothy said. "Warren, get out of here," Reitman ordered. Over his protests, Jennifer took her father to the dentist. Afterward, he liked the dentist: the pain was gone.

It would have been easy to make the on-screen exchanges between Murray and Oates exaggerated, but Murray, impressed by the actor's chops, asked Reitman if he could underplay their scenes. Hulka was originally scripted to die in his fall from the high platform, but the character—and the actor who played him—was so beloved that the decision was made to keep him. Hulka would return, injured but unbowed, in the second half of the movie, which did not keep the promise of the first. Out were any subtlety and human plot. In were nonsensical action and paltry payoff.

By the time filming shifted to Los Angeles, Murray and Oates had become friends, and they shared a drunken evening beside Strother Martin's grave—the actor and Oates contemporary had died on August 1—in the Court of Remembrance at the Forest Lawn Hollywood Hills Cemetery.

Stripes, released in mid-1981, was the summer's unexpected sensation, making $58,826,082 in its first eight weeks. Kevin Thomas found, "If anything, Oates has a natural warmth that makes him almost too sympathetic." Robert Osborne observed in the *Hollywood Reporter*, "Watching Oates is comparable to a year's course in drama school; his reactions keenly scaled to camera size, are priceless." But the last word is from Ted Strong. "Yep, it's Bill Murray's movie, but watch the old pro Oates as he does slow double takes in the barracks or grins through his threats. This isn't the drill sergeant as monster—it's the giant monster who has come to accept the lunacy of the military." Piggybacking on the runaway success of *Stripes*, army recruitment numbers went up.

At Briar Knoll, Oates had a new tenant. Dennis Hopper rented the one-bedroom house with a pool for about a thousand dollars a month. "Russ Tamblyn, Dean Stockwell, and I did a lot of swimming in that pool," Hopper attested. Oates stopped by now and then, to clean around the pool and do some gardening, but Hopper expected his landlord had an ulterior motive. He wanted, Hopper felt, "to see if the house was still there. I'd moved in at the height of my unfortunate decline."

Oates had a decline of his own, which led to his being let go from a television show and a movie of the week—unprecedented for the accomplished, professional actor. He was set to appear in an episode of *The Gangster Chronicles*, a seminal series starring Michael Nouri, and then to do a movie of the week called *Killjoy* with Robert Culp. For the latter, they were shooting atop the bluffs that drop off from the Pacific Coast Highway to Santa Monica Beach. The popular filming spot has several palm trees, a little white picket fence, a winding footpath through golf-course grass, and a dramatic view of the vast blue Pacific.

The day's work was over and it was already dark when Oates approached Culp and said, "They just canned me."

"They can't do that!" Culp replied. Oates shrugged and acted as if he did not care.

But he did. Talking under a bunch of palm trees in the late night, he confided in his friend about a run-in he had had with Peckinpah, during which Sam had insulted first Oates and then Judy. "At that point Warren told me their relationship was severed permanently," Culp said. He added, "I'm not sure Warren was doing OK; otherwise he wouldn't have taken the role from which he was fired in the first place." In the case of the movie of the week, Oates was replaced by a nonactor.

Money was tighter than it had been in the past, and Oates told Bob Watkins he could not continue paying his caretaker's salary at Six-Mile. Watkins and his wife returned to Taos. But in Los Feliz, the financial struggle was not discussed, as Jennifer Oates found out when she came for a visit. Jennifer sat in the backseat as her father drove her and Judy to dinner. Judy told Oates that one of the maids was going to be off the coming week. "I'm going to need you home," she said.

"What?" Jennifer exclaimed. "Are you nuts? You have three maids. One is going to be gone and you want my father to stay home because you'll only have two there and you need help to take care of your kids?"

Oates laughed like crazy. Then he told his wife he would be going in a couple of weeks to Santa Fe, where a print of *The Hired Hand* would be screened for the first time in almost a decade. The Santa Fe Film Festival, held April 24–30 and focusing on westerns, was shaping up to be a big event. *The Hired Hand* program, with Peter Fonda and Oates in attendance, sold out the 850-seat Lensic Theater well in advance.

At his home in Taos, Bob Watkins got a call. "Bob, you've got to come down and hang out," Oates told him. Watkins said, "At Santa Fe, we were having so much fun, we went in and out of the theater, outside for a cigarette, then someplace else. They also went out to eat. Writer Boyd Majers spotted Oates and a friend turning up an alley and going into a restaurant. He hesitantly approached Oates to compliment his work. "Sit down, have a bite to eat," Oates ordered Majers, and he did.

There was a Friday night screening of *High Noon* followed by *Shane*, and there were appearances by Katy Jurado and Jack Palance. Palance told the audience that George Stevens had wanted him to make his dramatic entrance into the film at full gallop, but Palance was an uneasy rider at best. "Jack," his director finally told him, "walk the damned thing."

Other events showcased Tom McGuane's *Rancho Deluxe* and Monte Hellman's unreleased (in the United States) *China 9, Liberty 37*; Charlton Heston discussed *Will Penny*; and a Saturday night tribute to Ben Johnson was a stomping, unqualified success. "But another Western image is equally stunning," Sheila Benson wrote in the *Los Angeles Times*: "Peter Fonda's almost-lost first feature, 'The Hired Hand,' in which he stars with Warren Oates. A difficult and less conventional work dealing with love and enduring friendship in a real and fiercely unfriendly West, it is the first great festival discovery." The critical and audience response must have been gratifying. However, Benson added, "The shocking print quality is another matter; no festival print should be as scratched as this."

On the last night, Oates was joined by Watkins and his wife Sandy at his motel room in Santa Fe. Watkins had brought along some cloths that his teacher had inscribed. Watkins explained, "A lot of times monks are really good calligraphers, so their parishioners will gift them with tea towels. Monks wear them around their heads when they're doing work, and laypeople use them for tea towels because they're the right size. Gaben did one that said, 'Compassionate mind pervades the universe,' four or five characters plus these red seals."

Oates leaped off the sofa and placed his omnipresent camera on the coffee table. He asked Watkins to tie the cloth around his head. Then he set the timer on the camera and jumped back on the couch with Sandy and Watkins. "He had this great big, outrageous smile on his face," Watkins said. "And that's the last time I saw this rascal."

Another Montana summer lay ahead, but only after a movie in Texas with Dennis Quaid. In late April, *Tough Enough* got under way in Dallas–Fort Worth. Part of it was filmed during a Writers Guild strike, and the movie would be investigated for scab activity, since the script was not written by a union member. In fact, the script was reportedly so bad that Quaid admitted ad-libbing most of his dialogue. The Twentieth Century–Fox production was an attempt to cash in on the novelty of the Toughman Contest, in which amateurs boxed each other for money.

The story follows hard-luck country singer Art Long (Quaid), who dislikes his job trimming trees. He has a wife and child to feed, so he enters a boxing contest for prize money and a possible recording career. As promoter James Neese, Oates looks fashionable in a T-shirt worn over a long-sleeved top, and he seems to enjoy both judging a wet T-shirt contest and prowling the boxing ring.

Tough Enough was directed by Richard Fleischer, who replaced John Leone when the president of American Cinema Productions did not like the coverage he was getting. "He wasn't directing the actors," said Andy Pfeffer, the firm's thirty-five-year-old president. Oates was quick to side with Leone. "John is brilliant. He established a good rapport with all of us and then they zapped him." Quaid was supportive, if less proactive. "I really liked him, but what can I do?" he said. Stan Shaw, who played the oddly named street hustler PT 109, shook his head in disbelief. "These people don't know what they're doing," Shaw said.

Somehow, *Tough Enough* manages a good-natured bluster that carries it away from hokum. Its female cast—Carlene Watkins as Quaid's less than supportive wife and Pam Grier as Shaw's girlfriend—are almost invisible, as it is essentially Quaid's turn, and he comes through, whether singing or packing punches. *People* wrote, "If he can work such magic with a derivative script like this, imagine what he ought to be able to do with 'The Right Stuff.'" *People* found Oates's Neese "terrific, gravelly," and *Playboy* traversed the same unpaved road. "Bristling with grit, as always," the reviewer wrote of his performance. But as *Z* magazine noted, *Tough Enough* opened on "the same day as eight other films [one was Steve Martin's *The Man with Two Brains*] in Spring 1983 and hasn't been heard from since."

"Working with Warren was the greatest," Quaid told the press at the time. "All you had to do was look in his eyes and everything was for real. He put you right there in the scene. You didn't have to act because he could just make you believe it was happening." The film's spirit had much to do with their friendship. "We had a blast doing *Tough Enough*," Quaid said. "We were together every day; we just really had a fun time. We'd drink a little whiskey and play guitars. He was a no bullshit kind of guy." And when Oates went to Montana, Quaid, who had been giving serious thought to living there, soon followed. "I stayed at his place—I never really thought of it as much of a house. The doors are short, but Warren really liked all that. We'd wind up going to Chico about every night because there wasn't much cooking going on back here," Quaid noted.

At his table, Oates had placed a framed photograph of little Torrey wearing a velvet dress with a lace-trimmed collar. He kept it there, he said, so he would not miss her as much.

Oates took Quaid trout fishing and initiated him into the Oates pace of life. "He loved to get in the truck and just drive real slow up the mountain to Sam's place and look for animals," Quaid said. Along the way, he would impart business advice, suggesting Quaid use his business manager. "My career was taking off—I was starting to make money. He loved to give me financial advice especially. He was definitely a mentor."

There were now two rules at Six-Mile. "He didn't like people parking on his grass," Quaid said. The other rule was, "You can do anything you want to, but you don't have to." These were rules that worked better in the absence of Sam Peckinpah. As Ben Johnson observed, Oates was "trying to come back into the business and make a new start with the new family and everything, and when Peckinpah got around him, he just couldn't do it. I don't like to talk about them taking pills and all that kind of stuff, you know. I never did do that and I know they did, but I never seen them. But it was a bad scene when they both got together. Peckinpah was such a fatalist."

Timothy, who had just graduated from high school, spent much of that summer with his father. They would cook lamb chops, and Timothy would watch Oates gobble up "pork chops, fat on his steak . . . also packs of cigarettes, drinking." There was not a lot of exercise going on either, as Oates's method of walking his dog illustrated. "My dad would hop in whatever vehicle he had at the time and drive down Six-Mile Creek Road. It's about six miles to the paved road. And J.D. would run along—he'd exercise him that way." Timothy continued, "We had a lot of coyotes. The coyote pack would send the female down to try to lure J.D. to the male coyotes waiting to do him in. Dad would watch J.D. follow the girls for a little bit till he got to a bend in the road, where he'd stop, turn around, and come back."

One day, Tom McGuane saw Oates in Livingston on one of his frequent trips to the car dealer. It involved a Suburban he had bought that was a lemon. "He concluded that they were going to run over him as a Hollywood guy, and he would come to town almost daily to do battle with the car dealer," McGuane said. Afterward Oates stopped by Joe Swindlehurst's office on Second Street. "He had a slouch hat and a beard and a fatigue jacket on," Swindlehurst said. "If you looked at him from the right perspective, he looked a little bit like a bum." Oates saw Swindlehurst's partner coming in the door with his suit and tie on. Warren looked over at his attorney and put his fingers to his lips. "Watch this," Oates whispered. Oates went to the door, stumbled out, and got tangled up with the partner. Then he got in his car and drove off. Swindlehurst had to convince his bewildered partner that it was only Warren Oates.

When the summer was over, Oates flew down to join Teddy for Timothy's college orientation at Northern Arizona University in Flagstaff. Afterward, they went to dinner at Denny's, where Oates ordered chicken fried steak and potatoes with gravy. From across the table, Timothy saw his father wince. "It's nothing," Oates said.

Teddy and her ex went back to their motel. The next day, during the long drive back to Phoenix, they were laughing about occasions when Oates, on location, would call her. "Teddy, where are you?" he'd say. "Warren, you called me," she would reply. Suddenly, Oates asked her, "Did you mean what you said, that once the last kid goes to school and is out of the house, we can talk about living together again?"

"It sounded like he was planning to leave Judy," Teddy said. "We'd gone out to dinner and stayed at a motel, and [he thought] I was taking him back."

That autumn, Oates would be in Los Angeles long enough to turn around and go to Arkansas for a dual role in a much-ballyhooed miniseries. Playing both a preacher and a Confederate major, Oates had the time of his life.

The Blue and the Gray was a sprawling, $15 million Civil War yarn with movie aspirations and miniseries limitations. The eight-hour CBS program was filmed in Van Buren, Arkansas, with additional sequences shot at Fort Smith and at Prairie Grove and Pea Ridge battlefields. Andrew McLaglen, who had been present at the beginning of Oates's career, directing him in *Have Gun—Will Travel*, now presided over the story, which pivoted around artist John Gentry (John Hammond), who sketched war scenes and vignettes for *Harpers Illustrated Weekly*.

The Blue and the Gray opens as a horse is struck by a mortar in Vicksburg. As the animal hits the ground, residents descend on the body to cut away at its flesh for sustenance. The scene set a realistic tone that carried forward throughout the eight hours. Among the 750 speaking roles (and 4,500 extras) were names: Geraldine Page, Colleen Dewhurst, Gregory Peck (in his first television role), Sterling Hayden, Paul Winfield, Rip Torn, and Stacy Keach.

"I saw Warren in the Los Angeles production of 'One Flew Over the Cuckoo's Nest,'" Paul Winfield told Stacy Keach. "It was one of the most memorable performances I've ever seen on stage." Colleen Dewhurst, who had worked with Oates in the recent *Baby* television movies, had been looking for him on one of the battlefields. When she found him, he was on a hilltop, conversing loudly with a flock of turkeys.

There was a palpable excitement about the project, as McLaglen noted. "There are wonderful things in the story—like the war stops so two brothers from opposite sides can talk over conditions at home. At one point, the Rebs sail a toy boat over to the Union side, offering to trade tobacco for coffee. And you give me soldiers, horses, cannons, that's my kind of film. That's the fun of this business."

Oates played both a villainous Virginia preacher who becomes unhinged after his son is killed and Major Welles, a Confederate leader with whom he felt a particular affinity. "I can relate to the story we're telling here because my own family split over the War," he said. "Kentucky was a border state, and some of my family fought for the North, and some for the South. Not only that, but my family also owned slaves. I used to be embarrassed about it, but I'm not any more. I just accept it as part of our history." He sighed, "Oh, my family was an intricate part of the progress of the great change that has gone on in this country for 200 years."

Stacy Keach met Oates as he came galloping onto a scene, taking Keach aback. "It was like this demon," he said. "He was playing this crazed Confederate officer who was leading his man into the jaws of death. I mean, he was in character right there. He was letting us all know that this was how he was going to play this part. It was like seeing a winged Mercury. This horse became him; horse and rider became this absolute hurricane of energy."

Oates was having a great time. "I would have done anything to be in a Civil War film," he said. "Doing this part is a fulfillment of my fantasy, which is to lead the brigade, to be in a battle, and to ride the horse back and forth behind the barricades. That's why I got into this business in the first place."

When *The Blue and the Gray* aired in November, *Variety* felt Oates approached the role of "twisted avenger with admirable restraint." But Howard Rosenberg in the *Los Angeles Times* played it for laughs. "The English excel in period dramas. On the other hand, we put on a good World Series." He concluded that the miniseries "does no irreparable damage. The North still wins." The *Los Angeles Weekly* submitted the show to an "accuracy in haircuts" test. *The Blue and the Gray* did not pass.

One night in early November, Oates met Charlton Heston and

some stuntmen and day players in the Formosa Café. Heston and crew had been picketing the Screen Actors Guild offices, opposing the guild's plan to admit extras who did not already have SAG cards and benefits. The referendum was up for a vote on what happened to be president Edward Asner's first night in the chair. Asner said, "They were picketing the Guild and Heston was half in his cups and of course the news crews were there. And I had a couple of stout hearts surrounding me, and one of my stout hearts described that Warren was there, drunk as well, and parading with the anti-absorption of the extras. My friend said a few unflattering things to him and Warren did his cackle and drifted away."

On November 28, William Holden was found dead in his apartment—a passing that Peckinpah would blame on coffee table edges. Oates took Holden's death personally. "Time is running out for me," he said. "Tragedies have struck down too many of the people in my life. It scares me. I'm afraid I might be next."

There was trouble with *The Border*. Previews were not going well; audiences did not take to the downbeat ending, in which Charlie (Jack Nicholson) blows up the border police headquarters and is sent to prison. In December, Tony Richardson called his entire cast back to El Paso to film a new conclusion. When the final version was released, Arthur Knight wrote that Oates lent "yet another masterful characterization as the canny, corrupt border police chief."

At Judy's suggestion, Oates spent Christmas in Louisville with his brother, as well as Teddy, Jennifer, and Timothy. His other family, his wife believed, needed to know they had not been usurped by Torrey and Cody. When Oates flew back to L.A., Timothy and his friend John Robinson came along and spent a few days in the house on Bonvue, playing chess and going out to dinner.

Making his next movie was a struggle for Oates. "His health was so bad," Judy said. "He was very ill during *Blue Thunder*." In John Badham's film, Oates played another ornery police official, Captain Jack Braddock, and Roy Scheider was Frank Murphy, commander of the titular police helicopter. *Blue Thunder* was intended to stave off the threat to movies posed by video games, and the erratic, frantic, stuttering result courted controversy. *California* magazine called it "a crass, smarmy roller coaster of a movie that besmirches everything it touches," but Tina Daniels at the *Hollywood Reporter* singled out Oates, who, "playing a type—the gruff captain . . . never slips into caricature. He's given some of the best dialog and delivers flawlessly."

In February 1982, Oates went to Montana and, on impulse, gathered his troops for a Chinese banquet at Chico Hot Springs. As was his custom, he brought a gift for Mike Art's wife, Eve, and then sat down with friends including Gatz Hjortsberg, Becky McGuane Fonda, Russell Chatham, Sam Peckinpah, and Joe Swindlehurst. Tom McGuane had seen Oates earlier that day, and although he attended many a Richard Brautigan spaghetti dinner, he confessed to not being a banquet kind of guy and declined the invitation.

There were aperitifs, cocktails, oysters Rockefeller, wine, egg rolls, Peking duck, jasmine rice, chop suey, chow mein, paper-wrapped chicken and spare ribs, fortune cookies, brandy, and cigars. The laughter went long and almost reached Emigrant Peak. As they said good night, Joe Swindlehurst had the farthest to go but was without a heavy coat. Oates was wearing the glitzy fur coat he had bought in Paris, "not one that you'd want to wear too much in public," Swindlehurst said. "One thing led to another, and I wound up in the coat."

Swindlehurst called Oates the next day. "I've got your coat."

"Oh, I know, I know, but I'm going back to L.A., and I'll get it from you the next time I come back," Oates said.

Before he left, Becky McGuane Fonda took Oates aside to express her concern about his health. "You gotta watch it, take care of yourself," she insisted.

"You kind of felt the kettledrums roll when he returned to California," said Tom McGuane.

A few winters previous, the writer William Kittridge was dining at Chico with his partner and her eleven-year-old twin boys. A few tables away, Oates, in his cups, had ordered flaming crêpes suzettes, and the children gaped, their eyes lit. Soon, a shimmering plate all their own arrived, compliments of Oates.

Flaming desserts and juveniles are not the wisest combination, unless you are a child—or dream of being one. Torrey Oates has fleeting memories of her father coming in at four in the morning, visiting her and her brother in their tiny beds, and feeding them Gummi Bears, rose petals, cotton candy, and—once—morsels from a pouch of cat food.

In March 1982, Gordon Oates flew out to Los Angeles on a business trip and visited his brother. Warren had been sick: the flu was going around, and he could not seem to shake it. "Warren did not like doctors, would not go to one, but I talked him into going, and he said he would," Gordon said.

Ted Markland called to a cool reception from Judy, and Warren called back. "I'm not Warren Oates," he told Markland; "I'm Worn Out."

Oates and Judy went to a gallery opening for artist and friend John Powell, one of whose outsize paintings Oates had obtained by trading Powell his red Mazda pickup truck. The showing was at the Deauville Gallery in West Hollywood near the Pacific Design Center, affectionately known to Angelenos as the blue whale. Before attending, Oates and Judy had popped into the Bodhi Tree to look at spiritual books and accoutrements. Afterward they went for drinks and dinner on restaurant row with Powell and his wife, Wendy. Throughout the evening, Oates said he was having trouble breathing, but when his wife and friends pressed him on it, he laughed it off, saying it was only indigestion.

Dennis Hopper's brother David arrived in Los Angeles with a documentary he had made about Russell Means and Dennis Banks and the Wounded Knee tragedy. Dennis was away in Paris, but David invited Oates and a couple of friends to come over and see the film. Afterward, they smoked a little grass. Oates, complaining about chest pains, folded early. "I've been smoking too much grass, and I think I better lay off," he said.

"You should probably go to a doctor," David Hopper advised.

It rained most of the day on Friday, and, feeling trapped by anxiety and cabin fever, Oates called Monte Hellman for a chat. In the course of the conversation, Oates said, "I think I've had a heart attack."

"What? Get to a doctor!" Hellman ordered.

"Nah, just kidding," he said. "I had some bad indigestion last night."

Becky Fonda also called Oates. Her husband was in Manila filming, and he requested a photograph of Oates inscribed, "To Harry, Thanks for the ride, Warren." Fonda wanted to place the photo in a helicopter he was flying in the movie, and as his children, Justin and Bridget, would be joining him in the Philippines in a few days, the plan was for Bridget to pick up the photo and bring it with her. When Becky reached Oates by phone, he told her he had not been feeling well.

"You didn't see a doctor, did you?" she scolded.

"Well, now, Becky . . ." he began.

The morning of Saturday, April 3, was intermittently cloudy and cool, with the promise of sunshine later in the day. The news made Judy happy because she was having a luncheon for several of her friends. Oates had been outside for a time, looking over the well-tended garden that did not really afford him much to do. Suddenly tired, he came in and told his wife he was going upstairs to lie down. "Call me when lunch is ready," Oates told her.

At noon, when she went to fetch him, he did not respond. Moving closer, Judy found his body "still and cool to the touch," as she would tell the team of paramedics who arrived bedside at 12:17 p.m. Their valiant, if routine, attempts to revive him were futile.

Lunch would have to wait. Warren Oates was dead.

24

No Magic Hour

The cluster of emergency vehicles on the narrow street had howled on their way up the hill. Now they were still, with only their lights flashing a steady beat. Judy's luncheon friends had scattered. A couple of them looked after the children while she dealt with the paramedics and fire department officials. Battalion chief Robert Ewert had made the pronouncement, but it would take more than that for it to sink in.

Oates's neighbor David Peckinpah phoned to alert his uncle. Judy had forbidden Sam to call, so he contacted Becky Fonda.

"Something's going on at Warren's house," Peckinpah told her. "I don't know what's going on over there, but things are bad." He asked if she would call Judy.

"Warren's dead," Judy told her. Becky's devastation was immediate, pierced by the realization that she would now have to tell her husband.

"I didn't know how I was ever going to tell him," she said.

Meanwhile, Judy phoned Gordon. Someone phoned Peter Boyle, who told Verna Bloom and Lee Purcell.

Vickery Turner began a long letter to Nick Georgiade, whom she had never met. She wrote about the circumstances of Oates's death and how much she knew Georgiade had meant to him.

Gordon called Teddy in Atlanta. "I had been to the Steeplechase. I lived in a house that had a basement with its own bath and own entrance. I rented it to a guy from Phoenix named Mike; he worked at night for CNN. I came in the front door, the phone rang, and it was Gordon. He told me. I ran outside the house—there was a stairway to go into Mike's place from the house, but for some reason I went outside and ran to knock on Mike's window."

"Mike, get up!" Teddy shouted. "Go upstairs and sit at the dining room table and don't say anything. Just sit there." He did. "Warren died," Teddy told him. "I have to think. I don't know what to do."

Judy had called Jennifer; Teddy had to call Timothy in Flagstaff. When his roommate answered, Teddy asked him his name. "Can you stay with Tim for the next eight hours no matter what he says?" The roommate agreed and got Tim on the phone.

"What do you mean he died? How dare he?" his son protested.

Monte Hellman was angry. "I felt that he literally killed himself," Hellman said. Because Oates had joked with him about a heart attack, Hellman insisted, "Those kinds of jokes are not kidding. He was telling me something, so telling himself something."

Becky Fonda reached her husband in Manila, where it was afternoon. "I'd been waiting for the call," he said. Fonda's father had been ill, and he had cultivated a resigned acceptance. But what she told him next caught him totally unprotected.

"Warren's just died."

"I burst into tears," Fonda said. "I was prepared for my father's dying. He'd been dying for the last eight years, but certainly not Mr. O. It was a major blow for me for the day, for the year, for my life. And of course I had to go tell the rest of the crew that Mr. O had taken the big hike."

Fonda and his crew gathered in his room for a wake. "In the Philippines, the sun sets about 6:15 and it's dark by 6:30. There's no magic hour," Fonda said. "All the crew came, we got tequila, and we all sat there. As the sun sank into the ocean, red-colored, we toasted to Warren. Needless to say," he added, "none of us went to work the next day." Oates's passing, he concluded, "was more than a death to me."

As Teddy, Jennifer, and Timothy booked their flights, L. Dean Jones drove to the Forest Lawn Hollywood Hills Mortuary to deliver Oates's favorite pair of cowboy boots. "He had this joke about being buried with his boots on," Jones said.

Word spread like a prairie fire. Robert Culp was heartbroken. The network newscasts devoted twenty seconds to his passing. First Jane Pauley on NBC and then, at 6:14 p.m. on CBS, Morton Dean read copy that misidentified Oates as one of the actors from *Bonnie and Clyde*. In print, the *New York Times*' obituary erroneously cast him in *Easy Rider*.

The *Times* of London believed Oates moved from "white collar respectability to hippydom, only to end up a John Wayne substitute and pillar of orthodoxy." But virtually all accounts praised his extraordinary acting ability and down-to-earth persona. *Rolling Stone* ran a column-length tribute, and the *Los Angeles Weekly* devoted a full page in which F. X. Feeney described him as "a genuine artist and a solid presence, a rare and authentic masculine grace. . . . He was always a star among the discerning." In his role as SAG president, Edward Asner paid tribute, saying Oates was "a highly gifted actor whose work I enjoyed enormously. He was a sweet, generally gentle person who had a great sense of humor and great respect for his craft."

Dennis Hopper was in Paris, where he had taken his mother and his ailing father for a European tour. Seeing Oates's obituary in a newspaper, Hopper's parents deliberated as to whether they should tell their son. "It was a total shock. I never saw him sick or even thought of him as being sick," Hopper said.

Dana Ruscha was on the crowded London Underground. Looking over someone's shoulder, she saw a tabloid headline, "Warren Oates Dead."

"It makes me think his karma was just right: when fate gives you a death where you get to die in your sleep without long medical turmoil and suffering, and disease," Gatz Hjorstberg said.

Stacy Keach was in a sound studio. "I always think of Warren as somebody I'm going to meet when we all pass to the other side," he said, "because that day I was doing the postproduction on *The Blue and the Gray*, and we were looping a particular scene, the one line I had as I was standing over his body. We were looping that scene, and there was a picture of Warren dead on the screen. Two minutes after that moment, a phone call came in saying that Warren Oates had just passed away."

Warren Oates would have more memorial services than he had marriages, and they would be equally eventful and emotional, with a twist thrown in for good measure. The funeral itself would be held in the quaint Old North Church (a replica of the one in Boston) at Forest Lawn Hollywood Hills, a stone's throw from the Warner Brothers lot, NBC Studios, Walt Disney Studios, and the River Bottom Bar.

Judy had obtained the services of Reverend Douglas Johnson of the Advanced Spiritual Church in Hollywood, a metaphysical group that put stock in world peace and reincarnation. At four o'clock in the afternoon on Tuesday, April 6, Douglas was to oversee the service of memory in the diminutive church that looked as if it had been plucked from a collector's train set. The green oblong felt of the graveyard surrounded it.

The man who was born the year the Academy Awards began but who never received a nod was also denied an autopsy by the coroner to the stars, Dr. Thomas Noguchi. The flamboyant Los Angeles coroner had recently begun a thirty-day suspension, and his troubles were only starting. Instead, Dr. Ronald Kornblum performed the procedure, and spokesman Bill Gold pronounced Oates dead of a heart attack brought on by natural causes. He also had chronic obstructive pulmonary emphysema.

"He smoked; he did drink. It was just a combination of a lot of things," Monte Hellman said. "It was as much that he liked to eat well as anything else. He wasn't willing to be told he had to give up any of those pleasures." Peter Fonda said, "Warren was not an abuser. No matter what it was—alcohol, grass, a little cocaine—I don't think it contributed to his early demise. He smoked too much, and he lived in Los Angeles too much, and he had emphysema. Sometimes we'd drink too much. . . . We liked life and we liked being there. We did smoke marijuana, but I was never worried about smoking marijuana with him; I was worrying about his cigarettes that he'd smoke all the time. The tobacco."

Harry Dean Stanton was not sure he was invited to the funeral, so he called Gordon Oates to see if he could get permission to attend. "Harry Dean, if you're not supposed to be there, I can't imagine who is," Gordon insisted.

Sam Peckinpah was another matter. "I'm sure Sam never thought he'd outlive Warren," Garner Simmons said. The last good talk he and Oates had, Peckinpah had repeated to him something Oates had told him four years before: "I don't want to possess or be involved with something I cannot enjoy with my friends or loved ones." The sentiment hit Peckinpah hard, and although he was resoundingly not invited to the service at the Old North Church, nothing would keep him away.

There was, however, one very notable absence. It was not Dennis Quaid, who was unable to attend because he was filming *The Right Stuff*. Nor was it the Fondas, the Montana contingent, or Jack Nicholson, who sent the largest floral tribute, so big it dwarfed the church as its blossoms reached toward the rafters. Instead, it was Teddy. In Atlanta, she had been packed and ready to go, but when it came time to board, she could not get on the plane. "I had maybe an anxiety attack," she said. She urged Jennifer to go ahead, saying she would fly with Timothy's friend Peter French. When French arrived at the airport, she still could not get on the plane bound for Los Angeles. "My clothes came, but I didn't," Teddy said.

The night before the funeral, Jennifer had finally managed to fall asleep. She remembered,

> The only place they had for me to sleep was the bed he died in, and I slept in that bed. That night, I must have been dreaming, I'm sure, but I felt like I saw this white gauziness, that kind of feeling. J.D. started barking his head off. In the morning, I woke up to my father's voice. It was on the TV, a *Gunsmoke*, and he was behind bars, going off, "Ya laa la la laa," yelling at the jailer. That's the time I realized that was the way it's going to be. I'm going to hear his voice. He'll never be older than fifty-three, and I can always hear his voice any time I want. I'm lucky. Kids of actors are lucky.

When Sam Peckinpah was recovering from heart surgery in Montana, a well-meaning young woman who had her eye on him showed up at his bedside with *The Tibetan Book of the Dead* in her purse. Peckinpah promptly threw her out, instructing she come back next time with spirits of the bottled variety. Warren Oates would have appreciated both.

Before the service, Judy joked that she should place "a fifth in every pew," but that might have left some gasping: the 185-seat church was packed to the gills, and people were standing outside. Timothy Hutton came, as did Strother Martin's widow. Eileen Brennan, Robert Culp, Stacy Keach, Shelley Winters, Monte Hellman, Allen Goorwitz, Rift Fournier, and Millie Perkins were there. Harry Dean Stanton and Sam Peckinpah came. Everyone came—everyone, that was, except the minister.

A half hour passed, then forty-five minutes. Nearing the hour mark, Judy had to make a decision. She approached the podium. "Until this nice gentleman gets here—if he gets here—why don't we each share some kind of memory—good, bad, indifferent—of the way we remember Warren?"

Harry Dean Stanton was first on his feet, with a story from *92 in the Shade*. Stacy Keach went up, with an anecdote from *The Blue and the Gray*. "He was brandishing his sword and riding around, and it accidentally fell out of his hand and almost hit one of the dead soldiers on the ground. He yelled, 'Cut, cut, cut, cut!' and got off his horse. His first concern was whether or not one of those extras that was lying on the ground had been hurt. Aside from being a wonderful actor—we all know that—he was real people."

Warren Miller spoke, lamenting all the chess games they had yet to play before concluding, "I wasn't finished with him as a friend."

Another person walked to the podium, and another, and then another with stories that were funny, touching, poignant, wild. As they spoke, Robert Culp watched Sam Peckinpah. "If he's going to go up there and shoot his mouth off, I will," Culp thought. But Peckinpah did not.

"I had a terrible time getting through it, but I wanted to be able to talk," Monte Hellman said. "I was so overwhelmed by emotion, and it was very difficult to speak. But we all managed to get it out. And I think we all were really moved by that community experience."

In all, about twenty-five people spoke. Right before the end, Timothy Oates took the podium. He later said, "I do not know what came out of me. Harry Dean was fairly visible, and I said, 'You, Harry Dean,' and here's this tough old bastard, and I see him get a little tear in his eye. I looked at the audience; they went from a mood of happiness to a period of sadness. People finally started crying." Timothy managed a story about his father calling his freshman son bright and early on a Saturday morning and scolding him, "Son, what are you doing in bed? Get outside. It's a beautiful day. Go out and do something."

A newspaper snippet in the now-defunct *Los Angeles Herald-Examiner* reported that the story that got the loudest response was "the one about the actor getting up and gliding back to grab a beer from the fridge in the rear of the camper—he happened to be *driving* at the time."

But for those who knew him differently, the rowdy note did not always ring true. "The funeral was horrible," Howard Dayton said. Warren Miller had a similar take. "It seemed like a lot of actors looking for work," he said. Armand Alzamora, noting that Jesse James had died one hundred years before on April 3, agreed. "It was a lot of actors paying tribute. Many of them didn't really know him," he said.

Not one person referenced a shy man with an essential loneliness, a man who would inscribe a photograph with his poem "The whole world went to bed early / leaving me up alone / with words for my friends / to speak for myself."

But at the end of the service, the mourners rose to their feet and burst into spontaneous rounds of applause. For someone who considered himself "the last person in the world to get into acting," it appeared he had made an awfully good choice. "And then all of a sudden, it just sort of petered out," Culp said. "And we all went out into the sunlight and took a deep breath and went to our cars." Looking over, Culp saw the profile of Peckinpah against the darkening sky.

There was no filing past the closed casket where Oates lay in his boots and a white linen suit. Those who chose to attend the wake drove slowly down the hill to the Smoke House, that darkest of dark restaurants where the gathered quickly got drunk. "He was there with us," Hellman said. "It was beautiful and it was tragic." From the pay phone, Jennifer called her mother.

Teddy and her friend Micki would hold their own wake the next day at a bar in Atlanta. "One minute we're laughing, and one minute we're crying over some stupid thing Warren did," Teddy said.

Warren Oates was to be cremated on April 7. Gordon felt his remains should be interred in Louisville, at Cave Hill Cemetery (where he would eventually place a headstone), but Jennifer and Timothy were not so sure. Judy only knew she was exhausted. "Why don't we just chop him up?" she snapped before regaining her composure and telling his two oldest children that it was their call. They decided pretty quickly: Montana.

"Ask me," Oates says in 1959's *Yellowstone Kelly*, "that major's in a hurry tuh be buried on a Montana mountain."

"Nobody asked yuh," comes the reply.

St. John's Episcopal Church on the upper Yellowstone River was tiny, holding about forty people, although fifty would attend the service for Oates led by Rector Michael Morgan. This time shop owners, ranchers, and colleagues got up and shared memories of Oates coming in to buy fly-fishing equipment or talk to the waitresses. Dobro Dick played music by Woody Guthrie, and others joined in with their own guitars and instruments. "It wasn't a hoedown but a real intimate, casual, Montana-style send-off," Timothy said. The minister got a laugh when he said a few words about the time Oates came to church.

"So many people got up and remembered small, intimate things about him, funny, inconsequential things, and it really brought him back to life and enlarged our regret of his departure," Tom McGuane said. He later told the *Bozeman Daily Chronicle*, "I was distressed when Oates was described in our local paper as a character actor and part-time resident. I felt that it gave a diminishing view of the man."

At Six-Mile, Timothy and Jennifer located their father's favorite spot on the hill, a berm where there was a campfire ring and benches. It was around this campfire that Steve Lim saw his most enduring image of Oates, "sitting comfortably back, light casting shadow across that face, his head cocked, crooked impish smile, and shining eyes as he would take a beat and then toss off some comment that put us all into laughter at the wonder and absurdity of ourselves and life. He was a brother."

Oates's children did not know what they were going to do. "We were drinking wine and toasting my dad, putting a little sip in the fire," Timothy said. "And all of a sudden, I started walking in a circle. I said, 'Jennifer?'" His sister helped scatter the ashes, and there they remained, for a time.

Driving fast through Yellowstone National Park, Timothy and his friend Peter French were zooming on their way to Atlanta, going way beyond the speed limit. They got to a curve in the road where a bison was standing. Timothy slammed on the brakes. "He kind of poked his head at us, blinked, and walked away. 'Maybe that's my dad saying, boys, slow down, take a look at what's here,'" Timothy said to his friend. Oates, after all, was a firm believer in reincarnation.

"I have a photo from *China 9* on my wall," Monte Hellman said. "My mother had just died; she died after Warren did, and I went back to Palm Springs for the service. The rabbi didn't show, and of course a month before, I'd been in the same situation. So I decided to hold my own service, and I mentioned Warren. When I came home, I saw that the photo of him had fallen off the wall."

There are ghosts at Chico Hot Springs, ghosts in the Palace Theater in Greenville who turn the lights off and on. There are ghosts everywhere. "Even Larry Girdler, who's at the ranch, says sometimes he knows somebody's watching him," Teddy said. "He'd just whirl around and go, 'Ah, it's probably just Warren.'"

"People who stay here are convinced they've seen Warren's ghost around here," Dennis Quaid said. "I've never seen him, but there's some strange things that happen. Somebody took a photo of us in the front yard, and somebody else with a different camera took another picture. We got the photo back and there's this crystal ball hovering, it's huge, in the foreground. We couldn't figure it out. Then our friend called. They had the same ball, only in blue."

In July, Sam Peckinpah wrote a letter to Judy from Livingston. "Watched the July 4th Parade with Timothy and Jennifer, which was a bright moment. I watched Ol' Joe [Swindlehurst] catch a trout out of high water and we were talking about you and Warren, your kids and the trout just jumped out."

When it came time to move Oates's ashes, Timothy called a couple of friends. "So now me and my buddies are all around this campfire looking for bone fragments of my dad, and it was like, 'Hey man, I got a big one!' and we're putting it in this jar. We filled it up with what we could and put some dirt from the area in there and we had a jar of Dad. We had that hanging around the house for a while." They eventually had a rescattering ceremony.

"Warren's bones are up on the knob," said Quaid. "His bones were scattered on the hill by the fire pit, but we moved them 'cause they were kind of getting trampled on. It's a good hike up there; you can see the whole valley. Warren's bones are there under a tree." The ashes are now mixed with those of J.D., who died shortly after Warren did.

A forest fire would imperil the acreage that surrounds what Quaid has named Warren Oates Camp, with its logo of crescent moon, mountain, and rising sun. Quaid said,

> The flames were headed, wind-blown, right here toward the house. We had three hundred firefighters, helicopter-landing pads. . . . Three days later, when they let us back up here, I go to the back of the property at Warren's, and the fire had stopped right at the property line. I thought Sam's had definitely got to be burned away. We drove back there, it's really heavily forested, and right there at the entrance to Sam's place, the fire had stopped. The firefighters had done nothing to do that. It's like Warren and Sam had both come at either end and stopped it.

"I have a picture of Sam and Warren together," said Joe Swindlehurst. "I always liked the picture because it captured the cynical questioning of Sam Peckinpah and the blathering of Warren. Warren's over here blathering and Sam's over here thinking,

'You're full of shit, Warren.' They're both of course at the bar; they're both smoking. The two buddies."

"A eulogy for Warren Oates is Warren Oates," Peckinpah wrote in *Rolling Stone*. "Anybody who knew him is richer for the experience. He was a superb actor who left us with a lot of values that none of us will ever forget. He saved my life both figuratively and literally and I regret that I wasn't in the position to return the favor."

Acknowledgments

At one point during the writing of this book, my friend Barney Hoskyns introduced me as someone doing "the coolest thing in the world." I did not have to think about it for very long: writing a book about Warren Oates *was* the coolest thing. What began as a suggestion (thank you, Chris Bohn aka Biba Kopf) to an expat writer beneath gray skies at the covered Spitalfields Market, London E1, eventually took me on the scenic route through Kentucky, Montana, North Carolina, Taos, and Los Angeles: Venice Beach, a couple of Starbucks, the topmost peaks of the Hollywood Hills, the "trafficated" lulls in the San Fernando Valley, and a whole expanse of seafoam green folding chairs at Farmers Market at Third and Fairfax.

I received early encouragement from Steve Connell, Nigel Matheson, Harry Northup, Aram Saroyan, and Jake Lingwood. Wide-open generosity from Peckinpah Dog Brothers Nick Redman, David Weddle (whose *If They Move . . . Kill 'em! The Life and Times of Sam Peckinpah* was my bible), and Garner Simmons still astounds me.

I worked with the most threadbare of shoestring budgets—a G-string one could have been better, but despite the efforts of my fantastic yoga instructor Diane Smith, it is a little late for that. Instead I relied on friends and family, taking sustenance and love from stepparents par excellence Helen and Gordon Anderson and my sister Mary Cabral, with whom I shared a night beneath pear-cut stars in Pioneertown as our glasses of red wine quickly froze on the sloping hood of the Prius. We did not notice, as Holly in *Badlands* might have said.

"I'm forty-three. . . . No, wait, I'm seventy-four," is perhaps my favorite quote from any interviewee; it is from Ted Markland, who sums up the agelessness of every single one. I thank them all—they dropped everything for the love of Warren. I am especially grateful to Gordon Oates (and the incomparable Lucille Barnett), Howie Dayton, Bob Watkins, Warren Miller, Armand and Betty Alzamora, Judy Oates, Nick Georgiade, and Bertie Rutter.

I wrote the book in the unsociable hours between four o'clock in the morning and noon, which meant I often started around the time Warren Oates might have been thinking about calling it a night. Staying up to attend Harry Dean Stanton's eightieth birthday party, which kicked off at midnight, would not have been possible without Peter Wilson, who also helped immeasurably with photos and the cover's concept.

On the late, lamented bluegrass and country music show *Wildwood Flower*, host Ben Elder always seemed to know when to play "Paradise" by John Prine. Donna Sugimoto and Phyllis Robichaud gave rides to an Angeleno who hates to drive. Chris Wallace, Scott Portnoy (whose "sad sack" adjective for Bennie in *Alfredo Garcia* I lifted), Toni Plummer, and Zach Locklin taught me more than I ever did them. Bliss plus Joe and Juliette Sehee were ready with phone numbers, scanning prowess, and downright good vibes. Susan Kallenbach was a great neighbor (and good friend).

Pretty much every biographer worth his or her salt thanks Ned Comstock at the University of Southern California's Cinematic Arts Library, and he is definitely worth his, as are librarians far and wide, including Libby Wirten and Jenny Romero at the Margaret Herrick Library; Martin Gostanian at the Paley Center for Media; Caroline Sisneros at the American Film Institute; Janis C. Test in Abilene, Texas; Danny Gonzalez at El Paso Public Library; and Coni Theios Wallace at Muhlenberg County Public Library in Greenville, Kentucky. Thanks also to the librarian at Edwards Air Force Base, who bent the rules a little bit in loaning me *Tough Enough*. California State University at San Bernardino's library had the prescience to give a home to *Cockfighter Journal* in its special collections and the good grace to allow me access. Information Services at the British Film Institute saved the day, as did Manola Madrid at the Autry National Center of the American West. Susan Andres was there at the eleventh hour.

Eddi Fiegel provided friendship, French translation, and standards to live up to. Jon Krampner offered mentorship even after his face drained of color when I told him I was working without an outline. Dudley Saunders gave a great walking tour of Louisville—and then I left him at the Magic Corner in the threatening rain.

Kathryn Jones, Ben Johnson's biographer, spurred me on. Oates's on-screen brother and real-life ideal got, in Jones, a writer who was witty, pretty, chic, Texan, and just the right amount of scholarly. Oates, on the other hand, got stuck with me, a model subdivision tumbleweed.

There were moments when the work lapsed into the uncharted, as when I made a *Wild Bunch* tableau using an array of Guatemalan trouble dolls. Then it spiraled into a kind of method biography as I found myself in a seedy pool hall, drinking and smoking (I have never smoked) at nine o'clock in the morning. The surroundings might have been spartan even for Oates, but the simpatico was there.

I received one marriage proposal (albeit couched) and a couple of lasting accolades: an actor hoped I would not be offended when he told me I reminded him of Bette Davis, and another person suggested I might be an "honorary Peckinpah."

Thanks to an eclectic grab bag of people including Dan Herron, Steven Farber, Mike Art, Logan Sparks, Tom Thurman, Brian Meacham (at the Academy of Motion Picture Arts and Sciences' Pickford Center), Sharon Nardin, Katie Lanegran, and Michael Aushenker, whose description of *Alfredo Garcia* as "a brutal, dark odyssey equal parts road movie, thriller, and black comedy" opened eyes momentarily glued shut by shoveled sand.

When Oates's younger son, Cody, said I would know him by the western shirt and sunglasses he would be wearing, I told him to stop right there. If I could not recognize Warren Oates's son in aviator shades, I did not deserve to write this book. Timothy, Jennifer, and Torrey—wonderful Torrey—Oates were equally identifiable.

The enduring memory of my father, Leroy Gordon Compo, a young marine who shared a drink or two with a hopeful actor from Kentucky checking coats in the 21 Club in 1955, is all around me. That marine's baby, landlocked in a crib in Bay Ridge, grew up to take one look at the actor on the drive-in screen who was seated in a gridlocked parked car in *Two-Lane Blacktop*. When he stared into the rearview mirror and asked his straggly-haired passenger, "Where to?" I thank the heavens and the open roads I answered.

Credits and Broadcast Appearances

Nonprofessional Stage

(All performances at the Playhouse, University of Louisville, Louisville, Kentucky, unless otherwise noted.)

Book Collecting. Student union building, Mar. 1949 (Snippling, a hillbilly).

The King's Bedchamber. Student union building, Mar. 1949 (sentry).

Fine Pretty Things. May 1949 (Guy Hill, a hillbilly).

The Boar. Nov. 1949 (character unknown).

Bury the Dead. Nov. 1949 (Private Dean, a soldier).

Nightmare. Fall 1949 (a horse).

Village Green. May 1950 (Walter Godkin).

Golden Boy. Mar. 1952 (Tokio).

Affairs of State. Mar. 1953 (Lawrence, an older man).

Remains to Be Seen. May 1953 (Waldo Walton, an aspiring musician).

Dark of the Moon. Director: Lamar Crask; written by Howard Richardson, William Berney. Brown-Forman Distillery, Louisville, Kentucky, spring 1953 (Conjur Man and Marvin Hudgens, a bully).

Macbeth. Director: Douglas Ramey. Central Park, Louisville, Kentucky, summer 1953 (character unknown).

Dark of the Moon. Director: Douglas Ramey. Church of the Advent, Louisville, Kentucky, Feb. 1954 (Conjur Man and Marvin Hudgens).

Professional Stage

The Tall Kentuckian. Director: Douglas Ramey; written by Barbara Tunnell Anderson. Louisville Amphitheater, Louisville, Kentucky, June 18, 1953 (character unknown).

The Wisteria Trees. Director: Joshua Logan; from *The Cherry Orchard* by Anton Chekhov. City Center Theater, New York, Feb. 2, 1955. Cast: Helen Hayes, Walter Matthau, Warren Oates (guest at party).

One Flew over the Cuckoo's Nest. Director: John Erman; written by Dale Wasserman, from the book by Ken Kesey. Players' Ring Gallery, Los Angeles, Jan. 12, 1965. Cast: Warren Oates (Randle P. McMurphy), Priscilla Morrill, Robert Doyle.

Who's Happy Now? Director: Gordon Davidson; written by Oliver Hailey. Center Theatre Group, Mark Taper Forum, Los Angeles, Oct. 13, 1967. Cast: Warren Oates (Horse), Betty Garrett, Peggy Pope, Warren Berlinger.

Film

Warren Oates worked on *Shenandoah* (1965) and *Chubasco* (1971) but does not appear in the films.

Up Periscope (Warner Brothers, 1959). Director: Gordon Douglas; producers: Aubrey Schenck, Howard Koch, Edwin F. Zabel; screenplay: Richard Landau; cinematography: Carl Guthrie. Cast: James Garner, Edmond O'Brien, Andra Martin, Warren Oates (uncredited, Seaman Kovacs).

Yellowstone Kelly (Warner Brothers, 1959). Director: Gordon Douglas; screenplay: Burt Kennedy; cinematography: Carl Guthrie. Cast: Clint Walker, Edward Byrnes, John Russell, Claude Akins, Warren Oates (Corporal).

Private Property (Citation, 1960). Director: Leslie Stevens; producer: Stanley Colbert; screenplay: Leslie Stevens; cinematography: Ted McCord. Cast: Corey Allen, Kate Manx, Warren Oates (Boots).

The Rise and Fall of Legs Diamond (Warner Brothers, 1960). Director: Budd Boetticher; producer: Milton Sperling; screenplay: Joseph Landon; cinematography: Lucien Ballard. Cast: Ray Danton, Karen Steele, Dyan Cannon, Warren Oates (Eddie Diamond).

Hero's Island (United Artists, 1962). Director, producer, and screenplay: Leslie Stevens; cinematography: Ted McCord. Cast: James Mason, Kate Manx, Neville Brand, Rip Torn, Warren Oates (Wayte Giddens).

Ride the High Country (MGM, 1962). Director: Sam Peckinpah; producer: Richard E. Lyons; screenplay: N. B. Stone Jr.; cinematography: Lucien Ballard. Cast: Randolph Scott, Joel McCrea, Mariette Hartley, Ron Starr, R. G. Armstrong, James Drury, Warren Oates (Henry Hammond).

Mail Order Bride (MGM, 1964). Director: Burt Kennedy; producer: Richard E. Lyons; screenplay: Burt Kennedy, from a story by Van Cort; cinematography: Paul C. Vogel. Cast: Buddy Ebsen, Keir Dullea, Lois Nettleton, Warren Oates (Jace).

The Rounders (MGM, 1965). Director: Burt Kennedy; producer: Richard E. Lyons; screenplay: Max Evans; cinematography: Paul Vogel. Cast: Henry Fonda, Glenn Ford, Chill Wills, Warren Oates (uncredited, Harley Williams).

Major Dundee (Columbia, 1965). Director: Sam Peckinpah; producer: Jerry Bresler, screenplay: Harry Julian Fink, Oscar Saul, Sam Peckinpah; cinematography: Sam Leavitt. Cast: Charlton Heston, Richard Harris, James Coburn, Michael Anderson Jr., Warren Oates (O. W. Hadley).

The Shooting (Proteus, 1967). Director: Monte Hellman; producer: Roger Corman; screenplay: Carole Eastman; cinematography: Greg Sandor. Cast: Warren Oates (Willet Gashade), Jack Nicholson, Millie Perkins, Will Hutchins.

Return of the Seven (United Artists, 1966). Director: Burt Kennedy; producer: Ted Richmond; screenplay: Larry Cohen; cinematography: Paul C. Vogel. Cast: Yul Brynner, Robert Fuller, Julian Mateos, Warren Oates (Colbee).

Welcome to Hard Times (MGM, 1967). Director: Burt Kennedy; producer: Max E. Youngstein; screenplay by Burt Kennedy, from the novel by E. L. Doctorow; cinematography: Harry Stradling Jr. Cast: Henry Fonda, Janice Rule, Keenan Wynn, Warren Oates (Leo Jenks).

In the Heat of the Night (United Artists, 1967). Director: Norman Jewison; producer: Walter Mirisch; screenplay: Stirling Silliphant; cinematography: Haskell Wexler. Cast: Sidney Poitier, Rod Steiger, Lee Grant, Warren Oates (Sam Wood).

The Split (MGM, 1968). Director: Gordon Flemyng; producers: Irwin Winkler, Robert Chartoff; screenplay: Robert Sabaroff; cinematography: Burnett Guffey. Cast: Jim Brown, Diahann Carroll, Ernest Borgnine, Julie Harris, Warren Oates (Marty Gough).

The Wild Bunch (Warner Brothers/Seven Arts, 1969). Director: Sam Peckinpah; producers: Phil Feldman, Roy N. Sickner; screenplay: Walon Green, Sam Peckinpah; cinematography: Lucien Ballard. Cast: William Holden, Ernest Borgnine, Robert Ryan, Edmond O'Brien, Jaime Sanchez, Ben Johnson, Warren Oates (Lyle Gorch).

Smith! (Buena Vista, 1969). Director: Michael O'Herlihy; director, Indian Actors Workshop of Hollywood: Jay Silverheels; producer: Bill Anderson; screenplay: Louis Pelletier, from the book by Paul St. Pierre; cinematography: Robert Moreno. Cast: Glenn Ford, Nancy Olson, Chief Dan George, Warren Oates (Walter Charlie).

Crooks and Coronets (Warner Brothers/Seven Arts, 1970). Director: Jim O'Connolly; producer: Herman Cohen; screenplay: Jim O'Connolly; cinematography: Desmond Dickinson. Cast: Telly Savalas, Edith Evans, Warren Oates (Marty Miller).

There Was a Crooked Man (Warner Brothers, 1970). Director, producer: Joseph L. Mankiewicz; executive producer: C. O. Erickson; screenplay: David Newman, Robert Benton; cinematography: Harry Stradling Jr. Cast: Kirk Douglas, Henry Fonda, Hume Cronyn, Burgess Meredith, Warren Oates (Floyd Moon).

Barquero (United Artists, 1970). Director: Gordon Douglas; producer: Aubrey Schenck; screenplay: George Schenck, William Marks; cinematography: Gerald Finnerman. Cast: Lee Van Cleef, Forrest Tucker, Kerwin Mathews, Warren Oates (Remy).

The Hired Hand (Universal, 1971). Director: Peter Fonda; producer: William Hayward; executive producer: Stanley A. Weiss; screenplay: Alan Sharp; cinematography: Vilmos Zsigmond. Cast: Peter Fonda, Warren Oates (Arch Harris), Verna Bloom, Robert Pratt.

Two-Lane Blacktop (Universal, 1971). Director: Monte Hellman; producer: Michael S. Laughlin; screenplay: Rudolph Wurlitzer, Will Corry; cinematography: Jack Deerson, Gregory Sandor (uncredited). Cast: James Taylor, Dennis Wilson, Laurie Bird, Warren Oates (GTO).

Chandler (MGM, 1971). Director: Paul Magwood; producer: Michael S. Laughlin; screenplay: John Sacret Young; cinematography: Alan Stensvold. Cast: Warren Oates (Chandler), Leslie Caron, Alex Dreier, Mitch Ryan.

Kid Blue (Twentieth Century–Fox, 1973). Director: James Frawley; producer: Marvin Schwartz; screenplay: Bud Shrake; cinematography: Billy Williams. Cast: Dennis Hopper, Ben Johnson, Warren Oates (Reese Ford), Peter Boyle, Lee Purcell.

Tom Sawyer (United Artists, 1973). Director: Don Taylor; executive producer: Walter Bien; producer: Arthur P. Jacobs; associate producer: Frank Capra Jr.; screenplay: Richard M. Sherman, Robert B. Sherman, from the book by Mark Twain; cinematography: Frank Stanley. Cast: Johnny Whitaker, Celeste Holm, Warren Oates (Muff Potter), Jeff East, Jodie Foster.

The Thief Who Came to Dinner (Warner Brothers, 1973). Director: Bud Yorkin; producers: Bud Yorkin, Norman Lear; screenplay: Terrence Lore Smith, Walter Hill; cinematography: Philip Lathrop. Cast: Ryan O'Neal, Jacqueline Bisset, Warren Oates (Dave), Ned Beatty.

Dillinger (American International, 1973). Director: John Milius; executive producers: Samuel Z. Arkoff, Lawrence Gordon; producer: Buzz Feitshans; screenplay: John Milius; cinematography: Jules Brenner. Cast: Warren Oates (John Dillinger), Michelle Phillips, Ben Johnson, Cloris Leachman.

Badlands (Warner Brothers, 1973). Director, producer: Terrence Malick; executive producer: Edward R. Pressman; screenplay: Terrence Malick; cinematography: Tak Fujimoto, Steven Larner, Brian Probyn. Cast: Martin Sheen, Sissy Spacek, Warren Oates (Sargis).

The White Dawn (Paramount, 1974). Director: Philip Kaufman; producer: Martin Ransohoff; screenplay: Thomas Rickman, James Houston, from the book by James Houston; cinematography: Michael Chapman. Cast: Warren Oates (Billy), Timothy Bottoms, Lou Gossett.

Bring Me the Head of Alfredo Garcia (United Artists, 1974). Director: Sam Peckinpah; producer: Martin Baum; screenplay: Frank Kowalski, Sam Peckinpah, Gordon Dawson; cinematography: Alex Phillips Jr. Cast: Warren Oates (Bennie), Isela Vega, Helmut Dantine, Gig Young.

Cockfighter (New World, 1974). Director: Monte Hellman; producer: Roger Corman; screenplay: Charles Willeford, from his book; cinematography: Nestor Almendros. Cast: Warren Oates (Frank Mansfield), Richard B. Shull, Harry Dean Stanton, Ed Begley Jr.

Rancho Deluxe (United Artists, 1975). Director: Frank Perry; producer: Elliott Kastner; screenplay: Tom McGuane; cinematography: William A. Fraker. Cast: Jeff Bridges, Sam Waterston, Elizabeth Ashley, Warren Oates (uncredited harmonica player).

Race with the Devil (Twentieth Century–Fox, 1975). Director: Jack Starrett; producers: Wes Bishop, Paul Maslansky; screenplay: Wes Bishop, Lee Frost; cinematography: Robert C. Jessup. Cast: Peter Fonda, Warren Oates (Frank Stewart), Loretta Swit, Lara Parker.

92 in the Shade (United Artists, 1975). Director: Tom McGuane; producer: George Pappas; screenplay: Tom McGuane; cinematography: Michael C. Butler. Cast: Peter Fonda, Warren Oates (Nichol Dance), Margot Kidder, Harry Dean Stanton.

Drum (United Artists, 1976). Director: Steve Carver; producers: Dino de Laurentiis, Ralph B. Serpe; screenplay: Norman Wexler, from the book by Kyle Onstott; cinematography: Lucien Ballard. Cast: Warren Oates (Hammond Maxwell), Isela Vega, Ken Norton, Pam Grier.

Dixie Dynamite (Dimension, 1976). Director: Lee Frost; producer: Wes Bishop; screenplay: Wes Bishop, Lee Frost; cinematography: Lee Frost. Cast: Warren Oates (Mack), Christopher George, Jane Anne Johnstone, Kathy McHaley.

Sleeping Dogs (Satori, 1977 [U.S. release 1982]). Director, producer: Roger Donaldson; screenplay: Ian Mune, Arthur Baysting, from the book by Christian Stead; cinematography: Michael Seresin. Cast: Sam Neill, Nevan Rowe, Warren Oates (Colonel Willoughby), Ian Mune.

Prime Time (Danton, 1978). Director: Bradley Swirnoff; executive producer: Robin French; screenplay: John Baskin, Stephen Feinberg; cinematography: Matthew Leonetti. Cast: Mel Carter, Joanna Cassidy, Warren Oates (celebrity sportsperson), Harry Shearer.

China 9, Liberty 37 (Allied Artists, 1978). Directors: Monte Hellman, Tony Brandt; producers: Monte Hellman, Gianni Bozzachi, Valerio De Paolis; screenplay: Ennio De Concini; cinematography: Giuseppe Rotunno. Cast: Warren Oates (Matthew Sebanek), Fabio Testi, Jenny Agutter, Sam Peckinpah.

The Brink's Job (Universal, 1978). Director: William Friedkin; producers: Dino de Laurentiis, Ralph B. Serpe; screenplay: Walon Green, from the book by Noel Behn; cinematography: Norman Leigh. Cast: Peter Falk, Peter Boyle, Warren Oates (Specs O'Keefe), Paul Sorvino.

1941 (Universal, 1979). Director: Steven Spielberg; producer: Buzz Feitshans; screenplay: Robert Zemeckis, Bob Gale, John Milius; cinematography: William A. Fraker. Cast: Dan Aykroyd, John Belushi, Warren Oates (Colonel Maddox), Ned Beatty.

Stripes (Columbia, 1981). Director: Ivan Reitman; producer: Dan Goldberg; screenplay: Len Blum, Daniel Goldberg; cinematography: Bill Butler. Cast: Bill Murray, Harold Ramis, Warren Oates (Sergeant Hulka), P. J. Soles.

The Border (Universal, 1982). Director: Tony Richardson; producer: Edgar Bronfman Jr.; screenplay: David Freeman, Walon Green, Deric Washburn; cinematography: Ric Waite. Cast: Jack Nicholson, Harvey Keitel, Warren Oates (Red), Valerie Perrine.

Blue Thunder (Columbia, 1983). Director: John Badham; producer: Gordon Carroll; screenplay: Dan O'Bannon, Dan Jakoby; cinematography: John A. Alonzo. Cast: Roy Scheider, Warren Oates (Captain Braddock), Candy Clark.

Tough Enough (Twentieth Century–Fox, 1983). Director: Richard Fleischer; executive producers: Michael Leone, Andrew Pfeffer; producer: William Gilmore; screenplay: John Leone; cinematography: James A. Contner. Cast: Dennis Quaid, Warren Oates (James Neese), Stan Shaw, Carlene Watkins.

Television Movies and Miniseries

Something for a Lonely Man (NBC, Nov. 26, 1968, 120 min.). Cast: Dan Blocker, Susan Clark, Warren Oates (Angus Duren).

The Movie Murderer (NBC, Feb. 2, 1970, 120 min.). Cast: Arthur Kennedy, Tom Selleck, Warren Oates (Alfred Fisher).

The Reluctant Heroes (ABC, Nov. 23, 1971, 120 min.). Cast: Ken Berry, Jim Hutton, Warren Oates (Corporal Leroy Sprague).

The African Queen (CBS, Mar. 18, 1977, 50 min.). Cast: Mariette Hartley, John Sekka, Warren Oates (Captain Charlie Allnut).

Black Beauty (NBC, Jan. 31, 1978, 300 min.). Cast: Edward Albert, Peter Breck, Warren Oates (Jerry Barker).

True Grit (ABC, May 19, 1978, 100 min.). Cast: Warren Oates (Rooster Cogburn), Lisa Pelikian, Lee Meriwether.

And Baby Makes Six (CBS, Oct. 29, 1979, 120 min.). Cast: Timothy Hutton, Colleen Dewhurst, Warren Oates (Michael Cramer).

My Old Man (ABC, Dec. 7, 1979, 120 min.). Cast: Warren Oates (Frank Butler), Eileen Brennan, Kristy McNichol.

Baby Comes Home (CBS, Oct. 16, 1980, 120 min.). Cast: Colleen Dewhurst, Warren Oates (Michael Cramer).

East of Eden (ABC, Feb. 19, 1981, 480 min.). Cast: Jane Seymour, Timothy Bottoms, Warren Oates (Cyrus Trask).

The Blue and the Gray (CBS, Nov. 14, 1982, 381 min.). Cast: John Hammond, Stacy Keach, Colleen Dewhurst, Warren Oates (Preacher/Major Welles).

Television Appearances

Warren Oates made several uncredited appearances on episodes of *Studio One* (CBS) and *Lamp unto My Feet* (CBS) in 1955–1956.

The Jackie Gleason Show (CBS, Mar. 6, 1954). Guest host: Art Carney. Cast: Warren Oates (uncredited juvenile delinquent in skit).

The Philco Television Playhouse (NBC, 1956, 60 min.). Cast: Warren Oates (character unknown).

The United States Steel Hour, "Operation Three Rs" (CBS, July 4, 1956, 60 min.). Cast: Robert Culp, Paul Mazursky, Warren Oates (Private Lear).

Studio One, "A Day before Battle" (CBS, Sept. 3, 1956, 60 min.). Cast: Jack Lord, Susan Oliver, Warren Oates (the prisoner).

Kraft Television Theatre, *Murder of a Sand Flea* (NBC, Oct. 10, 1956, 60 min.). Cast: Rip Torn, Warren Oates (marine).

Studio One, "The Night America Trembled" (CBS, Sept. 9, 1957, 60 min.). Cast: Edward Asner, Warren Beatty, Warren Oates (card player).

Have Gun—Will Travel, "Three Sons" (CBS, May 10, 1958, 30 min.). Cast: Richard Boone, Warren Oates (John Bosworth).

Rescue 8, "Subterranean City" (syndicated, Oct. 14, 1958, 30 min.). Cast: Jim Davis, Lang Jeffries, Warren Oates (Pete).

The Rifleman, "The Marshal" (ABC, Oct. 21, 1958, 30 min.). Cast: Chuck Connors, Johnny Crawford, Warren Oates (Andrew Sheltin).

The Adventures of Rin Tin Tin (ABC, Nov. 21, 1958, 30 min.). Cast: Lee Aaker, James Brown, Warren Oates (Deke).

Wanted: Dead or Alive, "Die by the Gun" (CBS, Dec. 6, 1958, 30 min.). Cast: Steve McQueen, John Larch, Warren Oates (Jesse Cox).

Playhouse 90, "Seven against the Wall" (CBS, Dec. 11, 1958, 90 min.). Cast: Tige Andrews, Walter Barnes, Warren Oates (Ted Ryan).

Gunsmoke, "Snakebite" (CBS, Dec. 20, 1958, 30 min.). Cast: James Arness, Andy Clyde, Warren Oates (Jed Hakes).

Trackdown, "Bad Judgment" (CBS, Jan. 28, 1959, 60 min.). Cast: Robert Culp, Lee Farr, Warren Oates (Lute Borden).

Wanted: Dead or Alive, "The Legend" (CBS, Mar. 7, 1959, 30 min.). Cast: Steve McQueen, Warren Oates (Billy Clegg).

Tombstone Territory, "Whipsaw" (ABC, Mar. 13, 1959, 30 min.). Cast: Pat Conway, Warren Oates (Bob Pickett).

Trackdown, "Fear" (CBS, Mar. 18, 1959, 30 min.). Cast: Robert Culp, Warren Oates (Kelly).

Black Saddle, "Client: Steele" (NBC, Mar. 21, 1959, 30 min.). Cast: Peter Breck, Warren Oates (Deputy Simms).

Buckskin, "Charlie, My Boy" (NBC, Apr. 6, 1959, 30 min.). Cast: Freeman Lusk, Edgar Stehli, Tom Nolan, Warren Oates (Charlie).

The Rough Riders, "The Rifle" (ABC, May 7, 1959, 30 min.). Cast: Kent Taylor, Warren Oates (Frank Day).

Wanted: Dead or Alive, "Amos Carter" (CBS, May 9, 1959, 30 min.). Cast: Steve McQueen, Warren Oates (Seth Blake).

Bat Masterson, "Lottery of Death" (NBC, May 13, 1959, 30 min.). Cast: Gene Barry, Warren Oates (Sonny Parsons).

Trackdown, "Back to Crawford" (CBS, Sept. 9, 1959, 30 min.). Cast: Robert Culp, Nancy Asch, King Calder, Warren Oates (Norvil).

The Rifleman, "Bloodlines" (ABC, Oct. 6, 1959, 30 min.). Cast: Chuck Connors, Paul Fix, Warren Oates (Jud Malackie).

Wagon Train, "The Martha Barham Story" (NBC, Nov. 4, 1959, 60 min.). Cast: Larry J. Blake, Ann Blyth, Warren Oates (Silas Carpenter).

The Rebel, "School Days" (ABC, Nov. 15, 1959, 30 min.). Cast: Nick Adams,

Gabe Dellitri, Warren Oates (Troy Armbruster).

Wanted: Dead or Alive, "Angela" (CBS, Jan. 9, 1960, 30 min.). Cast: Steve McQueen, Warren Oates (George Aswell).

Tombstone Territory, "The Target" (ABC, Jan. 29, 1960, 30 min.). Cast: Pat Conway, Warren Oates (Vic Reel).

The Twilight Zone, "The Purple Testament" (CBS, Feb. 12, 1960, 30 min.). Cast: Dick York, William Reynolds, Warren Oates (driver).

Hotel de Paree, "Hard Luck for Sundance" (CBS, Feb. 19, 1960, 30 min.). Cast: Earl Holliman, Jeanette Nolan, Warren Oates (Charlie Aiken).

Bronco, "Every Man a Hero" (ABC, Feb. 23, 1960, 30 min.). Cast: Ty Hardin, Patricia Berry, Warren Oates (Private Hurd Maple).

77 Sunset Strip, "Blackout" (ABC, Mar. 11, 1960, 60 min.). Cast: Efrem Zimbalist Jr., Roger Smith, Warren Oates (Dink Strahman).

Rawhide, "Incident of the Dancing Death" (CBS, Apr. 8, 1960, 60 min.). Cast: Eric Fleming, Clint Eastwood, Warren Oates (Marco).

The Rifleman, "The Prodigal" (ABC, Apr. 26, 1960, 30 min.). Cast: Chuck Connors, Rhys Williams, Warren Oates (Santos).

Johnny Ringo, "Single Debt" (CBS, May 12, 1960, 30 min.). Cast: Don Durant, Mark Goddard, Warren Oates (Burt Scanlon).

Tate, "Before Sunup" (NBC, Aug. 17, 1960, 30 min.). Cast: David McLean, Richard Whorf, Warren Oates (Cowpoke).

Wrangler, "Affair at the Trading Post" (NBC, Aug. 18, 1960, 30 min.). Cast: Jason Evers, Eli Boraks, Warren Oates (Shep Martin).

Gunsmoke, "Small Water" (CBS, Sept. 24, 1960, 60 min.). Cast: Trevor Bardette, Rex Holman, Warren Oates (Seth Pickett).

Outlaws, "Thirty a Month" (NBC, Sept. 29, 1960, 60 min.). Cast: Robert Culp, Steve Forrest, Warren Oates (Billy Hooten).

The Westerner, "Jeff" (NBC, Sept. 30, 1960, 30 min.). Cast: Brian Keith, Warren Oates (uncredited drunk).

Have Gun—Will Travel, "The Poker Fiend" (CBS, Nov. 12, 1960, 30 min.). Cast: Richard Boone, Eric Alden, Warren Oates (Harrison).

The Rifleman, "Miss Millie" (ABC, Nov. 15, 1960, 30 min.). Cast: Chuck Connors, Joan Taylor, Warren Oates (Marty Ryan).

Lawman, "The Second Son" (ABC, Nov. 27, 1960, 30 min.). Cast: John Russell, Kim Charney, Warren Oates (unnamed character).

Hawaiian Eye, "The Contenders" (ABC, Nov. 30, 1960, 60 min.). Cast: Robert Conrad, Anthony Eisley, Warren Oates (Al).

Thriller, "Knock Three-One-Two" (NBC, Dec. 13, 1960, 60 min.). Cast: Boris Karloff, Charles Aidman, Warren Oates (Benny).

Stagecoach West, "Object: Patrimony" (ABC, Jan. 3, 1961, 60 min.). Cast: Tim McBride, George N. Neise, Warren Oates (Billy Goe).

Wanted: Dead or Alive, "The Last Retreat" (CBS, Jan. 11, 1961, 30 min.). Cast: Steve McQueen, John Cliff, Warren Oates (Clem Robinson).

Gunsmoke, "Love Thy Neighbor" (CBS, Jan. 28, 1961, 30 min.). Cast: Jeanette Nolan, [Harry] Dean Stanton, Warren Oates (Jep Scooper).

The Case of the Dangerous Robin, "Baubles and Bullets" (syndicated, Feb. 20, 1961, 30 min.). Cast: Rick Jason, Dean Blake, Warren Oates (unnamed character).

Laramie, "Two for the Gallows" (NBC, Apr. 11, 1961, 60 min.). Cast: John Smith, Robert Fuller, Warren Oates (Pete).

Bat Masterson, "Meeting at Mimbers" (NBC, Apr. 13, 1961, 30 min.). Cast: Gene Barry, Warren Oates (Cat Crail).

Stagecoach West, "The Renegades" (ABC, June 20, 1961, 60 min.). Cast: Richard Devon, Ed Kemmer, Warren Oates (Tom Lochlin).

The Lawless Years, "Artie Moon" (NBC, Aug. 25, 1961, 30 min.). Cast: George Bremlin, Warren Oates (Brown).

The Dick Powell Show, "Somebody's Waiting" (NBC, Nov. 7, 1961, 60 min.). Cast: Tige Andrews, Mickey Rooney, Paul Mazursky, Warren Oates (Bruno).

Gunsmoke, "Marry Me" (CBS, Dec. 23, 1961, 60 min.). Cast: Amanda Blake, Don Dubbins, Warren Oates (Sweet Billy Cathcart).

Gunsmoke, "The Do-Badder" (CBS, Jan. 6, 1962, 60 min.). Cast: Abraham Sofaer, Strother Martin, Warren Oates (Chris Kelly).

Thriller, "The Hollow Watcher" (NBC, Feb. 12, 1962, 60 min.). Cast: Boris Karloff, Lane Bradford, Warren Oates (Hugo Wheeler).

The Rifleman, "Day of Reckoning" (ABC, Apr. 9, 1962, 30 min.). Cast: Chuck Connors, L. Q. Jones, Warren Oates (Willie).

Target: The Corrupters, "Journey into Mourning" (ABC, Apr. 13, 1962, 60 min.). Cast: Parley Baer, Royal Dano, Warren Oates (Billy Joe).

Bonanza, "The Mountain Girl" (NBC, May 13, 1962, 60 min.). Cast: Lorne Greene, Pernell Roberts, Warren Oates (Paul Magruder).

The Untouchables, "Pressure" (ABC, June 14, 1962, 60 min.). Cast: Robert Stack, Nick Georgiade, Warren Oates (Artie "the Firecracker" Krebs).

Stoney Burke (ABC, Oct. 1962–Sept. 1963). Regular cast: Jack Lord, Bruce Dern, Warren Oates (Ves Painter), Robert Dowdell.

77 Sunset Strip, "Terror in a Small Town" (ABC, Oct. 26, 1962, 60 min.). Cast: Kathy Bennett, Warren Oates (Orville).

The Travels of Jamie McPheeters, "The Day of the First Suitor" (ABC, Sept. 29, 1963, 60 min.). Cast: Dan O'Herlihy, Kurt Russell, Warren Oates (Eldon Bishop).

Rawhide, "Incident of the Prophecy" (CBS, Nov. 21, 1963, 60 min.). Cast: Clint Eastwood, Warren Oates (Rabbit Waters).

The Virginian, "Stopover in a Western Town" (NBC, Nov. 27, 1963, 90 min.). Cast: James Drury, Warren Oates (Corbie).

The Twilight Zone, "The 7th Is Made Up of Phantoms" (CBS, Dec. 6, 1963, 30 min.). Cast: Ron Foster, Randy Boone, Warren Oates (Corporal Richard Langsford).

Combat! "The Pillbox" (ABC, Jan. 7, 1964, 60 min.). Cast: Vic Morrow, Rick Jason, Warren Oates (Stark).

The Fugitive, "Rat in a Corner" (ABC, Feb. 18, 1964, 60 min.). Cast: David Janssen, Virginia Vincent, Warren Oates (Herbie).

Gunsmoke, "The Bassops" (CBS, Feb. 22, 1964, 60 min.). Cast: Robert Wilke, Warren Oates (Deke Bassop).

The Outer Limits, "The Mutant" (ABC, Mar. 16, 1964, 60 min.). Cast: Larry Pennell, Walter Burke, Warren Oates (Reese Fowler).

Rawhide, "The Race" (CBS, Sept. 25, 1964, 60 min.). Cast: Clint Eastwood, Eric Fleming, Warren Oates (Weed).

The Reporter, "No Comment" (CBS, Oct. 30, 1964, 60 min.). Cast: Harry Guardino, Garry Merrill, Warren Oates (Mickroe).

The Fugitive, "Devil's Carnival" (ABC, Dec. 22, 1964, 60 min.). Cast: David Janssen, Warren Oates (Hanes McClure).

Slattery's People, "Question: What's a Requiem for a Loser?" (CBS, Jan. 8, 1965, 60 min.). Cast: Richard Crenna, Barbara Feldon, Warren Oates (Eugene Henson).

Gunsmoke, "Circus Trick" (CBS, Feb. 6, 1965, 60 min.). Cast: Elizabeth Mac-Rae, Ken Scott, Warren Oates (Speeler).

The Virginian, "A Slight Case of Charity" (NBC, Feb. 10, 1965, 90 min.). Cast: James Drury, Doug McClure, Warren Oates (Roy Judd).

Bob Hope Presents the Chrysler Theatre, "The War and Eric Kurtz" (NBC, Mar. 5, 1965, 60 min.). Cast: Lloyd Bochner, David Carradine, Warren Oates (Joe Grover).

Branded, "Judge Not" (NBC, Sept. 12, 1965, 30 min.). Cast: Chuck Connors, Warren Oates (Perce/Frank Clampett).

A Man Called Shenandoah, "The Fort" (ABC, Sept. 27, 1965, 30 min.). Cast: Ed Binns, Warren Oates (Sergeant Ryder).

Gunsmoke, "Ten Little Indians" (CBS, Oct. 9, 1965, 60 min.). Cast: Nehemiah Persoff, Bruce Dern, Warren Oates (Al Tresh).

Slattery's People, "Rally round Your Own Flag, Mister" (CBS, Oct. 15, 1965, 60 min.). Cast: Lloyd Nolan, Warren Oates (Stu Burns).

Twelve O'clock High, "The Hot Shot" (ABC, Oct. 18, 1965, 60 min.). Cast: George Brenlin, Walter Brooke, Seymour Cassell, Warren Oates (Lieutenant Colonel Jerry Troper).

Rawhide, "Hostage for Hanging" (CBS, Oct. 19, 1965, 60 min.). Cast: Steve Raines, Warren Oates (Jesse Gufler).

Lost in Space, "Welcome Stranger" (CBS, Oct. 20, 1965, 30 min.). Cast: Guy Williams, June Lockhart, Warren Oates (Jimmy Hapgood).

The Big Valley, "The Murdered Party" (ABC, Nov. 17, 1965, 60 min.). Cast: Barbara Stanwyck, Lee Majors, Linda Evans, Warren Oates (Korbie Kyles).

The Virginian, "One Spring like Long Ago" (NBC, Mar. 2, 1966, 90 min.). Cast: Warren Oates (Bowers).

The Virginian, "Ride to Delphi" (NBC, Sept. 21, 1966, 90 min.). Cast: Randy Boone, Warren Oates (Buxton).

The Monroes, "The Forest Devil" (ABC, Sept. 28, 1966, 60 min.). Cast: Michael Anderson Jr., Barbara Hershey, Warren Oates (Buxton).

Shane, "An Echo of Anger" (ABC, Oct. 1, 1966, 60 min.). Cast: David Carradine, Jill Ireland, Warren Oates (Kemp Spicer).

Gunsmoke, "The Mission" (CBS, Oct. 8, 1966, 60 min.). Cast: Robert F. Simon, Bob Random, Warren Oates (Lafe).

The Big Valley, "The Great Safe Robbery" (ABC, Nov. 21, 1966, 60 min.). Cast: Barbara Stanwyck, Linda Evans, Peter Breck, Warren Oates (Duke).

Dundee and the Culhane, "The Turn the Other Cheek Brief" (CBS, Sept. 6, 1967, 60 min.). Cast: John Mills, John Drew Barrymore, Warren Oates (unnamed character).

Gunsmoke, "The Wreckers" (CBS, Sept. 11, 1967, 60 min.). Cast: Edmund Hashim, Warren Oates (Tate Crocker).

Cimarron Strip, "Battleground" (CBS, Sept. 28, 1967, 90 min.). Cast: Stuart Whitman, Telly Savalas, Warren Oates (Mobeetie).

The Iron Horse, "The Return of Hode Avery" (ABC, Nov. 4, 1967, 60 min.). Cast: Dale Robertson, Warren Oates (Hode Avery).

Cimarron Strip, "Nobody" (CBS, Dec. 7, 1967, 90 min.). Cast: Stuart Whitman, Warren Oates (Mobeetie).

Run for Your Life, "One Bad Turn" (NBC, Jan. 10, 1968, 60 min.). Cast: Ben Gazzara, Strother Martin, Warren Oates (Deputy Potter).

Walt Disney's Wonderful World of Color, "The Mystery of Edward Sims," parts 1 and 2 (NBC, Mar. 31, Apr. 7, 1968, 60 min. each). Cast: Roger Mobley, John McIntire, Warren Oates (John Blythe).

Lancer, "The Man without a Gun" (CBS, Mar. 25, 1969, 60 min.). Cast: Andrew Duggan, James Stacy, Warren Oates (Sheriff Val Crawford).

Lancer, "The Buscaderos" (CBS, Mar. 17, 1970, 60 min.). Cast: Warren Oates (Drago).

The FBI, "Turnabout" (ABC, Mar. 7, 1971, 60 min.). Cast: Efrem Zimbalist Jr., Warren Oates (Richie Billings).

The Name of the Game, "The Showdown" (NBC, Mar. 19, 1971, 60 min.). Cast: Anthony Franciosa, Warren Oates (Lew Weatherford/John).

The Virginia Graham Show (syndicated, Oct. 15, 1971, 60 min.). Host: Virginia Graham. Guests: Morey Amsterdam, Alisha Kashi, Warren Oates (himself).

Police Story, "Day of Terror, Night of Fear" (NBC, Mar. 4, 1978, 60 min.). Cast: Malcolm Atterbury, Tom Simcox, Warren Oates (Richey Neptune).

Insight, "The Man Who Mugged God" (syndicated, Apr. 21, 1979, 30 min.). Cast: Harold Gould, Warren Oates (unnamed character).

Tales of the Unexpected, "Nothin' Short of Highway Robbery" (ITV [UK], July 21, 1985, 60 min.). Cast: Bud Cort, Jennifer Adams, Warren Oates (Harry).

Notes

1. Population Boom

1 "I was due . . ." CBS Entertainment, *The Blue and the Gray* news release, November 2, 1982, television clipping files, Cinematic Arts Library, University of Southern California, Los Angeles

1 Major Jesse Oates's history from Otto Arthur Rothert, *The History of Muhlenberg County* (Louisville, KY: Morton, 1913), 91–92

2 Bayless E. Oates's history from W. L. Winebarger, "The James Wallace Oates Family" (unpublished manuscript, 1982), 6, private collection

3 "That's my favorite . . ." *Owensboro Messenger-Inquirer*, May 21, 2004

3 "I feel always . . ." Universal News, *The Border* news release, December 10, 1981, *The Border* clipping files, Cinematic Arts Library, University of Southern California

3 "You start moving . . ." Don Alpert, "Bad Guy Never Had It So Good," *Los Angeles Times*, August 6, 1967

3 "rolling hills, trees . . ." *Newsweek*, "Actor's Actor," September 20, 1971, 89

4 History of Depoy from Paul Complin, *A New History of Muhlenberg County* (Greenville, KY: Caney Station Books, 2006), 35–37

6 "Well, see . . . all around Depoy" Gordon Oates, telephone interview by the author, July 30, 2004

6 "My dad was . . ." Warren Oates, interview by Larry Byrd, "I'm Just a Dummy Actor," *Classic Images*, pt. 1, August 1987, p. 20

6 "a splendid place . . ." Universal News, *Border* news release

7 "Our upbringing was . . ." Bobby Coleman, telephone interview by the author, August 27, 2004

7 "Still, I would . . . ran Buren off!" Gordon Oates, interview, July 30, 2004

8 "When I was . . ." Universal News, *Border* news release

8 "In the wintertime . . ." Warren Oates, interview by Byrd, pt. 1, p. 20

8 "learned to paddle . . ." Gordon Oates, interview, July 30, 2004

8 "I would dread . . ." Coleman, interview by the author

9   "'Lasses, boys, 'lasses" Bobby Coleman, interview by Tom Thurman for *Warren Oates: Across the Border*

9   "made things much . . ." Warren Oates, interview by Alain Garel, *Image et Son*, April 1974, 83

9   "Warren and I were . . ." Coleman, interview by the author

9   "I wish I was . . ." Universal News, *Border* news release

9   "The most impressive . . ." MGM, *Chandler* press book, November 1971, MAT no. 2B, *Chandler* clipping files, Cinematic Arts Library, University of Southern California

10   "passionate attention . . . fascinating person" *Dillinger* press book, 1973, *Dillinger* production files, Core Collection, Margaret Herrick Library, Academy of Motion Picture Arts and Sciences, Beverly Hills, CA

10   "everybody listening to . . ." Dudley Saunders, "Wandering Warren Oates," *Louisville Times*, February 20, 1972

10   "you couldn't keep . . ." Gordon Oates, interview, July 30, 2004

10   "I'm going to chase . . ." Thomas McGuane, telephone interview by the author, November 4, 2006

11   "I don't know how . . ." Saunders, "Wandering Warren Oates"

11   "When the doors . . ." Gordon Oates, interview, July 30, 2004

11   "I had an . . ." Warren Oates, interview by Garel, 84

11   "Mr. Pittman . . . the big day" Coleman, interview by the author

12   "I think it . . ." Warren Oates, interview by Byrd, pt. 1, p. 20

12   "Daddy, when are . . ." Thelma Yates, interview by the author, December 5, 2005, Greenville, KY

12   "My father moved . . ." Warren Oates, interview by Byrd, pt. 1, p. 20

12   "I knew everything . . ." Sidney Skolsky, "Money Is Damned Important," *Singles Register*, November 1, 1973, 9

12   "There was nothing . . ." Charles Dickens, *American Notes* (New York: St Martin's, 1985), 152

13   "It was about . . ." Universal News, *1941* news release, 1979, *1941* production files, Core Collection, Herrick Library

13   Louisville during the war from Bruce M. Tyler, *Louisville in World War II* (Charleston, SC: Arcadia, 2005), 1–128

14   "The other kids . . ." John Sandilands, "Warren Oates Collects," *Honey*, February 1972, 44

14   "They didn't trust . . . made [Louisville] bearable" Saunders, "Wandering Warren Oates"

15   "When I went . . . out West" Warren Oates, interview by Byrd, pt. 1, p. 20

16   "He would always . . ." Joseph Altsheler, *The Young Trailers* (New York: Appleton-Century-Crofts, 1932), 325

16   "mean English teacher . . ." Warren Oates, interview by Garel, 84

16   "I don't know . . . gun wasn't loaded" Saunders, "Wandering Warren Oates"

17   "Probably my being . . ." Warren Oates, interview by Byrd, pt. 1, p. 20
17   "He used to . . ." Universal News, *1941* news release
18   "I wasn't a great . . ." Warren Oates, interview by Byrd, pt. 1, p. 20

2. A Good Horse

20   "I was a total hick . . ." Alpert, "Bad Guy Never Had It"
20   Weldon Stone's history from Criseyde Jones, interview by the author, January 18, 2008, Pasadena, CA
20   "authentic American folk fantasy" Stephen M. Shearer, *Patricia Neal: An Unquiet Life* (Lexington: University Press of Kentucky, 2006), 33
21   "Mr. Stone has left . . ." Ernest C. Hassold to John W. Taylor, memorandum, August 12, 1947, Boyd Martin Papers, University Archives, University of Louisville, Louisville, KY
21   Edgar Boyd Martin's history from Martin Papers and Jean Howerton Coady, "A Playbill of Memories," *Playhouse*, November 13, 1980, in the author's possession
21   "would rather work . . ." Boyd Martin, Show Talk, *Louisville Courier-Journal*, March 3, 1959
21   "We didn't break . . . drank a bit" Mitzi Friedlander, telephone interview by the author, November 7, 2007
22   "I felt strange . . ." *Newsweek*, "Actor's Actor," 89
22   "Have you ever . . . and try out?" Teddy Oates in *Across the Border*
22   "I didn't get the lead . . ." Boyd Martin, "Warren Oates Was One of My Boys," *Louisville Courier-Journal*, February 14, 1960
23   "a pretty bad play . . . from the audience" Ibid.
23   "Portrait of Boyd Martin . . ." *Fine Pretty Things* playbill, May 1949, Martin Papers
23   "The audience laughed . . ." Bill Ladd, "Louisvillian Is Rising Movie and TV Actor," *Louisville Courier-Journal*, February 14, 1960
23   "even at the manly . . . in a sense" Warren Oates, interview by Byrd, pt. 1, p. 20
24   "His vocabulary . . ." Ann Marshall, interview by the author, December 6, 2005, Louisville, KY
24   "The world is . . . in many ways" United Artists, *Bring Me the Head of Alfredo Garcia* news release, 1975, *Bring Me the Head of Alfredo Garcia* production files, Core Collection, Herrick Library
25   "He was a good horse" Friedlander, interview
25   "was an odd duck . . . pretty incredible" Bekky Schneider, telephone interview by the author, March 8, 2007
26   "Doug gave a lot . . ." Dudley Saunders, "Hoping for Another Hot Year: Ex-Louisvillian Warren Oates Now Has Co-Star Film Status," *Louisville Times*, December 6, 1968

26   Oates would be a sophomore from *Village Green* playbill, May 1950, Martin Papers

26   "I knew then ..." Warren Oates, interview by Byrd, pt. 1, p. 20

27   "Special recognition should ..." *Cardinal*, Winter 1950

27   "Your wish ... quiet, gentle" Alberta Waddell Rutter, telephone interview by the author, August 13, 2007

29   "They said everybody ..." Warren Oates, interview by Byrd, pt. 1, p. 20

30   "Bertie, I'm thinking ... in the world" Rutter, interview

31   "Mr. Warren Oates ..." *Affairs of State* playbill, March 24, 1953, Martin Papers

31   "I just couldn't ..." Warren Oates, interview by Byrd, pt. 1, p. 20

31   "I'd read there ... a normal life" Gordon Oates, interview by the author, December 5, 2005, Louisville, KY

31   "Since Waldo ..." Martin, "Warren Oates Was One"

32   "I thought, 'What ...'" Rutter, interview

32   "HELLO" in eyeliner pencil from Friedlander, interview

33   "Did you hear ..." Ibid.

33   "We had four ..." Mitchell Ryan, telephone interview by the author, September 12, 2007

33   "If we have ..." Warren Oates, interview by Byrd, pt. 1, p. 21

34   "Put it in ..." Gordon Oates, interview, December 5, 2005

34   "So they forced me ... helluvan actor" Warren Oates, interview by Byrd, pt .1, p. 21

3. Hi, I'm Warren

37   "The chicks were wilder ..." William F. Nolan, *McQueen* (New York: Congden and Weed, 1984), 16

38   "learning the talk ..." David McGinty, "The Top Is in Sight: Slow-Starting Warren Oates Moves Up," *Louisville Times*, September 30, 1967

38   "She told me ... my life" Armand Alzamora, telephone interview by the author, January 24, 2006

39   "The first two ..." *TV Guide*, May 11, 1963, 16–17

39   "Warren was broken up ... know why" Howard Dayton, interview by the author, July 21, 2004, Los Angeles

40   "I was struggling along ..." "Picture Cowboys: The Star, The Posse, and the Reel West," Western Movies: Myths and Images, July 3, 1976, Sun Valley Center for the Arts and Humanities, MS 582, folder 10, box 21, Institute of the American West Records, Sun Valley, ID

40   "All we wanted ..." Dayton, interview, July 21, 2004

40   "For some reason ..." *TV Guide*, May 11, 1963, 17

40   "Preston Foster would ..." Dayton, interview, July 21, 2004

41   "They were almost ..." Gordon Oates, interview, December 5, 2005

41   "We lived two blocks . . . in for coffee?" Howard Dayton, interview by the author, June 11, 2006, Los Angeles

41   "They allowed very . . ." Warren Oates, interview by Garel, 64

42   "to find the truth . . ." Wynn Handman, telephone interview by the author, July 21, 2005

42   "You're just like . . ." *TV Guide*, May 11, 1963, 17

43   "I met Warren . . ." Millie Perkins, interview by the author, June 8, 2005, Hollywood, CA

44   "All the girls . . ." Dayton, interview, June 11, 2006

44   "Six foot one . . ." *New York News*, 1975, clipping, private collection

44   "I think . . . about anything" Dayton, interview, June 11, 2006

45   "Kraft-TV's 'Murder . . .'" Quoted in Jim Kepner, *Rough News, Daring Views: 1950s Pioneering Gay Journalism* (Binghamton, NY: Haworth, 1997), 168

45   "I played a stuck-up . . ." Robert Culp, interview by the author, October 17, 2006, West Hollywood, CA

45   "We watched a tape . . ." Howard Dayton, interview by the author, November 16, 2006, Los Angeles

46   "We realized that . . . were never apart" Culp, interview by the author

46   "One day I got . . ." Dayton, interview, November 16, 2006

46   "I had a part . . ." *TV Guide*, May 11, 1963, 17

47   "like a producer's . . . a scary ride" *The Making of "Studio One,"* DVD (Gold Hill Media, 2004)

48   "Didn't you used to . . ." Rutter, interview

48   "I'm married now." Martin, "Warren Oates Was One"

48   "It was doomed." Armand Alzamora, interview

48   "He probably agreed . . ." Dayton, interview, July 21, 2004

48   "I have very little . . ." Ryan, interview

48   "I had every actor . . ." Nick Georgiade, telephone interview by the author, June 12, 2007

49   "Come to think of it . . ." Joan Crosby, "Rather Be a Character Actor," *TV Scout*, September 1962, clipping, private collection

49   "sitting, drinking, reading . . ." Dayton, interview, July 21, 2004

50   "Before I can turn . . ." James Bacon, *How Sweet It Is: The Jackie Gleason Story* (New York: St. Martin's, 1986), 150

50   "The appetite of . . ." Jon Krampner, *Man in the Shadows: Fred Coe and the Golden Age of Television* (New Brunswick, NJ: Rutgers University Press, 1997), 90

50   "These people don't . . . of this fact" Culp, interview by the author

50   "I kept hearing . . ." Georgiade, interview

50   "everything we owned . . ." Anita Khanzadian, telephone interview by the author, June 7, 2007

50 "I was between jobs . . ." CBS Entertainment, *Blue and the Gray* news release

51 Oates's leaving Bobbie from Teddy Oates Chase, interview by the author, July 17, 2006, Charlotte, NC

51 "Nick, you and . . . Why not?" Georgiade, interview

51 "like the Okies" *Newsweek*, "Actor's Actor," 89

51 "a hang-up sack . . ." David Castell, "Wild Oates," *Films Illustrated*, December 1971, 20

51 "to fly with . . ." Warren Oates, interview by Garel, 84

4. Have Gumption—Will Travel

53 "sucked up oil . . ." Georgiade, interview

53 "the smartest move . . ." McGinty, "Top Is in Sight"

53 "If you're going to succeed . . ." CBS Entertainment, *Blue and the Gray* news release

54 "It was a . . ." Khanzadian, interview

54 "He got hot . . ." Dayton, interview, July 21, 2004

54 "Warren got work . . ." Armand Alzamora, interview

54 Western series information from Richard West, *Television Westerns: Major and Minor Series, 1946–1978* (Jefferson, NC: McFarland, 1987), 1

56 "I kept pushing . . ." Culp, interview by the author

56 "Warren learned to ride . . ." Loren Janes, telephone interview by the author, November 9, 2006

56 "I had just gotten . . ." Castell, "Wild Oates," 84

56 "walked up and down . . . you'll do" Warren Oates, interview by F. Albert Bomar and Alan J. Warren, *Film Comment*, January–February 1981, 41

57 "You know something? . . ." *Up Periscope* press book, 1958, *Up Periscope* film clippings, Cinematic Arts Library, University of Southern California

57 "I was a city . . ." Edd Byrnes, telephone interview by the author, February 8, 2007

58 "Gordon told him . . ." Ibid.

58 "I was the guy . . ." Warren Oates and Peter Fonda, interview by David Castell, November 16, 1971, British Film Institute National Library, London

58 "I took the script . . ." Castell, "Wild Oates," 18

59 "Warren Oates, tyro thesp . . ." *Variety*, August 4, 1958, 6

59 "Lent is blamed . . ." *Hollywood Reporter*, March 10, 1959

59 "The New York Steaks . . ." *Los Angeles Times*, October 26, 1960

60 "We came in . . ." Armand Alzamora, interview

61 "a long table of . . ." Warren Oates, interview by Bomar and Warren, 41

61   "the first of many . . ." David Weddle, *If They Move . . . Kill 'em! The Life and Times of Sam Peckinpah* (New York: Grove Press, 1994), 152

62   "I've got to try . . ." Teddy Oates Chase, interview by the author

62   "I look out . . ." Nolan, *McQueen*, ix

63   "in a big . . . long as we are" Teddy Oates Chase, interview by the author

66   "a windbreaker . . ." Boots Le Baron, "Robert Culp Believes in Stanislavski and Realism," *Los Angeles Times*, December 14, 1958

66   "He nailed it . . ." Culp, interview by the author

66   "Television's western craze . . ." Cecil Smith, "Cowboy Writes Self into Play," *Los Angeles Times*, April 1, 1959

5. Bullfights and Boots

67   "I can't tell you . . ." Warren Oates, interview by Larry Byrd, "I'm Just a Dummy Actor," *Classic Images*, pt. 2, September 1987, 37

67   "At first, I played . . ." MGM, *Chandler* press book

67   "I was the fourth heavy . . ." *Newsweek*, "Actor's Actor," 89

67   "I was usually . . . black '49 Chevy" Sandilands, "Warren Oates Collects," 44

68   "I couldn't get . . ." Culp, interview by the author

68   "In my huge kitchen . . ." Georgiade, interview

68   "The premise of . . ." Tom Nolan, telephone interview by the author, January 25, 2007

69   "Strange thing . . ." Oates and Fonda, interview by Castell

69   "highly fictionalized" James Delameter, "Warner Bros.' Yellowstone Kelly," *Film History* 8 (1996): 176

70   "names may well bring . . ." *Motion Picture Daily*, August 13, 1959

70   "a throwback to those . . ." *Los Angeles Mirror-News*, August 30, 1959

71   "Are you going to come . . . to get lucky" Teddy Oates Chase, interview by the author

72   "You've been out . . ." Armand Alzamora, interview

72   "motorcycle-booted, switchblade-packing . . ." Arthur Jacobs Company, *Private Property* news release, April 1960, *Private Property* production files, Core Collection, Herrick Library

73   "We sometimes had . . ." *Newsweek*, "New Films: Seduction by Proxy," April 30, 1960, 22

73   "highly suggestive sequences . . ." *American Film Institute Catalog of Feature Films*, http://www.afi.com/

73   "America's only authentic . . ." Bernard Lewis, *Private Property* news release, April 25, 1960, *Private Property* production files

73   "At the time . . ." Stanley Colbert, e-mail message to the author, May 21, 2007

74   *Private Property* compared to *Marty* in *Daily Variety*, April 8, 1960, 3

74   "I began to write . . ." Cecil Smith, "Young Pros Shoot Tense Film Drama in Backyard," *Los Angeles Times*, August 16, 1959

74   "I didn't know Warren . . ." Colbert, e-mail message

74   "uniformly dreadful . . ." *New Yorker*, May 20, 1960

74   "unattractive and not quite bright" Arthur Jacobs Company, *Private Property* news release

74   "if he had any . . ." Colbert, e-mail message

75   "Warren Oates is Boots . . ." Richard L. Coe, "It's a Horror and It's Brilliant," *Washington Post*, May 6, 1960

75   "What will we do . . ." Smith, "Young Pros Shoot"

75   "two TV series . . ." Philip K. Scheuer, "Annakin's Ark Due for Swiss Family," *Los Angeles Times*, July 18, 1959

75   "He was enormously easy . . ." Colbert, e-mail message

76   "Warren called him . . . I was a wife" Teddy Oates Chase, interview by the author

6. A Diamond, a Daughter, and a Drunk

78   "sweet, uncomplicated, and . . ." Colbert, e-mail message

79   "How long do . . ." Dayton, interview, July 21, 2004

79   "that dear old mean . . ." John Mahoney, "Warren Oates Has a Face like a Country Road," *Hollywood Reporter*, February 16, 1968, 37

79   "Lucien Ballard was my . . . shot in 1920" Budd Boetticher, *When in Disgrace* (Santa Barbara: Neville, 1989), 110

80   "Warren Oates is perfect . . ." American Cinematheque at the Egyptian Theatre presents "Gangsters and Crime in the Big City," February 18, 2007, http://www.egyptiantheatre.com/archive1999/2007/Gangster_Films_2007.htm

80   "may cotton to Legs . . ." *Los Angeles Times*, March 24, 1960

80   "Warren loved my mother . . . I quit" Teddy Oates Chase, interview by the author

81   "Pupi's was the . . ." B. J. Merholz, telephone interview by the author, May 22, 2007

81   "Every now and then . . ." Teddy Oates Chase, interview by the author

82   "Our rent . . . $200 went away" Ibid.

83   "I'm looking over . . . Jennifer" Ibid.

84   "The first *Westerner* . . ." Garner Simmons, interview by the author, February 16, 2006, Encino, CA

7. Meanwhile, Back at the Raincheck

85   "Sam Peckinpah and Dennis Hopper . . ." Bob Watkins, interview by the author, May 5, 2006, Taos, NM

86 "I think he thought . . ." Harry Dean Stanton in *Warren Oates: Across the Border*, directed by Tom Thurman, written by Tom Marksbury (Fly by Noir Productions, 1992)

86 "My girlfriend Micki . . ." Teddy Oates, interview by Tom Thurman for *Across the Border*

87 "The Raincheck Room . . ." Alex Rocco, telephone interview by the author, March 30, 2007

87 "If Warren wasn't home . . . Oh, God" Teddy Oates, interview by Thurman

88 "way out . . . of America" Philip K. Scheuer, "Stevens Whips Up His Own New Wave," *Los Angeles Times*, June 5, 1961

88 "What we are . . . Bardot and sex" Ibid.

90 "a worthy effort . . ." *Hollywood Reporter*, September 19, 1962

90 Oates's sympathetic part from Boyd Martin, "Ex Louisvillian Moves Up," *Louisville Courier-Journal*, January 2, 1962

90 "To this day . . ." Teddy Oates Chase, interview by the author

91 Development of *Ride the High Country* from Weddle, *If They Move*, 197–201

92 "Inbred, lice-infested . . ." Ibid., 201

92 "'Now you guys . . ." Garner Simmons, *Peckinpah: A Portrait in Montage* (New York: Limelight Editions, 1998), 44

92 No such seclusion from John Davis Chandler, telephone interview by the author, March 23, 2007

92 "One of the things . . ." L. Q. Jones, interview by the author, February 20, 2006, Hollywood, CA

93 "They were really . . ." Mariette Hartley, telephone interview by the author, February 16, 2007

93 "I don't want to see . . ." Ibid.

93 "He had gone . . ." Chandler, interview

93 "Man, what a ride . . ." Hartley, interview

93 "Do you always . . . killing monks" Chandler, interview

94 "When he was . . ." Hartley, interview

94 "That scene came . . ." Simmons, *Peckinpah*, 47

95 "Sam told Frank Kowalski . . ." Chandler, interview

95 "Warren was one . . ." L. Q. Jones, interview

95 "I can tell you . . ." Hartley, interview

95 "salvation and loneliness" John Simons, "The Double Vision of Tragedy in *Ride the High Country*," in *Sam Peckinpah's West: New Perspectives*, ed. Leonard Engel (Salt Lake City: University of Utah Press, 2003), 63

96 "one of the last . . ." *Sam Peckinpah's West: Legacy of a Hollywood Renegade*, directed by Tom Thurman, written by Tom Marksbury (Fly by Noir Productions, 2004)

96 "Today the ranch . . ." Richard Whitehall, "Talking with Peckinpah," *Sight and Sound*, Fall 1969, 172

96   "dirty one of the group . . ." *Ride the High Country* script, December 18, 1961, Cinematic Arts Library, University of Southern California

96   "a diseased inbred . . ." Joe Neumaier, "Warren Oates: Living on the Edge," *Razor*, February 2004, transcribed on Ted Strong's personal Web site, http://www.tedstrong.com/oates-razor.shtml

96   "With the appearance . . ." John M. Marzluff, e-mail message to the author, June 12, 2007

97   "Instead of being . . ." Teddy Oates, interview by Thurman

8. It's Chicken One Day . . .

98   "I'm happy as a character . . ." Crosby, "Rather Be a Character Actor"

98   "full of fun . . ." *Charlotte (NC) News*, March 13, 1963

99   "doesn't ride, doesn't work . . ." *TV Guide*, May 11, 1963, 17

99   "Leslie Stevens had done . . ." John Erman, telephone interview by the author, September 2, 2007

99   "Ves Painter was . . ." Gordon Dawson, telephone interview by the author, September 8, 2006

99   "I knew his name . . ." Bruce Dern, telephone interview by the author, January 26, 2007

99   "Revue's WIDE COUNTRY . . ." William Morris Agency, "Television Pilots Sourcebook," March 19, 1962, Cinematic Arts Library, University of Southern California

100   "in a house on a big lot . . ." Walter Mirsch, "Warren Oates Biography," news release, June 1967, biography files, Core Collection, Herrick Library

100   "Warren smoked way . . ." Dern, interview

100   "Bruce Dern never stopped . . ." Michael Anderson Jr., telephone interview by the author, August 10, 2006

101   "Warren and I both . . ." Dern, interview

101   "I had just gotten . . . Warren Oates style" Hartley, interview

101   "professionalism and discipline" Ray Loynd, "Insights from a Gritty Actor," *Los Angeles Herald-Examiner*, October 13, 1974

102   "He was very fascinated . . ." Dern, interview

102   "honesty, realism, and respect" *TV Guide*, November 10, 1962, 16

102   "hang in with the Knights . . ." "Picture Cowboys," Western Movies, Institute of the American West Records

102   "Ben Johnson was the only . . ." Watkins, interview

103   "Coop, you know . . ." *TV Guide*, November 10, 1962, 16

103   "real old cracker barrel . . ." ABC-TV, *Stoney Burke* news release, September 18, 1962, Hal Humphrey Collection, Cinematic Arts Library, University of Southern California

103   "The worst of TV . . ." Hal Humphrey, "His Rodeo Series May Buck Trend," *Los Angeles Times*, September 16, 1962

103   "a classic hero . . ." *TV Guide*, November 10, 1962, 16

103   "Jack Lord stars . . ." *Los Angeles Times*, October 1, 1962

104   "Talented people, these" *Los Angeles Times*, October 3, 1962

104   "'Ben Casey' on the hoof . . ." *Variety*, October 3, 1962

105   "There really are characters . . ." *TV Guide*, May 11, 1963, 17

105   "It's like carnival people . . ." Ben Johnson, interview by Ronald Davis, April 10, 1992, no. 494, transcript, Ronald Davis Oral History Collection on the Performing Arts, DeGolyer Library, Southern Methodist University, Dallas

105   "I owe Warren . . ." *TV Guide*, May 11, 1963, 16

105   "Because Leslie was . . ." Erman, interview

105   "It was the first . . . No, Warren!" Anderson, interview

106   "cursed like a sailor" Edward Asner, interview by the author, March 15, 2007, Los Angeles

107   "That's Ves all right . . ." Donald Freeman, "That's Our Ves," *San Diego Union*, November 25, 1962

108   "the widow of . . ." *Louisville Courier-Journal*, "Mrs. Oates, Mother of TV Star, Dies," January 13, 1963

108   "I didn't want . . ." Rutter, interview

108   "As played to the hilt . . ." *TV Guide*, May 11, 1963, 16

109   "rube image . . ." Saunders, "Wandering Warren Oates"

109   "was my meat . . ." *Charlotte (NC) News*, March 13, 1963

110   "If it'd gone . . . in a movie" Oates and Fonda, interview by Castell

110   "I'm goin' fishing . . ." *TV Guide*, May 11, 1963, 17

9. . . . And Feathers the Next

111   "My brother Sam . . . cooked there" Fern Lea Peter, interview by the author, February 2, 2006, Malibu, CA

111   "He shot and wounded . . ." Jennifer Oates, interview by the author, August 17, 2006, Charlotte, NC

112   "It was the best . . ." Teddy Oates Chase, interview by the author

112   "Madame Pupi was . . ." Will Hutchins, telephone interview by the author, March 14, 2007

112   "Warren was a good . . ." Peter, interview

113   "Make sure you say . . . you're by yourself" Teddy Oates Chase, interview by the author

114   "The things I did . . ." Oates and Fonda, interview by Castell

114   "one of five . . ." Burt Kennedy, *Mail Order Bride* script, March 24, 1963, Museum of the American West, Autry National Center of the American West, Los Angeles

114   "He'd put his hand . . ." Georgiade, interview

115   "Warren Oates plays . . ." *Los Angeles Times*, April 10, 1964

115   "Oates is good . . ." *Hollywood Reporter*, January 15, 1964

115   "not very villainous . . ." *Films and Filming*, May 1964

115   "a generally enjoyable . . ." *Product Digest*, February 5, 1964, 9

115   "a merely colorfully ornery . . ." *Variety*, January 15, 1964

115   "Don't tell me . . ." Teddy Oates Chase, interview by the author

115   "Somebody had to . . ." L. Q. Jones, interview

116   "Dinner's off . . . something like that" Anderson, interview

116   "The money was . . ." L. Q. Jones, interview

118   "Warren Oates was playing . . ." Dawson, interview

118   Senta Berger on Peckinpah from Mike Siegel, "Sam Peckinpah: Passion and Poetry," *Major Dundee*, DVD (El Dorado Productions/Columbia Home Entertainment, 2005)

118   "Warren stayed at the Casablanca . . ." Anderson, interview

118   "There were two . . ." Dawson, interview

119   "I won four hundred bucks . . ." Anderson, interview

119   "Hadley, played brilliantly . . ." Matt Wanat, "'Fall In behind the Major': Cultural Border Crossing and Hero Building in *Major Dundee*," in Engel, *Sam Peckinpah's West*, 92

119   "O. W. Hadley is a great . . ." Simmons, interview

120   "That big river fight . . . the breadline" Chandler, interview

120   "I was talking . . . Brian Keith" Ibid.

121   "Everybody in our group . . ." L. Q. Jones, interview

121   "I can kill . . ." *Conversations with the Great Moviemakers of Hollywood's Golden Age at the American Film Institute*, ed. George Stevens Jr. (New York: Knopf, 2006), 113

121   "Sam was using . . ." Weddle, *If They Move*, 243

122   "the smoking ruin . . ." J. Hoberman, "The Charge of the Peckinpah Brigade," *New York Times*, April 3, 2005

122   "In the case of . . ." Richard L. Coe, "Disorder Dogs Major Dundee," *Washington Post*, April 9, 1965

122   "Mr. Peckinpah does have . . ." Eugene Archer, "Costly Western Opens at Capitol Theater," *New York Times*, April 8, 1965

122   "I remember the incident . . ." Castell, "Wild Oates"

122   "'Major Dundee' didn't . . ." Warren Oates, interview by Bomar and Warren, 42

122   "I think Mexico . . ." Warren Oates, interview by Byrd, pt. 2, p. 37

123   "It was an interesting . . . completely sure" Erman, interview

124   "We began to work . . ." Ibid.

124   "It is a vulgarization . . ." Philip K. Scheuer, "Hard Core Therapy for Cuckoo's Nest," *Los Angeles Times*, January 15, 1965

124   "Everybody came . . ." Erman, interview

125   "He was sensational . . ." Jack Klugman, interview by Tom Nolan, October 31, 2005, quoted in Tom Nolan, e-mail message to the author, February 14, 2007

125   "I imagine Jack . . ." Erman, interview

125   "John Erman asked . . . bouncing along" Richard Brander, telephone interview by the author, September 6, 2007

126   "Warren Oates (McMurphy) claims . . ." Players' Ring Gallery, *The Playgoer* (Hollywood, CA: Huber, 1964), 19, private collection

126   "I think the only . . . can remember" Burt Kennedy, *Hollywood Trail Boss: Behind the Scenes of the Wild, Wild West* (New York: Boulevard Books, 1997), 119

10. Cloudy and Cool

127   "I'm an actor . . ." Teddy Oates, interview by Thurman

127   "I don't truthfully know . . ." Sandilands, "Warren Oates Collects," 45

127   "I don't talk . . ." Skolsky, "Money Is Damned Important," 9

128   "The camera distorts . . ." Alpert, "Bad Guy Never Had It"

128   "a face like . . . happy to oblige" Mahoney, "Warren Oates Has a Face," 37

128   "I feel maybe most . . ." Warren Oates, interview by Bomar and Warren, 43

128   "I didn't intentionally . . ." Mahoney, "Warren Oates Has a Face," 37

128   "I believe what Camus . . ." United Artists, *Bring Me the Head* news release

128   "If I had to pick . . ." Dan Safran, "Oate's [*sic*] Violent Screen Life," *Dallas Times-Herald*, August 11, 1974

129   Camping trip with Timothy from Timothy Oates, interview by the author, July 18, 2006, Charlotte, NC

129   "I'm not sure how . . ." Lee Goldberg, *Unsold Television Pilots: 1955 through 1988* (Jefferson, NC: McFarland, 1990), 121

129   "something fuzzy to wear" Teddy Oates Chase, interview by the author

130   Teddy emptying wine bottles from Betty Alzamora, interview by the author, July 29, 2007, Franklin, TN

130   "This was a guy . . ." Teddy Oates Chase, interview by the author

130   "I somehow got elected . . . doesn't want me" Teddy Oates, interview by Thurman

131   "A Western is commercial . . ." Brad Stevens, *Monte Hellman: His Life and Films* (Jefferson, NC: McFarland, 1998), 53

131   "Several friends submitted . . ." Ibid., 54

132   "I don't know why . . ." Monte Hellman, interview by the author, June 8, 2004, Los Angeles

133   "It was one of those . . ." Monte Hellman, interview by Tom Thurman and Tom Marksbury for *Across the Border*

133   "He was a shy . . ." Culp, interview by the author

133   Perkins's coming to the role from Perkins, interview

134   "I liked my duds . . ." Hutchins, interview

134   "It was a real . . ." Chris Sanchez, telephone interview by the author, June 7, 2007

134   "I'd slip a nickel . . ." *Western Clippings*, A Touch of Hutch, January–April 2007, 38

134   "People were smoking . . ." Sanchez, interview

134   "We invented a drink . . ." Hellman, interview by the author

135   "I was aware . . ." Sanchez, interview

135   "Warren understood . . . have that horse?" Perkins, interview

136   "Warren would have been . . ." Perkins, interview

136   "He was too much . . ." Hutchins, interview

136   "He was a tough . . . weren't just fine" Merholz, interview

137   "Warren was *talking* . . ." Perkins, interview

137   "That's right, that's . . ." Oates and Fonda, interview by Castell

137   "You are speaking . . . got it all out" Hellman, interview by Thurman and Marksbury

138   "I realized . . ." Monte Hellman in *Across the Border*

138   "Just do it . . . that was it" Perkins, interview

138   "I don't remember . . ." Oates and Fonda, interview by Castell

138   "Warren said something . . ." Sanchez, interview

139   "I loved my . . ." Perkins, interview

139   "It's hard for . . ." Hellman, interview by Thurman and Marksbury

139   "They gave me . . ." Hutchins, interview

139   "We can't afford . . . we were there" Henry Cabot Beck, "Shooting at BAM," *New York Daily News*, August 1, 2004

139   "We loaded our . . ." Hutchins, interview

140   "Warren was my . . . it was heaven" Perkins, interview

141   "We thought they . . ." Stevens, *Monte Hellman*, 57

141   "What makes the film . . ." Ron Pennington, "Jack Nicholson Stars in Monte Hellman's Shooting," *Hollywood Reporter*, January 7, 1972

141   "The film has . . ." *Films Illustrated*, December 1971, 24

141   "He's a very careful . . ." Oates and Fonda, interview by Castell

141   "In *The Shooting* he . . ." Hellman, interview by the author

142   "shot at being . . ." Alpert, "Bad Guy Never Had It"

143   "That saved me . . ." *Time*, "The Story of Oates," September 6, 1971, 60

143   "Much hilarity comes . . ." *Los Angeles Herald-Examiner*, November 4, 1966

144   "best outing since . . ." *Hollywood Reporter*, November 11, 1966, 3

144   "Western style leisure . . ." *Return of the Seven* press book, November 1966, *Return of the Seven* clipping files, Cinematic Arts Library, University of Southern California

144   "That was Warren's . . ." Culp, interview by the author

144   "If Sam had made . . ." Ibid.

144   "I was afraid . . ." Kennedy, *Hollywood Trail Boss*, 118

144   "It was a beautiful . . ." Arlene Golonka, telephone interview by the author, September 10, 2007

146   "No, no, Norman . . ." Norman Jewison, *This Terrible Business Has Been Good to Me: An Autobiography* (New York: Dunne, 2005), 135

146 "It's very important . . ." Ibid., 136
146 "I didn't want . . ." Norman Jewison, telephone interview by the author, February 27, 2007
147 "I thought I made . . ." Asner, interview
147 "I was aware . . ." Jewison, interview
147 "Then Sidney Poitier . . ." Jewison, *This Terrible Business*, 140
148 "A lot of people . . . never going to" Patrick Gauen, "In the Heat of the Lights," *St. Louis Post-Dispatch*, July 30, 1989
148 "We had no . . ." Ibid.
148 "I introduced her . . ." Ibid.
148 "Sidney Poitier and . . ." Ibid.
149 Oates in Sparta from James DuBose to the author, October 1, 2007
149 "I tried to see . . ." Mahoney, "Face like a Country Road," 37
149 "was written . . . the Malamute Saloon" Jewison, interview
150 "I wanted Rod's . . ." Jewison, *This Terrible Business*, 143
150 "I think Warren . . ." Jewison, interview
151 *In the Heat of the Night* sound track decisions from Haskell Wexler, "Commentary," *In the Heat of the Night*, DVD, directed by Norman Jewison (United Arts Home Entertainment, 2007)
151 "Part of the lighting . . ." Ibid.
152 "I'm really one . . ." Alpert, "Bad Guy Never Had It"
152 "In 'In the Heat . . .'" Ibid.
152 "The locations are . . ." Teddy Oates Chase, interview by the author
153 "My first wife . . ." Ray Loynd, "Oates and Insights from a Gritty Actor," *Los Angeles Herald-Examiner*, October 13, 1974
153 "We were used . . ." L. Q. Jones, interview
153 "About two or three . . ." Teddy Oates, interview by Thurman

11. Beyond the Valley of the Summer of Love

154 "It really hurt . . ." L. Q. Jones, interview
154 "Warren was the only . . ." L. Q. Jones, interview
155 "Oates was a nice . . ." Norman Powell, telephone interview by the author, February 24, 2006
155 "I went out . . ." Jennifer Oates, interview
155 "famous bean suppers . . . along with Sam" Gordon Oates, interview, December 5, 2005
155 "Warren was a lot . . . more than enough" Peter, interview
156 "Mrs. Oates, do you . . . to be there" Teddy Oates Chase, interview by the author
156 "I got very friendly . . . show you're on" Georgiade, interview
156 "It seemed like . . ." Dayton, interview, July 21, 2004
157 "I get this . . . spirit he had" Anderson, interview
157 "Warren was totally . . . Is it?" Teddy Oates Chase, interview by the author

158   "Warren sent me . . ." Perkins, interview

158   "The twelve of us . . . up your film" Armand Alzamora, interview

159   "no one was . . . wearing it too" Hutchins, interview

159   "I've ruined the . . . *With* the movie" Jewison, *This Terrible Business*, 150

159   "word of mouth . . ." *Newsweek*, August 14, 1967, 83

160   "Oates's plight . . . just don't know" Alpert, "Bad Guy Never Had It"

160   "I don't get fan . . ." *Time*, "Story of Oates," 60

161   "He loved acting . . ." Teddy Oates in *Across the Border*

161   "Every now and then . . ." Dayton, interview, July 21, 2004

161   "Some people panic . . . go home again" McGinty, "Top Is in Sight"

162   "Oh, I'm so . . . he left again" Teddy Oates Chase, interview by the author

163   "Warren Oates as . . ." *Daily Variety*, November 29, 1968, 19

163   "He just couldn't . . . getting work" Nolan, interview

164   "Warren was wonderful . . ." Betty Garrett, telephone interview by the author, October 1, 2007

164   "There was one . . ." Peggy Pope, telephone interview by the author, October 1, 2007

164   "howlingly funny . . ." Cecil Smith, "'Who's Happy Now?' CTG Performs Hailey Play," *Los Angeles Times*, November 6, 1967

164   "He would talk . . ." Garrett, interview

165   "Warren Oates seemed . . ." Pope, interview

165   "What was his . . ." Garrett, interview

165   "He was a pretty . . ." Teddy Oates, interview by Thurman

165   "Where have you . . . He was hurting" Teddy Oates Chase, interview by the author

166   "This is dating? . . ." Teddy Oates, interview by Thurman

166   "which means above . . ." Saunders, "Hoping for Another Hot Year"

166   "wild . . ." Joyce Haber, "Vanessa's Pay Cut to Play in Cyril," *Los Angeles Times*, January 23, 1968

167   "Ah, Teddy." Teddy Oates, interview by Thurman

167   "We thought he . . ." Jewison, interview

167   "exciting and intriguing" *Soul Illustrated*, Fall 1968

167   Comparison to *The Killing* from *New Yorker*, November 23, 1968

167   "dreadful" *Time*, November 8, 1968

167   "impress, particularly . . ." *Hollywood Reporter*, October 2, 1968

12. All Sam's Films Are War Films

169   "No, Warren, do . . ." Teddy Oates Chase, interview by the author

170   "'Let's go. Why not' . . ." Charles Higson, "The Shock of the Old," *Sight and Sound*, August 1995, 38

170   "The whole book . . ." Robert Culp, "The Wild Bunch: An Appreciation Update," *Perfect Vision,* October 1, 1994, 32

170   "It had a lot . . ." Teddy Oates Chase, interview by the author

170   "Warren liked to party . . ." Ben Johnson in *Across the Border*

171   "Find me locations . . ." Chalo Gonzalez, telephone interview by the author, March 25, 2006

171   "For two days . . ." Bo Hopkins, interview by the author, January 25, 2007, Los Angeles

171   "I couldn't help . . ." L. Q. Jones, interview

172   "Warren opened up . . ." Johnson in *Across the Border*

172   "We would have . . ." L. Q. Jones, interview

172   "for about a week . . ." Gonzalez, interview

173   "That day, that . . ." Warren Oates, interview by Garel, 86

173   "By then I . . ." Simmons, *Peckinpah,* 98

174   "Bill Holden . . . embankment" Saunders, "Wandering Warren Oates"

174   "I'll be a son . . ." Dawson, interview

174   "I was alive . . ." Saunders, "Wandering Warren Oates"

174   "They'd been putting . . ." Hopkins, interview

175   "In 'The Wild Bunch' . . ." Oates and Fonda, interview by Castell

175   "Peckinpah would have . . ." Weddle, *If They Move,* 239

175   "Drinking was part . . ." Simmons, interview

175   "When Warren was . . ." Johnson in *Across the Border*

175   "Warren and Ben . . ." Gonzalez, interview

176   "They had cast . . ." Warren Oates, interview by Byrd, pt. 2, p. 37

176   Johnson laughing off the wine vat episode from Johnson in *Across the Border*

176   "Ben had a quiet . . ." Hopkins, interview

176   "When we were . . ." Johnson in *Across the Border*

177   "Sam . . . had a bad . . . that man has . . ." Warren Oates, interview by Bomar and Warren

177   "the toughest thing . . . a happier man" Ray Loynd, "Temperatures and Tempers Soared but Warren Oates Found Peace," *Hollywood Reporter,* July 16, 1968

178   "All Sam's films . . ." Universal News, *1941* news release

178   "The flashback scenes . . ." Oates and Fonda, interview by Castell

179   Divorce settlement details from Los Angeles County Hall of Records

180   "The movie insults . . ." Rex Reed, "Films for the Popcorn Brigade," *Holiday,* June 1969, 23

180   "a personal manager . . ." Kevin Thomas, "Warren Oates: A Candidate for the Big Leagues," *Los Angeles Times,* August 29, 1971

180   "I thought . . ." Castell, "Wild Oates, " 20

180   "She's great . . ." Saunders, "Hoping for Another Hot Year"

181 "Warren was in . . ." Nicky Henson, telephone interview by the author, December 5, 2006

182 "I need you . . ." Armand Alzamora, interview

182 Final divorce settlement details from Los Angeles County Hall of Records

182 "Hands jammed deep . . . good press agent" Saunders, "Hoping for Another Hot Year"

183 "When I met . . ." Thomas, "Warren Oates: A Candidate"

184 "My children got . . ." Ibid.

184 "From You Know Where . . ." Warren Oates to Teddy Oates, January 20, 1969, private collection

13. Leaving No Turn Unstoned

185 "a little crooked . . ." Alpert, "Bad Guy Never Had It"

185 "Warren's numerology number . . ." Teddy Oates, interview by Thurman

186 "In the '70s . . ." Simmons, interview

186 Oates bringing cocaine to Peckinpah's attention from Marshall Fine, *Bloody Sam: The Life of Sam Peckinpah* (New York: Fine, 1991), 278

186 "'Cable Hogue' was . . ." Warren Oates, interview by Bomar and Warren, 42

187 "I find it interesting . . ." Simmons, interview

187 "Men don't understand . . . bored" *Times* (London), "Vickery's Flick," May 18, 1970

187 "All I know . . . old" Sidney Skolsky, "Inside Hollywood," *Singles Register*, November 1, 1973, 9

187 "It was a bit . . . like that before" Culp, interview by the author

187 "I guess I'm . . ." Sidney Skolsky, "Inside Hollywood," *Singles Register*, November 1, 1973, 9

188 "Actors aren't citizens . . ." United Artists, *Bring Me the Head* news release

188 "In the Old West . . ." Harry Northup, interview by the author, June 4, 2004, Los Angeles

188 "It shocked the hell . . ." Warren Oates, interview by Bomar and Warren, 42

188 "I feel that some . . . of the bandoliers" Warren Oates, interview by Byrd, pt. 2, p. 38

188 "the second Mrs. DeWinter" Vickery Turner, e-mail message to the author, February 2, 2006

188 Cab ride to Indio from Howard Dayton, telephone interview by the author, May 24, 2007

189 "I always said . . ." *Los Angeles Times*, "Prison Springs Up in the Desert," May 5, 1969

190   "Things are looking . . ." Turner, e-mail message
190   "I think Vickery . . ." Armand Alzamora, interview
190   "Henry Fonda was . . . motel garden" Turner, e-mail message
191   "the Arizona Territorial Prison . . ." *Films and Filming*, January 1, 1971, 60
191   "The house is modern . . ." Skolsky, "Money Is Damned Important," 9
191   Briar Knoll Drive house details from Timothy Oates, interview
191   "one of the most . . ." Dorothy Manners, "Jack and Nancy Keeping in Touch," *Los Angeles Herald-Examiner*, June 23, 1969
192   "I'd never heard . . ." Turner, e-mail message
192   "I unfortunately didn't . . ." Stella Stevens, e-mail message to the author, March 3, 2006
192   "Crook Duo Marries" *Cleveland Plain Dealer*, June 27, 1969
192   "Julie Shaw . . . for three days" Unidentified clipping, July 8, 1969, private collection
193   "I've seen people die . . ." *Greenville (SC) Index-Journal*, July 8, 1969
193   Kim Novak's, Bryan Forbes's, and Danny Kaye's reactions from NEA Hollywood correspondent, July 8, 1969, private collection
193   "Imagine walking out . . ." *Greenville (SC) Index-Journal*, July 8, 1969
193   "The ladies, all these . . ." Warren Oates, interview by Bomar and Warren, 43
193   Ebert's speech from Weddle, *If They Move*, 7
193   "its many merits . . ." *Independent Film Journal*, June 24, 1969
193   "disconsolate" Abe Greenburg, *Los Angeles Westside Citizen*
194   "I was on . . ." Jennifer Oates, interview
194   "Between Marie Gomez . . ." Hartley, interview
195   "It was a wonderful . . ." Chandler, interview
195   "They got us both . . ." Warren Oates, interview by Byrd, pt. 2, p. 39
195   "Oates is a pot-smoking . . ." *Hollywood Reporter*, May 19, 1970
196   "a little Wild Bunchy . . . on the screen" Sam Pendergrast, "Barquero Is Good Bloody Fun Movie," *Abilene (TX) Reporter-News*, May 16, 1970
196   "Some scenes you . . ." Warren Oates, interview by Garel, 88
196   "Warren Oates takes . . ." *Hollywood Reporter*, May 19, 1970
197   "We both waited . . ." Turner, e-mail message
197   "After some prodding . . ." Vickery Turner, *Focusing* (London : Gollancz, 1984), 176
197   "Warren sometimes got . . ." Turner, e-mail message
197   "I almost had . . ." Chandler, interview
198   "Warren looks quite . . ." Simon Lee, "The Brontes," *TV Times*, October 4, 1973
198   "hillbilly redneck done . . ." Timothy Oates, interview
198   "Leon was never . . ." Turner, *Focusing*, 12
199   "somewhere between conception . . ." Saunders, "Wandering Warren Oates"

199   "Oates develops his . . ." *Daily Variety*, February 13, 1970, 18
199   "My impression was . . ." Hutchins, interview

14. Spread upon the Earth

202   "At six o'clock . . ." Oates and Fonda, interview by Castell
202   "Warren liked to . . ." Turner, e-mail message
202   "My dad was . . . an open thing" Timothy Oates, interview
203   Oates' nightly ritual, Turner, *Focusing*, 32
203   "fatty turnip" Lee, "Brontes"
203   "I ate an apple . . ." Armand Alzamora, interview
203   Organic foods for former drug addicts from Mary Reinholz, "Yin and Yang a la Carte," *Los Angeles Times*, February 14, 1971
203   "gravy on everything . . ." Hellman, interview by the author
203   "I just got off . . . while I washed" Turner, e-mail message
204   "'Two-Lane Blacktop,' 'Deadhead Miles' . . ." Thomas, "Warren Oates: A Candidate"
204   "No one's writing . . ." Universal News, *The Hired Hand* news release, June 11, 1971, *The Hired Hand* film clippings, Cinematic Arts Library, University of Southern California
205   "Peter and his wife . . ." Castell, "Wild Oates," 18
205   "I had watched . . ." Robert Nort, "My Kind of Western," *Santa Fe New Mexican*, November 29, 2002
205   "hand painted and collaged . . ." Peter Fonda, *Don't Tell Dad: A Memoir* (New York: Hyperion, 1998), 300
206   "I always take . . ." Oates and Fonda, interview by Castell
206   "If he won . . ." Turner, e-mail message
207   "inferior, incompetent . . ." *Los Angeles Times*, "100 Blacks, Chicanos, Picket Oscar Ceremony," April 8, 1970
207   "They're gaining attention . . ." Warren Oates, interview by Byrd, pt. 2, p. 38
207   "the girl least likely . . ." John Mahoney, "Oscars Sustain Glamour Infused with Tradition," *Hollywood Reporter*, April 8, 1970, 4
208   "If I won . . ." Skolsky, "Money Is Damned Important," 9
208   "Built in the '60s . . ." Frank Sheffield, telephone interview by the author, February 16, 2007
209   "He acts in Westerns . . ." *Times* (London), "Vickery's Flick"
209   "I'm Warren Oates . . ." Verna Bloom, telephone interview by the author, March 20, 2006
209   "'The Hired Hand' is . . ." Kevin Thomas, "Warren Oates," *Los Angeles Times*, August 29, 1971
209   "looked kind of like . . . haven't stopped" Peter Fonda, interview by Tom Thurman and Tom Marksbury for *Across the Border*

210 "reflected the influences . . ." Peter Collier, *The Fondas: A Dynasty* (New York: Putnam, 1991), 213

210 "A lot of those . . ." Ted Markland, interview by the author, April 18, 2007, Yucca Valley, CA

211 "He was actually . . ." Bruce Fessier, "Star Has Deep Spiritual Connection to Park Hill," *Desert Sun (Palm Springs, CA)*, July 10, 2005

211 "Warren was the most . . ." Bloom, interview

211 "There are not . . ." Watkins, interview

212 "This guy six years . . ." Warren Oates, interview by Byrd, pt. 1, p. 20

212 "Riding in the Land . . ." Bloom, interview

212 "No problem. He . . ." Oates and Fonda, interview by Castell

213 "the idyll is . . ." Castell, "Wild Oates," 22

213 "yearnings for a sagebrush . . ." *Village Voice*, August 26, 1971

213 "the most touching . . ." *Variety*, November 7, 1971, 14

213 "The fallout after . . ." Bloom, interview

213 "All I'd asked . . ." Northup, interview

213 "My friend Mr. Oates . . ." *Hired Hand* news release

213 "Only it was . . ." Stevens, *Monte Hellman*, 79

214 "I was interested . . ." Monte Hellman and Warren Oates, *Two-Lane Blacktop* panel moderated by George Stevens Jr., July 7, 1971, American Film Institute Library, Beverly Hills, CA

214 "the paralyzing orange . . ." Shelley Benoit, "On the Road with the New Hollywood," *Show*, March 1971, 16

214 "GTO is time . . ." Will Corry and Rudy Wurlitzer, *Two-Lane Blacktop* (New York: Universal/Award Books, 1971), 39

214 "I really cast . . ." Hellman and Oates, *Two-Lane Blacktop* panel

215 "Roger Corman had . . . got Warren Oates" Dern, interview

215 "Bruce Dern, younger . . ." Beverly Walker, telephone interview by the author, February 1, 2008

215 "I was at . . ." Warren Miller, interview by the author, June 11, 2004, Los Angeles

216 Stanton and Oates in *Waiting for Godot* from David Thomson, interview by Tom Thurman and Tom Marksbury for *Across the Border*

216 "We were up . . ." Stanton, interview

216 "There was a lot . . ." Hellman, interview by the author

216 "There weren't any . . . detrimental empathy" Hellman and Oates, *Two-Lane Blacktop* panel

216 Hellman harder to please than Antonioni from Benoit, "On the Road," 16

216 "The night before . . . and The Mechanic" Hellman and Oates, *Two-Lane Blacktop* panel

217 "I'm doing this . . ." Kevin Thomas, "Hellman's Best Kept Secret," *Los Angeles Times*, October 4, 1970

217 "It didn't bother . . ." Hellman and Oates, *Two-Lane Blacktop* panel

217   "grueling due to . . ." Hellman, interview by the author

217   "Warren was the sanest . . ." Walker, interview

217   "equipped with a stereo . . ." Hellman, interview by the author

218   "Hellman frequently scheduled . . ." Corry and Wurlitzer, *Two-Lane Blacktop*, 39

218   "It's almost magic . . . a beautiful day" Watkins, interview

218   "You couldn't point . . ." Jennifer Oates, interview

219   "I'm not an actor . . ." Thomas, "Hellman's Best Kept Secret"

219   "I thought there . . . knew each other" Hellman and Oates, *Two-Lane Blacktop* panel

220   "light, very expensive . . ." Rudolph Wurlitzer, *Two-Lane Blacktop* script, first draft, January 5, 1970, Scripts, Core Collection, Herrick Library

221   "The difference between . . ." Thomas, "Warren Oates: A Candidate"

221   "If it wasn't . . ." Benoit, "On the Road," 17

221   "I complained bitterly . . ." Thomas, "Warren Oates"

221   "The film company . . ." Michael Goodwin, "On Route 66, Filming Two-Lane Blacktop," *Rolling Stone*, October 15, 1970, 42

221   "a real endearing cat" Benoit, "On the Road," 23

222   "Dennis Wilson was . . ." Jennifer Oates, interview

222   Taylor never read the script from Benoit, "On the Road," 23

222   "You have a slight . . ." Hellman and Oates, *Two-Lane Blacktop* panel

222   "My favorite scene . . ." Hellman, interview by Thurman and Marksbury

223   "The normally reliable . . ." Benoit, "On the Road," 22

223   "If he likes it . . ." Hellman and Oates, *Two-Lane Blacktop* panel

223   "Laurie is really . . ." Benoit, "On the Road," 23

223   "Luckily he was . . ." Jennifer Oates, interview

223   "Warren Oates eases . . . but it hurts" Winfred Blevins, "Life Imitates the Movies," *Los Angeles Herald-Examiner*, October 11, 1970

224   "I only watch . . ." *TV Guide*, What I Watch, March 20, 1993

224   "The film slows . . . happening in society" Hellman and Oates, *Two-Lane Blacktop* panel

225   "I think he identified . . ." Hellman, interview by Thurman and Marksbury

225   "My agent in London . . ." Hellman and Oates, *Two-Lane Blacktop* panel

225   "I sang some . . . candy bar" Markland, interview

15. The Year of Warren Oates

226   "the year of . . ." *The Hired Hand* press book, *The Hired Hand* clipping files, Cinematic Arts Library, University of Southern California

226   "Warren Oates is . . ." *Daily Variety*, June 21, 1971

226 "has what it takes . . ." Thomas, "Warren Oates: A Candidate"

226 Oates as a double Oscar contender from Charles Champlin, "Rounding Last Curve in Oscar Stakes," *Los Angeles Times*, January 23, 1972

226 "I don't see . . ." Warren Oates, interview by Byrd, pt. 1, p. 19

226 "I don't think . . ." Walker, interview

227 "to watch the Fords . . ." *Time*, "Story of Oates," 60

227 "Anything I need . . . really loved it" Watkins, interview

228 "a tall and handsome . . ." Barbara Funkhouser, "Qualities of Film Outlined," *El Paso (TX) Times*, February 26, 1971

228 "Honk if you . . ." Hutchins, interview

228 "I've got to . . ." *Newsweek*, "Actor's Actor," 88

228 "He started to . . ." Merholz, interview

228 "pick up a beer . . ." *Time*, "Story of Oates," 60

228 "I know Bill . . . a wife, OK?" Jennifer Oates, interview

229 "Terry is playing . . ." Hellman and Oates, *Two-Lane Blacktop* panel

229 "Terry Malick had . . ." Dern, interview

230 "great sweeping things" *Newsweek*, "Actor's Actor," 88

230 "I'm not tired . . . it to you" Hellman and Oates, *Two-Lane Blacktop* panel

230 "It's a collage . . ." Thomas, "Warren Oates: A Candidate"

231 "Zero" Ryan, interview

231 "We didn't have . . ." Leslie Caron, telephone interview by the author, August 10, 2006

231 "I was in . . ." Ryan, interview

232 "I'm trying to live . . . affair with trains" MGM, *Chandler* press book

232 "play[ed] as if . . ." *Hollywood Reporter*, November 29, 1971

232 "walk dazedly through . . ." *Variety*, November 29, 1971

232 "50, bone-weary and . . ." *Chandler* script, 1970, Scripts, Core Collection, Herrick Library

232 "My husband has . . ." Caron, interview

233 "an attempt to do . . ." Thomas, "Warren Oates: A Candidate"

233 "a horrible film . . ." Saunders, "Wandering Warren Oates"

233 "On the strength . . ." Harold T. P. Hayes, Editor's Notes, *Esquire*, September 1971, 32

233 "'Esquire' magazine said . . ." Hellman and Oates, *Two-Lane Blacktop* panel

234 "What I liked . . ." *Chicago Sun-Times*, January 1, 1971

234 "shrugs off that . . ." Ernest B. Furgurson, "Filmmaker Shows What's Wrong in U.S.—Unwittingly," *Los Angeles Times*, August 13, 1971

234 "maybe as being . . . but we're not" Hellman and Oates, *Two-Lane Blacktop* panel

235 "As he did . . ." Charles Champlin, "Hired Echoes Rider Theme," *Los Angeles Times*, August 18, 1971

236 "The reviews for . . ." Thomas, "Warren Oates: A Candidate"

236   "a guy in the corner . . ." *Newsweek*, "Actor's Actor," 89
236   "That's the one . . . Fritz the Cat" Oates and Fonda, interview by Castell
237   "Timmy, if you don't . . ." Timothy Oates, interview
237   "After four days . . ." Fonda, *Don't Tell Dad*, 349
237   "For twenty feet . . ." Peter Fonda, interview by Thurman and Marksbury
237   "A German television . . ." Castell, "Wild Oates," 20
238   "It only hurt . . . which was perfect" Fonda, *Don't Tell Dad*, 357–62
238   "I've done my . . . It's about tribalism" Oates and Fonda, interview by Castell
239   "drawing room . . . next to him" *Evening Standard* (London), November 3, 1971
240   "He was wearing . . . An inspirational genius" Sandilands, "Warren Oates Collects," 45
240   "Up until this . . . of making films" Castell, "Wild Oates," 20
241   "'The Dirty Half Dozen' . . ." Jerry Beigel, "Berry Saves the Day with Indian Tactics," *Los Angeles Times*, November 23, 1971
241   "Warren Oates as the redneck . . ." *Daily Variety*, November 24, 1971

16. Secrets and Strengths

242   "Frawley's lady had . . ." Lee Purcell, interview by the author, February 15, 2007, Glendale, CA
243   "He went off . . ." Dennis Hopper, interview by the author, September 7, 2006, Venice, CA
243   "More than two . . ." Gary Cartwright, *HeartWiseGuy: How to Live the Good Life after a Heart Attack* (New York: Macmillan, 2001), 28
243   "Bud (Edwin) Shrake, apart . . ." Tom Milne and Richard Combs, "Kid Blue Rides Again," *Film Comment*, January–February 1976, 56
244   "Durango represented the peak . . . we were living" Steven L. Davis, *Texas Literary Outlaws: Six Writers in the Sixties and Beyond* (Fort Worth, TX: TCU Press, 2004), 256
244   "was not much . . . at the airport" Hopper, interview
245   "He may have . . ." Dawson, interview
245   "I think he'd . . . most amazing food" Purcell, interview
246   Oates's drug recipe from Cartwright, *Heartwise Guy*, 28
246   "and then I . . ." Purcell, interview
247   "Warren couldn't remember . . . and grass" Hopper, interview
247   "You know . . . definitely have noticed" Purcell, interview
248   "The funniest thing . . ." Hopper, interview
248   "They were in . . ." Purcell, interview
248   "Ben Johnson was . . ." Hopper, interview
248   "and not even . . ." Purcell, interview

248 "I recall a conversation . . ." "Picture Cowboys," Western Movies, Institute of the American West Records

249 "We had a lot . . ." Johnson in *Across the Border*

249 "Sometimes Oates talks . . . or a director" Saunders, "Wandering Warren Oates"

251 "We had a nice . . ." Purcell, interview

251 "a harrowing experience . . . are you wearing?" Saunders, "Wandering Warren Oates"

251 "It was changed . . ." Milne and Combs, "Kid Blue Rides Again," 54

252 "The first movie . . ." *Variety*, August 22, 1973

252 "It's no 'Deep Throat.'" *Kid Blue* press book, 1973, *Kid Blue* clipping files, Cinematic Arts Library, University of Southern California

252 "and it blew . . ." Milne and Combs, "Kid Blue Rides Again," 55

252 "Rotten" *New Republic*, October 27, 1973

252 "one of the nicer . . ." *Andy Warhol's Interview*, September 1973

252 "I for one . . ." Jon Landau, *Rolling Stone*, July 5, 1973

252 "manages to be both . . ." *Hollywood Reporter*, June 13, 1973

252 "a sweet, naïve . . ." Kevin Thomas, "Hopper as a Likeable Outlaw," *Los Angeles Times*, October 3, 1973

253 "Oates oscillates between . . ." *Newsweek*, June 9, 1973

253 "honest hatred of work . . ." *Village Voice*, August 2006

253 Beatty to Saunders from Dudley Saunders, interview by the author, July 25, 2007, Louisville, KY

254 "He would roll . . ." Turner, e-mail message

254 "I can't take . . ." Armand Alzamora, interview

255 Vickery's script for Jennifer from Jennifer Oates, interview

255 "Vickery Turner, for . . ." Dan Sullivan, "Chamberlain Makes Richard Work," *Los Angeles Times*, March 26, 1972

255 "We never had . . ." Ned Beatty, interview by Thurman and Marksbury

256 "This type of . . ." *QP Herald*, March 3, 1973

256 "performance typically keyed . . ." *Focus on Film*, Spring 1973, 18

256 "Oates lends the film . . ." Kevin Thomas, "Crook Aims High in Thief," *Los Angeles Times*, March 3, 1973

256 "Miller, you're wiser . . . raindrop that falls" Miller, interview

257 "a fine, wily . . ." *New York Times*, October 3, 1997

257 "Oates encapsulates whole . . ." James Morrison and Thomas Schur, *The Films of Terrence Malick* (Westport, CT: Praeger, 2003), 88

258 "I have this . . ." Thomson, interview by Thurman and Marksbury

258 "Times apart were . . ." Turner, e-mail message

259 "That's when I . . ." Richard Sherman, telephone interview by the author, January 12, 2008

260 "Warren did not . . ." Sherman, interview

260 "The way he . . ." Teddy Oates, interview by Thurman

260   "flings bottle and . . ." *Tom Sawyer* production notes, *Tom Sawyer* production files, Core Collection, Herrick Library
260   "Warren Oates is charming . . ." *Los Angeles Herald-Examiner*, May 25, 1973
261   "Warren Oates is sympathetic . . ." *Los Angeles Times*, May 23, 1973
261   "the most authentic . . ." *Variety*, March 6, 1973
261   "Warren was very . . ." Sherman, interview
261   "a blonde hussy . . . he said OK" Teddy Oates Chase, interview by the author
262   "Damn it, get . . ." Hopkins, interview

17. Three White Suits

263   "I was very . . ." Turner, e-mail message
263   "Leon looked quite . . ." Turner, *Focusing*, 86
263   Miller invited to stay from Miller, interview
263   "If he smoked . . ." Watkins, interview
264   "like the Indiana . . ." Bridget Byrne, "Oates Attempts Carbon Copy," *Los Angeles Herald-Examiner*, January 15, 1973
264   "In many respects . . ." Lee, "Brontes"
264   "I'm not happy . . ." Miller, interview
265   "I was lucky . . . He wasn't Clyde" Michelle Phillips, telephone interview by the author, July 28, 2006
265   "Warren Oates, the Dillinger . . ." *New Republic*, September 8, 1973, 24
265   "He had true . . ." Phillips, interview
265   "smokes filter-tipped . . ." Mary Murphy, "Strother Martin to Star in Sssssssss," *Los Angeles Times*, October 27, 1972
266   "We were really . . ." Phillips, interview
266   "I didn't read . . ." Byrne, "Oates Attempts Carbon Copy"
266   "I think *Dillinger* . . ." Johnson in *Across the Border*
267   "Warren Oates has never . . ." *Newsday*, August 2, 1973
267   "slack and derivative" *Time*, September 10, 1973
267   "masterful . . . as well-made . . ." Kevin Thomas, "Warren Oates Brings Dillinger Back Alive," *Los Angeles Times*, July 18, 1973
267   "more huckster than . . ." *New Yorker*, August 13, 1973, 49
267   "one more tarnish . . ." *Product Digest*, June 20, 1973
267   "I like Kurosawa . . ." Linda Strawn, "Blood and Guts Milius at War with Hollywood," *Los Angeles Times*, August 5, 1973
267   "a B-movie heavy . . ." *Village Voice*, August 16, 1973
267   "Warren Oates's excellence . . ." *Hollywood Reporter*, June 13, 1973
268   "He wasn't mean . . ." Dayton, interview, June 11, 2006
268   "I've had the flu . . ." Byrne, "Oates Attempts Carbon Copy"
268   Bogart and Oates pictures from Jack Bentley, "How Bogie #2 Won Fame and Lost his Wife," *Daily Mirror* (London), June 4, 1974

268   Mustached men from Earl Wilson, "Are Mustached Men Sexy?" *Dallas Morning News*, August 10, 1974

268   "intensely poetic style . . ." *Los Angeles Times*, December 3, 1972

268   "a city of oil . . . and look beautiful" Richard Cuskelly, "The Thief Who Came to Houston," *Los Angeles Herald-Examiner*, March 5, 1973

269   "How do you . . ." Philip Kaufman, "Commentary," *The White Dawn*, DVD, directed by Philip Kaufman (Paramount Home Entertainment, 2004)

269   "You aren't John . . ." Northup, interview

270   "Warren was very . . . ascot on his neck" Philip Kaufman, telephone interview by the author, January 16, 2007

270   "I knew this character . . ." Paramount, *The White Dawn* news release, no date, British Film Institute National Library

270   "Everybody was pushed . . . with the shaman" Kaufman, interview

271   "I'm standing on my head . . ." Miller, interview

272   "He was on his . . ." Kaufman, interview

272   "If the movie . . ." Ibid.

273   "He has a bad . . . attention she deserves" Skolsky, "Money Is Damned Important," 9

273   "He told a friend . . ." Turner, e-mail message

274   "When?" "Right now." Miller, interview

274   *"Worlds in Collision* and . . ." Watkins, interview

274   "When you get around . . ." Mahoney, "Face like a Country Road," 37

275   "Kowalski had the idea . . ." Dawson, interview

275   "But instead of . . ." *Sight and Sound*, April 1, 1975, 121

275   "The script deals . . ." Sam Peckinpah to Marty Baum, May 31, 1972, *Bring Me the Head of Alfredo Garcia* files, Sam Peckinpah Papers, Special Collections, Herrick Library

275   "Dillinger was a populist . . ." Simmons, interview

275   "If a director . . ." Warren Oates, interview by Garel, 88

276   "I am moving . . ." Sam Peckinpah to Aaron Stern, September 9, 1973, Peckinpah Papers

276   "There are certain . . ." Richard M. Mathison to Sam Peckinpah, October 3, 1973, Peckinpah Papers

276   "Call Warren Oates . . ." *Bring Me the Head of Alfredo Garcia* production notes, September 19, 24, 1973, *Bring Me the Head of Alfredo Garcia* files, Peckinpah Papers

276   "I don't know if . . ." Stanton, interview

277   "Many who came . . ." Simmons, interview

277   "Sam had such . . . Oh yeah" Gonzalez, interview

277   "Isela Vega did . . . burned my ass" Ibid.

277   "She was a pistol . . . butterfly net" Dawson, interview

278   "They had arguments . . ." Gonzalez, interview

278   "I went down to . . ." Simmons, *Peckinpah*, 195

279   Lessons learned from . . ." Sam Peckinpah, memorandum, September 1973, *Bring Me the Head of Alfredo Garcia* files, Peckinpah Papers

279   "The old Chevy . . ." Dawson, interview

279   "Sometimes you feel . . ." Miller, interview

279   "I really tried . . ." Warren Oates, interview by Bomar and Warren, 41

279   "I was writing Sam . . ." Dawson, interview

279   "In 'Alfredo Garcia' Warren . . ." Simmons, interview

280   "I got into . . ." Miller, interview

280   "He was really . . ." Dawson, interview

280   "I just knew . . ." Donnie Fritts in *Across the Border*

280   "I just hated . . . everybody on edge" Dawson, interview

280   "Sam had the uncanny . . ." Simmons, interview

281   "Sam did fall . . . the film justice" Dawson, interview

281   "genuine drinks . . ." *Bring Me the Head* production notes

282   "I don't think these . . . crews are great" Stanley Meisler, "Peckinpah Film under Studio Fire," *Los Angeles Times*, December 14, 1973

282   "It was an ugly . . . a bitch, Dawson!" Dawson, interview

283   "One day we . . . together fantastically" Gonzalez, interview

283   "I will show . . . neck gets tired" *Bring Me the Head of Alfredo Garcia* cast party, Tlaquepaque Bar, Mexico City, December 1973, audiotape, *Bring Me the Head of Alfredo Garcia* files, Peckinpah Papers

283   "We rented a van . . . along with anybody" Gonzalez, interview

284   "We were in . . . they got older" Miller, interview

284   "'Alfredo' has basic dramatic . . ." Loynd, "Oates and Insights"

285   "Put a man . . ." Simmons, interview

285   "We did mushrooms . . ." Dawson, interview

285   "Warren was very . . ." Simmons, interview

285   "Sam got pissed . . . Thank you" Gonzalez, interview

286   "We took a cast . . ." Dawson, interview

286   "I think because. . ." Safran, "Oate's [*sic*] Violent Screen Life"

286   "We were all . . ." Dawson, interview

287   "Dear Sam: . . ." Warren Oates and Emilio Fernandez to Sam Peckinpah, no date, Memorable Memos, Peckinpah Papers

288   "'Alfredo Garcia' was a real . . ." Simmons, interview

288   "We had a couple . . . Kill him" Dawson, interview

288   "I was playing cards . . ." Simmons, *Peckinpah*, 205

288   "The white suit was . . ." Dawson, interview

288   "Don't ever go . . ." Teddy Oates Chase, interview by the author

288   "I just used . . ." Northup, interview

288   "I never heard . . ." Dawson, interview

288   "If you look at . . ." Simmons, interview

18. Family Style

290   "Some things didn't jibe . . ." Warren Oates, interview by Bomar and Warren, 41

290   "When you find . . ." Teddy Oates Chase, interview by the author

290   "Atlanta was different . . ." Timothy Oates, interview

291   "Guess where my next . . ." Teddy Oates, interview by Thurman

291   "The story of . . ." Roger Corman, *How I Made a Hundred Movies in Hollywood and Never Lost a Dime* (New York: Random House, 1990), 200

291   "For several years now . . ." Charles Willeford, "From Cockfighter to Born to Kill," *Film Quarterly*, Fall 1975, 23

292   "The worst thing . . ." Loynd, "Oates and Insights"

292   "*Cockfighter*, I think . . ." Thomson, interview by Thurman and Marksbury

292   "Warren Oates, who plays . . ." Willeford, "From Cockfighter to Born to Kill," 21

292   "Oates was funky . . ." Donnie Fritts, telephone interview by the author, June 16, 2004

292   Fritts a better actor than Kristofferson from Don Herron, *Willeford* (Tucson, AZ: McMillan 1997), 365

292   "biscuits and grits . . . all the time" Watkins, interview

293   "Nestor Almendros is . . ." Charles Ray Willeford, *Cockfighter Journal: The Story of a Shooting* (Santa Barbara, CA: Neville, 1989), 10

293   "non-union crew . . ." Nestor Almendros, *A Man with a Camera*, trans. Rachel Phillips Belash (New York: Farrar, Straus, Giroux, 1984), 135

293   "We were from . . ." Watkins, interview

294   Willeford's memoir from Herron, *Willeford*, 201

294   "Laurie Bird, who . . . for the biscuits" Willeford, *Cockfighter Journal*, 15–42

296   "I was very new . . ." Ed Begley Jr., e-mail message to the author, August 17, 2006

296   "seem like a very . . . will be enhanced" Willeford, *Cockfighter Journal*, 36–43

277   "We had done . . ." Stevens, *Monte Hellman*, 110

277   "Warren and I took . . ." Watkins, interview

277   "They all look . . . you was stuck" Willeford, *Cockfighter Journal*, 48–84

299   "That was one . . ." Hellman in *Across the Border*

299   "Frank's stubbornness will . . . being a dentist" Willeford, *Cockfighter Journal*, 85

300   "I took *Cockfighter* . . ." Perkins, interview

300   "a master portrayer . . ." Kevin Thomas, "Warren Oates: Slices of Americana," *Los Angeles Times*, August 31, 1983

300   "not for sensitive . . ." *Variety*, June 4, 1975, F1

300 "eliciting an extraordinary . . ." *Films International*, September 1974, 12

301 "out into the night . . ." Willeford, "From Cockfighter to Born to Kill," 24

301 "pulled away from . . . am I gonna do?" Corman, *How I Made a Hundred Movies*, 201

301 "To Roger's credit . . ." Ibid., 202

301 "'Cockfighter' is about . . ." Loynd, "Oates and Insights"

301 "*Cockfighter* is as good . . ." Tom Thurman, interview of David Thomson for *Across the Border*

302 "I've given up . . ." Loynd, "Oates and Insights"

302 "I blame it . . . only true critics" Bentley, "How Bogie #2"

19. The Grand Experiment

303 "The Montana mountains . . ." Bentley, "How Bogie #2"

303 "Many of them . . ." William Clark, journal entry, July 15, 1806, quoted in Livingston (MT) Area Chamber of Commerce Walking Tour

305 "Warren knew that . . ." Peter Fonda, interview by Thurman and Marksbury

305 "I must have made . . ." Peter Fonda in *Across the Border*

305 "I thought I was . . ." Thomas McGuane, interview

306 "I met Warren . . ." William Hjortsberg, interview by the author, September 18, 2006, Livingston, MT

306 "It was such . . ." Thomas McGuane, interview

306 "I think they . . . in the Wrangler" Hjortsberg, interview

307 "It just seemed . . ." Becky McGuane Fonda, telephone interview by the author, March 28, 2007

307 "I thought he . . ." Thomas McGuane, interview

307 "I can get . . . back to work" Hjortsberg, interview

307 "Our little wave . . ." Ibid.

308 "memorabilia, guns, Eskimo . . ." Paramount, *White Dawn* news release

308 "Michelle Phillips" Becky McGuane Fonda, interview

308 "One time he . . ." Teddy Oates Chase, interview by the author

308 "Jack used to have . . ." Dana Ruscha, interview by the author, September 18, 2007, Los Angeles

309 "Roll the ball . . . to use it" Jennifer Lee, telephone interview by the author, September 10, 2007

309 "I know every . . ." Ruscha, interview

309 "Maybe I was . . ." Warren Oates, interview by Garel, 86

309 "What I really want . . ." Loynd, "Oates and Insights"

310 "saved my life . . ." *Dallas Sunday News*, "Sam Peckinpah: Bad Man and His Art," August 18, 1974

310 "Peter and I . . ." Markland, interview

310   "He was one . . ." *New York Post*, August 10, 1974

311   "I did not . . ." Lee, interview

311   "We hit New York . . ." Jennifer Lee, *Tarnished Angel: Surviving in the Dark Curve of Drugs, Violence, Sex, and Fame* (New York: Thunder's Mouth Press, 1991), 74

311   "It was a beautiful . . ." Dudley Saunders, "A Tale of Two Actors," *Louisville Times*, April 13, 1975

311   "This is a true . . ." Sam Peckinpah to Fred Goldberg and Buddy Young, May 15, 1974, Peckinpah Papers

312   "SAW THE ART WORK . . ." Sam Peckinpah to Martin Baum, telegram, June 29, 1974, *Bring Me the Head of Alfredo Garcia* files, Peckinpah Papers

312   "We met in . . ." Dawson, interview

312   "While I was . . ." *Der Spiegel*, September 18, 1974

312   Nosotros's reaction from Katy Haber to Sam Peckinpah, September 4, 1974, Peckinpah Papers

312   "What in the world . . ." *Product Digest*, August 14, 1974

313   "two middle-aged . . ." *Newsweek*, "Slay Him Again, Sam," August 26, 1974

313   "warmly played . . ." *Playboy*, November 1974

313   "an exercise in wood" Nora Sayre, "'Garcia,' a Film Portrait of Pessimism," *New York Times*, August 15, 1974

313   "instead of Chanel . . ." *Los Angeles*, September 1974

313   "doesn't make a great . . ." *New York Times*, September 15, 1974

313   "The second half . . ." *Hollywood Reporter*, August 7, 1974, 3

313   "We wish to . . ." Almer John Davis and Alicia Carol Hill to Charles Champlain, *Los Angeles Times*, August 15, 1974

313   "Up yours . . . all the time" John Bryson, "The Wild Bunch in New York," *New York*, August 19, 1974, 25

313   "When the girlfriend . . . authoritarian director" Tom Topor, "Head Hunting with Sam Peckinpah," *New York Post*, August 10, 1974

314   "All of us worked . . ." Bryson, "Wild Bunch in New York," 28

314   "Warren Oates, star . . . anything like that" *Box Office*, August 5, 1974

315   "There are a lot . . ." Elston Brooks, "Baddie Turns Goodie in New Oates Film," *Fort Worth (TX) Star-Telegram*, August 7, 1974

315   "It's not a suit . . . stood a chance" Safran, "Oate's [sic] Violent Screen Life"

316   "It was a very . . ." Warren Oates, interview by Bomar and Warren, 42

316   "We had a couple . . ." Dawson, interview

316   "I saw Sam . . ." Simmons, interview

316   "It was a lousy . . ." Culp, interview by the author

316   "I don't think . . ." Johnson in *Across the Border*

317   "I'm getting out . . ." Loynd, "Oates and Insights"

317   "It was too . . ." Saunders, "Tale of Two Actors"

317   "This will really turn . . ." Loynd, "Oates and Insights"

318   "McGuane cut short . . ." Peter Fonda, interview by Thurman and Marksbury

318   "We'd stop at . . ." Watkins, interview

319   "I'd admired it . . . friend of my wife's" Jerry Parker, "Writer Unlocks Film Career in Key West," *Los Angeles Times*, December 29, 1974

320   "He was so . . ." Thomas McGuane, interview

320   "Warren, I don't . . . is right" Stanton, interview

320   "There's been stuff . . ." Peter Fonda, interview by Thurman and Marksbury

321   "We decided that . . ." Elizabeth Ashley, *Actress: Postcards from the Road* (New York: Evans, 1978), 174

321   "None of us . . ." Watkins, interview

321   "A lot of . . ." Saunders, "Tale of Two Actors"

321   "When we were . . ." Peter Fonda, interview by Thurman and Marksbury

322   "Almost every man . . ." Ashley, *Actress*, 174

322   "Warren would say . . ." Watkins, interview

20. Another Wilderness

323   "I know he . . ." Ruscha, interview

323   "Vickery was good . . ." Bloom, interview

323   "I met Vickery . . ." Anderson, interview

323   "Vickery, I couldn't . . ." Ruscha, interview

323   "My parents almost . . ." Timothy Oates, interview

323   "The love of . . ." Ruscha, interview

324   "Warren and I . . ." Peter Fonda, interview by Thurman and Marksbury

324   "I was sitting . . . he did that" Jennifer Oates, interview

325   "Kesey never liked . . ." Jim Farber, "Cuckoo Chronicles," *Torrance (CA) Daily Breeze*, May 4, 2001

325   "I don't think . . . were high" L. Dean Jones, interview by the author, January 22, 2007, Los Angeles

325   "Listen to the wind . . . being illegal" Watkins, interview

325   "There were these . . . see that?" L. Dean Jones, interview

325   "The UFOs in . . ." Watkins, interview

326   "Just pay it . . . our rooms" L. Dean Jones, interview

326   "We drove from . . ." Watkins, interview

327   "We were in . . . get the room" Miller, interview

327   "*Deliverance*-inspired" Chris Poggalia and Robert Plante, "Remembering 'Race,'" *Fangoria*, August 2005, 71

327   "I'm not going . . ." L. Dean Jones, interview

327 "Relative to us . . ." Watkins, interview

327 "Warren was very . . ." L. Dean Jones, interview

328 "Everyone was just . . ." Poggalia and Plante, "Remembering 'Race,'" 72

328 "My agent burst . . ." Ibid., 73

328 "Now listen, Flyer . . . instead of just . . ." Peter Fonda, interview by Thurman and Marksbury

329 "We had a couple . . . drunk, I guess" Poggalia and Plante, "Remembering 'Race,'" 73

329 "my Ken Kesey . . ." Steve Lim, interview by the author, May 31, 2006, Los Angeles

329 "Flyer, you know . . . on Armistice Day" Peter Fonda, interview by Thurman and Marksbury

330 "disappeared pretty quickly . . . about that at all" *Race with the Devil* production notes, *Race with the Devil* production files, Core Collection, Herrick Library

330 "because they didn't . . ." Dudley Saunders, "Warren Oates: Busy, Busy, Busy," *Louisville Times*, June 3, 1978

331 "I looked at Warren . . ." Peter Fonda, interview by Thurman and Marksbury

331 "They came up . . ." Lara Parker, "Commentary," *Race with the Devil*, DVD, directed by Jack Starrett (Twentieth Century–Fox, 2007)

331 "The ending just sucked" Poggalia and Plante, "Remembering 'Race,'" 74

331 "If Warren didn't . . ." Watkins, interview

331 "Oates does his . . ." *Variety*, June 11, 1975

331 "AAA might use . . ." *Time*, August 18, 1975, 60

331 "Everyone does a great . . ." *Cinema Retro*, April 1, 2006, 59

331 "We drove back . . . biscuits and gravy" L. Dean Jones, interview

332 "The critics and people . . ." Saunders, "Tale of Two Actors"

333 "It was excruciating . . . smoke, and swear" Judy Oates, telephone interview by the author, August 26, 2004

334 "My next-door neighbor . . . he fits yet" Dern, interview

335 "I foresaw *The Missouri* . . . have been like" Thomas McGuane, interview

335 "Warren decided to scare . . ." Watkins, interview

336 "I'm from Houston . . ." Dennis Quaid, telephone interview by the author, September 26, 2006

336 "I think my dad . . ." Timothy Oates, interview

336 "Warren had a kind . . ." Thomas McGuane, interview

336 "United Artists dropped . . ." Vincent Canby, "They Dumped a Good One on Skid Row," *New York Times*, February 1, 1976

336 "I never really . . ." Thomas McGuane, interview

336 "I went to the 92 . . ." L. Dean Jones, interview

337   "We went up . . . down a drink" Mike Art, interview by the author, September 19, 2006, Pray, MT

337   "I couldn't say . . ." Quaid, interview

337   "Meet me in . . . prepared for winter" Becky McGuane Fonda, interview

338   "He had the hots . . ." Art, interview

338   "Warren, you've got . . . stole my act" L. Dean Jones, interview

339   Oates's call to television station from ibid.

339   "His status professionally . . . when I'm through" Dorothy Manners, "Film Violence Reflects the Streets," *Los Angeles Herald-Examiner*, May 23, 1976

340   "Is this enough? . . ." Judy Oates, telephone interview by the author, March 1, 2008

340   "In 'Drum' virtually . . ." Kevin Thomas, "Drum Rolls to a Slavery Beat," *Los Angeles Times*, August 4, 1976

340   "rarely seen to . . ." *Variety*, August 4, 1976

340   "Hell, we're shooting . . . lot of beers" Hopkins, interview

341   "Warren was on a quest . . ." Judy Oates, interview, March 1, 2008

21. Dog Days

343   "Warren would give . . ." Judy Oates, interview, March 1, 2008

343   "Everybody puts on . . ." Watkins, interview

343   "Now, that was . . ." Jennifer Oates, interview by Thurman

344   "It's hardly like . . ." Jennifer Oates, interview

344   "Man, I gotta . . ." Watkins, interview

344   "He was very . . ." L. Dean Jones, interview

344   Unexpected guest at Briar Knoll from L Dean Jones, interview

344   "I started building . . ." Saunders, "Warren Oates: Busy"

345   Oates and Peckinpah's agreement from Peter, interview; Montana files—general 1977, Peckinpah Papers; and property—Warren Oates 1977–1978, Peckinpah Papers

345   "When I was living . . . to talk about" "The Paradox of the Western Hero," Western Movies: Myths and Images, July 2, 1976, Sun Valley Center for the Arts and Humanities, MS 582, folder 10, box 21, Institute of the American West Records, Sun Valley, ID

346   "As far as me . . . follow Warren Oates" "Picture Cowboys," Western Movies, Institute of the American West Records

347   "It always reminded . . ." Hjortsberg, interview

347   Peckinpah's Montana lodgings from Peter, interview

347   "He didn't sell . . ." Joe Swindlehurst, interview by the author, September 18, 2006, Livingston, MT

347   "Back when it . . . of a bitch" L. Dean Jones, interview

348   "Chico was going . . ." Timothy Oates, interview

348   "Take off your . . ." Hjortsberg, interview

349   "The kitchen was . . ." Judy Oates, interview, March 1, 2008

349   "I had to drive . . . what you say" Toby Thompson, e-mail message to the author, February 4, 2007

350   "One day the . . ." Zak Zakovi, interview by the author, September 17, 2006, Bozeman, MT

351   "Judy had an elegance . . ." Lee, interview

351   "Judy was a kind . . ." Lim, interview

351   Oates's private rituals from Judy Oates, interview, March 1, 2008

351   "a pivotal part . . ." *Hollywood Press*, November 5–11, 1976, 7

351   Gilmore's choice of Oates from Norman Mailer, *The Executioner's Song* (Boston: Little, Brown, 1979), 658–59

352   "He frequently returns . . ." *Hollywood Press*, November 5–11, 1976, 7

352   "I know this actor . . . we're all in" *The Making of "Sleeping Dogs,"* directed by John Reid (Aardvark Productions, 2004)

353   "When Warren turned . . ." Roger Donaldson, "Commentary," *Sleeping Dogs*, DVD, directed by Roger Donaldson (Anchor Bay, 2004)

353   "Oates wasn't there . . ." *New Zealand Report*, October 19, 1977

354   "a warning to authority" Donaldson, "Commentary"

354   "maybe the silliest . . ." Cecil Smith, "African Queen on CBS Tonight," *Los Angeles Times*, March 18, 1977

355   "Warren and I tried . . ." Hartley, interview

355   "They seem at . . ." Smith, "African Queen on CBS Tonight"

355   "Both turn in . . ." *Variety*, "Hartley Oates Chemistry Doesn't Make It," March 18, 1977

355   "punk rock of . . ." *Los Angeles Times*, June 18, 1977

355   "become a lady . . . friends of mine" Jennifer Oates, interview by Thurman

356   "We looked pretty sad" Timothy Oates, interview

356   "acceptable children's fare" *TV Guide*, January 31, 1978

357   "a sentimental journey" Universal News, *Border* news release

357   "At a certain age . . ." Watkins, interview

357   "a slender, soft-spoken . . ." Saunders, "Warren Oates: Busy"

357   "Don't sit on . . . was very *correct*" Timothy Oates, interview

357   "I drank rum . . ." Judy Oates, interview, March 1, 2008

357   "When I'd go . . ." Teddy Oates, interview by Thurman

357   "We'll be eating . . ." Warren Oates to Timothy Oates, no date, private collection

358   "a taco western . . ." Saunders, "Warren Oates: Busy"

358   "Monte Hellman was very . . ." Judy Oates, interview, March 1, 2008

358   "*China 9* was . . ." Hellman, interview by the author

358   "Warren and Giuseppe . . . and almost did" Hellman, interview by Thurman and Marksbury

359   "Sam's just an asshole" Judy Oates, interview, March 1, 2008

359   "We could have set . . ." *China 9, Liberty 37* news release, 1977, Warren Oates clipping files, British Film Institute National Library

359   Midnight Mass from Judy Oates, interview, March 1, 2008

359   "the Coon Queen . . . ramble around" Hjortsberg, interview

360   "Judy had a big . . ." Watkins, interview

360   "I'll pretend I'm . . . Hollywood was in" Robert Story, interview by the author, September 18, 2007, Livingston, MT

360   "In this drama . . ." Cecil Smith, "TV Actors Take to Stage," *Los Angeles Times*, March 2, 1978

361   "We spend every . . ." Saunders, "Warren Oates: Busy"

361   "Now and then . . ." Dayton, interview, June 11, 2006

361   "I told him . . . but ornery" Northup, interview

361   "Only I could play . . ." L. Dean Jones, interview

361   "I had to be . . . recognized me" Saunders, "Warren Oates: Busy"

362   "I'll just do . . ." L. Dean Jones, interview

362   "A picture has . . ." *Los Angeles Times*, May 19, 1978

362   "Oates does a good . . ." *Variety*, May 19, 1978

362   "Oates scales his . . ." *Hollywood Reporter*, May 19, 1978

362   "point of saturation" Alpert, "Bad Guy Never Had It"

22. Something Incredible

363   "I made 'The Brink's Job' . . ." Nat Segaloff, *Hurricane Billy: The Stormy Life and Films of William Friedkin* (New York: Morrow, 1990), 180

364   "I was hired . . ." Rocco, interview

364   "His attention to detail . . ." Saunders, "Warren Oates: Busy"

364   "This was sufficient . . ." Nancy Pomerene McMillan, "Brink's Is Robbed in Boston Again," *New York Times*, July 2, 1978

365   "I'm ready to go . . . Old Man Brink" Clifford Terry, "Billy Friedkin and the Crime of the Century," *Chicago Tribune*, October 29, 1978

365   "He was watching . . ." Timothy Oates, interview

365   "Mike, Mike . . . need to do" Art, interview

365   "one of the most . . ." Universal News, *The Brink's Job* news release, November 30, 1978, *The Brink's Job* film clippings, Cinematic Arts Library, University of Southern California

365   "In *The Brink's Job* . . ." Thomson, interview by Thurman and Marksbury

366   "helpless heroism" Thomas D. Clagett, *William Friedkin: Films of Aberration and Obsession* (Jefferson, NC: McFarland, 1996), 184

366   "Warren Oates is . . ." *Los Angeles Herald-Examiner*, December 8, 1978

366   "Oates has a hell . . ." Frank Rich, "Light Work," *Time*, December 11, 1978

366 "It's a beautiful . . ." Universal News, *Brink's Job* news release

366 "We hear that . . . motorcycle rink" Art, interview

367 "I only hiked . . ." Becky McGuane Fonda, interview

367 "We all went . . . was in heaven" Hjortsberg, interview

368 Oates and friends' creek activities from Swindlehurst, interview

368 Peckinpah driving through the gate from Judy Oates, interview, August 26, 2004

368 "I lost it . . ." Ibid.

369 "a whole conundrum . . ." Lee, interview

369 "both good and bad . . ." Simmons, interview

369 "We share a place . . ." Warren Oates, interview by Bomar and Warren, 43

369 "Montana was very . . . else but Montana" Judy Oates, interview, August 26, 2004

370 "Judy was sweet . . ." Art, interview

370 "Judy was always . . ." Becky McGuane Fonda, interview

370 "I'm not coming . . ." Judy Oates, interview, March 1, 2008

370 "Warren, rather than . . . the whole deal" Hjortsberg, interview

371 "There was a road . . ." Swindlehurst, interview

371 "kind of tight . . ." Thomas McGuane, interview

371 "There's a saying . . ." Beatty, interview by Thurman

372 "It's astounding to me . . ." CBS Entertainment, *Blue and the Gray* news release

372 "a gung-ho soldier . . . this idealistic struggle" Universal News, *1941* news release

372 "He would have . . . everybody at ease" Chris Soldo, telephone interview by the author, January 24, 2007

373 "Let's see what . . ." Judy Oates, interview, March 1, 2008

373 "One man's banana . . ." *Sight and Sound*, July 1980, 194–95

374 "He was a completely . . ." Art, interview

374 "The mugger is . . ." "Insight: The Man Who Mugged God," episode overview, http://www.tv.com/insight/the-man-who-mugged-god/episode/333971/summary.html

374 "Warren didn't want . . ." Erman, interview

375 "He was very Dad-like . . ." Jennifer Oates, interview by Thurman

375 "That's the role . . ." Gordon Oates, interview, December 5, 2005

375 "What a pleasure . . ." Kevin Thomas, "My Old Man," *Los Angeles Times*, December 7, 1979

375 "haunting, crusty world-weariness" Tom Shales, "Girl Meets Horse," *Washington Post*, December 7, 1979

375 "technically competent . . ." *Hollywood Reporter*, December 7, 1979

375 Peckinpah's conversation with Judy Oates from Judy Oates, interview, March 1, 2008

375   "There's my dad . . ." Timothy Oates, interview by Thurman and Marksbury for *Aross the Border*

375   Peckinpah's antics at the Murray Hotel from Peter Bowen, placard, Murray Hotel lobby, Livingston, MT

376   "People would always . . ." Zakovi, interview

376   "This kid is . . ." L. Dean Jones, interview

377   "Warren really wanted . . ." Judy Oates, interview, August 26, 2004

378   "Another student, Ricardo . . . happen any time!" Rick Jewell, interview by the author, February 24, 2008, Los Angeles

380   "beyond belief" Dudley Saunders, "Warren Oates's Career Reflected Early Years in Kentucky," *Louisville Times*, April 5, 1982

380   "From what I know . . ." Watkins, interview

380   "The one thing I . . ." Judy Oates, interview, August 26, 2004

380   "credibly and affectionately played" *Hollywood Reporter*, October 20, 1980

380   "absolutely superb as . . ." *Daily Variety*, October 16, 1980

380   "TV trash-lover's delight" *Hollywood Reporter*, February 6, 1981

381   "Oates had the smell . . ." *Village Voice*, February 1981

381   "a crafty scene-stealer" *Time*, February 9, 1981

381   "Judy chose that house . . ." Teddy Oates Chase, interview by the author

381   "The housing difference . . ." Becky McGuane Fonda, interview

381   "I was driving up . . ." Purcell, interview

382   "It's been wonderful . . ." Universal News, *Border* news release

382   "'The Border' is basically . . ." *Los Angeles Herald-Examiner*, September 18, 1980

382   "It's a film . . ." Universal News, *Border* news release

23. Kettledrums Roll

385   "The *Animal House* era . . ." Judge Reinhold, "Commentary," *Stripes*, DVD, directed by Ivan Reitman (Columbia Tri-Star Home Entertainment, 2005)

385   "The Defense Department . . ." Mike Thomas, "Earning His Stripes," *Chicago Sun-Times*, June 7, 2005

385   "a cool, hip . . ." Harold Ramis, "Commentary," *Stripes*

385   "loved, respected, not . . ." Ivan Reitman, "Commentary," *Stripes*

385   "Ivan thought it . . . It was embarrassing" Ramis, "Commentary"

385   "'He didn't know . . . out of here" Timothy Oates, interview

386   "If anything, Oates . . ." *Los Angeles Times*, June 26, 1981

386   "Watching Oates is . . ." *Hollywood Reporter*, June 15, 1981, 3

386   "Yep, it's Bill . . ." Strong's personal Web site, http://www.tedstrong.com/

386   Army recruitment statistics from Reitman, "Commentary"

386   "Russ Tamblyn, Dean . . ." Hopper, interview
387   "They just canned . . . the first place" Culp, interview by the author
387   "I'm going to need . . ." Jennifer Oates, interview
387   "Bob, you've got . . ." Watkins, interview
388   "Sit down, have . . ." Boyd Majers, telephone interview, December 30, 2005
388   "Jack, walk the damned . . . scratched as this" Sheila Benson, "Santa Fe Roundup of Western Films," *Los Angeles Times*, April 28, 1981
388   "A lot of times . . . saw this rascal" Watkins, interview
389   Quaid ad-libbing his dialogue from Mike Greco, "Toughman America: The Movie," *Los Angeles Times*, June 28, 1981
389   "He wasn't directing . . . what they're doing" Ibid.
389   "If he can . . ." *People*, May 2, 1983, 14
389   "Bristling with grit . . ." *Playboy*, June 1983
389   "the same day . . ." *Z*, March 1984
390   "Working with Warren . . ." Twentieth Century–Fox, *Tough Enough* news release, June 1983, *Tough Enough* production files, Core Collection, Herrick Library
390   "We had a blast . . . don't have to" Quaid, interview
390   "trying to come . . ." Johnson in *Across the Border*
391   "pork chops, fat . . ." Timothy Oates, interview
391   "He concluded that . . ." Thomas McGuane, interview
391   "He had a slouch . . ." Swindlehurst, interview
391   "It's nothing" Timothy Oates, interview
391   "Teddy, where are . . . taking him back" Teddy Oates Chase, interview by the author
392   "I saw Warren . . ." CBS Entertainment, *Blue and the Gray* news release
392   Oates conversing with turkeys from ibid.
392   "There are wonderful . . ." Cecil Smith, "Yanks Meet the Rebs in Arkansas," *Los Angeles Times*, October 29, 1981
393   "I can relate . . ." CBS Entertainment, *Blue and the Gray* news release
393   "It was like . . ." Stacy Keach, interview by Tom Thurman and Tom Marksbury for *Across the Border*
393   "I would have done . . ." CBS Entertainment, *Blue and the Gray* news release
393   "twisted avenger with . . ." *Variety*, November 12, 1982, 14
393   "The English excel . . ." Howard Rosenberg, "Civil War Drama: CBS Rises Again?" *Los Angeles Times*, November 12, 1982
393   "accuracy in haircuts" *Los Angeles Weekly*, November 12, 1982
394   "They were picketing . . ." Asner, interview
394   "Time is running out . . ." *Globe*, "Wild Oates's Ordeal," April 27, 1982, Warren Wing, Chico Hot Springs, Pray, MT
394   "yet another masterful . . ." *Variety*, January 27, 1982, 16

394   "His health was . . ." Judy Oates, interview, August 26, 2004
395   "a crass, smarmy . . ." *California,* June 1983, 120
395   "playing a type . . ." *Hollywood Reporter,* January 31, 1983, 4
395   "not one that . . . I come back" Swindlehurst, interview
395   "You gotta watch . . ." Becky McGuane Fonda, interview
395   "You kind of felt . . ." Thomas McGuane, interview by Thurman and Marksbury
395   Crêpes suzettes at Chico Hot Springs from William Kittredge, e-mail message to the author, August 29, 2006
396   Early-morning snacks from Torrey Oates, telephone interview by the author, January 26, 2006
396   "Warren did not . . ." Gordon Oates, interview, July 30, 2004
396   "I'm not Warren . . ." Markland, interview
396   "I've been smoking . . . to a doctor" Hopper, interview
397   "I think I've . . . last night" Hellman, interview by the author
397   "You didn't see . . . now, Becky . . ." Becky McGuane Fonda, interview
397   "Call me when . . ." Judy Oates, interview, August 26, 2004
397   "still and cool . . ." Nicole Szulc, "Death of a Hollywood Tough Guy," *Los Angeles Herald-Examiner,* April 5, 1982

24. No Magic Hour

398   "Something's going on . . . to tell him" Becky McGuane Fonda, interview
398   "I had been . . . How dare he?" Teddy Oates Chase, interview by the author
399   "I felt that . . ." Hellman, interview by the author
399   "I'd been waiting . . . death to me" Peter Fonda, interview by Thurman and Marksbury
399   "He had this joke . . ." L. Dean Jones, interview
400   "white collar respectability . . ." *Times* (London), April 6, 1982
400   "a genuine artist . . ." F. X. Feeney, "Requiem for an Ordinary Hero," *Los Angeles Weekly,* April 30, 1982
400   "a highly gifted . . ." Szulc, "Death of a Hollywood Tough Guy"
400   "It was a total . . ." Hopper, interview
400   "It makes me think . . ." Hjortsberg, interview
400   "I always think . . ." Keach, interview by Thurman and Marksbury
401   "He smoked; he . . ." Hellman, interview by Thurman and Marksbury
401   "Warren was not . . ." Peter Fonda, interview by Thurman and Markbury
401   "Harry Dean, if . . ." Gordon Oates, interview, December 5, 2005
402   "I'm sure Sam . . ." Simmons, interview
402   "I don't want . . ." Sam Peckinpah to Judy Oates (draft), July 6, 1982, Peckinpah Papers

402 "I had maybe . . ." Teddy Oates, interview by Thurman

402 "The only place . . ." Jennifer Oates, interview

403 Peckinpah's response to his visitor from Hjortsberg, interview

403 "a fifth in every pew . . . we remember Warren?" Judy Oates, interview, August 26, 2004

403 "He was brandishing . . ." Keach, interview by Thurman and Marksbury

403 "I wasn't finished . . ." Miller, interview

403 "If he's going . . ." Robert Culp, interview by Tom Thurman and Tom Marksbury for *Across the Border*

403 "I had a terrible . . ." Hellman, interview by the author

404 "I do not know . . . do something" Timothy Oates, interview

404 "the one about . . ." *Los Angeles Herald-Examiner*, April 7, 1982

404 "The funeral was . . ." Howard Dayton, interview by the author, October 19, 2007, Los Angeles

404 "It seemed like . . ." Miller, interview

404 "It was a lot . . ." Armand Alzamora, interview

404 "The whole world . . ." Teddy Oates Chase, portrait of Warren Oates, private collection

404 "the last person . . ." Manners, "Film Violence Reflects"

404 "And then all . . ." Culp, interview by Thurman

405 "He was there . . ." Hellman, interview by Thurman and Marksbury

405 "One minute we're . . ." Teddy Oates Chase, interview by the author

405 "Why don't we just . . ." Judy Oates, interview, August 26, 2004

405 "It wasn't a hoedown . . ." Timothy Oates, interview

405 "So many people . . ." Thomas McGuane, interview

405 "I was distressed . . ." Joan Haines, "Friends Gather to Honor Warren Oates," *Bozeman (MT) Daily Chronicle*, April 18, 1982

406 "sitting comfortably back . . ." Lim, interview

406 "We were drinking . . . at what's here" Timothy Oates in *Across the Border*

406 "I have a photo . . ." Hellman, interview by the author

406 "Even Larry Girdler . . ." Teddy Oates, interview by Thurman

406 "People who stay . . ." Quaid, interview

407 "Watched the July 4th . . ." Sam Peckinpah to Judy Oates, July 6, 1982, Peckinpah Papers

407 "So now me . . ." Timothy Oates, interview by Thurman

407 "Warren's bones are . . . and stopped it" Quaid, interview

407 "I have a picture . . ." Swindlehurst, interview

408 "A eulogy for . . ." Sam Peckinpah, *Rolling Stone Yearbook*, December 23, 1982, 92

Index

CPSIA information can be obtained
at www.ICGtesting.com
Printed in the USA
BVOW04s0419260517

484448BV00012B/4/P

9 780813 193465